TRANSFORMATIVE LAW AND PUBLIC POLICY

This book explores the convergence of law and public policy. Drawing on case studies from Asia, Europe, the Middle East and Australia, it examines how judicial and political institutions are closely linked to the socio-economic concerns of the citizens. The essays argue for the utilization of both legislative and executive, private and public spheres of society as vehicles for transformative social change and to safeguard against violations of socio-economic rights.

The volume will be of great interest to both public and private stakeholders, as well as professionals, including NGOs and think tanks, working in the areas of law, government, and public policy. It will also be immensely useful to academics and researchers of constitutionalism, policymaking and policy integration, social justice and minority rights.

Sony Pellissery is Executive Director of the Institute of Public Policy, National Law School of India University, Bangalore.

Babu Mathew is Chairperson of the Institute of Public Policy, National Law School of India University, Bangalore.

Avinash Govindjee is the Executive Dean of the Faculty of Law at Nelson Mandela University in Port Elizabeth, South Africa.

Arvind Narrain is a human rights lawyer based in Bangalore, India, and an Honorary Professor of Practice at the National Law School of India University.

'Ranging from the local to the global, the contributions collected in this remarkable volume make a persuasive case for the alignment of public policy and law demonstrating that the notions of justice underpinning them are not revealed but constructed.'

Armando Barrientos, Professor Emeritus of Poverty and Social Justice, Global Development Institute, University of Manchester

'Grounded in empirical research and rooted in theories of social justice, *Transformative Law and Public Policy* explores the shifting intersections between law and public policy in the developing world. Its detailed case studies and reflective essays provide an engaging view of how those two realms can come together to address poverty and build more inclusive societies.'

Joan Dassin, Professor, Heller School for Social Policy and Management, Brandeis University

'The weaving together of different public policy areas and the application of the law offers a deeper understanding of the realities on the ground that resonates with many countries in the Global South. The book is a great resource not only for academia but public policy architects and implementers as well.'

Grace Bantebya-Kyomuhendo, Professor, Makerere University

'Critically important book to social scientists and legal scholars interested in current debates about international public policy and law. It contains up-to-date information and discerning commentaries that will be of value to scholars everywhere. It deserves to be widely read.'

James Midgley, Professor of the Graduate School, University of California, Berkeley

TRANSFORMATIVE LAW AND PUBLIC POLICY

*Edited by Sony Pellissery,
Babu Mathew, Avinash Govindjee,
and Arvind Narrain*

LONDON AND NEW YORK

First published 2020
by Routledge
2 Park Square, Milton Park, Abingdon, Oxon OX14 4RN

and by Routledge
52 Vanderbilt Avenue, New York, NY 10017

Routledge is an imprint of the Taylor & Francis Group, an informa business

© 2020 selection and editorial matter, Sony Pellissery, Babu Mathew, Avinash Govindjee and Arvind Narrain; individual chapters, the contributors

The right of Sony Pellissery, Babu Mathew, Avinash Govindjee and Arvind Narrain to be identified as the authors of the editorial material, and of the authors for their individual chapters, has been asserted in accordance with sections 77 and 78 of the Copyright, Designs and Patents Act 1988.

All rights reserved. No part of this book may be reprinted or reproduced or utilised in any form or by any electronic, mechanical, or other means, now known or hereafter invented, including photocopying and recording, or in any information storage or retrieval system, without permission in writing from the publishers.

Trademark notice: Product or corporate names may be trademarks or registered trademarks, and are used only for identification and explanation without intent to infringe.

British Library Cataloguing-in-Publication Data
A catalogue record for this book is available from the British Library

Library of Congress Cataloging-in-Publication Data
Names: Pellissery, Sony, 1972– editor. | Mathew, Babu, editor. | Govindjee, Avinash, editor. | Narrain, Arvind, editor.
Title: Transformative law and public policy / edited by Sony Pellissery, Babu Mathew, Avinash Govindjee, and Arvind Narrain.
Description: Abingdon, Oxon ; New York, NY : Routledge, 2020, | Includes bibliographical references and index.
Identifiers: LCCN 2019028214 (print) | LCCN 2019028215 (ebook)
Subjects: LCSH: Law—Social aspects—Congresses. | Public policy (Law)—Congresses. | Law—Social aspects—India—Congresses. | Public policy (Law)—India—Congresses.
Classification: LCC K555 .T73 2020 (print) | LCC K555 (ebook) | DDC 340/.115—dc23
LC record available at https://lccn.loc.gov/2019028214
LC ebook record available at https://lccn.loc.gov/2019028215

ISBN: 978-0-367-11139-7 (hbk)
ISBN: 978-0-367-34829-8 (pbk)
ISBN: 978-0-429-34465-7 (ebk)

Typeset in Bembo
by Apex CoVantage, LLC

 Printed in the United Kingdom by Henry Ling Limited

CONTENTS

List of illustrations	*vii*
List of contributors	*viii*
Preface	*xi*

1 Why is law central to public policy process in the Global South?   1
  Babu Mathew, Sony Pellissery and Arvind Narrain

2 The rise of an anti-global doctrine and strikes in public services   26
  Lilach Litor

3 Scrutiny of sovereign border policy for 'operational
  matters': a new political role for an old legal dichotomy in
  Australia?   49
  Suzanne Bevacqua and John Bevacqua

4 Sovereign debt restructuring: locating Indian law and
  jurisprudence in the contemporary international legal order   74
  Ansari Salamah

5 The legal and policy questions in Foreign Direct
  Investment: an assessment using Indian case   92
  Priya Misra and Praveen Tripathi

6 Politics of making and unmaking of the Indian Planning
  Commission: destiny of non-statutory institutions in a
  democracy   111
  Sony Pellissery, Sharada Srinivasan and Anusha Chaitanya

vi Contents

7 Constitutional promises vs practices of participation and
representation of minorities in South Asia 128
Mushtaq Ahmad Malla

8 Growing up in families with low income: the state's legal
obligation to recognize the child's right to adequate
standard of living 151
Julia Köhler-Olsen

9 Implementers of law or policymakers too? A study of
street-level bureaucracy in India 171
Amrutha Jose Pampackal

10 Production of space in urban India: legal and policy
challenges to land assembly 189
Varun Panickar

11 Rawls, Nozick and Dworkin in an Indian village: land
alienation and multiple versions of distributive justice 202
Naivedya Parakkal, Sony Pellissery and Rajesh Sampath

12 Concluding reflections: transformative constitutionalism
as a framework for law and policy integration in the
Global South 223
Avinash Govindjee

Index 239

ILLUSTRATIONS

Figures

9.1	Bureaucratic structure for TRDM implementation within STDD	175
11.1	Concept map of causal relations to deprivation	208

Tables

1.1	Policy-centric and law-centric institutional spaces to deal with public problems	17
5.1	Sectoral caps usually observed in FDI policy	95
5.2	Landmark judgements on FDI	97
6.1	Views of chief ministers on dismantling planning commission	119
7.1	Typology of the transformative constitutionalism vis-à-vis the participation of minorities in South Asian states	141
9.1	Increase in responsibilities of TEOs in Kerala from 1980–81 to 2013–14	183
11.1	Profiles of 12 interviewees	210
11.2	Contrasting views on land ownership from settlers and *adivasis*	215
11.3	Contrasting views among *adivasis* on compensation	218

CONTRIBUTORS

John Bevacqua is an Australian commercial lawyer with 20 years' experience and a senior lecturer at Monash University in Melbourne. John completed his PhD from the University of New South Wales and was awarded the CCH ATTA Doctoral Prize in 2011. John publishes extensively and is recognized as an international expert in the field of taxpayer rights, remedies and public policy. John teaches in subjects including taxation law, commercial law and business law to cohorts of predominantly international students.

Suzanne Bevacqua is an Australian legal practitioner with 20 years' experience. At the same time as engaging in full-time legal practice, Suzanne has pursued a passion for legal education, acting as mentor for Juris Doctor Students at Melbourne Law School and a sessional academic at La Trobe University, Melbourne since 2005. Suzanne is published frequently on legal, ethical and regulatory developments in legal industry journals and presents legal education seminars for continuing legal education providers.

Anusha Chaitanya is a doctoral candidate in the Organizations and Social Change PhD programme in the University of Massachusetts Boston. Her research is on non-governmental organizations in India and how they challenge or reinforce socio-economic hierarchies in the society within their own organizational structure and leadership. She is broadly interested in understanding organizations in the context of socio-cultural history.

Avinash Govindjee is Executive Dean of the Faculty of Law at Nelson Mandela University in Port Elizabeth, South Africa. He is a consulting attorney to the law firm Cliffe Dekker Hofmeyr and has served South Africa's Commission for Conciliation, Mediation and Arbitration (CCMA) for a number of years as a senior commissioner.

Julia Köhler-Olsen is associate professor in law at the Department of Social Work at Oslo Metropolitan University. She has a PhD and masters in law from the University of Oslo. Her research and teaching covers regards economic and social human rights, children's human rights, the right to non-discrimination, as well as digital public services and the rule of law.

Lilach Litor is a lecturer at the open university of Israel in law and public policy. She completed her L.L.B at the Hebrew University Faculty of Law, and her M.A. and PhD at the Tel Aviv University Department of Public Policy. Her main research interests include: public law, labour law, and public policy and regulation.

Mushtaq Malla is working as State Project Manager (J&K) with ActionAid. Before this he was working as assistant professor at the National Law School of India University (NLSIU) Bangalore. He has completed his PhD from JMI New Delhi, and MSc. in social policy from the London School of Economics and Political Science. His work and research is mainly focussed on social protection, poverty and dignity, political economy, collective livelihoods and minorities in South Asia.

Babu Mathew is with the Institute of Public Policy, National Law School of India University, Bangalore. He began his career through the trade union movement and various other social movements taking up issues of bonded labour, child labour, and displacement and destruction of the livelihoods of the marginalized. He combines teaching and practice of human rights. During 2004–10 he served as Country Director of Action Aid International in India.

Priya Misra is assistant professor of law at National Law School of India University, Bangalore. She teaches corporate law and specialized areas of business law at the university. She is a visiting faculty at National Academy of Direct Taxes and Indian Institute of Corporate Affairs. Her current areas of research include cross-border corporate insolvency law and takeovers.

Arvind Narrain is a human rights lawyer based in Bangalore, India. He is Honorary Professor of Practice at the Institute of Public Policy, NLSIU. He is a founder member of the Alternative Law Forum, a space devoted to human rights research and practice and where he worked from 2000 to 2014. He was also the Geneva Director of Arc International, an NGO which worked with the development of international human rights law and policy.

Amrutha Jose Pampackal is a PhD student in the Department of Development Sociology at Cornell University. She is also a research scholar at the Tata-Cornell Institute for Agriculture and Nutrition. Prior to joining Cornell, Amrutha was working at the International Food Policy Research Institute. Her research interests converge on the broad themes of state–society interaction, food security, land governance and social inequalities, with a primary focus on India.

x Contributors

Varun Panickar works as a senior associate at the Indian Institute for Human Settlements (IIHS). His work has focussed on various aspects of land governance, such as the push for a conclusive titling system, the workings of the real estate regulatory authorities and making policy advisories to state governments for making improvements to their property registration systems.

Naivedya Parakkal is a doctoral student at the University of Michigan School of Education. She is interested in issues of international development, empire and education, and in exploring decolonial alternatives to dominant educational paradigms. In her research, she examines how youth navigate the process of (un)learning local/indigenous epistemologies to accommodate, resist and transform hegemonic discourses around globalization, development and modernity.

Sony Pellissery is teaching at the Institute of Public Policy, National Law School of India University, Bangalore. His research on the question of politics of social policy, emotions in the public sphere and social rights in the informal sector have been published in leading journals. He has been awarded with IDRC India Social Science Award (2009) and Ram Reddy Memorial Social Science Award (2015).

Ansari Salamah completed her doctoral studies from the Indian Institute of Management Calcutta in public policy and management area. Prior to joining IIM Calcutta as a full-time fellow, she worked as an associate at IIM Ahmedabad, India. Her interest areas include issues of sovereign debt restructuring, urban governance and community-based development initiatives.

Rajesh Sampath is associate professor of the Philosophy of Justice, Rights, and Social Change at Brandeis University. Raj completed his PhD at the University of California, Irvine. His current research interests and disciplinary expertise include: moral and political philosophy, comparative constitutional law and legal philosophy, epistemology and the sociology of knowledge in comparative religious studies, and comparisons of Western philosophy and various philosophical traditions in the Global South.

Sharada Srinivasan is a research fellow at the Center for Technology, Innovation and Competition, University of Pennsylvania. As part of her research at *1 World Connected*, a global research project, she collects empirical data from grassroots-level Internet connectivity deployments around the world to synthesize insights using both qualitative and quantitative methods to drive decision making.

Praveen Tripathi is assistant professor at School of Law, Bennett University (The Times of India Group). Earlier, he worked as Assistant Professor at National Law School of India University (NLSIU) and as Research Associate at NLSIU under the project titled "Capacity Building Initiative in the Competition Area under Trade Development Programme" sponsored by the Delegation of European Union to India.

PREFACE

How does law interface with public policy? This is the single question that is pursued in this volume. The editors and authors use the lens of the constitution while answering this question. The constitutional lens frames the law as a site of values which should guide and modulate public policymaking. We argue that particularly in the Global South, where the legitimacy of the post-colonial state is based upon its ability to ensure social, economic and political justice to its people, constitutions become the source of values.

A constitution not only lists out a set of rights and corresponding state obligations, but also expresses an objective order of values (e.g. of dignity, equality etc.) that may be invoked not only against state action, but also have a "radiating effect", serving as background interpretive principles for adjudicating private law disputes as well as guiding the framing of public policy.

This is what we refer to as the idea of a transformative constitution which mandates that the role of the state is to function in accordance with the constitution and actively work towards fulfilling the constitutional mandate. Public policy in a constitutional democracy, rooted in the constitution, seeks to actualize constitutional values.

This approach has significant implications in many parts of the Global South as constitutional protections enable civil society groups to approach the judiciary to direct the state to fulfil its constitutional obligations. Thus, the judiciary has directed and ultimately compelled the state to take the requisite action in relation to many crucial questions of public policy. The questions have been in the arenas of providing safe drinking water, providing health care, providing food security and so on. Such examples demonstrate the way in which public policy and the law are both shaped by constitutional imagination.

The editors provide two framing chapters as part of this volume. The first chapter makes the argument that both policy and law have their origins in the idea of constitution. It further conducts an institutional mapping of law and policy to find where synergy exists between these two disciplines. In the final chapter, one of the editors provides an overview of the practice of transformative constitutionalism when policy questions have arisen. Apart from these two framing chapters, the rest of the chapters deal with how law interfaces with public policy in specific instances. Each of the chapters deals with specific dimensions of policy process. These dimensions include ideational influences on policies (Chapters 2 and 11), resources management (Chapters 4, 5 and 10), how institutions could be strengthened for policy effectiveness (Chapters 6 and 9), inclusive dimensions of public policy (Chapters 3, 7 and 8) and the role of actors in policy processes (Chapters 9 and 4).

The initial idea for this book germinated when the editors organized a conference panel on 'The Interface of Law and Public Policy' in 2017. Several chapters in this book were first presented during the Third International Conference of Public Policy, held between 28–30 June 2017 at Lee Kuan Yew School of Public Policy, Singapore. Selected chapters underwent several rounds of revisions before being included in this volume. Subsequently, many more scholars from across different schools working in the area of public policy were invited to contribute chapters. Our hope is that this collection will usher a new way of thinking about the sub-discipline of and interaction between law and policy in the post-constitutional dispensation. We wish you enjoyable reading!

Sony Pellissery
Babu Mathew
Avinash Govindjee
Arvind Narrain

1

WHY IS LAW CENTRAL TO PUBLIC POLICY PROCESS IN THE GLOBAL SOUTH?[1]

Babu Mathew, Sony Pellissery and Arvind Narrain

Introduction

Public policy discourses as well as education have mimicked many Western text books. Global consultancy firms that reproduce policy practices are reinforcing the mimics. This approach is without an iota of respect for context, which founding fathers of public policy emphasized. The context of the Global South presents a very different set of challenges centred around the interface of law with policy practices. In this chapter, we argue that due to the particular history emerging from colonial rule, law is central to public policy processes in Global South.

A review of academic journals dealing with the question of law and policy (Kreis and Christensen, 2013; Barclay and Birkland, 1998) fails to find a common ground between these two disciplines. Yet, independently, both these disciplines invoke each other's support for their own effectiveness. Policy clarity is considered as a precursor for a good law. In a similar vein, without translating policies into legal texts and authorities, there is very little force for policy. What exactly is the common ground between these two disciplines? How much of a boundary drawing is possible between the two? In this chapter we are attempting to answer these questions while arguing the case of law as central to policy process.

The chapter has two sections. In the first section of we have conceptually attempted to find the intrinsic link between law and public policy. In this section we argue how the constitution as fountainhead of law and policy gets rooted within the socio-economic context of a nation-state. The new constitutions in the Global South provide more space for policy-specific actions compared to traditional liberal constitutions. In the second section of the chapter, we undertake an institutional mapping of legal and policy domain to identify where policy and law interfaces in practice. In the conclusion we argue that in the context of multiple institutional crises that the world is facing, changes required are neither

2 Babu Mathew et al.

within law, nor within policy. An interaction between them is not an option, but a necessity to deal with problems comprehensively to keep the disciplines relevant in the contemporary world.

Law and policy: forward and backward linkages

What is law?

There are different understandings and theoretical approaches as to what is law. We review some of the most important positions on law to inform its connection with policy.

An early influential figure in conceptualizing law was John Austin (Austin, 1995)[2] who conceptualized law as the command of the sovereign. This notion has at least three characteristics:

1 Law as a command
2 Such a command is issued by a political superior to a political inferior
3 A political superior is one who is obeyed 'by and large'

The limitations of this understanding of the law, is that in effect it's a 'gangster' theory of the law, with obedience being based upon fear of the one issuing the command. Understanding the power of law to stem wholly from fear, may be totally inadequate for understanding the real power of law.

An important theorist who critiqued the narrowness of the 'gangster' vision of law was H.L.A. Hart who in his classic work, *The Concept of Law* (1961/2012), understood law as deriving its legitimacy and distinctiveness not merely from the fear that disobedience would lead to punishment, but really from a deeper acceptance of the legitimacy of law. Within Hart's understanding, law is a system of rules that imposes obligations which members of society accept and are in the habit of obeying.

Hart sees 'law as a union of primary and secondary rules' (p. 32). Primary rules are rules directed to all individuals in a social group telling them how they ought to act in certain circumstances. Secondary rules in the framework of Hart are the rules of recognition, rules of change and the rules of adjudication. A rule of recognition allows one to identify or recognize the actual rules of one's society. Rules of change will establish authoritative mechanisms (e.g. legislatures) for enactment and repeal of rules and will overcome the static character of a system of primary rules. Rules of adjudication will establish mechanisms (e.g. courts) to overcome the problem of efficiency present when controversy over primary rules exists (Murphy and Coleman, 1990).

The importance of Hart's framework is that systems of rules are those which the members of society accept and are in the habit of obeying. We move beyond the 'gangster' notion of law to make an argument for the legitimacy of law. Legitimacy of law depends upon the established system through which rules are established as

Why is law central to public policy process? **3**

well as what Hart called 'the internal point of view', which is the fact that people accept its legitimacy and are in the habit of obeying the rules.

However even within Hart's system, the legitimacy of the law lies primarily in the procedure through which it is created. The procedure for the creation of law can well create the rules of Nazi Germany as there is no external reference point for what the law should be. In fact, Hart's positivism is founded on a separation of law from morality. Thus while Hart's concept of law focusses on the procedure through which law comes into being, it has very little to say about the content of law.

It is Ronald Dworkin (1986), in *Law's Empire*, who sheds light on the content aspect of law.[3] Dworkin elucidates this important aspect of law through four cases. One of the cases Dworkin discusses pertains to whether Elmer, who murdered his grandfather knowing fully well that he was entitled to inherit the bulk of his estate, was entitled to inherit the estate. The minority opinion held that yes he was entitled to inherit the estate as the statute did not have any exception saying murderers of the testator cannot benefit from the testament. The majority opinion held that while there was no express statutory bar on murderers benefiting by way of testament from their actions, 'statutes should be constructed from texts not in historical isolation but against background of what he called general principles of law: he meant that judges should construct a statute so as to make it conform as closely as possible to principles of justice assumed elsewhere in the law' (Dworkin, 1986: 19).

The decision of the majority in Elmer's case leads Dworkin to conceptualize 'law as integrity'. It is not possible to see law as a series of discrete decisions but rather law should be seen as part of a coherent phenomenon which is animated by certain background principles. The idea that no person can benefit from his wrong is a part of the coherent whole of law and will have to be read into all other laws. Similarly the idea of equality before the law is a principle which should animate all laws (Teitel, 2013; Estrada-Tanck, 2016).

If one is to apply this idea of law as having integrity of its own in a constitutional democracy, what would it mean? Law within the context of a constitutional democracy can never be the command of the sovereign, neither can it be a system of primary and secondary rules divorced from background principles. The background principles within which law must be made are encoded in the constitution.[4]

Thus all law preceding the coming into force of the constitution and all law which is enacted post the coming into force of the constitution will have to conform to the constitutional commandment if it is to be considered law at all. This then is the essence of a Dworkinian vision of law wherein law is not merely any enacted piece, but has to be judged in the context of certain background principles. At the broad level, constitutionalism provides protection for the individual and civil liberties, by checking the political power as well as the authority of the state.

This overview on the different theoretical schools on law enables us to depart from a unitary understanding on law. Different schools (formalist, often referred to as 'black letter law', stands on one extreme while legal realists stand on the other extreme) view the role and function of law very differently. Legal realists advocate the use of social science knowledge and public opinion in order to apply the laws effectively. On the other hand, formalists consider superimposition of legal rationality in a top-down manner as the method. This formalist idea of law externalizes power, and approaches legal decisions as technically reached. Legal realism comes close to public policy, where the role of politics is acknowledged in public problem solving. Yet, they all converge on the centrality of the constitution. As we have seen the inseparability of law from the principle of constitutionalism, we now move to examine public policy's inherent connection to constitutionalism.

Constitutional mandate of public policy

The nature of the formation of the state is critical to the role and function of public policy for those contexts. The process of the state formation is hugely different in Global North and Global South. Enlightenment and subjugation of feudal forces to democratic and capitalist processes explain the origin of the modern state in most of the Global North (Moore, 1966). In most of the Global South, where colonialism was critical to the state formation, what brought the society together is two processes: a) mobilization against colonial forces, and b) the making of the constitution.[5] The second aspect is what makes law inseparable from public policy question in the countries of Global South.

Western liberal democratic traditions (where the discipline of public policy originated) gave shape to traditional liberal constitutions, which emphasized negative rights (Nussbaum, 2006). Within this framework, typically the judiciary is engaged in an adjudication process involving private interests.

On the other hand, new constitutions in the Global South gave space for positive action from the state. It is important to quote Nussbaum who makes this distinction:

> Often fundamental entitlements have been understood as prohibitions against interfering state action, and if the state keeps its hands off, those rights are taken to have been secured; the state has no further affirmative task. Indeed, the US Constitution demonstrates this conception directly in that negative phrasing concerning state action predominates, as in the First Amendment: "Congress shall make no law respecting an establishment of religion, or prohibiting the free exercise thereof; or abridging the freedom of speech, or of the press; or the right of the people peaceably to assemble, and petition the Government for a redress of grievances."
>
> Similarly, the Fourteenth Amendment's all-important guarantees are also stated in terms of what the state may not do: "No State shall make or enforce any law which shall abridge the privileges or immunities of citizens of the United States; nor shall any State deprive any person of life, liberty, or property, without due process of law; nor deny to any person within its jurisdiction the equal protection of the laws." This phraseology, deriving from the Enlightenment tradition of negative liberty, leaves things notoriously indeterminate as to whether impediments supplied by the market, or private

actors, are to be considered violations of fundamental rights of citizens. The Indian Constitution, by contrast, typically specifies rights affirmatively. Thus for example: "All citizens shall have the right to freedom of speech and expression; to assemble peaceably and without arms; to form associations or unions; . . . [etc.]" (Art. 19). These locutions have usually been understood to imply that impediments supplied by non-state actors may also be deemed violative of constitutional rights. Such an approach seems very important for the state needs to take action if traditionally marginalized groups are to achieve full equality. Whether a nation has a written constitution or not, it should understand fundamental entitlements in this way.

(Nussbaum, 2006: 54)

This departure from traditional constitutions in the Global South is what is termed as transformative constitutionalism (Vilhena et al., 2013). Close examination of the judgements of Supreme Courts in the Global South shows how 'public interest' is deliberately built into legalism in those constitutions. Interestingly, in the Global South where impunity is high, the largest number of court cases are against the state. Therefore, how constitutionalism protects individual liberties against the authority of the state becomes more important in the Global South.

This approach had significant influence on public policy. In most of the Global South, since the state had little legitimacy and reach over societal forces, the constitutional provision gave a handle for the civil society groups[6] to approach the judiciary to gain justiciable action from the state to meet public policy objectives. Thus, in many public policy questions, the judiciary directed and thereby compelled the state to take requisite action. The questions have been in the arenas of providing safe drinking water, providing health care, providing food security etc. The Indian Supreme Court expanded the judicial framework through a path-breaking conceptualization that locus standi of the litigant does not matter to approach the Court for legal action. Thus, Public Interest Litigation (PIL), in which a civil society member or organization, who may not be directly aggrieved, could approach the Court for forcing the state to take action (Bhagwati and Dias, 2012). Alongside, developments took place to expand the 'right to life' clause in the constitution to include several socio-economic guarantees.[7] Similar developments took place in South African constitutional courts (Khosla, 2010).

In the South African case of *The Curators v. University of Kwa-Zulu Natal*[8] the court held – in language reminiscent of German constitutional doctrine – that "public policy 'is now rooted in our constitution and the fundamental values it enshrines, thus establishing an objective normative value system.'"[9] In other words, a Constitution or Bill of Rights not only lists out a set of rights and corresponding state obligations, but also expresses an *objective order of values* (e.g. of dignity, equality etc.) that may be invoked not only against state action, but also have a "radiating effect", serving as background interpretive principles for adjudicating private law disputes.[10]

The South African constitutional court directly linked public policy with the objective order of values embodied within the constitution, observing that "in considering questions of public policy . . . the Court must find guidance in the founding constitutional values of human dignity, the achievement of equality and the advancement of human rights and freedoms, non-racialism and non-sexism."[11] These public policy concerns, grounded in constitutional values, overrode the freedom of testation and did not unjustifiably deprive the individual of his property. It has become established norm that courts go to Constitutional Assembly debates and preamble to identify these values while public policy questions are settled in the court.[12] In other words, public policy decisions could not be arrived technocratically through an economic rationality. The economic logic should be subjected to the constitutional values (Pellissery and Mathew, 2018).

Most of the constitutions across the world profess some broad values[13] in their preamble, namely, equality, liberty, fraternity, justice, welfare and security. When legislation is interpreted by judges in the light of these broad principles, advancement of public interest takes place. It is not co-incidental to observe that stated goals of public policy are exactly these values (Stone, 2012). Thus, for law and policy, the constitution remains as the moral core and guiding principle.

Law and decisions for public good

At the core of the public policy is the question of 'public interest', and the question of 'what is the right thing to do' while dealing with a public problem. There is a tendency to view the law and services that the court provides as primarily to settle disputes between grieving parties. Landes and Posner (1979), by distinguishing private arbitrations and adjudication, refute this idea by showing how precedents created through the litigation process shape the behaviour of others.[14] As shown by Elster (1995), the very aim of a legal framework for a country is to bring about stability through established norms and expectations in a society.[15] But the question that emerges is about the route to achieve public good. Is law an appropriate route?

Deborah Stone (2012), while defining 'public', makes a distinction of market and polis. While market is the arena of self-interested individuals competing with each other, in polis an arena of shared interest, which seeks for arriving public interest goals through approaches of co-operation and collective decision making prevails. Kantian school, which views law as the highest expression of reason, and thus the primacy of self-interest, would find little relevance in the polis model. It is in this sense that law may not be the route to arrive at solutions keeping public interest as the goal. In an adjudicative approach law tends to hover around a sector – scuttling the public interest concern in that case. An example is useful to demonstrate this. In the court of law a case against an industrialist employing children will navigate around labour law, and may never examine the inefficiencies of schools around the industry (forcing parents to pull out children of school in favour of industry). On the other hand, policy interventions are excellent domains where inter-sectoral linkages are possible. Similar debates[16] exist as to whether economic efficiency logic

Why is law central to public policy process?   **7**

is a better approach, compared to the deliberative approach of politics, to achieve public interest.

Dworkin (1986) tends to think that constitutional interpretation suffices the criteria for deliberative decisions since rights-based philosophy is at the core of constitutional jurisprudence. However, Habermas (1996), evaluating the position of Dworkin, rejects this possibility. He argues that decision-making processes, both within the legal and economic domains, is 'monological' – lacking the corrective ability for misconceptions held by different members in the society.[17] This is possible only through political deliberations. As Ingram (2006: 188) argues, the primacy of politics, while making decisions on public good, emerges from the limitation of legal and economic rationality since "money-driven economic systems and law-driven administrative systems relieve us of responsibility for coordinating *all* our interactions through *ad hoc* face-to-face bargaining" (emphasis in the original).[18]

Dworkin's (1977) view regarding whether constitutional courts should engage with the question of public goods is negative. To be true to the founding legitimacy of the constitution, the interpretative role of courts should be limited to checking whether public policies violate the rights of citizens. Courts may not engage with the cost-benefit analysis of what policies should produce social goods.[19] An examination of the court judgements on public policy questions confirms this view. There are two conditions which trigger law to the domain of public policy. First is the inaction of the executive to take positive action to generate public good.[20] A second condition is legally wrongful action from the part of the executive. Typically, the court sets aside such actions as *ultra vires*. These could be through new legislation, administrative action which is not consistent with the constitutional values.

These two conditions need to direct us to conclude that court and law are the conscience keepers of the society. Often, when legal institutions have been weak then laws pertaining to distributive justice came into the picture. Several public policy initiatives of the legislature were overturned by judiciary through narrowly interpreting the cases through liberal traditions. 'Social' reasons of legislature were considered irrelevant for the courts. An oft-quoted example for this from India is the policy decision for land reforms. The large-size landlords succeeded to convince the Supreme Court that a liberal interpretation of private property was more important than the social aim of parliamentary decision for land reform. The liberal interests of landowners and social interests for the labourers and landless populations collided.[21] Constitutional amendments in the form of suspension of fundamental rights to property were necessary to integrate 'social citizenship' concerns (Davy and Pellissery, 2013; Davy, 2012).

Interface of law and policy in practice

In this section, our aim is to find similarities and dissimilarities between the legal and policy domains. Using this frame, towards the end of the chapter we will make an institutional mapping where law and policy could interface in practice realms. Literature acknowledges five areas where law is essential for public policy practice.

8 Babu Mathew et al.

We briefly provide an account of these domains. Particularly, last two sub-domains are undergoing tremendous transformation in the light of increasing privatization of public good in recent times.

Five sub-domains of law and policy interface

a   **Rights:** Citizens as right holders are widely celebrated in the literature of public policy (for instance, Stone, 2012: Chapter 15; Uhr, 2006). In the earlier part of the chapter we have shown how the limitations of economic efficiency arguments lead to further emphasize the importance of rights. This literature makes a distinction of *rights-attentive* bureaucracy which responsibly implements policies to advance welfare of the citizens and *rights-responsive* model which takes note of changing citizenship requirements. This domain gets a boost through operationalization of human rights through global bodies.[22] While the legal compliance is primarily focussed on protecting and respecting legal entitlements, the policy arena pushes the boundaries to ensure the creation of environment of promoting the realization of rights.[23]

b   **Role of legislature:** Lawmaking, as a responsibility vested with elected representatives, is widely acknowledged in the policy literature. Different processes of influencing lawmakers (advocacy,[24] public choice approach of direct accountability through voting mechanisms in democracy,[25] various strategies in bill readings in parliamentary processes, different types of committees which make interventions in the bill introduction process) are widely studied through cases.[26] The legal dimension of how the passage of a bill must occur, and its different steps are often adhered to scrupulously. However, when policy has to be implemented, executive decisions are challenged, leading to a standstill for the policies. Delegated legislation, which empowers the bureaucrats, is more contested in contexts where social heterogeneity is high.

c   **Administrative law:** In fact, the domain of administrative law predates public policy in the sense that public administration as a discipline precedes public policy. While the governmental activity translates legislated policies, there are chances of the abuse of governmental power. In this sense, administrative law is "the practical enforcement of the rule of law, meaning that the government must have legal warrant for what it does and that if it acts unlawfully the citizen has an effective remedy" (Wade, 1971: 1). Some of the institutions or processes that translate administrative law into policy practices are statutory inquiries, delegated legislation, special tribunals, judicial control of ministerial and administrative powers, application of principles of natural justice, and rule of law.

d   **Regulatory agency functions:** In the old regulatory approaches (Schwartz and Wade, 1972) government appointed agencies (e.g. electricity board) shaped the economic behaviour of individuals and businesses. While this principle of market correction remains the primary objective of regulation even today, there is tremendous churning that is happening in the domain of regulation. After

Why is law central to public policy process? **9**

the acceptance of Washington Consensus as economic policy, an increased reliance on market mechanisms for delivery of public services became the order of the day. Thus, the objective of regulation expanded to market allocation, protecting human rights and even to further social solidarity (Prosser, 2006; Baldwin et al., 2013). Regulatory functions through pricing, licensing, standard setting, preventing anti-competition, protecting clients by enforcing responsibility on producers and service-providers and regulating profits have played a role in reducing the negative impact of market inefficiencies on citizens. The emerging jurisprudence shows that these regulatory powers are subjected to the Supreme Court of the land. Bringing both economic analysis and legal analysis into a single frame of regulation, it is one of the sub-domains where law and policy interfaces in the true interdisciplinary sense.

e **Planning laws:** One arena, where probably the majority of legal battles against the state take place, is restricting the freedom of individual. This primarily happens when the state uses its planning control over private land property.[27] Planning laws are extremely complicated, since the public goals come in direct conflict with the private commercial interests. Infrastructural improvement for the state requires planning, which in turn boosts the economy. However, windfall benefits for private actors through planning activities are difficult to calculate (Alterman, 2014). These planning decisions are primarily policy directives, and the (typically) Town and Country Planning Act provides legitimacy and authority for planning. Increasing urbanization across the world, and pressure on municipal authorities to provide better services have brought planning laws to central focus of the policy arena in current times.

This approach of some legal domains having special significance is an instrumental use of law by public policy. It fails to identify the linchpin, which connects both of them. In fact, the closer connection between law and policy is through the nature of complexity of public problems – primarily through a process of globalization.

Globalization, law and policy

Perhaps there is no better field to interrogate the respective roles of law and policy than the current process of globalization. Globalization is the "intensification of economic, political, social and cultural relations across borders" (Braithwaite and Drahos, 2000: 9). In the area of business regulation it has meant giving primacy to the role of the self-regulating market which has translated into support for deregulation, privatization and disinvestment. This form of globalization always implies a form of war on both human and natural substance of society. As Polanyi (1944) presciently observed:

> Our thesis is that the idea of a self-adjusting market implied a stark Utopia. Such an institution could not exist for any length of time without

annihilating the human and natural substance of society; it would have physically destroyed man and transformed his surroundings into a wilderness.

(p. 43)

This war of the 'self-adjusting market' on people was always resisted by the people. The resistance took the form of public protests and also resorted to the law. The law included both statutory law, which embodied the promise of the Constitution, as well as the Constitution itself. For the movement of a self-adjusting market, there was a counter movement from society. As Polanyi (1944) put it:

> Inevitably, society took measures to protect itself, but whatever measures it took impaired the self-regulation of the market, disorganized industrial life, and thus endangered society in yet an other way. It was this dilemma which forced the development of the market system into a definite groove and finally disrupted the social organization based upon it.
>
> *(p. 43)*

The point to be made about both law and policy in this context is that globalization advances its agenda primarily by policy and it is left to social movements to counter the policy changes introduced by globalization using the law. As Upendra Baxi puts it, the human rights regime inaugurated by the Universal Declaration of Human Rights is being supplanted by a framework of trade-related, market-friendly human rights (Baxi, 2012: xliv).

The legal framework which we have identified as the source of the normative values of both law and public policy is slowly being supplanted. Perhaps in a slight modification of the Baxi thesis, the constitutional framework is being supplanted not by any one law but by a policy framework with its roots in adherence to the Washington Consensus in country after country.

In India this new model of a progressive divestment of state responsibility was announced through the 'New Economic Policy' inaugurated by Manmohan Singh in 1991, taking its guidance from the Washington consensus. In the Indian context it is this significant declaration of policy intent which has moulded the direction that the Indian state has taken since 1992, drifting away from its moorings in the Constitution (Pellissery and Mathew, 2018). In this case policy serves as the handmaiden of globalization and constitutional law serves as the heroic bulwark against these changes. Of course it should be noted that in many cases policy seems to have won over constitutional law.

This policy change is really a global process. Braithwaite and Drahos argue that the world is witnessing an intensification of the globalization of rules and standards. This naturally means that global standards will regulate increasing areas of human life, right from what we eat, to the condition of the environment to the treatment of labour (Braithwaite and Drahos, 2000).

The point to be made is that these global standards, which can often originate in needs of a few corporations (as Drahos and Braithwaite demonstrate), become the law for many millions of people, completely supplanting the constitutional framework.

Thus a study of globalization and its impacts on law and policy can only lead us to conclude that the constitution as source of values and as the embodiment of a certain policy consensus is very much under threat today in most regions of the Global South. While activists have sought to defend the vision of the constitution through movements such as the Movement to Save the Constitution in India, there might very well be a need for a policy articulation at a wider level than the defence of the values of the constitution alone.

In this context one can note the emergence of new policy frameworks which have arisen out of the struggles of the global movement for climate justice. This has found policy recognition through a resolution moved in the US House of Representatives by newly elected member, Alexandria Ocasio-Cortez and others popularly referred to as the 'Green New Deal'. The name itself invokes both the New Deal of FDR as a model of state intervention as well as a crisis of the environment. The Green New Deal acknowledges the impacts of globalization on jobs, environment, health etc., and rather than seeking to mitigate its worst effects through the use of the legal framework, seeks to articulate a new policy framework.

The policy document acknowledges the environmental, social and economic ill effects of climate change, notes the problem of persistent inequality by stating that, "the top 1 percent of earners accruing 91 percent of gains in the first few years of economic recovery after the Great Recession" and calls for new socio-economic programmes which can deal with the severe crisis in which the country finds itself.

As the authors note:

> Whereas the House of Representatives recognizes that a new national, social, industrial, and economic mobilization on a scale not seen since World War II and the New Deal era is a historic opportunity –
>
> (1) to create millions of good, high-wage jobs in the United States;
> (2) to provide unprecedented levels of prosperity and economic security for all people of the United States; and
> (3) to counteract systemic injustices:[28]

The Green New Deal is still a policy proposal moved in the House of Representatives and not yet anywhere close to being accepted. The articulation itself emerges from an older articulation by the global activism around climate justice, which has repeatedly stressed that the way forward in these times of environmental crisis is to see the crisis as a moment of opportunity to transform existing socio-political structures and respond to issues of continuing injustice, be it attacks on workers' rights, environmental rights or refugee rights.[29]

In this conundrum of the link between law and policy, the most significant global shifts have emerged from the policy consensus referred to as the Washington consensus. The efforts to constrain the negative efforts of the Washington consensus

12 Babu Mathew et al.

has led to a stress on the frameworks of the constitution in the Global South. However the question to be asked is, is the time right for a global articulation of a counter policy which can displace the Washington consensus and began a shift towards a policy rooted in climate, social and economic justice?

Law and policy: practice models of reasoning

Beyond the worldview, practice elements bring us close to the ground. Both in positivist law as well as positivist policymaking 'causal' models operating in respective disciplines determine the 'reasoning' they put forward for solving a case or a public problem.[30] But, how decisions are in practice really arrived at for future course of action, backed by a creative logic of human mind,[31] is in conflict with deterministic models. We find divergences in policy and law when we move out of formalist and positivist models of decision making. For instance, theory of evidence and theory of precedent (along with theories of subsidiarity) play crucial roles in decision making in the legal domain.[32] Through these limitations discretionary role is limited, to ensure predictability (Kreis and Christensen, 2013) and stability of the system that law intends to uphold. In contrast, public policy allows discretionary social and political choices given a wide range of evidence. Though the positivist model counts statistics and numbers as evidence, in post-positivist models what counts as evidence is often influenced by the ideas and values that prevail in a given society and time, rather than governed by a clear theory of evidence. It is for this reason, the policy making process often is art than reason to deal with public problems, whose emergence is not based on rational models (Wildavsky, 1979).

The practice model of law, where discretion is limited, raises a question of how effective judiciary and legal domain could be to engage with public problems. It is here that judiciary's co-existence with other institutions in the polity becomes relevant. There are two models while responding to this issue: the American model of *separation of powers* and the European model (practiced in Germany, Italy, Japan, Canada, India and South Africa) of *mediation of powers* (see Lijphart, 1999 for an account from the perspective of political science and see Ingram, 2006 for a legal account). These two models are debating a knotty problem of whether legislature or judiciary has an upper hand in deciding the rules that affect us all. Classical philosophers such as Rousseau, Hegel and Kant viewed that legitimacy of law, in terms of obligation by an individual to obey the law, came when he or she has freely consented to the same. This is possible when elected representatives discuss and debate laws first, *mediated* by the other branches of executive and judiciary. This mediational approach rejects the American model of checks and balances between three separate institutions of executive, legislature and judiciary. The American model has been under strain after the famous Bush vs Gore election judgement[33] (see also Ackerman, 2000).

A procedurally perfect democracy and constitutional institutions alone do not legitimize public policy. Laswell's (1951: 4) articulation of "policy sciences of democracy . . . directed towards knowledge to improve the practice of democracy" refers to substantive democracy. The supremacy given to the elected representatives assumes a well-functioning democracy. This is one aspect where the democracies in the Global South are contrasted with the Global North. The incentive structure (arising from a variety of asymmetries of power and information between citizens and politicians) of political economy of public problems evinced least interest by the elected government to solve them (Keefer and Khemani, 2005). Further, in several sectors, crony capitalist arrangements served public interest decisions to favour private interests. It is for this reason, the state is the defendant in more than one third of the cases in most of the courts in the Global South. In such a scenario, citizens fight against the state in the court on a range of policy issues such as access to health care and drugs, access to school education, access to food grains etc. Several scholars have argued that a court-led judgement cannot replace the public policy approach, due to monological decision making as noted in the previous section.

Yet, democratic institutions in the Global South allow very limited space for reasoned deliberations[34] (Sen, 2009) since the traditional institutions of religion, society and feudal political structures still overshadow the state. In the West too, the origins of law and policy were precisely for these institutions. However, a historical break[35] happened in Western societies through the formation of citizenship and state (Marshall, 1950; Turner, 1990). Democracy as a form of governance and its interface with capitalist forms of accumulation, mediated through markets (facilitated by the state), required "merging of State and Society as common expressions of a set of shared values" (Clapham, 1985: 12). Most of the nation-states in the Global South did not have this historical break. State formation occurred through post-colonial processes. Huge social and economic inequality that existed in the Global South reinforced the absence of a historical break. Thus, 'public' space was predominantly occupied by society, religion and elite political voices in the Global South.

Two suggestions are made to respond to this apathy. The first suggestion is to improve the deliberations in the policymaking process. This is to improve the pre-legislative processes through wider participation of the public. Very often, this is limited to elite sections of society. A participative pre-legislative process backed up with statutory requirements could mandate politicians to adopt certain standard operating procedures before legislation is introduced in the parliament. A second suggestion is to introduce Legislative Impact Assessments (LIA). In some countries in the Global North this is a pre-requisite for the introduction of legislation. LIA undertakes prospective assessments about the costs that a particular legislation would incur. Once the feasibility assessment is conducted, the argument of impracticality is reduced to a great extent.

Who asks, when, how and what

While defining politics, public policy founding scholar Harold Laswell (1936) opined "Politics is who gets what when and how." To capture the difference and similarities between law and policy in terms of demands for the same, we found nothing better than paraphrasing the same expression. Both legal and policy scholars are in agreement on the reasons for demanding new legislation, constitutional amendments and new policies. When norms change in society then 'felt-needs' are changed. The driving force behind such change is through re-composition of social class, when existing frameworks that govern the society are found to be outdated. A friction between different sections of society on values typically happen in such a context, leading to either collective agreement on status quo or to demand changes.[36] While this broad agreement between law and policy is a matter of common sense, how interests are represented is contrasting.

At the core of professional practice of law, different lawyers representing the interest of their clients in the court of law become central. A range of trained legal actors (judges, prosecutors, attorney generals, notaries, registrars etc.) shape the outcome of particular cases. The hiring capacity of a litigant (firm or individual) for experienced and expert lawyers plays a key role in the litigation process. Compared to this adversarial process, when conflict between two legal entities arises (typically termed as private law[37]), in the matter of public law the demand is for new norms and rules, to which government needs to be adhered (rather than making citizens comply with rules and laws). Judges in the Global South have taken cognizance of the insufficiency of private incentives to litigate in the matters of public good. These factors are execution delays, inadequacy of representation, absence of market driven fee-sharing etc. Therefore, within the framework of transformative constitution (discussed in the previous section) several judges have assumed a role of 'norm entrepreneurs'. This has led to judges setting norms and raising policymakers up to those norms. One very well-cited example for this is how Delhi High Court forced the state government to take actions to improve the air quality in Delhi by instituting regulations on vehicles.[38]

Adversarial nature of judicial system is often misused by private interests who could afford litigation to scuttle the public interest. Very often, decisions to advance public interest are challenged on procedural grounds of decision, rather than substantive matter. Executive action being challenged through the parameters of judicial lens falters. When the court sets aside a project for public good citing non-compliance of 'due process', frustration occurs in the citizen groups, who have limited resources to follow up the litigation.

Another judicial remedy at the disposal of powerful private interests to deal with executives is through 'contempt of court' litigations. This provision is considered as the 'nightmare of an executive'. Through this process, an executive is forced to carry out an action. At the outset, this remedy may look like a powerful tool to discharge the statutory duties. However, as a matter of fact, the private interests use this remedy to cause bureaucrats to promote profiteering aims over public goods. It is in this context that the accountability tools advocated by civil society groups for achieving public goods become important.

An emerging interface of law and policy is through the increasing demands of accountability in the Global South. This aspect is not very pronounced in the Global North, where the shared expectations between citizens and the state are

Why is law central to public policy process? **15**

largely complementary through institutional arrangements. In the Global South several service protests have disturbed the public space, and rampant corruption has demoralized the legitimacy of the state (Pellissery and Bopiah, 2019). It is in this context that demand for accountability has risen. Right to information (to share relevant information with citizens instead of office holders wielding more power through information asymmetry), right to service (if services are not provided in timely manner the officers are fined), or social audit (beyond the financial audit, the accountability to citizens ensured by checking if the objectives of the spending was met) are recent expressions of how law is used to realize policy objectives promised by the state.

Implementability of decisions

Luhmann (1993) points out the self-reproductive capacity of law, by way of simple classification of everything into legal and illegal through a process of judgement. Law achieves its penultimate fruition through this self-reproduction of norms and laws. Compared to this, policy's fruition is through its implementability, not decisive judgement. Policy cannot be subjected to a test of 'right or wrong' on the ground of its decision alone.[39] It is in this sense of inseparability of implementation from policy decision, the famous dictum of 'policy is what it does' emerges (Clay and Schaffer, 1984; Harriss-White, 2003). Policy has to be deliberated with different stakeholders, through which an implementable solution is generated. Similar consultative responsibility does not lay with judges. If implementability is a consideration of judgements, they are often accused of public opinion biases.[40]

Though this key difference between law and policy may be found to be contrastingly stark, at the structure of decision making they are guided by pragmatism. Weber (1922) attributes this distinct development of legalism as justified, since politics (as well as religion) has different ways of reasoning. In other words, universal principles may be sacrificed for particular cases when power decides. This is the bedrock of pragmatic philosophy. Charles Pierce and John Dewey, who spearheaded this movement in the late nineteenth and early twentieth centuries, spoke of the limitations of deductivist and inductivist logic while solving practical problems. They proposed abduction as the method to arrive at context-specific solutions (for an overview see Bromley, 2006). Legal traditions, which acknowledge the presence of politics, have similarly found abduction (though not sufficient) as a method not to scuttle justice by purely adopting logic of the law. How do we evaluate decisions and claims (both in law and policy) with pragmatic orientation?

Sunstein (1995) finds an answer in what he terms as incompletely theorized agreements in legal decisions. In other words, different judges agree on the decision, but not the reasons for the decision. Similarly, orientation of public policy postponing 'hard decisions' is termed as "the science of the muddling through" (Lindblom, 1959). Public policy decisions inspired by purist theoretical orientations are often unrealistic. The decisions often arise from compromises reached by different parties. Yet, for a policymaker, the solace is in the incremental approach of the decision

16 Babu Mathew et al.

making. In other words, a series of decisions in different systems could be managed to produce a positive outcome. This comfort may not be possible for a judge while deciding legal cases. In other words, a litigant stands to lose or win through a judgement, rather than hoping to achieve public good incrementally through his or her case.

It is widely agreed that implementation of court judgements and policy decisions have a life of their own through executive actions. As two separate arms of government, coherence is theoretically expected. This is a matter of legitimacy of the state. In less-legitimate states, norms of local justice prevails (Mathew and Pellissery, 2009). In the Global South on several occasions, executives facing stiff opposition or non–co-operation from politicians claim 'non-implementability'. In contexts where society is much stronger than the state forces (Myrdal, 1968; Riggs, 1964; Migdal, 2001), this is matter of fact. On rare occasions, a court-supervised implementation through *continuous mandamus* is carried out.[41]

Institutional mapping to find the intersectionality of law and policy

Having seen the foundational assumptions within both law and public policy, we could ask the question as to 'what is possible within law' and 'what is possible within policy' in order to address public problems. While approaching a public problem, *possibility of law* is defined through eight conditions of legal processes (Raz, 1979): a) prospective, b) relatively stable, c) made in conformity with clear secondary rules, d) applied by an independent judiciary, e) applied in open and fair hearings, f) susceptible to judicial review by higher courts, g) applied in a timely manner, without excessive court delays, costs etc. and h) free from arbitrary discretion of crime prevention agencies. Compared to this, *possibility of politics* opens up the problem for a diagnosis both for short-term solutions as well as long-term solutions. Thus, creative possibility places policy clarity as a pre-requisite before legal framework could be brought in.

These comparative strengths of each discipline enable us to map the institutions and functions where both of these domains converge and diverge. We classify the functions and institutions broadly into three: Judicial, Constitutional and Statutory. We notice the policy spaces increase progressively in these institutions. We also have arranged institutions from least policy space to high policy space. This arrangement is with a specific aim. We like to show institutional spaces available if a public problem is approached purely legally (more on left side of Table 1.1) or approached in policy-centric manner (more on the right side of Table 1.1).

To elucidate the table for the reader, let us take the first row where the approach towards resolving economic/social conflicts in law and policy are explained. A civil suit between two citizens or between citizens and the state may take place in a civil court when conflicting issues arise. Resolving the issue at that level sets some predictable ground rules for other citizens and the state functionaries (see the discussion in the earlier part of this section). This public good generated through legal

TABLE 1.1 Policy-centric and law-centric institutional spaces to deal with public problems

	Function ↓	Less policy space	→	More policy space
Judicial	Economic/social conflict resolutions	Civil courts	Competition commission	Regulatory agencies Planning laws
	Law administering towards protection of Body and property	Criminal courts	Institutions with promotive functions (e.g. legal services, legal literacy and education)	High courts/Supreme courts Constitutional benches
	Law enforcing	Police	Inquiry agencies Customs	Anti-corruption wing Mediation
Constitutional	Lawmaking	Law department scrutinizing and clearing or changing all the bills to be presented in legislature	Writ orders to government Declaring a legislation as *ultra vires*. Law commission/commissions of inquiry	Constitutional amendments and introduction of new legislation through floor activities in the legislature Pre-legislative processes including LIA statutory committees
	Critical law	Law commissions	Civil society responses	People's tribunals
	Transformative role	Vulnerable sections of society seeking legal protection Deviating sections of society from normative frames	Dealing with diversity and inequality Prevention of crime and promotion of healthy society	Translating the goals of progress and economic growth for the country Distributive justice through budgetary instruments and allocative roles of government
Statutory	Executive functions	Administrative law and delegated legislation	Civil service appointments and transfers	Improving governance indicators
	Electoral	Legislation pertaining to procedures of people's representation (elections)	Election commission	Base unit where citizens interact and bargain with elected representatives for realization of substantive democracy
	Counter-veiling institutions	Vigilance commission	Comptroller and auditor general	Social audit institutions Public Accounts Committee
	International legal regimes and statutory responsibility of country	International court Human rights commissions (within country)	Shadow reports to UN bodies	Bilateral and multilateral agreements Foreign policy and trade agreements

Source: Generated by authors primarily considering the law and policy institutions in the Global South. Typically, this excludes civil law tradition.

18 Babu Mathew et al.

processes is subjected through limited deliberation. The occurrence of conflict may be minimized by way of explicated rules of competition. This rule-making process provides increased chances of deliberation. Further, economic rationality of the citizens could be taken into consideration through the regulatory agencies.

The table proves the complementarity between two domains and a continuum that is possible to achieve the greater public good through synergy of law and policy.

Conclusion

In this chapter, we have reviewed the dimensions where law and policy converge and diverge. The review has shown how different traditions of conceptualizing public interest exist in both law and policy. This unpacking of disciplines enables us to find arenas where interdisciplinarity could be fostered both in theory and practice. The striking point is how constitutional principles provide guidance (both legal and policy) when conflicting value frameworks emerge on public problems. When policy alone (or law alone) is viewed as a vantage point, the space where they overlap becomes less fertile for intervention. Rather than seeing these two disciplines as 'policy vs law' we have shown shared arenas of practice through examples where they often interface.

Is interdisciplinarity a desirable objective between law and policy? Our review has shown that left to themselves, these disciplines become counter-productive to public interest. Therefore, interdisciplinarity is not a choice. Within the frameworks of democracy and capitalism, both law and public policy play a complimentary role while advancing public interest.

The institutional crisis that is looming large across nation-states points out that mono-rationalities of disciplines may aggravate the problem rather than solving it. Existing frameworks of disciplines are not sufficient to advance public interest. They have, rather, contributed to the making of crises. The crisis of corporate-funded democratic processes, limitations of capitalism, and the search for responsive bureaucracy all indicate that society moves ahead faster than the institutions which are designed for the wellbeing of society. This institutional crisis compels us to search for novel ways to make law and public policy relevant for society. The traditional approach of policy as a vision to solve the public problems, and the legal approach as a compliance mechanism to generate stability within this vision, is no longer tenable. This redefined prophetic role has the potential to humanize the profession of problem solving itself beyond a managerial approach to public problems.

Notes

1 We acknowledge the review comments by Des Gaspers and N. Jayaram on the earlier version of this chapter, which have tremendously helped us to improve this chapter. We also thank the discussants and participants of the panel on 'Interface of Law and Public Policy' organized during the third international conference of Public Policy 28–30 June 2017 at Lee Kuan Yew School of Public Policy, Singapore. We also have benefited

Why is law central to public policy process? **19**

from various rounds of discussion with Master of Public Policy students of National Law School of India University, Bangalore where ideas of this chapter were consulted on different occasions. An earlier version of this chapter was published as Occasional Paper 05/2019 of the Institute of Public Policy, National Law School of India University, Bangalore.

2 We are not neglecting the contributions from earlier philosophers such as Montesquieu (eighteenth century). Our focus here is to trace the foundations for legitimacy of systematic account of law in public decision making.

3 Dworkin is leaning towards the Hegelian school of thought about law. Hegel opposed Immanuel Kant's conceptualization of law as a Categorical Imperative that emerges from rational certainty. Kantian position says "these universal principles obligate us without exception; indeed they reduce the substance of law to the unitary form of logical consistency: treating the persons and situations the same way" (Ingram 2006: 35). Hegel challenges this and demands for integration of morality and legality. Refer to Waldron (1988) for comparison of Hegel and Kant.

4 For instance, the Indian Constitution makes it explicit through Article 13. Law to be considered valid law will have to conform to the mandate of the Constitution. Article 13 of the Constitution states:

13. (1) All laws in force in the territory of India immediately before the commencement of this Constitution, in so far as they are inconsistent with the provisions of this Part, shall, to the extent of such inconsistency, be void.

(2) The State shall not make any law which takes away or abridges the rights conferred by this Part and any law made in contravention of this clause shall, to the extent of the contravention, be void.

(3) In this article, unless the context otherwise requires, –

(a) "law" includes any Ordinance, order, bye-law, rule, regulation, notification, custom or usage having in the territory of India the force of law;

(b) "laws in force" includes laws passed or made by a Legislature or other competent authority in the territory of India before the commencement of this Constitution and not previously repealed, notwithstanding that any such law or any part thereof may not be then in operation either at all or in particular areas.

5 Note that in some of the countries in the Global North, where colonial rule for a sustained period took place, similar situations occurred (e.g. United States of America).

6 Several civil society movements approach the Constitution as a moral guiding principle, rather than a document to rely for arguments in the Court. Such movements infuse life into policy domain, taking inspiration from the Constitution. Some of the grassroots organizations have been able to translate these moral musings into radical legal alternatives. For example, the slogan of *hamara paise, hamara hisab* (our money, our account) of Mazdoor Kisan Shakti Sangatan was used while demanding the legislation for the right to information through a citizen campaign in India.

7 Article 21 of the Indian Constitution reads: "Protection of life and personal liberty – No person shall be deprived of his life or personal liberty except according to procedure established by law."

8 The key contention was whether freedom to dispose of one's property was a right which had to function within the limits of the constitutional protection of equality of all persons. The court held in the affirmative. Refer to Curators v. The University of Kwa-Zulu Natal, 2011 (1) BCLR 40 (SCA).

9 Ibid., at para 38.

10 See Ralf Brinktine (2001), "The horizontal effect of human rights in German constitutional law", (2001) *European Human Rights Law Review* 421. See the famous *Luth* case: BVerfGE 7, 198.

11 Curators, *supra* note 8, para 38.

12 If one expects solutions for newer problems from a constitution, are we not looking backward for solutions? Where do constitutional assemblies get legitimacy? These are classical questions debated by scholars (ref. Arendt, 1973; Ackerman, 1991; Derrida 1992; Habermas, 1996; 2001; Hegel, 1991; Michaelman, 1998).

13 Primarily inspired by European enlightenment and the French revolution.

14 Refer also McAdams (2005) and Ware (2013).

15 Accountability, stability, predictability, protection against time inconsistency, protection against short-term passions and prevention of economic suicide are the impacts of constitutionalism to which Elster alludes. Even when legal processes lead to punishment for individuals and firms, it has a clear aim of public good. Different reasons for punishment such as deterrence, rehabilitation, societal protection through incapacitation, retribution, restoration and education all show how public good is clearly attempted.

16 Miller and Hammond (1994) show politics is more fundamental than economics when decisions of public good are taken. Literature on welfare maximization through an economic efficiency approach is also critiqued by several scholars. Among this literature, Sen (1984) identifies the weaknesses of both consequentialist and deontological approaches when decisions of public good are taken. In subsequent writings, Sen has advocated human rights approach. None of these approaches alone, in itself, including the human rights approach, meets the sufficiency condition as a method of decision making for public good.

17 On this idea of 'consent for the constitution', there is no agreement among scholars. Wicksell (1896) considered a constitution passes the universal consent test. But, Tullock and Buchanan (1962) were convinced that some coercion is required if constitutional morality has to be operationalized. Unanimous consent was nearly impossible due to a Rawlsian veil of ignorance. Yet, since citizens are unlikely to foresee their future interest, they would prefer rules that did not favour any particular interest (Rawls, 1971).

18 Critics of Habermas do not agree that democratic deliberation is the best way to arrive at decisions. They point out the inefficiencies of democracy, particularly in divisive societies. When public issues are deeply divisive, no political party is ready to bring such issues into the agenda for deliberation. Such delay tactics deepen the problem to an extent of finding a solution. A good example is how both liberals and right-wing political parties agreed on contentious issues of citizenship registry questions (conflict between migrants and settlers in North-East India) and temple construction (conflict between Hindus and Muslims) to be decided by the Supreme Court, rather than politically settling them.

19 A validating example is when the South African court aimed to settle the question of how much water should be provided to citizens by municipal authorities to enable citizens to lead a decent life. Where consensus could be achieved was to ensure the municipality takes adequate measures to provide water. There was no consensus achieved through legal process as to how much water should be provided. On the other hand, public policy frameworks do take up these questions. In India, while providing permissions for new housing areas, Delhi Development Authority follows the guidelines to check the capacity to provide water by the municipality.

20 This was articulated by former Chief Justice of India as follows: "Extent of judicial interference in governmental issues depends on how effectively and efficiently the government does its job. Which court would want to intervene if the government works efficiently and sincerely? The courts only fulfil their constitutional duty and need would not arise if the governments do their job" (Justice T. S. Thakur reported in *Indian Express* dated 7 June 2016).

21 This history is sufficiently studied in the literature, particularly that of land policies. Refer to Allen (2007), Pellissery and Sattwick (2012) and Mitra (2017) for an overview.

22 For instance, special rapporteurs of the UN who visit countries to prepare a status report on several sectors in which countries have signed UN Conventions interact with a range of stakeholders, citizens and civil society groups.

23 For instance refer to the literature on property rights as human rights (Pellissery et al., 2017).

Why is law central to public policy process? **21**

24 There are some countries (for instance the U.S.) where lobbying in a policy domain is legitimated. In contexts where lobbying is not legitimated, the art of influencing is opaque (Sabatier, 1988).

25 Representation of public policy demands are primarily through elected politicians. Beginning with Tiebout (1956) the scholarship on how a public choice approach influences policy decision making is presented as a paradigmatic opponent to rational choice approach, where policy options are transitively ranked to facilitate decision making.

26 See Lowi's (1972) seminal study which summarizes different case studies of bill introduction processes.

27 The principle of eminent domain – the State has sovereign control over the territory – allows private property to be acquired for public purposes.

28 H.Res 119, available at: www.congress.gov/116/bills/hres109/BILLS-116hres109ih.pdf

29 Klein (2015) argues that one cannot think of the climate crisis outside the framework of social and economic justice and any solution to climate justice must encompass fundamental changes in both social and political structures.

30 Refer to chapter 1 of Bromley (2006) for the distinction of reason and cause.

31 Read Arendt (1958) for the distinction of action and behaviour in public space.

32 However, a judge decides to break this precedent in some landmark cases (e.g. Brown vs the Board of Education of Topeka, 1954).

33 On the question of re-counting the votes in the state of Florida, where Bush had marginal victory being challenged by Al Gore on the reason of uncounted votes, while the state secretary and Supreme Court of Florida ordered for re-counting, Supreme Court of America intervened and cancelled re-counting on a narrow 5–4 decision.

34 In the sense of 'government by discussion' through a public exchange of reasons and 'open impartiality' (Sen 2009: 321–54). Public opinion and different frames of valuation that the public hold influence the quality of deliberations. It is in this sense the ideas and ideational approach in public policy framework (for different ideational frameworks in public policy refer Campbell, 1998) becomes the equivalent to the Constitutional values within the legal approach.

35 On state formation refer to Tilly (1975), Skocpol (1979). On democracy see Moore (1966), Huntington (1968).

36 Giving credence to the definition of "Policy is what government choose to do not to do" (Dye, 1992).

37 The distinction and theorization of private law and public law is classical (refer Jolowics and Nicholas, 1967). Private law referred to 'natural' rights, which could be arrived through reason in an apolitical manner. Compared to this, public law was concerned with public good, which essentially involved consultation and participation of people. However, this distinction lost its credibility since the early decades of the twentieth century, when formalist interpretations of law were shown to be favouring the business interests. Yet, some die-hard formalists prefer to maintain this distinction. Some scholars have introduced the concept of 'social law' to transcend this distinction (refer to Gurvitch, 1941). Also see how private law affecting Constitutionalism in Indian context is argued by Balganesh (2016).

38 Chapter 4 of Mathur (2013) is an excellent case study on this. He summarizes the lessons from this case as:

> "Political leadership may agree to the enactment of laws but block their implementation. When activist environmentalist groups do not see enough action in the enactment of laws, they search for ways that can force the government into implementing laws. Realising that it is futile to work through political leadership that has already demonstrated its resistance, they began to search for state institutions outside the electoral arena that enforce implementation" (p. 118).

39 There are several policies which are bad at the decision-making stage. See for instance, Scott (1998). What we are refuting is the pessimistic argument of good policy as unimplementable (Mosse, 2004).

22 Babu Mathew et al.

40 Yet, several judgements are shelved by executives because they are impractical. As we have seen earlier in the chapter, this is a classical tension of formalism and realism. Habermas (1996: 201) acknowledges that the value considerations politicians are engaged with – not merely facts of the case – enters into legal domain: "One can no longer clearly distinguish between law and politics . . . because judges, like future-oriented politicians, make their decisions on the basis of value orientations they consider reasonable . . . [or] justified on utilitarian or welfare-economic grounds."

41 Refer to Sturm (1991) for a range of remedies when public law is decided in the courts. In 2002 the Supreme Court of India appointed two commissioners for the purpose of monitoring the implementation of all orders relating to the right to food (PUCL vs Union of India and others, Writ Petition 196 of 2001). In the context of persistent hunger in the states of Orissa and Jharkhand, this court intervention had tremendous impact in localities where particular dominant societal forces colluded with the state forces for siphoning the public provisions.

References

Ackerman, B. (1991) *We the people – vol. 1: Foundations*. Cambridge, MA: Harvard University Press.

———. (2000) "The new separation of powers", *Harvard Law Review,* 113(3), 633–729.

Allen, T. (2007) "Property as fundamental right in India, Europe and South Africa", *Asia Pacific Law Review*, 15(2), 193–218.

Alterman, R. (2014) "Planning laws, development controls, and social equity: Lessons for developing countries", *The World Bank Legal Review,* 5, 329–350.

Arendt, H. (1958) *Human condition*. Chicago: University of Chicago Press.

———. (1973) *On revolution*. New York: Viking Press.

Austin, J. (1995) *The province of jurisprudence determined*. Cambridge: Cambridge University Press.

Baldwin, R., Martin, C. and Martin, L. (2013) *Understanding regulation: Theory, strategy and practice*. Oxford: Oxford University Press.

Balganesh, S. (2016) "The constitutionalization of Indian private law", Faculty Scholarship. Paper 1557. Available at: http://scholarship.law.upenn.edu/faculty_scholarship/1557 (Accessed 10 October 2018).

Bhagwati, P. N. and Dias, C. J. (2012) "The judiciary in India: A hunger and thirst for justice", *NUJS Law Review,* 171.

Barclay, S. and Birkland, T. (1998) "Law, policymaking, and the policy process: Closing the gaps", *Policy Studies Journal,* 26, 227–243.

Baxi, U. (2012) *The future of human rights*. Delhi: Oxford University Press.

Braithwaite, J. and Drahos, P. (2000) *Global business regulation*. Cambridge: Cambridge University Press.

Brinktine, R. (2001) "The horizontal effect of human rights in German constitutional law", *European Human Rights Law Review,* 421.

Bromley, D. W. (2006) *Sufficient reason*. Princeton: Princeton University Press.

Campbell, J. L. (1998) "Institutional analysis and the role of ideas in political economy", *Theory and Society,* 27(5), 380–392.

Clapham, C. S. (1985) *Third world politics: An introduction*. Wisconsin: University of Wisconsin Press.

Clay, E. J. and Schaffer, B. J. (1984) *Room for Manoeuvre: An exploration of public policy planning in Agricultural and Rural Development*. London: Heinemann Educational Publishers.

Davy, B. (2012) *Land policy: Planning and spatial consequences of the property*. London: Ashgate.

Davy, B. and Pellissery, S. (2013) "The citizenship promises (un) fulfilled: The right to housing in informal settings", *International Journal of Social Welfare,* 22, S68–S84.

Derrida, J. (1992) "The force of law: The mystical foundation of authority", in D. Cornell, M. Rosenfield, and D. G. Carlson (eds.), *Deconstruction and the possibility of justice.* New York: Routledge.

Dworkin, R. (1977) *Taking rights seriously.* Cambridge, MA: Harvard University Press.

———. (1986) *Law's empire.* Cambridge, MA: Harvard University Press.

Dye, T. (1992) *Understanding public policy.* Englewood Cliffs, NJ: Prentice Hall.

Elster, J. (1995) "The impact of constitutions on economic performance", in Proceedings of the World Bank Annual Conference on Development Economics 1994.

Estrada-Tanck, D. (2016) *Human rights and human security under international law.* London: Hart Publishing.

Gurvitch, G. (1941) "The problem of social law", *Ethics,* 52(1).

Habermas, J. (1996) *Between facts and norms: Contributions to the discourse theory of law and democracy.* Cambridge, MA: MIT Press.

———. (2001) "Constitutional democracy: A paradoxical union of contradictory principles?" *Political Theory,* 29(6), 766–781.

Harriss-White, B. (2003) "Development, policy and agriculture in India in 1990s". QEH Working Paper Series WPS78.

Hart, H. L. A. (1961/2012) *The concept of law.* Oxford: Clarendon Press.

Hegel, G. W. F. (1991) *Elements of philosophy of right* (ed. A. Wood, trans. H. B. Nisbit). Cambridge: Cambridge University Press.

Huntington, S. (1968) *Political order in changing societies.* New Haven: Yale University Press.

Ingram, D. (2006) *Law: Key concepts in philosophy.* London: Continuum International Publishing Group.

Jolowics, H. F. and Nicholas, B. (1967) *Historical introduction to the study of Roman law.* Cambridge: Cambridge University Press.

Keefer, P. and Khemani, S. (2005) "Democracy, public expenditures and the poor", *The World Bank Research Observer,* 20(1), 1–27.

Khosla, M. (2010) "Making social rights conditional: Lessons from India", *International Journal of Constitutional Law,* 8(4), 739–765.

Klein, N. (2015) *This changes everything.* New York: Penguin.

Kreis, A. M. and Christensen, R. K. (2013) "Law and public policy", *Policy Studies Journal,* 41(s1), S38–S52.

Landes, W. M. and Posner, R. A. (1979) "Adjudication as a private good", *Journal of Legal Studies,* 8, 235–238.

Laswell, H. (1936) *Politics: Who gets what, when, how.* London: McGraw-Hill Book Co.

———. (1951) "Policy orientation", in D. Lerner and H. D. Lasswell (eds.), *The policy sciences: Recent developments in scope and method.* Stanford: Stanford University Press, pp. 3–15.

Lindblom, C. E. (1959) "The science of muddling through", *Public Administration Review,* 19(2) 79–88.

Lijphart, A. (1999) *Patterns of democracy.* London: New Haven.

Lowi, T. (1972) "Four systems of policy, politics, and choice", *Public Administration Review,* 32(1), 298–310.

Luhmann, N. (1993) *Law as a social system.* Oxford: Oxford University Press.

Marshall, T. H. (1950) "Citizenship and social class", in Thomas H. Marshall (ed.), *Citizenship and social class and other essays.* Cambridge: Cambridge University Press, pp. 1–85.

Mathew, L. and Pellissery, S. (2009) "Enduring local justice in India: An anomaly or response to diversity", *Psychology and Developing Societies,* 21(1).

Mathur, K. (2013) *Public policy and politics in India*. New Delhi: Oxford University Press.
McAdams, R. H. (2005) "The expressive power of adjudication", *University of Illinois Law Review*, 1043–1114.
Michaelman, F. I. (1998) "Constitutional authorship", in L. Alexander (ed.), *Constitutionalism: Philosophical Foundations*. Cambridge: Cambridge University Press.
Migdal, J. (2001) *State in society: How states and societies transform and constitute*. Cambridge: Cambridge University Press.
Miller, G. and Hammond, T. (1994) "Why is politics more important than economics", *Journal of Theoretical Politics*, 6(1).
Mitra, M. D. (2017) "Evolution of property rights in India", in S. Pellissery, B. Davy, and H. M. Jacobs (eds.), *Land Policies in India*. Singapore: Springer, pp. 35–50.
Moore, B. (1966) *Social origins of dictatorship and democracy*. London: Beacon Press.
Mosse, D. (2004) "Is good policy unimplementable? Reflections on the ethnography of aid policy and practice", *Development and Change*, 35(4), 639–671.
Murphy, J. G. and Coleman, J. (1990) *Philosophy of law: An introduction to jurisprudence*. New York: Routledge.
Myrdal, G. (1968) *Asian drama*. New Delhi: Kalyani Publishers.
Nussbaum, M. C. (2006) "Poverty and human functioning: Capabilities as fundamental entitlements", in D. B. Grusky and R. Kanbur (eds.), *Poverty and inequality*. Stanford: Stanford University Press, pp. 47–75.
Pellissery, S. and Bopiah, P. (2019) "Corruption and social policy", in *Oxford handbook of public administration for social policy* (forthcoming).
Pellissery, S. and Mathew, B. (2018) Relevance of constitutional economics in post-neoliberal India" Occasional Working Paper Series 1/2018, Institute of Public Policy, Bangalore.
Pellissery, S, and Sattwick Biswas (2012) "Emerging property regimes in India: What it holds for the future of socio-economic rights?" IRMA Working Paper No. 234.
Pellissery, S., Davy, B. and Jacobs, H. (2017) *Land policies in India*. Singapore: Springer.
Polanyi, K. (1944) *The great transformation*. London: Farrar & Rinehart.
Prosser, T. (2006) "Regulation and social solidarity", *Journal of Law and Society*, 33, 364–387.
Rawls, J. (1971) *Theories of Justice*. Harvard: Harvard University Press.
Raz, J. (1979) *The authority of law*. Oxford: Clarendon Press.
Riggs, F. W. (1964) *Administration in developing countries: Theory of prismatic societies*. London: Houghton Mifflin.
Sabatier, P. (1988) "An advocacy coalition framework of policy change and the role of policy-oriented learning therein", *Policy Sciences*, 21(2–3), 129–168.
Schwartz, B. and Wade, H. W. R. (1972) *Legal control of government*. Oxford: Clarendon Press.
Scott, J. C. (1998) *Seeing like a state*. New Heaven: Yale University Press.
Sen, A. (1984) "Rights and agency", *Philosophy and Public Affairs*, 11(1), 3–39.
Sen, A. (2009) *The idea of justice*. Harvard: Harvard University Press.
Skocpol, T. (1979) *States and social revolutions*. Cambridge: Cambridge University Press.
Stone, D. (2012) *Policy paradox*. New York: W. W. Norton & Co.
Sturm, S. P. (1991) "A normative theory of public law remedies", *The Georgetown Law Journal*, 79, 1355–1446.
Sunstein, C. (1995) "Incompletely theorised agreements", *Harvard Law Review*, 108(7), 1733–1772.
Tiebout, C. M. (1956) "A pure theory of local expenditures", *Journal of Political Economy*, 64(5), 416–424.
Teitel, R. G. (2013) *Humanity's law*. Oxford: Oxford University Press.
Tilly, C. (1975) *The formation of national states in Western Europe*. Princeton: Princeton University Press.

Tullock, G. and Buchanan, J. (1962) *The calculus of consent*. Michigan: The University of Michigan Press.

Turner, B. (1990) "Outline of a theory of citizenship", *Sociology*, 24(2), 189–217.

Vilhena, O., Baxi, U. and Viljoen, F. (2013) *Transformative constitutionalism*. Pretoria: Pretoria University Law Press.

Waldron, J. (1988) "When Justice replaces affection: The need for rights", *Harvard Journal of Law and Public Policy*, 625.

Wade, W. (1971) *Administrative law*. Oxford: Clarendon Press.

Ware, S. J. (2013) "Is adjudication a public good? Overcrowded courts and private sector alternative of arbitration", *Cardozo Journal of Conflict Resolution*, 14, 899–921.

Weber, M. (1922) *Economy and society*. Berkeley, CA: University of California Press.

Wicksell, K. (1896) "Studies in the theory of public finance", translated as "A new principle of just taxation" [1896] in R. A. Musgrave and A. T. Peacock (eds.), *Classics in the theory of public finance*. London: Macmillan, 1958, pp. 72–118.

Wildavsky, A. (1979) *Speaking truth to power: The art and craft of policy analysis*. California, CA: Transaction Publishers.

Uhr, J. (2006) "Constitution and rights", in G. Peters and J. Pierre (eds.), *The handbook of public policy*. London: Sage Publications, pp. 169–185.

2

THE RISE OF AN ANTI-GLOBAL DOCTRINE AND STRIKES IN PUBLIC SERVICES[1]

Lilach Litor[2]

Introduction

The chapter explores the application of international labour standards in a context of different constitutions – in Canada, Germany and Israel – and its implications on the freedom to strike in public services and the capacity of the state to regulate labour disputes. It discusses the transformation of the rule of law in the age of globalization and the role of international labour standards in relation to constitutionalism within the nation-state.

The chapter distinguishes between two approaches – a global integrative doctrine and a political doctrine. According to the latter a constitutional right to strike should not be recognized unless included specifically in domestic constitutional documents, while according to the former global constitutionalism is based on the application of international labour standards. This chapter also presents a third approach: an anti-global doctrine, which includes local constitutionalism and emphasizes the role of the nation-state. It includes a protection of labour interests, irrespective of possible restrictions in international labour standards. The chapter suggests the embracement of the anti-global approach, which strengthens domestic institutions and their capacity to design public policy.

The chapter is divided into eight sections. The first section discusses the implications of the potential conflict of law and policy design on the issue of labour. The second section discusses the interface of public policy and labour law, with regard to the right to strike in public services. The third section discusses the freedom to strike and international labour standards. The fourth section discusses the effects of the globalization process on public employees and then presents the three different doctrines for constitutionalism in public services: a political doctrine, an anti-global doctrine and a global integrative doctrine, within global human rights governance. The fifth section presents the development of an anti-global doctrine and local constitutionalism in Israeli jurisprudence. The sixth section presents the German jurisprudence. The seventh section presents the jurisprudence of the Supreme Court of Canada and the embracement of a global integrative doctrine and global constitutionalism. The eighth section discusses the issue of the application of an anti-global doctrine in the age of globalization vis-à-vis the other doctrines.

The potential conflict of law and policy and its implications on labour

The issue of applying a right to strike is related to the interplay of law and public policy. In the case of collective disputes in public services, recognizing a fundamental right to strike is related to the capacity of unions as interest groups within the public policy arena to be heard. Nevertheless, recognizing a right to strike interferes with the state's attempt to address the public interest in the continuation of the supply of public and essential services. The legal recognition of a fundamental right to strike therefore could be considered as undermining the capacity of the state to design public policy regarding public services' supply (Etherington, 2009).

Recognizing a right to strike on the basis of international standards influences the ability of the state to freely design public policy. It weakens the domestic political institutions and the effect of local agendas. Hence, basing constitutionalism on local constitutional documents bears advantages.

These conflicts revolve around the issue of recognition of the freedom to strike as a constitutional right. The application of constitutionalism regarding strike action in public services lays a burden on the state to enable a wide possibility of collective action. The recognition of a constitutional status of the right to strike might also be a basis for judicial review over legislation and decisions of the executive branches that limit strike action, in regard to certain public services or specific public tasks. This raises the question of what kind of approach the courts should embrace regarding these conflicts.

Different scholars have discussed the transformation of the rule of the law and constitutionalism in the age of globalization (Jayasuriya, 2001). Some of them emphasized that the wider role of international law in the globalization era should be captured as the rise of a new mode of governance (Kumm, 2004). Others emphasized that in the globalization era supranational labour institutions, such as the International Labor Organization (hereinafter ILO) play a bigger role (Mundlak and Finkin, 2015). In regard to these issues Judy Fudge (2015) discussed the development of a global integrative doctrine. According to this doctrine, global constitutionalism – in which international human rights standards are applied – is used in order to recognize a constitutional right to strike.

The rise of a new mode of governance with regard to the specific issue of constitutionalism in the age of globalization accentuates this problematic issue. In the framework of different varieties of constitutionalism in the globalization era, this chapter presents a new notion – that of an anti-global doctrine. According to the anti-global doctrine, the right to strike is derived from other constitutional rights, which are included in domestic constitutional documents. The anti-global approach applies local constitutionalism, while denying the application of various international standards. Hence, an important development in the age of globalization is not only the embracing of a global integrative doctrine and a global labour governance by some courts, but also the development of local anti-global doctrine by other judiciaries. It is important to systematically examine how courts in different countries, with different constitutions, differ in the application of integrative global doctrine and its implications on the capacity of the state to regulate collective disputes and supply public services.

According to the global integrative approach, constitutionalization of strike action is based on the application of international labour standards of the ILO in the interpretation of domestic constitutional documents, while according to the anti-global approach, the constitutionalization of strike action is based on existing domestic constitutional documents.[3] Whereas, according to the political doctrine, strike action is considered mostly as a negative freedom, and constitutionalism is denied, as long as the freedom to strike is not included specifically in domestic constitutional documents.

The interface of labour law, the right to strike in public services and public policy

Recognizing a right to strike in the arena of public services' supply is related to the interface of labour law and public policy. Dye defines public policy as the things governments choose to do, including regulating behaviour, in order to resolve social problems (Dye, 2013). Others emphasize that public policy is made on the public's behalf and is oriented towards a desired state in achieving social goals and addressing the needs of the citizens (Birkland, 2016; Peters, 2010). Law, on the other hand, is a system of rules that are designed and enforced by the state through formal institutions such as laws and constitutions, and contains the rights granted by the state to groups and individuals. A law is therefore the means by which the state fulfils its public policy, including its policy regarding the labour market and collective disputes. Nevertheless, a law that grants individuals and groups with fundamental rights could impose obligations on the state and limit its ability to design public policy.

The application of constitutionalism in a given law system regarding strikes in public services raises a conflict between collective interests and the democratic responsibility of the state to regulate strikes and design public policy. In this respect, mainly a few interests are in collision – the interest of employees, whose work is considered essential or important to have decent terms of employment, and the public interest in receiving public services. It also involves the nation-state's prerogative to manage and regulate the labour market in the globalization era (Etherington, 2009).

That is, there is a conflict between strengthening union rights via constitutionalism based on international standards and the capacity of the nation-state to

The rise of an anti-global doctrine and strikes **29**

independently regulate the labour market. Hence, the implication of international labour standards of the ILO on constitutionalism in the nation-state should be explored.

It could be claimed that recognizing a fundamental right to strike enhances democracy and the possibility of trade unions, as part of civil society, to influence public policy design. The public policy field includes theories that refer to various policy actors. The group theory refers to interest groups as policy actors and their participation in the public policy design (Dye, 2013). According to the group theory, public policy is the equilibrium reached in the group struggle of different interest groups. The task of the law is to manage group conflicts within the public policy design by establishing the rules of the game in the group struggle and enacting compromises in the form of public policy.

Trade unions are interest groups that represent the interests of the working class. Recognizing a plurality of interests and of different interest groups in society could lead to the understanding that these interests cannot be eclipsed merely by the election of a government by a majority vote. Instead effective government should appreciate the particular capability of different interest groups, including trade unions, and grant them representation in decision making (Novitz, 2003). In the case of trade unions, recognizing a right to strike in public and essential services will grant trade unions the possibility to influence public policy design in regard to the labour market.

In this respect we should consider the state's capacity to design public policy regarding strikes vis-à-vis the influence of international labour standards of the ILO. One could claim that basing constitutionalism on international standards of the ILO enhances democratic values. Drawing on deliberative democratic justification, Novitz claimed that discussing controversial issues at the international level achieves an improved quality of debate (Novitz, 2003). In this vein it could also be claimed that the interests of trade unions and employees are best served by applying international labour standards.

Nevertheless, applying international labour standards as a basis for constitutionalism undermines the capacity of the state to design labour policy according to the local political agenda. Hence, we should keep in mind that local cultures, political agendas and the characteristics of domestic labour relations are best served via local constitutionalism.

The specific international principles of the ILO, regarding strikes in public services, are discussed in the following section.

Collective action and international law

Collective freedoms are stated in the United Nations International Covenant on Social Economic and Cultural Rights 1967. Article 8 of the covenant includes the right to organize – the right to form and join trade unions and the right of trade unions to function freely. Article 8 also includes the right to strike. According to this convent, a citizen is entitled not only to political and civil rights but also to social rights including labour-related social rights (Marshall 1992). In regard to public services, the covenant specifically states that it does not prevent the imposition of lawful restrictions on the exercise of these rights by members of the armed forces or the police or by the administration of the state. The right to organize is also included in international treaties of the ILO, such as ILO Convention 87 on the Freedom of Association and Protection of the Right to Organize 1948 and ILO Convention 98 on the Right to Organize and Collective Bargaining 1949. That is, strike action by itself is not included directly in the ILO conventions. Yet the ILO committees have recognized in their decisions and resolutions a right to strike, which is derived from the right to organize (Lorewz, 2016).[4] Even though the ILO committees on the application of ILO conventions have recognized the right to strike in their decisions, the dispute over the status of collective action still continues within the ILO institutions and beyond (Swepston, 2013).

Nevertheless, ILO standards enable the regulation of collective action of public employees, whose tasks are likely to impact the supply of public services. According to the ILO principles, legislative restrictions could define certain public servants whose right to strike is limited due to their special duties and the implication of these duties on the supply of public services. Thus, it is possible to establish limitations on specific public servants who exercise authority in the name of the state due to their special tasks.[5] It was also stated by the ILO committees that the right to strike could be denied or restricted in essential services. Essential services are defined as those services of which interruption would endanger the life, health or personal safety of the whole or part of the population.[6] Furthermore, in strikes in public utility services of general interest, according to the ILO standards it is possible to demand a minimum supply of services by the striking workers.[7]

Indeed, international bodies disagree upon the extent to which the right to strike is protected under international labour law. The question of the enforcement of a right to strike through the application of a global integrative approach versus political approach or an anti-global approach, is discussed in the following section.

Different approaches regarding strikes in public services and the globalization process

The effects of the globalization process

The globalization process describes growing cross-border relations between countries and designates a growth in interdependence. Rapid technological changes and heightening international competition characterize the labour markets, and the globalization process has created inequality and a retreat of the welfare state. Growing income inequality, job insecurity and unemployment are widely seen as the other side of globalization (Kapstein, 1996). The globalization process has also affected trade unions and union density has declined considerably in most industrialized countries (Mundlak and Finkin, 2015).

Within the public sector itself the globalization process has introduced new public management reforms (NPM) in which market practices are adopted into the public sector. NPM reforms include the process of downsizing the bureaucracy and embracing patterns of precarious employment (Cohen, 2016). Thus, NPM reforms are characterized by fragmentation of the public labour market, and temporary and part time work. The implementation of market-oriented practices and development of precarious employment in the public service have all affected public employees and the weekend labour force.

Hence, despite a growing boom in international trade and finance, inequality and job insecurity have grown larger and union density has declined. The negative effects of the globalization process have created a need for another method of regulation of the labour market and protection of employees' rights.

The development of different doctrines in the globalization era

Collective action has been a major tool in industrial relations ever since the industrial revolution. Despite their dominant role, labour freedoms – especially the freedom to strike – have not always been included in constitutional documents. Thus, strike action has been considered in various countries such as Israel and Canada up until the last few years merely as a negative freedom (Mundlak, 2012; Savage, 2009).

The enforcement of labour rights raises the issue of imposing duties on the state regarding public services, and of the horizontal application of collective rights on public employers (Tushnet, 2003).

Thus, it would be fruitful to distinguish between three approaches possible for addressing the issue of the application of a constitutional right to strike in public services: a political approach, an anti-global approach and a global integrative approach within human rights global governance. The global integrative approach within human rights global governance, applies international labour standards issued by international organizations – mainly the ILO – within the interpretation of constitutional documents in domestic law (Pegram, 2015; Tucker, 2012).

According to the political doctrine, collective freedoms should be treated as merely freedoms and not as rights, unless included specifically in domestic constitutional documents. The doctrine is related to a narrow model of labour freedoms (Bog and Ewing, 2012; Tucker, 2012). That is, the political doctrine includes the understanding that the distinction between freedoms and rights should be considered when dealing with labour disputes.

In general, the narrow concept of labour freedoms protects trade unions' interests to a lesser extent (Bog and Ewing, 2012; Tucker, 2012). The narrow conception means that these freedoms protect mainly individual rights of employees to join trade unions of their choice and act individually within labour associations (Langille, 2009). The political doctrine has embraced such narrow concept. According to the political doctrine, labour freedoms, including the freedom of association, collective bargaining and strike, are captured as negative individual liberties and not as fundamental rights, unless included in domestic constitutional documents.

Scholars note that the globalization process affected the approach of the nation-state and the judiciaries to constitutionalism. In this respect, Eric Tucker claimed that a multi-level constitutionalism regarding labour rights could be developed in which global constitutionalism would be dominant (Tucker, 2012). Judy Fudge, drawing on Eric Tucker's idea of labour's many constitutions, discussed the development of transnational global constitutionalism, in which international human rights standards are applied in order to recognize a constitutional status of the right to strike (Fudge, 2015).

Within the global integrative doctrine, constitutionalism is implemented via the application of international labour standards. Hence, international labour standards of the ILO are applied as a basis for the recognition of labour freedoms as constitutional rights. The embracement of ILO labour standards is used as a means of interpreting existing constitutional documents. Thus, the recognition of a constitutional right to strike via the application of human rights global governance enables the realization of labour rights. Nevertheless, the exercise of a global integrative approach also enables the applications of restrictions on the right to strike that are embodied in international standards, such as limitations on strikes in essential services, which have been established by the ILO.

As opposed to the global integrative doctrine, according to the anti-global doctrine, a phenomenon of local constitutionalism is prevalent. Local constitutionalism bases recognition of labour freedoms on other constitutional rights that are included in domestic constitutional documents.

According to the anti-global approach, constitutionalism is established in response to a few processes that occurred in the age of globalization, including demographic changes, the decline of union density and the phenomenon of precarious employment. The anti-global doctrine is based on the general rejectionism theory regarding globalization, which suggests a reaction against the harmful effects of the globalization process (Scholte, 2005). The rejectionist anti-global movement calls for a de-globalization process. For their part, rejectionists have extrapolated from the failing of laissez faire globalization to conclude that the globalization process has negative consequences. Hence, only with a revision to national and local spheres can people rebuild a good society.

The anti-global approach is a wide doctrine, which ensures a constitutional protection of the right to strike and imposes a duty on the state to ensure the implementation of this right. It denies the application of some international ILO standards, which enable the restriction of strike action in public services in various situations – including for instance the possibility to place restrictions on strikes in essential services or demand a minimum supply in utility services. It also emphasizes the role of domestic political institutions in establishing constitutionalism and public policy regarding the labour market.

Judiciaries differ in their willingness to embrace the global – integrative – doctrine. The Israeli judiciary will be discussed first, and it will be followed by a presentation of the German jurisprudence and the Supreme Court of Canada's jurisprudence.

Embracing an anti-global doctrine and local constitutionalism in Israel

The issue of recognizing a constitutional status of the right to strike in Israel

An unwillingness of Israeli courts to establish constitutionalism in regard to the freedom to strike has been apparent only up until the end of the first decade of the millennium. However, the right to strike has been enforced in the last few years in the Israeli labour market. Indeed, the field of constitutionalism regarding collective action demonstrates the movement of the Israeli judiciary away from a political doctrine towards the new embracement of an anti-global doctrine regarding strikes in public services.

In Israel, constitutionalism was adopted in response to changes within the labour market in the globalization era. Judges in Israel have responded to general changes, including the decline of union density and demographic changes, that affected the labour market (Mundlak, 2007). Historically, Israel was characterized by a high union density, corporatism and strong collective bargaining. Since the 1980s there has been a drastic decline in union density and in unions' political power, as well as in the corporatist regime (Mundlak, 2012). The reality in the labour market has influenced judges to develop new workplace protections. Changes in life expectancy and the retreat of the welfare state, which also have implications on the labor market, have also affected courts' rulings.

In the early 1990s two basic laws of human rights were constituted in Israel; Basic Law: Freedom of Occupation and Basic Law: Dignity and Liberty, which are considered as constitutional norms.[8]

Nevertheless, collective labour freedoms were not included in the Israeli basic laws, which include only individual freedoms, such as the right to dignity and property. Thus, the freedom to strike was not included and the traditional jurisprudence treated it merely as a negative freedom.[9]

Throughout the years, Israeli courts dealt with the issue of whether a constitutional right to strike should be recognized, especially within the area of strikes in public services. This jurisprudence will be discussed next.

Constitutionalism in Israel in the public services arena

Contrary to the traditional jurisprudence, the Israeli courts have recognized, in the last few years, the right to strike as a constitutional right, while applying an anti-global doctrine.

Constitutionalism of labour rights has been apparent in a few areas in regard to strikes in public services. Firstly, the enforcement of a constitutional right to strike was aimed at overcoming a legislation according to which strike action is not possible. One of these cases is the *Bar Ilan* case. The *Bar Ilan* case involved an attempt of the union to take collective measures to demand a raise in the pensions of the workplace's pensioners. The Israeli Collective Agreements Law 1957 and the Israeli Labour Disputes Law 1957 enabled the declaration of a strike only regarding employees' interests. According to the Israeli law, the union was not entitled to declare a strike regarding the pensioners' interests. Even though the law itself did not include the option of such a strike, the court ruled using constitutionalism that the labour organization was able to take such collective measures.

In the *Bar Ilan* case the right to strike was captured as an integral part of the right to human dignity, on the basis of the worker's autonomy to fulfill his goals and aspirations regarding the workplace by taking a positive collective action.[10] The Israeli Supreme Court held that the right to strike could be also derived from the statutory constitutional right to occupation.[11] The reasoning of the court referred to the fact that the freedom of occupation includes one's right to fair conditions at work. The court ruled that the right to strike is included in the statutory right for property as well, since workers have various economic interests regarding the working place. Thus, the right to strike could be derived from the right to property, since the struggle of workers to improve their employment terms involved property aspects.[12]

The court emphasized that in the age of globalization the protection of the rights of elderly people and pensioners is of special importance. The need for the protection of their rights has been accelerated due to the retreat of the welfare state in the globalization era. The recognition of the right to strike as a constitutional right was also considered as included in the constitutional freedom of expression, which by itself was considered as included in the right to dignity.[13] The strike is one of the major means for workers' voices to be heard and a means of presenting their common interests. That is, the court recognized the constitutional status of the freedom to strike, using various statutory rights and the principle of human dignity.

Thus, the Supreme Court applied an anti-global approach in the *Bar Ilan* case. The recognition of a constitutional right to strike was derived out of other existing constitutional rights and the court emphasized that the implementation of constitutionalism was established in response to the results of a few processes that took place in the age of globalization. Mainly, the age of globalization has brought with it a retreat of the welfare state model, which affects the interests of elderly people and their right to a decent standard of living, causing a rise in the poverty rate among the elderly population. This phenomenon, along with the rise in life expectancy, has created a need for the protection of the rights of workplace pensioners by the union, and a need for the application of constitutionalism.

Secondly, constitutionalism was applied as a basis for avoiding the restriction of strikes in essential services. In Israel, in principle the law does not restrict strikes in public services or even in essential services. Nevertheless, Israeli law denies a right to strike by members of the armed forces, namely the army, the police, prisons and the secret services.

The Israeli labour court held in the *Mekorot* case, which involved work stoppages in water supply services, that essential services workers enjoy a fundamental right to strike.[14] In the *Mekorot* case the court emphasized that even though a supply of a

The rise of an anti-global doctrine and strikes **35**

minimum service could be demanded, in principle the regular strike law – including the demand of proportionality – should also apply to strikes in essential services. Even though the Israeli national labour court mentioned the ILO conventions in the *Mekorot* case, it did not apply the specific ILO standards that enable the denial of the right to strike in essential services and concluded that in essential services workers enjoy in principle a regular right to strike.

In some cases, the court refrained from issuing an injunction against strike action in services that the court considered essential, while emphasizing that the freedom to strike is a fundamental right. For instance, in the *Teachers strike* case the labour court refrained for a period of two months from issuing an injunction against a general strike in the whole Israeli high school education system.[15] In this case the court rejected the claim that the strike, which involved a suggested reform in the education system, was an illegitimate strike. Education services are not likely to be classified as essential services according to the ILO principles. The court, however, emphasized that education services are considered essential services, although it let the collective action go on for two months before it issued an injunction. The court applied the anti-global doctrine and emphasized that the implementation of a fundamental right to strike in these public services was aimed at coping with processes that took place in the age of globalization, and in particular the decline in union density and in the capacity of unions to lead struggles.

Thirdly, the Israeli courts embraced an anti-global doctrine and the application of a constitutional right to strike regarding strikes in utility services and the issue of replacing striking employees. Hence, the application of constitutionalism of labour strikes has reflected on the issue of hiring replacement for the workers who are involved in a strike in public services. One of the cases in which an anti-global doctrine was embraced is the *Metrodan* case.[16] In the *Metrodan* case, drivers of a private bus company who were not organized started a strike aimed at starting negotiations with the employer over collective bargaining. Because of the strike, the transportation minister gave another bus company a temporary license to operate bus services in the city of Beer Sheva. Although bus transportation services have not been considered as essential services, they are utility services of great importance to the public.

Even though in that case the stoppage of bus services was very long, as the strike lasted three months, the court did not issue an injunction against the strike. The court ruled, using constitutionalism, that the minister's decision was void. The decision of the transportation minister to give a temporary license was aimed at addressing the public need of bus transportation. The court implemented the anti-global approach and did not apply the specific ILO standards that enable a minimum service supply demand. The court noted that hiring a temporary replacement for the unorganized workers that were involved in the collective action violated their fundamental right to strike. The denial of the option to hire temporary replacement was based on the constitutional status of strike action and was aimed at the protection of the interests of unorganized employees.[17]

Germany – embracing a partial anti-global doctrine regarding strikes in public services

The German judiciary has embraced partial anti-global doctrine regarding strikes in public services. The German courts have not applied the ILO principles in the interpretation of domestic constitutional documents and hence have embraced a doctrine which is mostly anti-global and relies on local constitutionalism. The freedom to strike has been captured as a constitutional right in Germany, based on other domestic constitutional rights and not on the application of ILO international standards. Thus, a constitutional right to strike has been applied in principle regarding strikes in public services.

The context of the application of labour fundamental rights in Germany is a social corporatist regime. The corporatist regime enabled the regulation of many collective disputes and strikes in public services within the private sphere. The German Constitution Article 9 paragraph 3 of The Basic Law of the Federal Republic of Germany includes the freedom of association.[18] This article relating to the right to form associations has been perceived through the years by the constitutional court as guaranteeing the right to strike, in addition to the right to collective bargaining.[19] The constitutional court held that article 9(3) of the German constitution protected the right to strike as long as it was related to an economic strike aimed at enhancing negotiations regarding collective agreements.[20]

In Germany there is a distinction between regular public service employees and civil servants, including teachers, policemen, judges, soldiers and municipal workers. Whereas civil servants are not considered as workers and their relationship with the state as an employer is not based on employment contracts, regular public employees work according to a collective agreement (Schubert, 2013). Some of these regular public employees supply public utility services of general interest, such as waste disposal and transport services.

As long as regular public service employees are involved, the collective working terms are set up in Germany in two parallel ways – collective bargaining between trade unions and employers and social dialogue between works councils employee committees and employers.

Even though the right to strike has been considered a constitutional right, the courts approved of the application of severe restrictions on strike action by the specific class of public employees who are considered civil servants. Hence, civil servants and regular public-sector employees differ in their ability to take collective action (Lorewz, 2016). Whereas public sector employees are not excluded from the scope of protection of Article 9 paragraph 3 of the Basic Law, civil servants are not allowed to strike, and their working conditions are set up by public law. Thus, regular public employees who are not classified as civil servants are entitled to strike and enjoy a constitutional right to strike. Nevertheless, courts use proportionality tests in order to ensure the supply of public services. The judiciary applies the proportionality tests regarding third-party interests, ensuring that the population's needs are satisfied (Weiss, 2016).

The proportionality test is also used in utility services of general interest – including waste disposal and collection, health care services and transport services, airline services and railway services. Furthermore, the labour court ruled that public workers were under the obligation to supply the so-called emergency services – a minimum supply of services during strikes.[21] The German federal constitutional court also stated a limitation on employee committees' actions concerning strikes in public services. The federal court held that the principle of democracy demanded a parliamentarian legitimization on decisions that have implications on the supply of public services. That is, whenever the state wishes to regulate the supply of public services, the rights of the working committees are limited.[22]

Contrary to the conception of the freedom to strike by the ILO, in the German constitutional jurisdiction there has been a general denial of the right to strike of civil servants. The ILO principles state that the right to strike may be subject to certain restrictions that are necessary in a democratic society. This principle is mainly relevant to public service employees. Nevertheless, according to ILO principles, the restrictions should be limited to certain categories of civil servants (Weiss, 2016). Furthermore, the legislature should define the concerned category as narrowly as possible. Article 33 sec. 5 of the German Basic Law has been interpreted in a way that states that the law governing the public service shall be developed with due regard to the traditional principles of the professional civil service.[23] It was held that this ban should apply to all staff members in the public sector who were considered as belonging to the legal status of civil servants.

Thus, notwithstanding the international treaties ratified by Germany – mainly ILO Convention 87 – it has been held that civil servants generally have no right to strike, irrespective of their specific duty (Weiss, 2016). The ratified international law is considered statutory law that is overridden by the higher ranking constitutional domestic norms, as interpreted by the constitutional court. Hence, it was held that the Basic Law imposed a general ban on civil servants' strikes, although it contained no such explicit limitation on the right to strike (Weiss, 2016). Thus, the German judiciary applied a partial anti-global approach. Even though the international ILO standards were ratified and accepted, the general denial of the right to strike is contrary to the concept of strike action as a fundamental right and the local domestic constitutional norms are captured as superior to ILO standards. It was held that the general ban on strike action was legitimate, even though the employees did not have any other means of conflict resolution and representation of their interests, and their working conditions were set by the law.

Yet, in recent years, the right to strike of public service employees and the general denial of the right to strike of civil servants have been at the center of a debate in Germany.

The debate mainly involved the issue of collective action of civil servants. A few years ago, the federal constitutional court claimed, with regard to the decisions of the European court of human rights,[24] that the Basic Law also had to comply with international law.[25] Following this case, one of the issues that arose was the question whether the general limitation on civil servants' strikes is problematic and does not comply with ILO standards. Another question that arose was whether restrictions on the right to strike of civil servants could only apply to specific functions and responsibilities (Weiss, 2016). Following this earlier case, the Dusseldorf administrative court held that teachers, although classified as civil servants, should have a right to strike.[26] Another federal administrative court held that these principles might allow for some adjustment in favour of strikes by civil servants without regulatory authority and without powers as to security or public order (Wolfrum and de Wet, 2015). Nevertheless, constitutional petitions on these administrative court rulings were recently decided by the federal constitutional court. Hence, the constitutional court dealt with petitions on these judgements regarding teachers that were punished for participating in strikes.[27] The unions claimed, by reference to international law, that a ban on strikes could only refer to officials with purely sovereign tasks performing core governmental functions, such as policeman, whereas other civil servants such as teachers should have been granted a right to strike.

In June 2018 the German federal constitutional court[28] rejected the constitutional complaint of the teachers directed against the ban on strike action of civil servants.[29] The court held that the legislative ban on strike action is constitutional since it is qualified as a traditional principle of the civil service system, within the meaning of article 33(5) of the Basic Law, declaring that "the law governing the public services shall be regulated and developed with due regard to the traditional principles of the professional civil service."[30] The court stressed that it was in accordance with both requirements necessary for being considered a traditional principle. Firstly, it complied with the requirement of traditionality, since it went back to a line of tradition established in the Weimar Republic. Secondly, it complied with the requirement of substantiality, since it had a strong link to the foundation of the German career civil service under constitutional law.

The court emphasized that a ban on strike action did not result in the complete irrelevance of the constitutional freedom to form and join trade unions. The legislature created provisions designed to help compensate for the restrictions of article 9(3) of the Basic Law regarding civil servants. For instance, there were participation rights for trade union organizations when legal provisions for the civil service were drawn up.

It was held that considering the traditional principles of the career civil service system, it was not required that the ban on strike action would be limited to civil servants whose main role was to exercise public authority. Dividing civil service into groups that have or do not have the right to strike based on their different functions would entail difficulties of distinction and create an unstable structure of administration.

The court held that the ban on strikes by civil servants was justified under article 11(2) first and second sentence of the European Convention on Human Rights (hereinafter ECHR).

Even though the court held that the general ban on strike complies with the ECHR, it could be claimed that the recent judgement does not comply with the principle of the Constitution's openness to international law, as long as ILO principles are concerned. Considering ILO principles, placing a comprehensive ban on all public employees in a given field, and not only a restricted limitation on certain civil servants, seems problematic.[31] Also, according to ILO principles a ban on strike action is legitimate as long as other effective means of resolving collective disputes are available.

Hence the social-corporatist constitutional context enabled the German judiciary to base their judgments regarding strike action on domestic constitutional documents, irrespective of ILO standards. Local constitutionalism included a recognition of a constitutional right to strike in regard to regular public service employees. Thus, it meant a protection on the interests of employees within the public sector. Nevertheless, the denial of ILO standards enabled the German judiciary to place a general ban on the right to strike of civil servants while embracing a partial anti-global approach.

The Supreme Court of Canada: embracing a global integrative doctrine and global constitutionalism

The jurisprudence of the supreme court of Canada in the last decade is characterized by the global integrative constitutional doctrine. The Canadian charter includes liberal oriented rights and does not include labour rights. Even though the charter does not include a right to collective bargaining and strike, the Supreme Court recognized a constitutional right to strike under the 2(d) right to freedom of association of the charter based on international labour rights governance. Nevertheless, leaning on international labour governance enables wide restrictions on strikes in essential services.

Canada is characterized by a regulatory pluralist regime in which the legislation itself addresses strikes in public services. In Canada the legislation regarding strikes is determined by each government. A restriction on strikes in certain essential services is considered as legitimate. The legislation of the different provinces therefore regulates strikes in essential public services. In most cases the legislation restricts strikes in essential services.

In the years prior to 2007, the Canadian Supreme Court has been reluctant to recognize collective rights as human rights with a constitutional status (Fudge, 2008). In a few cases known as the labour trilogy the Canadian Supreme Court had ruled, prior to 2007, that the right to collective bargaining and the right to strike were not constitutional rights.[32] The court held that these collective rights were not derived out of other statutory rights that were included in the Canadian charter, mainly the freedom of expression (Langille, 2009).

In the last few years, though, the Supreme Court of Canada has applied constitutional labour rights regarding essential services. The first step was the recognition of a constitutional right to collective bargaining in a case, involving legislation which invalidated provisions in collective agreements that prevented reorganizations in the workplace. The court interpreted the association right, acknowledged in the charter, in a way that enabled constitutionalism.[33] This was based on the application

40 Lilach Litor

of international labour standards. The Canadian Supreme Court ruled that the 2(d) article of the freedom of association in the Canadian Charter of Rights and Freedoms protected the ability of employees to request collective bargaining and to strike.

In the *Saskatchewan* case the Supreme Court had overruled its previous position held in the labour trilogy series of cases, that statutory rights of the charter did not include the freedom to strike.[34] The court referred to international labour standards and decisions of ILO supervisory bodies as a basis for constitutionalism of strike action.

The *Saskatchewan* case involved the essential services act introduced in 2008.[35] It was the first statutory scheme in Saskatchewan to limit the ability to strike of public sector employees who perform essential services. It prohibited designated essential services employees from participating in any strike action against their employer. The employees were required to continue the duties of their employment in accordance with the terms of the last collective agreement.

No meaningful mechanism for resolving bargaining impasses was provided in the act. Under the act a public employer had the unilateral authority to dictate whether and how essential services would be maintained, including the authority to determine the classification of employers who had to continue working during the work stoppage, the number and names of employees within each classification of employees who had to continue working during the work stoppage, the number and names of employees within each classification and the essential services that were to be maintained. Even when an employee has been prohibited from participating in a strike, the act did not determine his responsibility to the performance of essential services alone.

The court held that the provisions of the act went beyond what was reasonably required to ensure the uninterrupted delivery of essential services in strikes. Nor was there any access to a meaningful alternative mechanism for resolving bargaining impasses such as arbitration. The court emphasized that when strike action is limited in a way that substantially interferes with a meaningful process of collective bargaining, it must be replaced by one of the meaningful dispute resolution mechanisms, commonly used in labour relations.

The unilateral authority of public employers to determine whether and how essential services were to be maintained during a work stoppage with no adequate review mechanism and the absence of a meaningful dispute resolution mechanism to resolve bargaining impasses justified the conclusion that the act was unconstitutional. The Canadian Supreme Court ruled that in this case the prohibition on essential service employees participating in strike action accounted to substantial interference with a meaningful process of collective bargaining and therefore violated section 2(d) of the charter. It was held that a general ban on strikes of public employees was not legitimate.

The application of a constitutional right to strike enables judicial review over laws that limit the right to strike. Thus, the Canadian Supreme Court held that a constitutional right to strike should be applied in the context of public essential services. The ruling was based on the application of international labour standards of the ILO and on the fundamental status of the freedom to strike in ILO resolutions.

The application of the global doctrine enables placing restrictions on strikes in essential services, as long as other means to resolving collective disputes are introduced and as long as a general ban on strikes is not applied.

The legislation can demand such a restriction. Hence the application of a rather restricted right to strike in public services is likely to follow the application of the global doctrine, since it is in accordance with the ILO resolutions. The application of the ILO standards enables placing vast restrictions on strikes, as long as it is not a general ban on strikes in public services.

The issue of the application of an anti-global doctrine vis-à-vis a political approach and a global doctrine

As we suggested, it would be fruitful to distinguish between three approaches regarding the right to collective action in public services: a political approach, and an anti-global approach vis-à -vis a global integrative approach, which is based on global human rights governance. This raises the issue of which doctrine should be embraced.

There are a few claims that can be brought up in favour of a political doctrine. Firstly, industrial relations and labour interests have been originally set up in the private sphere by labour organizations and other interest groups. Thus, it could be claimed that collective struggles should indeed take place within the political arena and not through litigation (Tucker, 2012). Secondly, human rights are originally aimed at setting up obligations on the public authorities within the relationship of citizens and the state. Therefore, the fact that labour disputes usually occur in the private sphere and between employers and workers casts doubt on the ability to apply human rights obligations. Thirdly, embracing human rights discourse regarding the right to strike raises difficulties because it lays an extra burden on the state to consider labour rights. In fact, in the public sector, the concern over the ability of the state to design regulation regarding strike action is accelerated due to the fact that public sector employees and unions, which enjoy special power, may deprive society of a given set of services. Thus, the concern is that the application of constitutional litigation might place certain labour rights above the democratic fray (Oliphant, 2012).

Furthermore, whereas in the private sector strike is an economic weapon, strike in public services is often captured as a political tool (Malin, 1993). Working conditions of public employees frequently involve political questions. Unlike the private sector – where strikes cause the loss of revenues and therefore motivate the employer to settle labour disputes – in public services it does not have the same effect. Since the state as a public employer continues to collect taxes during a strike, the strike does not create an economic motivation to settle the dispute. In fact, the public union's goal in withdrawal of the supply of public services is to cause sufficient political costs, in a way that would motivate the government to settle the dispute in more favourable conditions. It could be claimed that a right to strike in public services affects the political process by empowering public service unions in a decision- making arena from which other interest groups have been excluded.

Fourthly, the enforcement of a constitutional right to strike requires courts to make decisions that have large-scale consequences, regarding governmental labour market policies (Tushnet, 2003), in a way that extends the role of courts beyond their original duty. A part of this intervention of courts is done by the declaration of legislation and executive decisions concerning strikes in public services as void (Tucker, 2012). Indeed, it might be claimed that the application of a constitutional right to strike restricts legislators by denying them the flexibility needed to ensure the proper balance of the three competing interests – those of employees, the public employers and the public in general.

Despite these claims, it seems that courts should reject the political doctrine. Hence, the rejection of the political doctrine means that constitutionalism regarding the right to strike could be applied, even when the freedom to strike is not included in domestic constitutional documents.

A few arguments can be brought up in support of the application of constitutionalism regarding strikes in public services and in response to the previously mentioned claims. Firstly, the gap between the bargaining power of the public employer and the power of the employees creates a need to recognize a constitutional right to strike. Secondly, due to the incapability of the individual worker to lead up struggles in the workplace on his own, the recognition of a constitutional right to organize is of great importance. In fact, the very recognition of a right to strike is needed in order to enable a meaningful right to organize and to bargain collectively. The recognition of a constitutional right to strike also promotes equality in the working place. It is therefore the possibility to strike which enables workers to negotiate their employment terms on a more equal basis. Thus, the recognition of a constitutional status of the right to strike is justified due to the crucial role of strike action in collective bargaining. Where negotiations break down, the ability to engage in a strike is a necessary component of the bargaining process.

Fourthly, the decline in unions' political power in the age of globalization stresses the need to strengthen collective rights. As long as labour unions have enjoyed substantial power and had the capacity to influence labour market policy, constitutionalism and the intervention of courts were not necessary. Nowadays when unions have lost their power and their ability to influence labour policy, it is crucial to embrace different ways to protect labour's interests. (Fudge, 2008).

When we wish to apply a constitutional right to strike, there are two doctrines that might be considered – the global integrative doctrine and the anti-global doctrine. Hence, there are a few claims that can be brought up in favour of a global doctrine which recognizes a constitutional right to strike, via the application of international labour standards. Firstly, the application of ILO standards usually presents a universal understanding and agreement regarding minimum just conditions for employees.

The rise of an anti-global doctrine and strikes 43

Secondly, the application of global labour human rights governance is justified in a globalized world since there is a need to further develop global unitarian standards of labour rights. In this respect, scholars stressed the need to extend principles of human rights and justice beyond the political boundaries of the nation-state (Dahan et al., 2016). Those scholars emphasized the advantage, in the age of globalization, in developing global justice principles of international labour rights.

Despite the previously mentioned claims, courts should embrace the anti-global doctrine. There are a few arguments that can be brought up to justify the application of the anti-global doctrine and in response to the preceding claims.

Firstly, as a few scholars have noted, the issue of the recognition of a right to strike depends on the particular features of the strike in question, which are variable (Sheldon, 2009). When dealing with strikes in public services or essential services there are a few specific factors that should be considered. One of the major concerns regarding the application of constitutionalism is over the sovereignty of the state to design regulation regarding strikes in public services (Oliphant, 2012). This concern is accelerated in the course of the application of a global approach, since the very application of human rights global governance undermines the capacity of the nation-state to act and determine the proper policy regarding public services.

Thus, the application of the global integrative approach is related to the issue of the changing role of the state in the globalization era and globalization's effect on the ability of the state to determine public policy regarding the labour market. The transformation of the role of the state in a globalized world challenges the perception of constitutionalism and the rule of law regarding labour relations. The transformation of the rule of law and constitutionalism in the age of globalization is reflected in the bigger role that international law takes vis-à -vis the nation-state (Jayasuriya, 2001). That is, the application of the global integrative approach and the adoption of international labour law in the interpretation of domestic constitutional documents undermines the capacity of the state, including the local judiciary itself, to regulate strike action and determine labour policy. Thus, it creates a democratic deficit which challenges the capacity to protect workers' interests and apply constitutionalism regarding labour rights.

Secondly, the anti-global doctrine is characterized by flexibility and allows a wide discretion for the domestic actors and the judiciary to regulate labour disputes in public services, regardless of international standards. Furthermore, the application of an anti-global doctrine based on domestic constitutional documents is characterized by a democratic legitimacy, since it does not undermine the sovereignty of the nation-state and thus enables a wider protection of labour's interests.

Thirdly, In the globalization era, the decline of union power and union density have raised new challenges for labour interests. The retreat of the welfare state, in which organized labour and workers' rights were central within the political arena, has created a need for another method of governance regarding collective disputes. It stressed the need for the application of a certain constitutionalism, which is aimed at responding to globalization's negative effects.

44 Lilach Litor

Furthermore, within the specific arena of the public sector, the age of globalization has also brought up the embracement of NPM reforms into the public sector (Cohen, 2016). The implementation of market-oriented practices and development of precarious employment in the public service, have all affected public employees. This phenomenon has weakened the labour force and reduced the capacity of unions to address struggles within the workplace, while stressing the need for new means of regulation of labour disputes. Thus, globalization's effect on the workforce has raised the need for the application of an anti-global doctrine. Indeed, constitutionalism could create a change in the reality of and strengthen the workforce, the state of individual employees in the retreat of the welfare state and in particular the ability of workers to organize.

Furthermore, In the age of globalization there is a growing inequality within the labour market. The outcome of the globalization process and NPM reforms have created inequality between different kinds of employees within the public sector. The growing of that inequality in the age of globalization justifies the application of an anti-global doctrine aimed at regaining equality. The socio-economic processes that took place in the age of globalization and their effect on the workforce – the weakening of unions and the decline in union density – justify the development of an anti-global doctrine. In the age of globalization when employees' interests are at stake, it is critically important to apply constitutionalism of labour rights. Furthermore, courts have a general role in protecting various kinds of human rights and the protection of labour rights is an integral part of it.

Conclusion

The challenges to labour interests and public employees in the age of globalization and the decline of the interventionist state raise the question of the proper doctrine that courts should embrace regarding collective action in public services. The chapter distinguished between different approaches: a political doctrine, and a global integrative doctrine. According to the political doctrine, strike action is a negative freedom, while the anti-global doctrine recognizes a positive protection of strike action as a fundamental right, even when such freedom is not included in constitutional documents.

The chapter introduced the notion of the anti-global doctrine, in which the right to strike is derived out of other constitutional rights which are included in local constitutional documents. As opposed to the global doctrine, which bases constiututionalism on global labour standards – ILO conventions and resolutions – the anti-global doctrine is based on interpretation of domestic constitutional documents.

The chapter reviewed the jurisprudence of three different jurisdictions and their willingness to apply constitutionalism regarding strikes in public services and the application of global human rights governance. As shown in the chapter, in some cases courts developed a dominant role regarding strikes in public services by applying an anti-global doctrine whereas other courts applied the global integrative doctrine. While the former applied extensive judicial review over laws and executive branches' decisions that limit collective action, the latter considered wide restrictions on strikes in public services embodied in international standards as necessary. Nevertheless, courts might embrace the political doctrine and deny the application of constitutionalism of the right to strike altogether, as long as it is not included in local constitutional documents.

In Canada a context of a regulatory pluralist regime led to laying on international standards of the ILO as a basis for constitutionalism of labour rights. It enabled the application of a constitutional right to strike, while restricting strikes in public services according to the restrictions prevalent in ILO standards. In Germany a context of corporatist regime led to the embracement of a partial anti-global doctrine regarding strikes in public services.

In Israel the judiciary embraced an anti-global approach. Hence, courts based constitutionalism on domestic constitutional documents, rejecting the restrictions on strikes in public services embodied in ILO standards. The decline of corporatism in Israel created the need to embrace an active judicial role. Basing constitutionalism on local constitutional documents enabled the Israeli courts a vast protection on labour's interests.

Courts should embrace the anti-global approach in interpreting current constitutional documents. In fact, the denial of a global integrative approach strengthens the capacity of the nation-state to regulate strikes in public services in a flexible manner in compliance with local agendas and culture regardless of international standards. Thus, the anti-global doctrine allows a wide discretion for the domestic actors and the judiciary to regulate labour disputes in public services. Furthermore, the application of an anti-global doctrine, which is based on domestic constitutional documents, is characterized by a democratic legitimacy since it does not undermine the sovereignty of the nation-state in a way that enables the establishing of a wider protection of labour's interests.

Notes

1 This chapter was originally presented in the panel of "Interface of Law and Public Policy" during the third international conference of Public Policy 28–30 June 2017 at Lee Kuan Yew School of Public Policy, Singapore. The author has benefited from comments during the conference presentation and from reviewer comments at different stages of publication.
2 The division of public law and public policy. The Open University of Israel.
3 The ILO standards enable the restriction of the right to strike in public and essential services in various circumstances. The anti-global approach enables a wider protection of human rights, since it does not necessarily apply the specific limitations of the right to strike in public services that are included in international law.
4 ILO Freedom of Association and collective bargaining: a general survey of conventions No. 87 and No. 98 conducted in 1994 by the Committee of Experts on the application of conventions and recommendations (hereinafter ILO 1994a); ILO CFA Digest – ILO Freedom of Association: digest of decisions and principles of the freedom of association. Committee of the governing body of the ILO (hereinafter ILO 1996a).
5 ILO 1994a, para 158.

46 Lilach Litor

6 ILO 1994a, pages 64-65, paras. 146, 159, 214; ILO 1996a; paras. 532, 534; ILO 1994a, para.164.
7 ILO 1996a, paras. 473, 474, 475, 532, 534.
8 Supreme Court case 6821/93 *Bank Hamizrahi v. Migdal.* supreme court cases vol. 49 (4), 221 (1995).
9 Supreme Court case 593/81 *Ashdod Vehicle planets v. Sizik* vol. 41 (3), 169, 190 (1987).
10 HCJ 1181/03 *Bar Ilan University v. The Israeli National Labor Court* (2011). The right to dignity is included in the Israeli Basic Law of Human Dignity and Liberty.
11 HCJ 1181/03 *Bar Ilan University v. The Israeli National Labor Court* (2011). The right to occupation is included in the Israeli Basic Law of Occupation.
12 HCJ 1181/03 *Bar Ilan University v. The Israeli National Labor Court* (2011). The right to dignity is included in the Israeli Basic Law of Human Dignity and Liberty.
13 The freedom of expression itself has been recognized as a constitutional right that is included in the statutory constitutional right to dignity. National Labor court case 1017/04 *The general health services.*
14 Labor collective dispute case 19/99 *Mekorot – the water company v. General Histadrut* (2001)
15 Labor Collective dispute case *20/07 The State of Israel v. The Teachers Organization* (2007).
16 Labor collective dispute 57/05 *The General Histadrut v. Metrodan* (2005).
17 The ILO standards mainly state that hiring permanent replacement for striking employees violate the right to strike- ILO 1994a, Para 175 (Compa, 2006).
18 Basic Law for the Federal Republic of Germany. Article 9(3) – Freedom of Association –

> The right to form association to safeguard and improve working and economic conditions, shall be guaranteed to every individual and to every occupation and profession. Agreements that restrict or seek to impair this right shall be null and void.

19 Bundesverfassungs gericht [BverfG] 103, 1993.
20 Bundesverfassungs gericht [BverfG] 212, 1991, June 26, 1991. Entscheidungen Des Bundesverfassungsgericht.
21 Bundesarbeitsarbeitsgericht [BAG] [Federal Labor Court] April, 21, 1971.
22 Bndesverfassungs gericht – German constitutional court – [BverFG] May 24, 1995, 93. Entscheidungen Des Bundesverf Assungsgericht [BverfGE] 37, 70 (1995). For a decision of a German federal administrative court, see BVerwG 27.2.2014–2 C 1/13. 52.
23 BverfGE 8,1 (17) 44, 249 (264). 119, 247(264) BVerwG No 2c 1/13, 27 Feb. 2014.Mn. 32.
24 Application no. 68959/01 *Enerji Yapi Yol v. Turkey* 21 April 2009; 2008-PARA-97 G.C. *Demir and Byarka v. Turkey* (2008).
25 Federal Constitutional Court. Decision 2004/10/14. 111/307.
26 Administrative Court of Dusseldorf 2010/12/15 Aur 2011, 74.
27 Petitions before the federal constitutional court – 2BVR 1738/12, 2bvr 1395/13, 2bvr 1065/14, 2bvr 646/15.
28 Bundesverfassungsgericht. 2 BVR 1738/12 2BVR 646/15, 2BVR 1068/14, 3 BVR 1395/13. Judgement of 12 June 2018, available at: https://www.bundesverfassungsgericht. de/SharedDocs/Pressemitteilungen/EN/2018/bvg18-046.html
29 The complaints were made by teachers with civil servant status. Disciplinary sanctions were imposed on these teachers for participating in a strike. The civil servants were regarded as breaching fundamental duties under civil service law and in particular the duty not to be absent from work.
30 The German Basic Law is available at: www.btg-bestellservice.de/pdf/80201000.pdf
31 This was also the interpretation of the European Court on Human Rights in regard to ILO principles. Application no. 68959/01 *Enerji Yapi Yol v. Turkey* 21 April 2009.
32 Reference re public service employee relations act (Alta) 1987. SCR 313 (Alberta reference); *PSAC v. Canada* (1987) 1 SCR 424; *Rwdsu V. Sakatchewan* (1987) 1 SCR 313.
33 Health Services v. British Columbia. 2007 scc 2007.
34 *32 Saskatchewan v. Saskatchewan Federation of Labor, [2015] S.C.R 245.*
35 Public service essential services act s.s. 2008 c. p-42.2.

References

Birkland, T. (2016) *An introduction to policy process: Theories, concepts and models of public policy making*. New York: Routledge.

Bog, A. and Ewing, K. (2012) "A muted voice at work? Collective bargaining in the supreme court of Canada", *Comparative Labor Law and Policy Journal*, 33, 379–416.

Cohen, N. (2016) "Forgoing New Public Management and adopting post New Public Management principles", *Public Administration and Development*, 36, 20–34.

Compa, L. (2006) *Striker replacement: A Human rights perspective*. Cornell university ILR collection. Available at: https://digitalcommons.ilr.cornell.edu/cgi/viewcontent.cgi?article =1181&context=articles

Dahan, Y., Lerner, H. and Milman, S. F. (2016) "Global labor rights as duties of justice", in Y. Dahan, H. Lerner and S. F. Milman (eds.), *Global justice and international labor rights*. Cambridge: Cambridge University Press.

Dye, T. R. (2013) *Understanding public policy*. 14th ed. Boston, MA: Pearson.

Etherington, B. (2009) "Does freedom of association under the charter include the right to strike after B.C. Health: Prognosis, problems and concerns", *Canadian Labor and Employment Law Journal*, 15, 315–332.

Fudge, J. (2008) "The supreme court of Canada and the right to bargain collectively: The implications of the health services and support case in Canada and beyond", *Industrial Law Journal*, 37(1), 25–48.

———. (2015) "Constitutionalizing labor rights in Canada and Europe: Freedom of Association, collective bargaining and strike", *Current Legal Problems*, 68, 267–305.

Jayasuriya, K. (2001) "Globalization, sovereignty and the rule of economic Constitutionalism", *Constellations*, 8(4), 442–460.

Kapstein, E. (1996) "Workers and the world economy", *Foreign Affairs*, 75(3), 16–26.

Kumm, M. (2004) "The legitimacy of international law: A constitutional framework analysis", *European Journal of International Law*, 15(5), 907–931.

Langille, B. (2009) "The freedom of association mess, how we got in to it and how we can get out of it?" *Mcgill Law Journal*, 54, 177–214.

Lorewz, S. (2016) "The right to strike between ILO labor standards and the European Convention on Human Rights", in R. Streinz and C. K. Suh (eds.), *Social dimensions of international law*. Munich: Herbert UTZ Verlag.

Malin, M. H. (1993) "Public employees' right to strike: Law and experience", *University of Michigan Journal of Law and Reform*, 26, 313–402.

Marshall, T. H. (1992) "Citizenship and social class", in T. H. Marshall and T. Bottomore (eds.), *Citizenship and Social Class*. London: Pluto Press, pp. 1–51.

Mundlak, G. (2007) *Fading corporatism: Israel's labor law and industrial relations in transition*. Ithaca and London: Cornell University Press.

———. (2012) "Human rights and labor rights: Why don't the two tracks meet?" *Comparative Labor Law and Policy Journal*, 34(1), 217.

Mundlak, G. and Finkin, M. (2015) "Introduction to comparative labor law handbook", in G. Mundlk and M. Finkin (eds.), *Comparative labor law*. Cheltenham: Edward Elgar publishing, pp. 20–21.

Novitz, T. (2003) *International and European protection of the right to strike*. Oxford: Oxford university press.

Oliphant, B. (2012) "Existing the freedom of association labyrinthine: The parliament liberty standard and saving the freedom to strike", *Toronto Law Review*, 36, 36–89.

48 Lilach Litor

Pegram, T. (2015) "Global human rights governance and orchestration: National human rights institutions as intermediators", *European Journal of International Relations,* 21(3), 595–620.

Peters, G. B. (2010) *American public policy: Promise and performance.* 8th ed. Washington, D.C.: CQ Press.

Savage, L. (2009) "Workers' rights as human rights", *Labor Studies Journal,* 34(1), 8–20.

Scholte, J. A. (2005) *Globalization: A Critical Introduction.* Hamphshir: Palgrame Macmillan, pp. 13–84.

Schubert, J. M. (2013) "Public sector collective bargaining and the distortion of democracy: Do public sector unions have too much power? The German perspective", *Comparative Labor Law and Policy Journal,* 34, 443–456.

Sheldon, L. (2009) "Can you derive a right to strike from the right to freedom of association", *Canadian Labor and Employment Law Journal,* 15, 271–296.

Swepston, L. (2013) "Crisis in the ILO supervisory system: Dispute over the right to strike", *Journal of Comparative Labor Law and Industrial Relations,* 29(2), 199–218.

Tucker, E. (2012) "Labor's many constitutions", *Comparative Labor Law and Policy Journal,* 33, 355–378.

Tushnet, M. (2003) "Social welfare rights and the forms of judicial review", *Texas Law Review,* 82, 1895–1920.

Weiss, M. (2016) "The development of industrial relations from the perspective of labor law", in A. Ingrid, B. Martin, K. Berndt, W. Matiasue, N. Werner, R. Britta, and W. Carsten (eds.), *Developments in German industrial relations.* Cambridge: Cambridge Scholars Publishing. 221–252.

Wolfrum, R. and Etika, de W. (2015) *Implementation of the international law in Germany and South Africa.* Pretoria: Pretoria University Law Press.

3

SCRUTINY OF SOVEREIGN BORDER POLICY FOR 'OPERATIONAL MATTERS'

A new political role for an old legal dichotomy in Australia?[1]

Suzanne Bevacqua and John Bevacqua

Introduction

Tightening of border control policy to 'protect' sovereign borders and own citizens has become common practice across the world over the past two decades. However, a question that is rarely scrutinized by governments in this framework is, where does policy end and operational matters begin? The Australian approach to stricter border control highlights the many policy concerns that emerge when this distinction is not routinely applied. In the Australian context, the federal government consistently refers to the need to keep 'operational matters' associated with implementation of its Operation Sovereign Borders (OSB) offshore immigration control policies secret. This insistence on secrecy has drawn significant and sustained criticism from media, academic commentators and refugee advocates who have called for greater transparency and scrutiny of operational aspects of these policies. This chapter adds to these calls by examining the government's use of the term 'operational matters' through the lens of the substantial body of legal precedent associated with the use of that term as a central tool for delineating the limits of sovereign immunity from suit and judicial scrutiny. It calls for the government to adopt a use of the term more consistent with long-term legal precedent in delineating which aspects of its Operation Sovereign Borders offshore immigration control policies should be disclosed for public scrutiny. In doing so, this will clearly define where policy ends and operational matters begin, including which aspects justify continuing to be protected by a cloak of non-disclosure and where the traditional legal usage of 'operational' is misapplied.

In the first part of the chapter, we unravel the concept of 'operational matters'. Here, the legal meaning and history of the use of the term 'operational' is more closely examined. We introduce the policy/operational dichotomy as a legal tool for delineating the proper boundaries for scrutiny of government activities. It also assesses the use of the term 'operational matters' in the context of OSB. The Australian government's current approach to disclosure of information relating to OSB 'operational matters' is examined here. It also sets out the apparent justifications for the government's stance. In so doing, it demonstrates the ever-expanding breadth of the government's definition of 'operational matters'. The analysis of the traditional legal use of 'operational matters' shows that the use of the term in this context is completely inconsistent with its traditional legal formulation as a tool for aiding in delineating the boundary between matters properly capable of being subjected to judicial scrutiny.

Finally, resultant recommendations make the case for using the categorization of OSB matters as 'operational' or otherwise in a manner more consistent with the legal heritage of such delineations in order to assist in credibly determining what details and aspects of the policy and its implementation should be subject to public disclosure and scrutiny and which should legitimately continue to be protected by a veil of secrecy.

'Operational matters': the problematique

It is trite but true that the Australian government's Operation Sovereign Borders (OSB) immigration border control policies are extremely controversial. Whilst key aspects of the policy have enjoyed significant public support,[2] OSB has also been subjected to intense criticism from parts of the media, a range of academic commentators[3] and human rights and refugee advocacy groups.[4] Criticisms of the merits of the policy extend from concerns about its effects on asylum seekers, particularly children held in long-term detention (Australian Human Rights Commission, 2014), regional geopolitical relations (Chambers, 2015) and Australia's international human rights obligations (Dechent, 2014; Australian Human Rights Commission, 2013). Adding to the criticisms has been the Australian government's insistence on the need to keep OSB 'operational matters' out of the public eye. Recent criticisms have centred on the introduction of the federal *Australian Border Force Act 2015* and the further entrenchment of secrecy of OSB facilitated by that act.[5]

This chapter proposes a different type of challenge to the secrecy surrounding OSB and the government's grounds for insisting on secrecy. The challenge posed is to the defensibility of the government's continuing use of the term 'operational matters' to describe OSB activities it considers inappropriate for public scrutiny. This exercise is more than a mere semantic exercise, because the term 'operational matters' has a long legal history associated with delineation of the limits of sovereign immunity from suit and judicial scrutiny as part of what is known as the 'policy/operational dichotomy'.

Viewed through this lens, a number of important issues can be addressed which extend beyond merely challenging the secrecy surrounding OSB. One such issue is whether, if a legal challenge to the implementation of OSB arose, the government would be able to rely on its categorization of OSB activities as 'operational' to aid in resisting any such challenge. The key issue for the purposes of this chapter, however, is whether the government could use the term 'operational matters' in a manner more consistent with its rich legal history to assuage its critics and more appropriately delineate which OSB operational matters should properly be subject to public disclosure and scrutiny and those which should remain secret.

Origin of the 'operational matters' in OSB

Operation Sovereign Borders was announced as a formal Liberal/National Coalition policy prior to the 2013 election. The policy was described as a 'military-led response to combat people smuggling and to protect our borders' (Liberal Party of Australia, 2013). The policy was described as being in response to a 'border protection crisis' and 'national emergency'. A leading and acclaimed Defence Force General was appointed to lead the operation.[6] This military-led approach has informed the government's approach to disseminating information about OSB activities.

Equally, there has been significant rhetoric characterizing the issue as a matter of 'national sovereignty' in terms of Australia's rights to determine the conditions of entry to the country. Tactical reasons around not wishing to broadcast to people smugglers the details of OSB activities have also been cited as reasons for secrecy and non-disclosure of OSB activities, especially in relation to 'people smugglers'. This part of the chapter elaborates on each of these bases for denial of public access to information about OSB activities. The discussion then extends to an introduction of how the 'operational matters' rhetoric has been used by the Australian government to delineate the boundaries of permissible disclosures of OSB information to the public.

'Operational matters' and the grounds for OSB secrecy

The Australian government has been quick to employ military rhetoric as a justification for resisting public disclosure of details of the implementation of OSB. For instance, in 2014 then Prime Minister Tony Abbott observed: "If we were at war we wouldn't be giving out information that is of use to the enemy just because we might have an idle curiosity about it ourselves."[7] The rhetoric has even extended to referring to OSB operations in intercepting asylum seeker vessels as the 'battle-space'.[8]

Hodge (2015: 127) summarizes the government's approach:

> Since their election success in September 2013, the coalition government has readily adopted the language of war to characterise their border protection policy and struggle against people smugglers. The lack of transparency and secrecy on 'on-water operations' is deemed necessary and prudent given the ongoing fight to secure our borders.

However, to what extent can OSB properly be characterized as a military operation? The question is worth asking given that, in evidence before the Senate's inquiry into navy vessel incursions into Indonesian sovereign waters when turning back asylum-seeker boats as part of OSB, Michael Pezzullo, Chief Executive Officer of the Australian Customs and Border Protection Service, confirmed that "matters pertaining to the management of illegal maritime arrivals is executed under civil legislation – the Customs Act and the Migration Act" (Commonwealth of Australia, 2014a: 10). In the enforcement of these two pieces of legislation, Mr Pezzullo described Australian Defence Force personnel conducting OSB operations as acting as "civilian law enforcement officers" (Commonwealth of Australia, 2014a: 10) and confirmed "it [OSB] is absolutely a civil operation" (Commonwealth of Australia, 2014a: 9).

An interesting question that flows from this characterization is whether military personnel engaged as civilian law enforcement officers should be entitled to claim the same protection from scrutiny afforded to military personnel when engaged in military combat operations. A comprehensive answer to this question is beyond the scope of this chapter, although there is precedent for distinguishing between different types of military engagements.

For example, the federal *Work Health and Safety Act 2011* declaration draws a distinction between 'warlike' and 'non-warlike' operations for the purposes of exemptions from various workplace health and safety requirements under that act. A similar approach to the disclosure of information would see greater disclosure in the OSB non-combat context than in warlike OSB operations. But there is no evidence of any intention of the Australian government to adopt such a nuanced approach to disclosure of OSB information.[9] The use of the term 'operational matters' does not appear to be an attempt by the Australian government to add any such nuance to its approach to disclosure of OSB information. Arguably, the use of the term serves simply to further infuse OSB activities with the rhetoric of a military 'operation'.

However, this effort is probably unnecessary given the already significant and well-tested Australian legal concessions against public disclosure of information on national security or defence grounds. A good example of such a legal concession is contained in section 33 of the *Freedom of Information Act 1982* (Commonwealth) which exempts from disclosure documents that affect Australia's national security, defence or international relations.[10] There is a body of case law which could be drawn upon in applying this exemption from disclosure in the OSB context. Instead the indications to date are that the government is taking a blanket approach to non-disclosure in the OSB context, aided by a largely unchallenged and unexplained use of the term 'operational matters'.[11]

For example, the government has refused to supply a range of information sought by the Senate in relation to OSB operational matters on the basis of a blanket public interest immunity claim.[12] Despite the joint concession to the Senate Foreign Affairs, Defence and Trade Committee in 2014 by the Australian Customs Service and the Australian Defence Force that "[t]he release of information relating to operational matters needs to balance the public's legitimate right to be aware of such matters with operational requirements"[13] there is no explicit evidence to date

Scrutiny of sovereign border policy **53**

of any such weighing-up process in seeking to withhold OSB information from the Senate and other interested bodies.

Whilst the justification for this apparent blanket approach to secrecy of OSB information is elusive, some grounds for restriction of information on national security grounds is easy to appreciate.[14] As Bateman (2013), observed, "[t]hese relate to the modus operandi of the Special Forces (SF) in boarding refugee boats and using force as necessary to turn them around." However, Bateman concedes that such concerns have their limits and in some circumstances may be outweighed by countervailing policy concerns. This is a valid and insightful observation which is examined in detail here in the context of discussing how the policy/operational dichotomy *could* be utilized to weigh up these countervailing policy concerns. For present purposes it suffices to note that there is no express evidence of the Australian government making any concerted effort to utilize the use of the term 'operational matters' as part of such a weighing up process (Liberal Party of Australia, 2013).

As noted previously, the government has also characterized OSB as a matter of national sovereignty and this is an equally fertile basis for claiming immunity from public scrutiny. The pre-election policy document itself characterizes the need for OSB as a matter of 'national sovereignty', even harking back to former Prime Minister John Howard's declaration that "we decide who comes to this country and the circumstances in which they come" (Liberal Party of Australia, 2013. Setting aside the politics of such statements,[15] at first glance the national sovereignty argument appears unimpeachable as a basis for resisting exposure to public scrutiny.

However, as with the national security argument outlined earlier, such imperatives still need to be weighed against possible countervailing policy considerations. The concept of national sovereignty is not a simple one – it is a matter of 'profound complexity' (Maley, 2003). Accordingly, national sovereignty cannot operate as an impenetrable veil against public scrutiny of governmental action. For example, as one commentator has pertinently observed:

> it is arguable that in the globalised spaces of the twenty-first century, sovereignty is increasingly illusory and identity is increasingly transnational, so that the old dichotomy between 'national sovereignty' and transnational values – especially 'universal human rights' – is becoming steadily less tenable.
>
> *(McMaster, 2002: 279–80)*

Again, though, the constant references by the Australian government to 'operational matters' as a basis for non-disclosure of OSB activities does not signal an appreciation of the complexities of using national sovereignty as a justification for governmental action or secrecy when dealing with asylum seekers. It also ignores the global movement towards greater transparency and government accountability.

The third main basis for denial of access to OSB information cited frequently by the Australian government is a tactical concern to ensure OSB activities are not signalled to potential people smugglers. At his first OSB briefing to the media, then

Immigration Minister Scott Morrison was clear about this concern: "This briefing is not about providing shipping news to people smugglers."[16]

There are many questions that can and have been raised about this justification. Maxwell summarizes some of the questions which have been raised in the media:

> The Abbott Government has asserted broadly that the release of information gives 'aid and comfort to the people smugglers'. . . . How does particular information provide 'comfort' to people smugglers? Why is this relevant? . . . What kind of information – boat arrivals, turn-back procedures, conditions in detention – 'aids' the smuggling trade, and how? In failing to answer these questions, the Abbott Government has failed to make the case for the sweeping secrecy of Operation Sovereign Borders.
>
> *(Maxwell, 2014: 26–27)*

Some have also been quick to point out the futility of this reasoning for suppression of information. For example, Bateman notes:

> It is most unlikely that the policy of suppressing information will work. The refugees have mobile phones and will try to tell their version of operations before their phones are seized by SF personnel on boarding a vessel. The residents of Christmas Island will also have a fair idea of what is happening. When the leaks about actual operations occur, the rumours may do more harm to Australia's international image than the actual facts.
>
> *(Bateman, 2013: 1–2)*

However, there is no evidence of any of these arguments dissuading the Australian government from its current approach. The only real limit on the policy of non-disclosure of OSB information has been through a willingness to limit non-disclosure to 'operational matters'. However, in the absence of clarity as to what that term is actually intended to mean in the OSB context, it is difficult to appreciate how this chosen terminology specifically aids in balancing the objective of depriving people smugglers of information relevant to their illegal activities with the need for public transparency and scrutiny.

'Operational matters' and the limits of OSB secrecy

As noted repeatedly, since the introduction of OSB, government spokespersons have consistently resisted answering questions about the details of the policy on the basis that such matters are 'operational matters'. However, it is unclear precisely what the Federal government considers to be an 'operational matter.' The term has variously been used to resist disclosure of a range of information spanning from details about any asylum-seeker vessel turn-back activities(ABC News, 2013), boat arrivals[17] and to relatively mundane matters such as whether Navy patrols carry GPS location devices (discussed further ahead).

In the first briefing to the media on 23 September 2013, then Immigration Minister Morrison made the government's initial position clear:

> We want to make it crystal clear: operational and tactical issues that relate to current and prospective operations . . . will not be the subject of public commentary from these podiums. . . . We will tell you what vessels have arrived and have gone into the care of the Department of Immigration and Border Protection. . . . Those updates will be provided as well as transfers and other key policy decisions and announcements and implementation issues regarding this policy, but we are not getting into the tactical discussion of things that happen at sea.[18]

The only notable initial apparent qualification on the concept of 'operational' matters was the qualification of 'things that happen at sea' – which has subsequently been refined to 'on-water' operational matters. However, this qualification appears to have been progressively relaxed. The prohibition now appears to extend to information about matters that 'may be used on water' and as innocuous as training of OSB personnel as the following exchange between Labor Senator Stephen Conroy and Vice-Admiral Ray Griggs Chief of Navy, before Senate Estimates Committee on 26 February 2014 indicates:

SENATOR CONROY: It cannot be a matter of national security what training is being provided to our service personnel. It is by definition not actually in Operation Sovereign Borders.

VICE ADM. GRIGGS: Yes, but if I talk about the type of training I will be going to on-water matters and the techniques and procedures *that may be used on water* (Commonwealth of Australia, 2014b: 64). [emphasis added]

The following exchange from the Senate Committee hearing into incursions by Customs vessels into Indonesian Sovereign waters in towing asylum-seeker boats out of Australian waters as part of OSB between Mr Martin Bowles, Secretary of the Department of Immigration and Border Protection, and the Committee Chair, ALP Senator Sam Dastyari, provides further insight into the generality of the approach as to what constitutes 'operational matters':

CHAIR: Are there vessels that do not have the basic function of GPS?

MR BOWLES: We cannot go into capability issues of specific vessels.

CHAIR: You cannot tell me whether or not we have GPS on vessels that are in the Royal Australian Navy?

MR BOWLES: That is not what I said.

CHAIR: What is it that you said?

Mr BOWLES: I said we are not going to go into the capability of our vessels. It is a sensitive issue from a security perspective.

CHAIR: You cannot tell me whether we have GPS on our vessels or not?

MR BOWLES: That is not what I said.

(Commonwealth of Australia, 2014a)

In light of these types of farcical exchanges, the characterization in some parts of the media of the 'operational matters' exemption as a "tumour" that has "metasta-sised" and "spread further into ever more improbable areas"(Keane, 2014) is under-standable. It has led one commentator to conclude:

> Exemptions to the public release of information designed for operational and national security measures have been extended beyond their legitimate realm. Parliament and its committees have been unable to obtain information – their requests for information often remain unanswered, rejected on the basis of operational security.
>
> *(Reilly et al., 2014)*

Notwithstanding this sentiment and the apparent ambiguity of the intended scope of the government's use of 'operational matters' terminology, the question remains as to whether the Australian government's use of that terminology is consistent with the historical legal development and use of that term. The question is impor-tant in that although a use of the term consistent with its legal heritage may not assuage the critics, it would provide some justification or explanation for its use in the OSB context, and provide some further clues as to the intended meaning of the term in the OSB context.

Policy-operational dichotomy

The preceding analysis has shown a lack of clear government directive as to pre-cisely what constitutes an 'operational matter' for OSB purposes. This lack of a clear directive is, arguably, unsurprising as arriving at an all-encompassing definition of what constitutes an 'operational' matter is notoriously difficult. Whilst a useful start-ing point is the proposition that "[t]he word itself seems to imply something that is mechanical in nature . . . rather than discretionary" (Baker, 1985: 219), the best guidance is to look for indicators as definitional guides.

The most likely indicator used by the federal government in the context of OSB is that operational activities are more concerned with *implementation* than *decision-making*. This description perhaps provides the best clues as to the government's original interpretation when employing this terminology, based upon statements made shortly after the 2013 federal election by then Immigration Minister Scott Morrison when introducing the communication policy surrounding the central policy plank of OSB of turning around asylum-seeker vessels. Minister Morri-son stated that decisions about whether to turn around asylum-seeker boats are

Scrutiny of sovereign border policy **57**

"operational decisions for those operationally in control of *implementing* the government's policies. . . . These are decisions politicians would only be involved in where policy guidance is sought" (Ireland and Hall, 2013) [emphasis added].

However, even with this general guidance, the main definitional complexity remains – the fact that in many cases it will not be possible to draw a 'bright-line' distinction between policymaking and 'implementation'. For example, is the OSB decision to tow an asylum-seeker boat back to Indonesia simply an act of implementation of a government policy, or does it require the making of a discretionary policymaking decision by those in command of 'on-water' activities? In order to answer that question it is helpful to have a basic understanding of the substantial body of case law, which has been developed to address such difficulties.

In the context of defining what constitutes governmental 'operational' activity, undoubtedly the most intensive scrutiny of the term and its complexities has arisen in the context of tortious claims against government and statutory authorities and officials. In negligence claims, the issue has been addressed as part of the discussion of what has been described as the 'policy/operational dichotomy'. The dichotomy has traditionally operated as an attempt to demarcate the boundary between liability and immunity from suit where negligence of a public body or official is alleged.

The policy/operational dichotomy was first expressly enunciated in Commonwealth courts[19] by the UK House of Lords in *Anns v Merton London Borough Council*[20] (*'Anns'*). In that case, Lord Wilberforce described the distinction as follows:

> Most, indeed probably all, statutes relating to public authorities or public bodies, contain in them a large area of policy. The courts call this "discretion" meaning that the decision is one for the authority or body to make, and not for the courts. Many statutes also prescribe or at least presuppose the practical execution of policy decisions; a convenient description of this is to say that in addition to the area of policy or discretion, there is an operational area.[21]

In Australia, Mason J. in *Sutherland Shire Council v Heyman*[22] (*Sutherland*) subsequently explained the distinction between policy and operational acts in the following terms:

> The distinction between policy and operational factors is not easy to formulate, but the dividing line between them will be observed if we recognise that a public authority is under no duty of care in relation to decisions which involve or are dictated to by financial, economic, social or political factors or constraints . . . But it may be otherwise when the courts are called upon to apply a standard of care to action or inaction that is merely the product of administrative direction, expert or professional opinion, technical standards or general standards of reasonableness.[23]

Applied in the OSB context, questions involving allegations that the minister has made an error in interpreting the federal *Migration Act 1958* would clearly fall within the exercise of the minister's *policy* or *discretionary* powers. Applying the policy/operational distinction, this characterization would afford those activities immunity from suit. In contrast, a simple example of an operational failure would be if the minister intended to give a directive to turn around an asylum-seeker boat to Indonesia, but due to a purely administrative oversight such as a typographical or computer error, communicated the opposite position to the Navy or Customs personnel charged with implementing this directive.

This type of activity is far more likely to be considered justiciable because in such a situation there is arguably no challenge to the minister's power to exercise her or his *discretion* to interpret the migration laws however she or he considers appropriate within the scope of her or his statutory mandate. The only challenge is to the faulty implementation of that exercise of discretion. The application of the distinction in these circumstances is enlightening as clearly no challenge to any policymaking powers is posed in this case. Accordingly, any judicial fears of undue judicial intervention in the legislative or executive sphere in enforcing any aggrieved asylum seeker's private law rights to seek compensation for any ensuing loss in such a case are more readily allayed.

However, determining whether an act is operational or administrative in nature is often more complex.[24] The obvious problem with the policy/operational distinction is that any act, even one that is fundamentally operational or administrative in nature, may expressly or implicitly involve the exercise of *some* degree of discretionary power. This is because "even knocking a nail into a piece of wood involves the exercise of some choice or discretion and yet there may be a duty of care in the way it is done."[25]

A simple example in the OSB context can readily illustrate complexities such as these. Assume a Customs official or Australian Navy officer boarding an asylum-seeker vessel gives incorrect information to an asylum seeker about their asylum claim. Can giving this incorrect information confidently be characterized as an exercise of discretionary power or a simple operational activity? To answer the question would require a complex and detailed inquiry into the decision-making processes and internal workings of the Customs and/or the Navy.

A relevant issue would be an assessment of the role and level of authority of the official. The lower the level of authority of the official the more likely it will be that the advice given is administrative in nature. Conversely, it would be expected that a very high-ranking officer would be concerned almost entirely with high-level policy or discretionary decision making.

However, classification of the offending officer alone would not be conclusive (Reynolds, 1968). There also needs to be consideration of whether the information is wrong *but consistent* with Customs or Navy guidelines or internal policies. The giving of the information in these circumstances is likely to be characterized as the exercise of a policymaking or discretionary power. This is because a challenge to the decision in such a case would be tantamount to a direct challenge to the exercise of policymaking power in arriving at the erroneous guideline or internal policy. Alternatively, if the information is wrong *and inconsistent* with any internal or public guideline issued by Customs or the Navy, it is possible to mount a stronger argument that this is a characteristically operational error. In this instance, the policymaking power was exercised when the relevant guideline or internal policy was drafted. The error resulted purely from faulty implementation of that policy decision.

Also relevant, however, would be questions of whether the error arose as a result of "financial, economic, social or political factors or constraints."[26] It is these factors or constraints which render attempts to devise neat, comprehensive lists of operational activities or all-encompassing definitions impossible. Any of these factors or constraints might transform an otherwise apparently administrative act into a clear exercise of policymaking power. This might be the case if, for example, a delay in processing a refugee's claim for asylum (a frequent basis for complaint[27]) was due to a deliberate policy of directing resources and senior staff away from the processing of claims and into OSB border control activities due to internal, high-level budgetary decisions.

These definitional challenges associated with attempting to determine whether a matter is 'operational' exposed by the preceding discussion have led judicial and academic thought, both in Australia and overseas, to gradually (albeit far from uniformly)[28] swing against support for the retention of the policy/operational dichotomy as a guide on the limits of government legal accountability, especially in the tort law context (Oliver, 1980; Smillie, 1985; Todd, 1986; Woodall, 1992). However, the definitional challenges of defining whether a matter is 'operational' are undoubtedly exacerbated in the minds of analysts by virtue of the fact that appellate courts will usually be dealing with the more problematic cases. In the vast majority of cases, determining whether a matter is 'operational' remains possible.

For example, consider the allegation in 2014 that asylum seekers were injured through being forced to put their hands against an exhaust causing burns to their hands when boarded by Navy officers as part of OSB.[29] If this allegation was true, it is difficult to conceive of this activity as involving any conscious policymaking decision on the part of the Navy officers involved to cause such physical injury. Instead, the result is almost certainly due to an operational mistake, capable of being subjected to judicial scrutiny to determine if the mistake happened because of a failure to meet the standard of care expected of reasonably competent officials.[30]

There are many similar examples which readily come to mind. For example, the decision of whether to turn an asylum-seeker vessel back to an Indonesian port could be considered a discretionary policy decision. However, again, once that decision is made, the actions taken in order to effect that policy – for example, the speed at which to tow the boat in light of its possible fragility, decisions on whether to leave sick passengers on the boat for the return trip, the route to take for the tow-back, precautions that should be taken to ensure the safety of those on board the vessel during that manoeuvre etc., are all distinctly operational matters at first glance. There may well be other public policy reasons for resisting disclosure of information about those matters (for example national security concerns) but the operational nature of those matters per se provides no such justification.

60 Suzanne Bevacqua and John Bevacqua

Notwithstanding, however, it is clear that the government's use of the term 'operational' to describe matters which should *not* be scrutinized is completely opposite to the manner in which the term has traditionally been used in a legal context. Certainly, if the government sought to rely solely on the 'operational' nature of an activity as a basis for resisting its subjection to judicial scrutiny, that argument would likely fail.

Operational matters and public disclosure – the case for change

In light of the preceding discussion, the government may be best advised to completely abandon its confusing use of the term 'operational matters' in the context of resisting releasing information about OSB activities to the public. Alternatively, the government could modify its use of the term to a use which is more consistent with the legal meaning and use of that term. The latter approach is preferable for a number of reasons.

The first of these reasons is that despite the apparent loss of legal favour of the policy/operational dichotomy, distinguishing between matters which are 'operational' and matters which are 'policy' remains an important factor in determining whether matters should be subjected to judicial scrutiny in tortious contexts,[31] equitable contexts[32] and administrative law contexts.[33] Perhaps most significantly, however, it is the legal foundation blocks of justiciability which the dichotomy has come to represent in this range of legal contexts which provide a strong, credible basis for the government delineating the boundary between matters concerning OSB which it is prepared to disclose to the public and those which it is not.

The fact that that difficult borderline cases might arise from time to time is no reason for abandoning the distinction as a potentially useful guide for determining matters appropriate for public disclosure just as it has served for determining matters appropriate for judicial scrutiny. As Gleeson J has extra-judicially observed, "[t] wilight does not invalidate the distinction between night and day (Gleeson, 2000)." This is especially true when no more satisfactory principle has emerged (Buckley, 2000: 41).

As one United States commentator has pointed out:

> [T]he terms "planning" and "operational" are indefinite; the problem of drawing a line remains. But all interpretations involve drawing distinctions. The present situation is aided by terms which have a considerable history of application. They have been used, with varying degrees of consciousness. . . . It is true that formulation is mixed with implementation and application in government workings, but separation and classification are not impossible.
> *(Reynolds, 1968: 129)*

Fairgrieve also rebuts the uncertainty argument, concentrating on the fact that some degree of uncertainty is unavoidable. He points to the justiciability underpinning

Scrutiny of sovereign border policy **61**

of the policy/operational distinction as the basis for the unavoidable uncertainty in applying the test, given the lack of any "acceptable bright-line method of delimiting justiciable and non-justiciable issues (Fairgrieve, 2003: 62)." In effect, Fairgrieve sees a role for the policy/operational distinction as just *one* among a number of tools to assist in determining the justiciability issue in claims involving statutory authorities.

Many critics have ignored the fact that the policy–operational distinction, and the justiciability dilemma which it represents, is but one of a number of tools which has been used to determine liability. Buckley points this out, arguing that this misconception has led in large part to the perception that the distinction has been discredited. Buckley notes that "this perception seems to have been based, at least in part, on the fallacious assumption that the distinction purported to be a *comprehensive* statement of the conditions required for the imposition of negligence liability upon public authorities (Buckley, 2000: 43)."[34]

However, even if the views of the critics were to be accepted without qualification, the difficulty of devising some alternative approach which resolves the problems raised remains. To date this has proved an intractable problem. For example, Davies (2000) in his article discussing one of the leading recent Australian negligence cases concerning statutory authority liability, *Crimmins v Stevedoring Industry Finance Committee*,[35] identifies one of the dangers of using an alternative test to take the place of the policy/operational dichotomy. Davies (2000: 11–12) notes:

> [T]he majority appears to take the view that the standard of care required of a statutory body that has failed to act positively in exercising statutory powers is that of the reasonable authority with the powers and resources of that body. If that is right, trial courts will be required to consider what would have been reasonable budgetary and resource priorities at the time the statutory body made its decision. That would amount to more intrusive scrutiny of the decision-making processes of statutory bodies than the classical policy/operational distinction supposes.

Consequently, the use of the policy/operational dichotomy provides an opportunity for the government to take an approach which falls short of a blanket ban on release of any information associated with OSB and which has a significant legal history upon which to draw in order to make defensible assessments as to what information should be released.

There is, however, a further very practical reason for utilizing the distinction between policy and operational matters as a basis for delineating matters appropriate for public disclosure. This justification stems from the fact that characteristically operational matters have in recent times been the most common bases for legal complaint in the immigration context. The Commonwealth Ombudsman spends much of his time in his capacity as Immigration Ombudsman investigating instances of alleged Immigration Department operational failures. For example, the Commonwealth Ombudsman, in his 2014–15 Annual Report observes that "[t]he largest category of complaints was delays in visa application processing. The second largest was complaints about delays or the refusal of citizenship applications (p. 51)." This continues ongoing complaint trends. For example, in his 2013–14 report the Commonwealth Ombudsman observed, "[a]s in previous years, delay is the most common cause of complaint, particularly in relation to the processing of some visa categories" (p. 51). Delays such as those identified as leading causes of complaint in the 2014 and 2015 Ombudsman Annual Reports are characteristically procedural or operational issues.

The Ombudsman's 2014–15 Annual Report also points to other systemic complaint themes which are similarly characteristically operational in nature. "property issues are a common area of complaint, including detainees' property going missing or not being transferred when detainees are moved within the detention network, as well as complaints about compensation claims for lost or damaged property" (p. 52). Again, this echoes similar statements in the 2013–14 Annual Report: "Management of detainee property in detention is also a concern, with these complaints mostly concerning property that is damaged or lost while it is in the custody of the detention facility management" (p. 52). Past Ombudsman Annual Reports reveal similar significant operational themes. For example the Ombudsman's 2011–12 Annual Report notes that: "The complaint themes we observed in 2011–12 were similar to those in the previous year with delay being the main cause of complaints" (p. 75). The 2011–12 Annual Report elaborates further pointing to many more characteristically operational matters as key concerns, particularly for those in mandatory detention. These include delay in processing protection claims, problems with property management and loss of property and concerns about the skill and accuracy of some interpreters (p. 76–77). Reports such as these indicate that these operational matters are significant contributors to the mental harm experienced by mandatory detainees – a systematic approach to disclosure and discussion of these issues is an important step in addressing them (Commonwealth Ombudsman Report, 2012).

Similar operational themes are echoed in the findings of the Commonwealth Ombudsman 2013 investigation into suicide and self-harm of persons held in immigration detention. The Ombudsman found that mandatory immigration detainees are particularly vulnerable and that "[t]hese vulnerabilities can also be exacerbated by anxiety about, and frustrations with immigration decision-making processing."[36] In its conclusions the Ombudsman's report repeatedly refers to the need for the Department of Immigration and Border Protection to engage more strategically in addressing its operational functions and pressures.[37] Again the link between operational activities and significant and serious unaddressed concerns is highlighted.

Accordingly, application of the policy/operational dichotomy to determine matters to expose to the public would introduce transparency into the immigration systems in those areas which are presently causing significant harm to detainees. It would allow the government to demonstrate a commitment to dealing with these operational matters in a more strategic and systematic manner as called for by the

Commonwealth Ombudsman. It allows a conscious and systemic focus on operational matters.

Adopting a policy of disclosure that is more consistent with legal principles would also demonstrate a systemic shift towards a more pro-disclosure approach and directly address possible perceptions of a culture of secrecy associated with immigration matters. This would be consistent with the recent recommendations of an independent comparative review of the Immigration and Citizenship Department Freedom of Information procedures by Robert Cornall AO. The Cornall Report found that:

> the Department's current level of performance in regard to freedom of information is unacceptable. It is not an option to maintain the status quo, particularly given the Government's recent FOI reforms and its expectation that all agencies will adopt a more pro-disclosure approach.[38]

The Cornall Report also found that the Department "presently appears to have more of an attitude of resistance to disclosure."[39] The current confused approach to refusing to disclose operational matters as part of OSB is unlikely to be aiding in changing that attitude of resistance to disclosure.

A related incentive for shifting to a more systematic and legally defensible approach to disclosure of operation matters associated with OSB might also address the department's current enormous FOI application workload. The department consistently receives the largest number of freedom of information requests of any Australian government agency – as high as 34% of all claims and almost twice the number of any other department.[40]

Further, the Cornall Report found that in addressing FOI concerns there is an apparent lack of understanding within the Department of Immigration and Citizenship of national security and non-national security classifications – these are not effectively or consistently applied.[41] The application of the policy/operational dichotomy would allow the government to focus on the underpinning public policy matters which have informed the development and judicial application of that dichotomy, including matters which are not justiciable due to national security and similar overriding public policy concerns.

The more systemic approach to disclosure of information surrounding OSB which the adoption of the policy/operational dichotomy would signal to the community is also likely to have further benefits in terms of enhancing public confidence and trust in the immigration detention system. There is a large body of work developing in other fields which clearly links community trust and confidence in government instrumentalities and officials when the system is perceived to be fair, even-handed and transparent.[42] The conclusion of much of this work is that "[i]f individuals perceive an authority to be acting fairly and neutrally, and they feel treated with respect and dignity, they will be more willing to trust that authority and will voluntarily obey and defer to its decision and rules."[43]

On a related point, the report also alludes to reputational harm associated with current shortcomings in its approach to public disclosure which the adoption of a systemic and widely recognized approach to delineating matters appropriate for disclosure which the policy/operational dichotomy would facilitate:

> The Department's current level of performance in regard to freedom of information is unacceptable. DIAC is not complying with its legal obligations. It is in bad standing with the FOI regulator. Its FOI shortcomings damage the Department's relationship with the Minister and his Office and reflect adversely on the Department's reputation within the Australian Government.[44]

The link between operational failures such as these and the public and government reputation of the department was also highlighted by the Public Service Commission in their recent review. They found "perceptions that DIAC is crisis prone have an effect on the department's public and parliamentary reputation and are a legitimate concern for the minister and the government."[45]

A further basis for adopting a reputable approach to dealing with disclosure and scrutiny of operational matters is the fact that operational standards of the Department of Immigration and Citizenship are also clearly a concern of the government. There have been numerous recent inquiries into various aspects of the operational performance of the department. The most damning of these was the recent KPMG Report[46] into an operational failure in February 2014 which saw "the information of up to 10,000 adults and children in Australian immigration detention inadvertently made available. The database included their full names, nationalities, location in Australia, arrival date and their boat arrival information."[47] That review found a range of operational failures contributed to the release of the information and made numerous procedural change recommendations including that "the department develop procedures for 'cleansing' personal data, update review procedures, develop an IT security training programme and incorporate privacy training in connection with the Australian Privacy Principles."[48]

A Public Service Commission Report also made major findings into operational performance of the department pointing to the continuing failure of the Department to develop control mechanisms "to reduce the risk of future failures of *process*"[49] (emphasis added). All of this adds to a compelling case for the government radically reframing its current use of 'operational matters' as a filter for determining appropriateness for public disclosure of OSB information.

Conclusions

This chapter has demonstrated that the Australian government's present use of the term 'operational matters' as a distinction for determining OSB activities which should not be revealed to the public is entirely inconsistent with the substantial body of legal analysis which has built up around that term in the context of appropriateness of governmental activity for judicial scrutiny. It has demonstrated that this continued inconsistent and largely unexplained use is unlikely to stand up to judicial scrutiny if challenged as part of a civil law claim arising out of OSB activities. This raises several significant general law and policy issues from both a national and international viewpoint.

Firstly, there is a demonstrable need nationally and globally for governments to reconsider the use of this doctrine in border control and either explain the reasoning for non-adherence to the doctrine in accordance with established legal principle or begin using the term in a manner that accords more closely with legal authority. Reconsidering the use of the term can add to the credibility of the government's claims for immunity from public scrutiny of certain OSB activities and enhance trust and confidence of the public and other stakeholders in the Immigration system. The latter has been shown to be the preferable course for many substantive policy reasons. Perhaps the most significant of these is that continued use of the terminology in a manner consistent with the legal approach to the term would allow the government to introduce an element of transparency and order to the operational aspects of the immigration system which have been consistent themes in complaints to the Australian Commonwealth Ombudsman and the cause of significant harm to mandatory immigration detainees to date. It would allow the government to achieve these objectives while remaining cognoscente of the various global public policy concerns around various aspects of OSB which warrant protection both from public scrutiny and judicial scrutiny. These include policy concerns around national security, preserving life at sea, ensuring the safety of staff charged with implementing OSB and meeting international human right obligations and greater transparency.

Applying a well-established approach such as the policy/operational dichotomy to determine whether matters should be disclosed for public scrutiny also allows for public policy concerns such as these to be dealt with in a more direct, express and questioning manner. It is conceded that the policy/operational dichotomy is not a perfect solution. The dichotomy would require case-by-case consideration of whether to release information in difficult cases. This is simply unavoidable in a complex and polycentric policy area such as immigration. However, the dichotomy establishes a useful framework for a more systematic approach which would foster consideration of both positive and negative policy concerns and the *demonstrability* of these concerns. In effect, adopting this consistent systemic approach would require the government to subject public policy concerns such as national security concerns to some degree of evidentiary scrutiny rather than accepting them according to their inherent logical appeal or political expediency. This has the potential to not only define a clearer line between policy and operational matters within Australia but provide a more consistent and transparent standard and framework for border control that could be modelled elsewhere.

Notes

1 This chapter was originally presented in the panel of "Interface of Law and Public Policy" during the third international conference of Public Policy 28–30 June 2017 at Lee Kuan Yew School of Public Policy, Singapore. The author has benefited from comments during the conference presentation and from reviewer comments at different stages of publication.

2 For example, the 2014 Lowy Institute Poll found majority support for key planks of the OSB policy, including the turn-back of asylum-seeker boats (71% support) and the processing of asylum seeker claims offshore (59% support), available at: www.lowyinstitute. org/publications/lowy-institute-poll-2014 (accessed 3 May 2016).

3 Noteworthy examples, touched upon later in this chapter, include McAdam, 2013), Dechent (2014) and Hodge (2015).

4 Including the United Nations High Commission for Refugees, (UNHCR) which has repeatedly criticized the treatment of refugees in detention in reports on visits to offshore asylum claim processing facilities, and Amnesty International, who has called for a Royal Commission into OSB and lists its complaints in its publication (the Australian Human Rights Commission, Human Rights Law Centre, Refugee Council of Australia, 2015).

5 See, for example, the ABC Four Corners expose entitled 'Bad Blood' screened on 25 April 2016, available at: www.abc.net.au/4corners/stories/2016/04/25/4447627.htm (accessed 4 May 2016). Section 42 of the *Australian Border Force Act 2015* (Commonwealth) (entitled 'Secrecy') provides that a person who is an 'entrusted person' commits an offence punishable by up to two years imprisonment if he or she makes a record of, or discloses, 'protected information'. An 'entrusted person' is defined in section 4 of the Act to include an 'Immigration and Border Protection worker', which includes consultants or contractors as well as government employees. Under section 4 'protected information' is defined expansively as 'information that was obtained by a person in the person's capacity as an entrusted person.'

6 Lieutenant-General Angus Campbell headed OSB until Major-General Andrew Bottrell took over command in March 2015.

7 Jonathan Swan, 'Tony Abbott Compares Secrecy Over Asylum Seekers to War Time', 11 January 2014, *Sydney Morning Herald,* available at: www.smh.com.au/federal-politics/political-news/tony-abbott-compares-secrecy-over-asylum-seekers-to-war-time-20140110-30lyt.html (accessed 2 May 2016).

8 Chief of the Defence Force David Hurley in testimony before Senate Estimates 26 February 2014. Commonwealth of Australia, *Official Committee Hansard, Senate Foreign Affairs, Defence and Trade Legislation Committee*, 26 February 2014, 64. For an example of media reaction see Bernard Keane, 'Training, lifeboats and asylum Seekers in the 'battle-space", 6 March 2014, *Crikey,* available at: www.crikey.com.au/2014/03/06/training-lifeboats-and-asylum-seekers-in-the-battle-space/ (accessed 2 May 2016).

9 In fact, the only distinction made is the special exemption granted to OSB operatives from the requirement under sections 28 and 29 of the *Workplace Health and Safety Act 2011* (Commonwealth) to take reasonable care of themselves and other persons in the workplace. This is a concession not available even to frontline troops. For a detailed critique see Keane (2014). Keane summarizes the distinction between military personnel engaged in OSB activities and frontline troops succinctly: "Only those engaged in turning back unarmed people in wooden boats don't have to exercise reasonable care."

10 The exemption comprises two distinct categories of documents: a) documents which, if disclosed, would, or could reasonably be expected to, cause damage to the Commonwealth's security, defence or international relations; and b) documents that would divulge information communicated in confidence to the Commonwealth by a foreign government, an agency of a foreign government or an international organization.

11 The creation of the 'Australian Border Force' by the *Australian Border Force Act 2015* (Commonwealth) and the broad secrecy obligations imposed on employees and contractors engaged in work to implement OSB by section 42 of that act (discussed further in

Scrutiny of sovereign border policy **67**

note 7, *supra*) further indicates no softening of the government's expansive approach to non-disclosure of information surrounding OSB.

12 Made pursuant to Senate Order made on 9 May 2009, well before the commencement of OSB.

13 This concession was made by the Head of the Australian Customs and Border Protection Service, Michael Pezzullo, and General David Hurley, the Chief of the Defence Force on 21 March 2014 before a Senate inquiry into an incursion by the Australian Navy into Indonesian waters (Commonwealth of Australia, 2014a).

14 There is judicial precedent for being wary of impinging on matters of national security which is relatively uncontroversial. For example, Wilcox noted in his judgment in *Minister for Arts Heritage and Environment v Peko-Walsend* (1987) 15 FCR 274 at 304, that the relevance of a decision to questions of national security would render a matter 'inappropriate' for judicial review.

15 There are many examples (see for instance Devetak, 2004) of well-reasoned challenge to the relatively recent Australian conceptualization of refugee issues as a national security and sovereignty risk rather than a humanitarian concern.

16 The Hon. Scott Morrison MP, *Transcript of joint press conference: Sydney: 23 September 2013: Operation Sovereign Borders,* 23 September 2013, available at: http://parlinfo.aph.gov.au/parlInfo/download/media/pressrel/3099126/upload_binary/3099126.pdf;fileType=application%2Fpdf#search=%22media/pressrel/3099126%22 (accessed 5 May 2016).

17 Initially the subject of a complete 'media blackout' and subsequently restricted only to announcements made at the weekly OSB media briefings (Martin, 2013).

18 The Hon. Scott Morrison MP, *Transcript of joint press conference: Sydney: 23 September 2013: Operation Sovereign Borders* 23 September 2013, available at: http://parlinfo.aph.gov.au/parlInfo/download/media/pressrel/3099126/upload_binary/3099126.pdf;fileType=application%2Fpdf#search=%22media/pressrel/3099126%22 (accessed 5 May 2016).

19 The original source is usually credited as the case law concerning a similar test contained in the United States *Federal Tort Claims Act of 1948,* 28 USC Pt IV Ch 171 (1948), most notably *Dalehite v United States* 346 US 15 (1953); *Indian Towing Co v United States* 350 US 61 (1955); and, more recently, *United States v Gaubert* 499 US 315 (1991). Hink and Schutter (1965: 721–722) have extensively detailed the relevance of the policy/operational distinction in respect of the *Federal Tort Claims Act* and how it has been applied in the case law. On the former, they note:

> Section 421 of the *Federal Tort Claims Act* sets out a number of classes of claims as to which the United States does not waive its immunity. The most important of these is a non-waiver of claims "based upon the exercise or performance or the failure to exercise or perform a discretionary function or duty on the part of a federal agency or an employee of the Government." Clearly the intention was retention of immunity for high-level policy decisions, analogous to the "Act of State" doctrine adopted in European countries.

20 *Anns v Merton London Borough Council* [1977] 2 All ER 492. Although, as Bailey and Bowman point out, prior to the *Anns* decision, Lord Diplock in *Dorset Yacht Co. Ltd v Home Office* [1970] AC 1004 clearly had in mind drawing a line between statutorily authorized damage and damage caused by negligent exercise of statutory power. For a detailed discussion see Bailey and Bowman (1986).

21 *Anns v Merton London Borough Council,* [1977] 2 All ER 492, 501.

22 *Sutherland Shire Council v Heyman* (1985) 157 CLR 424.

23 *Sutherland Shire Council v Heyman* (1985) 157 CLR 424, 469.

24 Although, perhaps not as often as might appear from the cases which have examined the issue. Naturally, it is only the most difficult cases which reach the appellate courts. It is also only those cases in which the parties have the financial resources to judicially pursue the matter.

25 *Barrett v Enfield London Borough Council* [2001] 2 AC 550, 571. This reference to 'knocking in a nail' is derived from the United States case of *Ham v Los Angeles County* 46 Cal App 148 (1920) in which it was noted, at 162, that: "It would be difficult to conceive of

any official act, no matter how directly ministerial that did not admit of some discretion in the manner of its performance, even if it involved only the driving of a nail."

26 This is a return to the terminology of Mason J in *Sutherland Shire Council v Heyman* (1985) 157 CLR 424.

27 Discussed at length in the final recommendations that follow.

28 Notable judicial proponents include Mason J and Gibbs J in *Sutherland Shire Council v Heyman* (1985) 157 CLR 424, where their Honours used the words "logical and convenient" to describe the distinction. Kirby J in *Pyrenees Shire Council v Day* (1998) 192 CLR 375 also gave qualified support noting that although the distinction is 'far from perfect' it has 'some validity'. There was also High Court support from Gaudron J in *Crimmins v Stevedoring Committee* (1999) 200 CLR 1. Also see academic works on this aspect in Kneebone (1998) and Woolf (1990).

29 Asylum seekers recounted their allegations on current affairs programme ABC 7:30, televised on 24 March 2014, available at: www.abc.net.au/7.30/content/2014/s3970527. htm (accessed 2 May 2016).

30 Of course, there would remain other policy and practical matters which could legitimately be raised at this point which might determine the matter in court. However, these are no basis for a wholesale rejection of any opportunity to test those policy and practical matters in a public or judicial setting. This is an issue addressed further in the final recommendations that follow.

31 For example, Hayne J in *Crimmins v Stevedoring Committee* (1999) 200 CLR 1 in acknowledging that 'quasi-legislative' functions should be immune from private law tortious suit recently affirmed the link between the public/private law friction encapsulated in separation of powers concerns and the policy/operational distinction observing, at 101:

> Put at its most general and abstract level, the fundamental reason for not imposing a duty in negligence in relation to the quasi-legislative functions of a public body is that the function is one that must have a public rather than a private or individual focus. To impose a private law duty will (or at least will often) distort that focus. This kind of distinction might be said to find reflection in the dichotomy that has been drawn between the operational and the policy decisions or functions of public bodies.

32 In the equitable context, the relevance of the policy/operational distinction has come to the fore as a qualification to the *Southend-on-Sea* principle (that an estoppel should not be raised to prevent the performance of a statutory duty or to hinder the exercise of a statutory discretion) and has been applied in a number of cases. The most notable example is *Minister for Immigration, Local Government and Ethnic Affairs v Kurtovic* (1990) 21 FCR 193. In that case, at 215, Gummow J stated:

> The planning or policy level of decision making wherein statutory discretions are exercised has, in my view a different character or quality to what one might call the operational decisions which implement decisions made in exercise of that policy . . . where a public authority makes representations in the course of implementation of a decision arrived at by the exercise of its discretion, then usually there will not be an objection to the application of a private law doctrine of promissory estoppel.

It is probable, given His Honour's shift away from application of the policy/operational dichotomy in cases such as *Crimmins v Stevedoring Committee* (1999) 200 CLR 1, that Gummow J would today be more equivocal in his support for applying the distinction in estoppel claims too.

33 The relevance of distinguishing operational functions from those that are discretionary in nature also extends to public law cases where judicial review is sought and the reviewability of a decision of a public authority is at issue. For instance, it has been suggested that the policy/operational distinction may be utilized in some judicial review cases in conjunction with the concept of *ultra vires* to assist in delineating between 'impeachable and unimpeachable discretion.' Hayne J also discusses the issue, in the context of

explaining the *Wednesbury* unreasonableness test, in his judgment in *Brodie v Singleton Shire Council* (2001) 206 CLR 512. His Honour notes, at 628:

> In public law, decisions may be examined for error of law, but statute apart, there is no review of the merits of decisions made by such bodies. The closest the courts come to such a review is what is usually called *Wednesbury* unreasonableness, where the test is whether the decision is so unreasonable that no reasonable decision-maker could have made it. What the *Wednesbury* test reflects is that the courts are not well placed to review decisions made by such bodies when, as is often the case, the decisions are made in light of conflicting pressures including political and financial pressures.

While his Honour does not take the step explicitly, the terminology used by his Honour to delineate between reviewable and non-reviewable decisions is similar to terminology used in tort cases to explain the policy/operational distinction. Noteworthy, for instance, is the similarity between the Hayne J reference to 'political and financial pressures' and the 'financial, social, economic or political factors or constraints' referred to by Mason J in *Sutherland Shire Council v Heyman* (1985) 157 CLR 424.

34 The fact remains that the distinction was never intended to be applied exclusively. It was simply intended as one of a number of considerations which might be relevant to the question of imposition of liability on a statutory authority, including the danger of fettering future discretion of that authority and the relevant statutory context. In fact, in *Anns*, the first stage of the Court's analysis was detailed consideration by Lord Wilberforce of the statutory setting – the *Public Health Act 1936* (UK). His Lordship also considered (albeit briefly) the question of proximity and public policy arguments around adverse motivational effects of finding the existence of a duty of care. See the discussion by Lord Wilberforce in *Anns v Merton London Borough Council* [1977] 2 All ER 492, especially at 499–502.

35 *Crimmins v Stevedoring Committee* (1999) 200 CLR 1.

36 Report by the Commonwealth and Immigration Ombudsman, Colin Neave, under the *Ombudsman Act 1976, Report No, 02/2013 – Suicide and Self-Harm in the Immigration Detention Network* (May 2013), 27.

37 Ibid., 32.

38 Ibid., 3. The report further notes, at 35, that: "It is not an option to maintain the status quo, particularly given the Government's recent freedom of information reforms and its expectation that all agencies will adopt a more pro-disclosure approach."

39 Ibid, 24.

40 Robert Cornall AO, *Independent Comparative Review of the Department of Immigration and Citizenship's Freedom of Information Procedures Report*, 30 August 2012, 2, available at: www.border.gov.au/ReportsandPublications/Documents/reviews-and-inquiries/independent-comparative-review-foi-procedures.pdf (accessed 5 May 2016), citing Office of the Australian Information Commissioner, *Processing of Non-Routine FOI Requests by the Department of Immigration and Citizenship – Report of an Own Motion Investigation*, 3, available at: www.oaic.gov.au/images/documents/migrated/oaic/repository/publications/reports/DIAC_FOI_own_motion_report_FINAL.pdf (accessed 5 May 2016).

41 Robert Cornall AO, *Independent Comparative Review of the Department of Immigration and Citizenship's Freedom of Information Procedures Report*, 30 August 2012, 5, available at: www.border.gov.au/ReportsandPublications/Documents/reviews-and-inquiries/independent-comparative-review-foi-procedures.pdf (accessed 5 May 2016).

42 This body of literature is particularly developed in fields such as tax, where many studies have demonstrated a link between transparency and fairness and taxpayer trust and confidence translated into increased willingness to voluntarily comply with tax obligations. For examples see John Scholz, 'Trust, taxes and compliance' in Valerie Braithwaite and Margaret Levi (eds.), *Trust and Governance* (1998), 135; Jenny Job and Monika Reinhart, 'Trusting the Tax Office: Does Putnam's Thesis relate to Tax?' (2003) 38 *Australian Journal of Social Issues* 307; Valerie Braithwaite, *Taxing Democracy: Understanding Tax Avoidance and*

Evasion (2003) Aldershot: Ashgate; Kristina Murphy, 'Procedural Justice and Tax Compliance' (2003) 38 *Australian Journal of Social Issues* 379; John T. Scholz and Mark Lubell, 'Trust and Taxpaying: Testing the Heuristic Approach to Collective Action' (1998) 42(2) *American Journal of Political Science* 398; and Benno Torgler, Ihsan C. Demir, Alison Macintyre and Markus Schaffner, 'Causes and Consequences of Tax Morale: An Empirical Investigation' (2008) 38(2) *Economic Analysis and Policy* 313.

43 Kristina Murphy, 'The role of trust in nurturing compliance: A study of accused tax avoiders' (2004) 28 *Law and Human Behaviour* 187, 190.

44 Robert Cornall AO, *Independent comparative review of the department of immigration and citizenship's freedom of information procedures report*, 30 August 2012, 35, available at: www.border.gov.au/ReportsandPublications/Documents/reviews-and-inquiries/independent-comparative-review-foi-procedures.pdf (accessed 5 May 2016).

45 Sean Parnell, 'Department of Immigration and Citizenship culture heavily risk averse, says Australian Public Service Commission' 4 December 2012, *The Australian*, available at: www.theaustralian.com.au/news/foi/department-of-immigration-and-citizenship-culture-heavily-risk-averse-says-australian-public-service-commission/story-fn8r0e18- (accessed 5 May 2016).

46 KPMG, *Management initiated review, privacy breach – data management*, 20 May 2014, available at: www.immi.gov.au/pub-res/Documents/reviews/kpmg-data-breach-abridged-report.pdf (accessed 3 May 2016).

47 Emma Griffiths, 'Immigration Minister Scott Morrison demands answers from his department after it accidentally disclosed asylum seeker personal details online' 19 February 2014, *ABC News*, available at: www.abc.net.au/news/2014-02-19/personal-details-of-asylum-seekers-published-by-immigration-dept/52694 (accessed 2 May 2016).

48 Paul Farrell and Oliver Laughland, 'Review blames Immigration for data breach exposing 10,000 detainees' 12 June 2014, *The Guardian*, available at: www.theguardian.com/world/2014/jun/12/review-blames-immigration-data-breach-detainees (accessed 5 May 2016).

49 Sean Parnell, *supra* note 83.

References

ABC News (2013) Emma Griffiths, "Scott Morrison says government won't reveal when asylum seekers boats turned back", 24 September 2013. Available at: www.abc.net.au/news/2013-09-23/government-won27t-reveal-when-boats-turned-back/4975742 (Accessed 2 May 2016).

Anns v Merton London Borough Council [1977] 2 All ER 492.

Ashgate, A. and Murphy, K. (2003) "Procedural justice and tax compliance", *Australian Journal of Social Issues,* 38, 379–395.

Australian Broadcasting Commissioner, 7:30 Report, Asylum seekers recounted their allegations, televised on 24 March 2014. Available at: www.abc.net.au/7.30/content/2014/s3970527.htm (Accessed 2 May 2016).

Australian Broadcasting Commission, Four Corners, "Bad blood", screened on 25 April 2016. Available at: www.abc.net.au/4corners/stories/2016/04/25/4447627.htm (Accessed 4 May 2016).

Australian Human Rights Commission. (2013) "Human rights standards for immigration detention". Available at: www.humanrights.gov.au/our-work/asylum-seekers-and-refugees/publications/human-rights-standards-immigration-detention (Accessed 3 May 2016).

———. (2014) "Inquiry into children in detention", *The forgotten children: National inquiry into children in immigration detention 2014.* Available at: www.humanrights.gov.au/our-work/asylum-seekers-and-refugees/publications/forgotten-children-national-inquiry-children (Accessed 4 May 2016).

Scrutiny of sovereign border policy **71**

————. (2015) *By Hook or By Crook; Australia's Abuse of Asylum Seekers at Sea* (2015), Caritas Australia, UNICEF Australia, Worldvision, Children's Rights International, and the Human Rights Council of Australia.

Bailey, S. and Bowman, M. (1986) "The policy-operational dichotomy – cuckoo in the nest", *Cambridge Law Journal,* 45, 430–451.

Baker, D. (1985) "Maladministration and the law of Torts", *The Adelaide Law Review,* 10, 201–253.

Barrett v Enfield London Borough Council [2001] 2 AC 550.

Bateman, S. (2013) "Should operations to turn the boats around be kept secret?" *The Conversation,* 27 September 2013. Available at: http://ro.uow.edu.au/cgi/viewcontent.cgi?article=2572&context=lhachapter (Accessed 2 May 2016).

Braithwaite, V. (2003) *Taxing democracy: Understanding tax avoidance and evasion.* Sydney: Routledge.

Brodie v Singleton Shire Council (2001) 206 CLR 512.

Buckley, R. (2000) 'Negligence in the public sphere: Is clarity possible?' *Northern Ireland Legal Quarterly,* 51, 25–41.

Chambers, P. (2015) "The embrace of border security: Maritime jurisdiction, national sovereignty, and the geopolitics of operation sovereign borders", *Geopolitics,* 20(2), 404–425.

Colin Neave, under the *Ombudsman Act 1976, Report No, 02/2013 – Suicide and Self-Harm in the Immigration Detention Network,* (May 2013).

Commonwealth of Australia, (2012) Commonwealth Ombudsman, *Annual Report 2011–2012.*

———— (2013) Report by the commonwealth and immigration Ombudsman.

———— (2014a) Senate Foreign Affairs, Defence and Trade References Committee, *Official Committee Hansard – Breach of Indonesian Foreign Waters,* (21 March 2014).

———— (2014b) *Hansard, Senate Foreign Affairs, Defence and Trade Legislation Committee – Estimates,* (26 February 2014).

———— (2014c) *Official committee Hansard, senate foreign affairs, defence and trade legislation committee,* 26 February 2014.

———— (2014d) Senate Foreign Affairs, Defence and Trade References Committee, *Official Committee Hansard – Breach of Indonesian Foreign Waters,* (21 March 2014).

———— (2014e) Commonwealth Ombudsman, *Annual Report 2013–2014,* (2014).

———— (2015) Commonwealth Ombudsman, *Annual Report 2014–2015,* (2015).

Commonwealth of Australia, Australian border force act 2015.

Commonwealth of Australia, work health and safety act 2011 (application to defence activities and defence members) Declaration 2012.

Crimmins v Stevedoring Committee (1999) 200 CLR 1.

Dalehite v United States 346 US 15 (1953).

Davies, M. (2000) "Common law liability of statutory authorities: Crimmins v Stevedoring Industry Finance Committee", *8 Torts Law Journal,* 1, 11–12.

Dechent, S. (2014) 'Operation sovereign borders: The very real risk of refoulement of refugees' *Alternative Law Journal,* 39(2), 110–121.

Devetak, R. (2004) "In fear of refugees: The politics of border protection in Australia", *The International Journal of Human Rights,* 8(1), 101–109.

Fairgrieve, D. (2003) *State liability in Tort: A comparative law study,* (Oxford Scholarship Online). ISBN: 9780199258055.

Farrell, P. and Laughland, O. (2014) "Review blames Immigration for data breach exposing 10,000 detainees" 12 June 2014, *The Guardian.* Available at: www.theguardian.com/world/2014/jun/12/review-blames-immigration-data-breach-detainees (Accessed 5 May 2016).

Gleeson, M. (2000) "Judicial legitimacy", *20 Australian Bar Review,* 4.

Griffiths, E. (2014) "Immigration Minister Scott Morrison demands answers from his department after it accidentally disclosed asylum seeker personal details online" 19 February 2014, *ABC News*.Available at:www.abc.net.au/news/2014-02-19/personal-details-of-asylum-seekers-published-by-immigration-dept/52694 (Accessed 2 May 2016).

Ham v Los Angeles County 46 Cal App 148 (1920).

Hink, H. and Schutter, D. (1965–1966) "Some thoughts on American law of government tort liability", *Rutgers Law Journal,* 29, 710.

Hodge, P. (2015) 'A grievable life? The criminalisation and securing of asylum seeker bodies in the 'violent frames' of Australia's operation sovereign borders", *Geoforum,* 58, 122–135.

Indian Towing Co v United States of America 350 US 61 (1955).

Ireland, J. and Hall, B. (2013) "Tony Abbott evokes John Howard in Slamming doors on Asylum Seekers", 15 March. Available at: https://www.smh.com.au/politics/federal/tony-abbott-evokes-john-howard-in-slamming-doors-on-asylum-seekers-20130815-2rzzy.html (Accessed 2 May 2016).

Job, J. and Reinhart, M. (2003) "Trusting the tax office: Does Putnam's thesis relate to tax?" *Australian Journal of Social Issues,* 38, 307.

Keane, B. "Operation secretive bureaucrats: It just keeps expanding", 24 March 2014, *Crikey.* Available at: www.crikey.com.au/2014/03/24/operation-secretive-bureaucrats-it-just-keeps-expanding (Accessed 5 May 2016).

———. "Training, lifeboats and asylum seekers in the 'battle-space", 6 March 2014, *Crikey.* Available at: www.crikey.com.au/2014/03/06/training-lifeboats-and-asylum-seekers-in-the-battle-space/ (Accessed 2 May 2016).

KPMG, "Management initiated review, privacy breach – data management", 20 May 2014. Available at: www.immi.gov.au/pub-res/Documents/reviews/kpmg-data-breach-abridged-report.pdf (Accessed 3 May 2016).

Liberal Party of Australia, "The coalition's operation sovereign borders policy – our plan: Real solutions for all Australians", July 2013. Available at: http://lpaweb-static.s3.amazonaws.com/Policies/OperationSovereignBorders_Policy.pdf (Accessed 2 May 2016).

———, "The coalition's operation sovereign borders policy", July 2013. Available at: www.nationals.org.au/Portals/0/2013/policy/The%20Coalition%E2%80%99s%20Operation% 20Sovereign%20Borders%20Policy.pdf (Accessed 16 January 2015).

Maley, W. (2003) "Asylum-seekers in Australia's international relations", *Australian Journal of International Affairs,* 57(1), 187–201.

Martin, P. (2013) "Weekly briefings will end boat arrival blackout, says minister", 23 September 2013, *Sydney Morning Herald*.Available at:www.smh.com.au/federal-politics/political-news/weekly-briefings-will-end-boat-arrival-blackout-says-minister-20130922-2u81u.html (Accessed 5 May 2016).

Maxwell, J. (2014) "The unjustified secrecy of the Abbott government", *Eureka Street,* 24(15), 26.

McAdam, J. (2013) "Australia and asylum seekers", *International Journal of Refugee Law,* 25(3), 435–444.

McMaster, D. (2002) "Asylum-seekers and the Insecurity of a Nation", *Australian Journal of International Affairs,* 56(2), 279.

Minister for Arts Heritage and Environment v Peko-Walsend (1987) 15 FCR 274.

Minister for Immigration, Local Government and Ethnic Affairs v Kurtovic (1990) 21 FCR 193.

Murphy, K. (2004) "The role of trust in nurturing compliance: A study of accused tax avoiders", *Law and Human Behaviour,* 28, 187.

Office of the Australian Information Commissioner, "Processing of non-routine FOI requests by the department of immigration and citizenship – report of an own motion investigation". Available at: www.oaic.gov.au/images/documents/migrated/

oaic/repository/publications/reports/DIAC_FOI_own_motion_report_FINAL.pdf (Accessed 5 May 2016).

Oliver, D. (1980) "Anns v London borough of Merton reconsidered", *Current Legal Problems*, 33, 270.

Pyrenees Shire Council v Day (1998) 192 CLR 375.

Reilly, A., Applebye, G. and Laforgia, R. (2014) "'To watch, to never look away': The public's responsibility for Australia's offshore processing of asylum seekers", *Alternative Law Journal*, 39(3), 163–178.

Reynolds, O. (1968) "The discretionary function exceptions of the federal torts claims act", *Georgetown Law Journal*, 57, 81–101.

Robert Cornall, A.O. "Independent comparative review of the department of immigration and citizenship's freedom of information procedures report", 30 August 2012. Available at: www.border. gov.au/ReportsandPublications/Documents/reviews-and-inquiries/independent-comparative-review-foi-procedures.pdf (Accessed 5 May 2016).

Scholz, J. (1998) "Trust, taxes and compliance", in V. Braithwaite and M. Levi (eds.), *Trust and governance*. New York: Russell Sage Foundation.

Scholz, J. and Lubell, M. (1998) "Trust and taxpaying: Testing the heuristic approach to collective action", *American Journal of Political Science*, 42(2), 398–415.

Sean Parnell, "Department of immigration and citizenship culture heavily risk averse, says Australian Public Service Commission", 4 December 2012. *The Australian*. Available at: www.theaustralian.com.au/news/foi/department-of-immigration-and-citizenship-culture-heavily-risk-averse-says-australian-public-service-commission/story-fn8r0e18-1226529744381 (Accessed 5 May 2016).

Smillie, J. (1985) "Liability of public authorities for negligence", *University of Western Ontario Law Review*, 23, 213–240.

Sutherland Shire Council v Heyman (1985) 157 CLR 424.

Swan, J. (2014) "Tony Abbott compares secrecy over asylum seekers to war time", 11 January 2014. *Sydney Morning Herald*. Available at: www.smh.com.au/federal-politics/political-news/tony-abbott-compares-secrecy-over-asylum-seekers-to-war-time-20140110– 30lyt.html (Accessed 2 May 2016).

The Honourable Scott Morrison Member of Parliament, "Transcript of joint press conference: Sydney: 23 September 2013: Operation Sovereign Borders", 23 September 2013. Available at: http://parlinfo.aph.gov.au/parlInfo/download/media/pressrel/3099126/upload_binary/3099126.pdf;fileType=application%2Fpdf#search=%22media/pressrel/3099126%22, (Accessed 5 May 2016).

Todd, S. (1986) "The negligence liability of public authorities: Divergence in the common law", *Law Quarterly Review*, 102, 370–385.

Torgler, B., Demir, I. C., Macintyre, A. and Schaffner, M. (2008) "Causes and consequences of tax morale: An empirical investigation", *Economic Analysis and Policy*, 38(2), 313.

United Kingdom, Public Health Act 1936.

United Nations High Commission for Refugees, (UNHCR), (2015) *By Hook or By Crook; Australia's Abuse of Asylum Seekers at Sea*.

United States of America, *Federal Tort Claims Act of 1948*, 28 USC Pt IV Ch 171 (1948).

United States v Gaubert 499 US 315 (1991).

Woodall, K. (1992) "Private law liability of public authorities for negligent inspection and regulation", *McGill Law Journal*, 37, 83–102.

Woolf, H. and Woolf, B. (1990) *Protection of the public – A new challenge, 60*. London: Stevens. Available at: https://trove.nla.gov.au/work/17317269?q&versionId=45411863

4

SOVEREIGN DEBT RESTRUCTURING

Locating Indian law and jurisprudence in the contemporary international legal order[1]

Ansari Salamah

Introduction

Distressed sovereign debt ceases to be a rarity. Sovereign debt crisis has become a contemporary international problem affecting not just the state in crisis but also nations at large. The protracted history of sovereign debt crises and associated problems is not restricted to the developing world and includes developed countries like France and the United Kingdom which defaulted during the Great Depression of the 1930s (Dodd, 2002). Specifically, the developing countries have been facing the hazard of sovereign debt crisis for a long time now as post-1950s most debt crises occurred in developing or emerging market economies. Latin American countries hit the crisis during the 1980s: Brazil defaulted in 1980 followed by Mexico in 1982[2] and several other Latin American countries followed suit in a decade-long debt crisis. A majority of the Asian countries grappled with a financial crisis during the 1990s, followed by other countries across the globe. Starting with Thailand in 1997 the debt crisis spread to Indonesia, South Korea, Philippines, Malaysia and Singapore, and soon spread to Russia (1998).

Argentina's default during 2001 is considered the largest in history, amounting to more than US $100 billion in private debt and has brought back to the front many of the conventional problems related to sovereign debt restructuring. Other countries that faced similar issues include Cote d'Ivoire, Democratic Republic of Congo, Ecuador, Pakistan, Panama, Peru, Turkey, Uruguay and Vietnam, with Greece being the latest to join the list. Moreover, several countries in Europe[3] are in the primary moments of a sovereign debt crisis (Wright, 2012), which validates that problems associated with sovereign debt crises and restructuring are not the exclusive preserve of Highly Indebted Poor Countries (HIPC) or developing countries (Lumina, 2011). Since 1975, the amount of distressed external debt peaked in 1990 at an estimated more than $335 billion issued by 55 countries (Hatchondo et al.,

2007). Practically all voluntary lending by commercial banks ceased in 1982 after Mexico's moratorium on external debt repayments (Buchheit, 1999); resultantly the 1980s became famous as the '*lost decade*' for the Latin American sub-continent (Ghosal and Miller, 2003) owing to the absence of economic growth in that part of the world (Dodd, 2002).

Variable factors that can lead to a debt crisis are weak macroeconomic policies, worsening terms of trade, adverse environmental conditions, political and institutional factors (Das et al., 2013) and other external factors that are frequently coupled with protracted civil unrests and armed conflicts[4] and occasionally ill-advised lending–borrowing decisions. Another important reason for the debt crisis can be odious and illegitimate debt. There have been several instances when the debt has been illegally issued by past governments (Porzecanski, 2010; Feibelman, 2010). Missing transparency and tainted by corruption, often these debts have been proved to be in violation of domestic laws and international treaties. During the Cold War, many developed countries lent money to corrupt and oppressive regimes in return for support, while private companies extended loans in return for over-valued contracts that had negligible worth for the sovereign borrower's citizens (Lumina, 2011). There is an international consensus "for a debt to be odious it is sufficient that the debt is incurred without the consent of the people" as in the case of dictatorship (Wright, 2012). In such a circumstance, the debt seldom accrues any benefit to the people, and these facts are not unknown to the creditors lending at that time (Wright, 2012).

Sovereign debt crisis leads to a fall in domestic output, economic dislocation, domestic political disorder and foreign trade sanctions along with a loss of access to capital markets (Krueger, 2002). Explicit or clandestine trade sanctions have been experienced by countries in default. Martinez and Sandleris (2011) have shown empirical evidence that countries in default experience a significant decline in foreign trade, which may indicate the imposition of trade sanctions or the loss of access to trade credit facilities. Debt crisis can reduce the amount of foreign credit available to private domestic firms via a decline in supply because lenders' perceptions of country risk worsen (Drudi and Giordano, 2000). Further, the domestic costs associated with default include damages to domestic financial system by inducing a domestic banking crisis and fall in domestic output (Wright, 2012).

Unable to pay back its debt; to free up public resources, a country is forced to choose between two options: a) default on payment and subsequent debt restructuring or b) receive an International Monetary Fund (IMF)–funded bailout and accept the conditionalities that are attached to bailout loans (Eurodad, 2014). More often than not, the debtor country is reluctant to default on payment, and they choose the latter option and accept IMF's conditionalities. Theoretically, a sovereign decides to seek IMF financing voluntarily, but it should be borne in mind that a country facing a crisis seldom has any other option owing to the economic constraints that a distressed debt situation imposes (Paliouras, 2017). Nonetheless, the history of sovereigns is replete with numerous incidences of debt defaults. As discussed earlier, a country facing a debt crisis has limited options: either to default on payment and then request debt restructuring or consent to the conditionalities that come along with IMF–funded bailout.

The conditionalities or austerity policies are costlier for all the parties concerned as they are more disruptive for the national economy and also internationally (Stichelmans, 2015). The debt crisis lasts longer and has a negative impact on economic recovery as the first step usually undertaken is reduction in public expenditure and a raise in taxes in order to reduce public debt. This leads to lower tax revenues instead of higher as there is a reduction in economic output, plus a government is forced to spend even more on social assurance benefits (Ibid). This can induce recession which affects the level of employment. Increased unemployment in turn creates new conditions of poverty. Further, as debt crises often lead to decline in economic output, the resultant drop in a government's capacity to ensure basic social services threatens the enjoyment of socio-economic rights moreso for the underprivileged citizens who are disproportionately affected by such financial incapacity of the state (Goldmann, 2012).

Often sovereign debt crisis grows into a perpetual nightmare for nations as the process of sovereign debt restructuring is relegated to ad hoc mechanisms of resolution. As there is no legitimate system of rule of law or internationally recognized codified procedure for sovereign debt restructuring (Herman et al., 2010; Calitz, 2012) that can prescribe fair and equitable resolution mechanism, restructurings are mostly done on a case-to-case basis, directed mainly by the IMF and occasionally by other international lenders. Frequently loss of market access triggers a debt restructuring and hence the primary aim of most of the initiatives is to restore market access (Stichelmans, 2015). Non-economic factors or human rights criteria get relatively insignificant consideration.

Despite a long history of financial crisis, there is lack of adequate safeguards and international policy framework to ensure timely and equitable restructuring of sovereign debt. Nevertheless, sovereign debt restructuring has met with varied response from multilateral and domestic initiatives in the last few decades. The majority of these initiatives are voluntary in nature, with no legal entity or statutory rules of procedure. Although geared towards debt relief, the process continues to be case based and ad hoc, often left to the discretion of the creditors. Taking advantage of this inadequacy in the legal framework, several creditors have resorted to litigations to realize their contractual claims. Instead of accepting a reduction in their claims, some creditors resort to legal remedies to enforce their contractual claims and get 100 dollars a cent.

On facing a distressed debt situation, it is in the best interest of the sovereign and its creditors that all the creditors accept a reduction in their claims. Restructuring becomes central as the sovereign is facing macroeconomic and financial crisis. It is imperative for the sovereign to regain financial sustainability before it can resume servicing its debt obligation. In such a situation, instead of co-operating several opportunistic creditors litigate to extract full repayments from the sovereign. Prevention and management of unsustainable sovereign debt and subsequent litigations continue to baffle the international institutions.

During the nineteenth century, under the prevailing doctrine of absolute immunity, a state enjoyed immunity while involved in commercial activity and so holdout litigation was restricted to national courts (Waibel, 2007). Over time there was a resolute decline in absolute sovereign immunity, partly due to a transition in the nature of international trade and partly due to the lack of an international forum for sovereign debt crisis resolution. A more restrictive code of sovereign immunity has materialized in response to government participation in commercial activities (Wright, 2012). As a result sovereigns fall prey to opportunistic litigations while restructuirng external debt.

Nations have acknowledged that nothing short of legislation is required to establish uniformity and certainty. Hence, a set of nations have proactively augmented the customary international law by national legislation, e.g. the US Foreign Sovereign Immunities Act 1976 (FSIA) and the State Immunity Act 1978 of the UK. For reasons unknown, several states have forgone the opportunity to pass national legislation and continue to rely on international customary law in determining the scope of immunity (Finke, 2010). India belongs to this category of nations. As India is emerging as an attractive destination for Foreign Direct Investment (FDI), the Indian government needs to set out appropriate rules and regulations that explicitly define the degree, scope and extent of state immunity. The process of sovereign debt restructuring is seldom straightforward. Each step involves considerable negotiations and is time consuming. Several conflicting interests interplay and the process is politically charged.

International initiatives

Sovereign debt restructuring has been met with a varied response from individual states as well as from the multilateral initiatives throughout the last few decades. Though mostly creditor/lender initiated, these international initiatives have led to a considerable increase in sovereign debt relief (Sookun, 2010). Several bilateral creditors have extended debt relief, which has restrained the sale of claims to private litigants in secondary markets which in turn has reduced the number of lawsuits.[5] Quite a few debt relief initiatives have curtailed the crippling debt of countries in the past three decades. Although the past decades have seen marked and significant improvement in the provision of debt relief to distressed sovereigns; the picture is not equally good when it comes to sovereign debt restructuring processes. The minimal support towards establishing a fair and equitable debt restructuring process is partly due to the interconnection between debt problems and political, economic and social factors of both the creditor and debtor countries. Legislative efforts have been undertaken by a few national governments like Belgium and UK but they have been less successful than expected in motivating other governments to adopt similar legislation.

The efforts by multilateral institutions and government include the HIPC debt relief initiatives (2006), Multilateral Debt Relief Initiative (MDRI, 2009) and Debt Reduction Facility (DRF); initiatives by Norway (1998); G8 (2005); initiatives by

China (2007); and the Paris Club Initiatives (1956, 2007). International initiatives have met with some success as far as debt relief is concerned. These multilateral and individual efforts of states have helped to reduce the indebtedness of countries and bring them back on the path of development. Creditor initiated and voluntary in nature with no legal entity and statutory rules of procedure the entire process is ad hoc.

More importantly, the debt relief initiatives have largely targeted poorer countries. For the other developing economies that have a distressed debt situation, there have not been enough measures. Also, when the amount is too considerably large to waive off or when there is involvement of bilateral private lenders, the debt relief would be substantially reduced. Moreover, debt write-off may not be the right step towards prudent financial management. There is a lack of a comprehensive approach towards sovereign debt restructuring that is based on a well-accepted international framework. A piecemeal approach does not suffice and fails to deal with the various problems of sovereign debt restructuring. It is imperative to cure the root cause of why nations become indebted in an unsustainable manner.

The impetus on developing an international legal framework for sovereign debt restructuring is not a recent phenomenon. The Paris Club initiative was undertaken in 1956 because the international community realized that sovereigns are facing distressed debt situation. A well-crafted proposal was made in 1979; the Group of 77 developing countries proposed the first policy initiative for sovereign debt restructuring to create an "International Debt Commission" (Rogoff and Zettelmeyer, 2002). It never materialized because of resistance from the creditor countries. The Group of 77 effectively championed the resolution at the United Nations General Assembly (UNGA) which recognized that a state's efforts to restructure debt should not be impeded by hedge funds that seek to profit from distressed debt. It remains an uphill battle to actually realize it as the US, Germany and the UK – key countries in global finance – are amongst those which objected (Khor, 2015), and in any event it would not have had powers other than making recommendations (Rogoff and Zettelmeyer, 2002).

In 2002, a recommendation from the IMF for an improved sovereign debt restructuring mechanism (SDRM) was made. It focussed more on preserving asset values in case of default and protects creditors' rights. Immediately thereafter the US Treasury Department proposed a framework for sovereign debt restructuring on the lines of US bankruptcy code for corporates. In 2012, the intergovernmental Group of Twenty-Four on International Monetary Affairs and Development Communiqué highlighted the need for further research on sovereign debt restructuring mechanisms[6] (Reddy et al., 2014). In 2012, under the aegis of the Centre for International Governance and Innovation (CIGI) and Institute for New Economic Thinking (INET), a five-point agenda for global arrangements for resolving sovereign debt crisis was proposed (Schadler, 2012).

With the emergence of sovereign debt crises in developing and developed countries, the United Nations Conference on Trade and Development (UNCTAD)

Sovereign debt restructuring **79**

made a proposal to improve the coherence, fairness and efficiency of sovereign debt workouts. It established an ad hoc Working Group on a Debt Workout Mechanism in 2013 composed of stakeholders and independent experts.[7] Most recently The South Summit of the G77 in Bolivia in June 2014 called for a proper global debt restructuring mechanism (Khor, 2015). In September 2015 the UNGA passed a binding resolution on the "Basic Principles on Sovereign Debt Restructuring Processes" (A/69/L.84). It laid down the basic guidelines for sovereign debt restructuring guided by customary law and basic international principles of law. The binding resolution was adopted in response to the exponentially growing concerns about sovereign debt crises and debt sustainability, particularly in the backdrop of transnational economic fragility.

Several proposals for an international legal framework for sovereign debt restructuring have been made but it still remains an unfinished task. There is a greater diversity of creditor claims and interests that need to be taken care of while restructuring sovereign debt. Additionally, as nations increasingly issue debt in a range of legal jurisdiction it is a herculean task to ensure creditor coordination in the event of default and restructuring. It should be borne in mind that there are other problems associated with restructuring sovereign debt like long-term access to capital, economic dislocation and political upheaval. However, the scope of the present chapter is limited to analyzing the doctrine of sovereign immunity in the context of litigations arising during sovereign debt restructuring.

Doctrine of sovereign immunity

Historically, states enjoyed absolute immunity based on the concept of sovereignty. Sovereignty refers to the internationally accepted principle of "non-intervention and mutual recognition that create the boundaries between independent States" (Guder, 2008). Ascending from the theoretical underpinning of sovereignty and sovereign immunity[8] is the qualification and validation for differential treatment of sovereign debt and subsequent debt restructuring. Sovereign has a special legal status "arising from the doctrine of sovereign immunity which precludes a lawsuit against a sovereign without its consent or waiver" (Wright, 2012). Sovereign immunity is a "procedural bar based on the status of the defendant as a sovereign State" (Foakes and Wilmshurst, 2005). The doctrine of absolute sovereign immunity seems to have originated during the nineteenth century as a state enjoyed protection while involved in commercial activity during that time. Hence, a creditor did not have a right to sue a nation-state and holdout litigation was limited to national courts (Waibel, 2007). If need be the creditor had to persuade her own nation to compel the debtor country to pay using moral suasion or political pressure. Diplomatic and political relations were not gravely affected by the private commercial interests (Panizza et al., 2009). The two principles which govern the soveign immunity follow.

Immunity from jurisdiction

Immunity from jurisdiction involves treating sovereigns with equality and dignity; a sovereign state cannot be sued in foreign courts without its consent (Panizza et al., 2009), a fragment of general principles of international law. This principle is derivative of the doctrine of equality of sovereign nations under international law which prescribes that "legal persons of equal standing cannot have their disputes settled in the courts of one of them" (Brownlie, 2003). An individual or a company can be hauled into court, but a sovereign cannot be treated similarly unless it has waived off its immunity explicitly. Presently, the involvement of state in commercial activity is an exception when such immunity gets annulled automatically. This exception gets suspended only to the degree that a state's property has been used in execution of sovereign activities.

A specific example of this is the case of *Donegal International Ltd v Republic of Zambia & Anor.*[9] In this case, in the original debt contract between Romania and Zambia mutual sovereign immunity was respected. However, Romania sold its claims to Donegal International Ltd. Donegal made Zambia sign a supplementary agreement under which Zambia was forced to waive off its sovereign immunity. Instead of accepting all the previous terms and conditions as assigned to the primary lender, Zambia waived off its sovereign immunity. Had Zambia appropriately negotiated with Donegal, Donegal would be forced to respect the original agreement.

Immunity from execution

Immunity from execution is a check against indiscriminate attachment of foreign state's property that can have adverse socio-political corollaries. This perhaps is a weaker defence as compared to the immunity against jurisdiction. This rule pertains to the attachment of a foreign state's property after a judgment has been obtained against a foreign state. A classic example of this is when a firm NML Capital[10] detained an Argentine naval vessel on a port of Ghana. Argentina approached the International Tribunal for the Law of the Sea, which held that Ghana should release the ship as UN convention "gives warships immunity from civil claims in foreign ports." The tribunal added that attachment of the ship was "a source of conflict that may endanger friendly relations among States."[11]

A restrictive interpretation of sovereign immunity started post–World War II when the US courts did not grant immunity to the Soviet Union corporations functional within the US In the context of commercial activities carried out within the US, or which would have a direct effect inside the US, the US government endorsed a restrictive approach of sovereign immunity and frequently foreign sovereigns were denied the protection of sovereign immunity. This paved the way for allowing commercial companies to litigate against a foreign sovereign if the claim was purusant to commercial activity and subsequently the Foreign Sovereign Immunities Act (FSIA) of 1976 embodied this restrictive approach (Panizza et al., 2009).

Post-1970s, the deregulation of the financial market in the UK and the US led to a rise in the use of negotiable instruments which could be traded in the international market. Demand for such instruments was created by design to accommodate the change in international trade. With the growth of negotiable instruments it became impossible to classify the acts of state into strict categories of *iure imperii* (public acts) and *iure gestionis* (commercial acts). This overlap in state functions happened deliberately. The parallel events in the financial and economic world impacted the legal system of countries and also internationally. These were not isolated arenas and worked in tandem, each one influencing the other. The supplementary legal framework further weakened the sovereign as compared to the private interests. The emergent pattern of international trade deliberately stripped the sovereign of the benefits of immunity and made it more vulnerable to litigations. Increasing incidences of litigations have perplexed the IFIs and nation-states alike.

Now creditors who are dissatisfied as to the terms of restructuring often resort to litigations to realize their contractual claims against a defaulting sovereign. This is of particular concern in sovereign debt restructurings, as in holdout litigation a minority of creditors chooses to sue for full repayment whilst the majority of creditors have accepted the terms of debt restructuring (Waibel, 2007). The resort to market forces for sovereign debt restructuring has led to this phenomenal increase in litigations targeting assets of defaulting sovereign nations, not only within the state but internationally across jurisdictions. Aggressive lawsuits haunt the distressed countries in dire need of restructuring. The private litigants that aggressively plague the distress nations, often upsetting the restructuring process, are generally called 'vulture funds'.

Commercial activity exception

Ostensibly both the immunities – immunity from suit and immunity against execution – should be a sufficient safeguard against litigation. However, a single exception quashes both the provisions: involvement of state in commercial activities. It is noteworthy that in the sovereign debt market, it is considered that sovereigns act much like private borrowers (Waibel, 2007). Due to the application of the commercial activity exception, the protection of sovereign immunity defence has regularly been suspended for the sovereign defendants following the 1980s Latin American Crisis (Blackman and Mukhi, 2010). Moreover, foreign states' property have been attached as and when it is being used for "commercial activity."

Overtime, it has become prevalent that the "immunity right must only be recognized where governments act in the exercise of their public authority and must be denied where governments act as any private person might" (Kupelian and Rivas, 2014). In most incidences of litigation, the sovereign has waived off such immunity in the debt contract. It has been held time and again in several judgments that a right cannot be waived off if "considerations of public policy or morals are involved" (Kupelian and Rivas, 2014) but still there have been numerous episodes when a sovereign has waived off immunity. This brings us to a loophole in the

82 Ansari Salamah

current legal framework pertaining to waiver of sovereign immunity. An exception has become a major deciding factor of the degree and extent of the principle of sovereign immunity in adjudicating an increasing number of litigations against a sovereign.

By de-politicizing the authority to grant sovereign immunity, attempts have been made to open up the courts to injured plaintiffs in need of relief (Ashe, 1992). Increasingly states engage in a plethora of activities and this increases the risk of running into disputes. States may undertake commercial contracts with foreign individuals and companies, or may own and run enterprises that cater to other countries' citizens. When disputes relating to such transactions are taken to the courts, questions pertaining to the scope of state immunity arise frequently (Foakes and Wilmshurst, 2005).

The rise of a restrictive approach to sovereign immunity

Over time there is a resolute decline in absolute sovereign immunity, partly due to a transition in the nature of international trade and partly due to the lack of an international forum for sovereign debt crisis resolution. The requisite legal machinery to buffer nations against economic and political shocks impairing their payment capacity is largely absent (Waibel, 2007). Over the years, states are either compelled to waive their immunity or consent to be sued, specifically when they enter into commercial contracts. It is now universally accepted that the doctrine of sovereign immunity is not applicable when a sovereign participates in commercial activity and behaves like a private player. A more restrictive code of sovereign immunity has materialized in response to government participation in commercial activities (Wright, 2012).

There have been several instances when the sovereign has waived off its immunity in commercial contracts. The decline in the strength of the protection over time, both through statutory changes and through case laws, has opened a window for legal enforcement of contractual claims against sovereign states (Panizza et al., 2009). Unfortunately, recent times have witnessed a phenomenal increase in litigation targeting assets of defaulting sovereign nations, not only within the state, but across jurisdictions. With the sovereign space eroding over time, the sovereign acts and assets which do not fall within the strict definition of 'sovereign' sphere have fallen prey to such litigation.

It is pertinent to note here that although the involvement of the state in commercial activity leads to the quashing of the privilege of sovereign immunity there remains a glaring difference between a sovereign doing business and a corporate. The two cannot be compared and hence cannot be treated in the same manner. Several lacunas in the international sovereign debt restructuring framework have led to avenues for litigations against the sovereign. As reported by the IMF and the World Bank (2007), there have been 47 litigations against 11 highly indebted poor countries (Wright and Pitchford, 2011). Since 2004, Africa and Latin America have been the most harassed by the litigating creditors as the number of claims has almost doubled with an average of eight cases per year; (Rossi, 2016). After its 2001 default, Argentina faced more than 100 lawsuits (Gelpern, 2005).

This recourse to litigation instead of participating in negotiations with the sovereign debtor threaten not only national but international political and financial stability whilst decreasing welfare for countries and their citizens (Waibel, 2007). Theoretically, litigation may be *legal*; it is to be noted that resort to these legal mechanisms evading negotiations is invigorated by the unsustainable debt positions of sovereign countries. A country's debt position is determined by not only the financial and economical but also political issues and these factors play an essential role in the choice of recourse by a creditor: arbitration or litigation (Sookun, 2010). Such creditors specialize in bringing suit against a country in default and enjoy greater bargaining power because of their experience in litigation.

Foreign state immunity: India

India is emerging as an attractive destination for Foreign Direct Investment (FDI). Several policy initiatives for promoting deregulation and liberalization have been undertaken to facilitate the FDI inflows. However, in cases where the investors are foreign-state[12]–controlled investors there is a growing concern as to the appropriate legislation in case of disputes as the foreign states enjoy sovereign immunity which provides them an advantage over private persons. Frequently disputes arise from non-sovereign activity and commercial transactions entered into by a state (Foakes and Wilmshurst, 2005). The rules of state immunity differ substantially across different countries and so should be appropriately known and deliberated as it can affect business and nations alike.

With the ongoing lawsuits against several nations, the Indian government needs to set out appropriate rules and regulations that explicitly define the degree, scope and extent of state immunity. Sovereign immunity is one of the most potent defences available to a sovereign state; it can help distressed debtors to avoid litigation while restructuring sovereign debt. Growth in government participation in business ought to be coupled with the corresponding evolution of legislation governing the issue. While India subscribes to the internationally accepted maxim of sovereign immunity, "*par in parem non habet imperium*"[13] meaning "an equal has no power over an equal", there is absence of any distinct domestic legislation for the same. Having domestic legislation is crucial as international law may outline the common rules pertaining to immunity; nonetheless, those rules are interpreted and executed by the national law (Foakes and Wilmshurst, 2005).

India, unlike its American, British and other common law counterparts, lacks a comprehensive statute dealing with sovereign immunity (Choudhary, 2010). Compared to developed countries the advent of this doctrine is relatively recent in India as it came with the British. It was believed that that the King of England ruled by divine right and thus could do no wrong; consequently the courts would not allow a lawsuit against the king. This English concept of sovereign immunity was transported to the Indian colony,[14] and it became ingrained in our law as well (Krishna,

2012). However, it has been evolving ever since as the international perception of immunity has been rapidly changing with changing forms of public administration. In India it has been subject to the different times and ideas pre- and post-independence theoretically. But practically in the absence of an exclusive code as to the extent of sovereign immunity, it still depends upon the decisions of the court as to what is the appropriate scope of state immunity in a case. Precedents serve as the principal source of understanding, hence judiciary predominantly employs cases to decide the scope of sovereign immunity (Krishna, 2012).

Post-independence efforts were made to codify India's legal status on the doctrine of sovereign immunity. An initial report by the Law Commission recommended the abolition of the doctrine of absolute immunity from the Indian legal system.[15] Even though the first report found the doctrine to be outdated, for numerous reasons the draft bill for the abolition of absolute sovereign immunity doctrine never passed. Thus, it was left to the discretion of courts to adjudicate the scope, extent and degree of immunity as well as its compatibility in accordance with the Constitution of India (Garje, 2009). In a later period, the Government (Liability in Tort) Bill, 1965 was passed. However, this too could not be enacted into law. Subsequently, a new bill was reintroduced in 1967 which also met the same fate. This led to the default employment of the courts as the final conciliators in the matter concerning the doctrine of sovereign immunity. This raises the question as to why the law has not been rationalized to take account of the changed situation of public administration (Garje, 2009). Post-independence the doctrine of absolute sovereign immunity became unsuitable to a republican welfare nation.

Nevertheless, the government of India in its Memorandum on State Immunity[16] in its "Final Report on Immunity of States in respect of Commercial and other Transactions of a Private Character" has taken the position that immunity shall be denied to commercial activities undertaken by another state or its trading organizations. The memorandum explicitly stated that no distinction should be made between commercial activities conducted directly by a foreign government from those undertaken through trading organizations. The status of the juristic personality of such trading organizations would be immaterial (Choudhary, 2010). Additionally, India has signed the UN Convention on Jurisdictional Immunities of States and their Property.[17] However, India is still to ratify the said treaty as it has not accepted, approved or acceded to it (Sharan 2016).

Section 86 – Code of Civil Procedure

The Code of Civil Procedure (CPC) prescribes any legislation against sovereigns and also "against the execution of any decree against the property of a foreign State" (Section 86). It also deals with the exception when a person is allowed[18] to litigate against a foreign sovereign in a court of law. The conditions under which such permission may be granted are deliberated upon in the same section.

Section 86 of the CPC lays down following conditions under which a suit can be initiated against a sovereign:

a   if the foreign State has instituted a lawsuit in the court against the applicant;
b   if the foreign State, by itself or another, trades within the local limits of the Indian court;
c   if the foreign State's immovable property, in respect of which the applicant wants to sue is situated in India;
d   if the foreign State has waived the privilege of Section 86.[19]

CPC is a "procedural law that comprises the rule by which a court hears and determines what happens in civil lawsuits, criminal or administrative proceedings" (Choudhary, 2010). The code is exhaustive on matters dealt explicitly by it, but unfortunately it does not have a comprehensive Sovereign Immunity Act. The section does contain a subsection entitled "Suits by Aliens and by or against Foreign Rulers, Ambassadors and Envoys" which deals with suits against a foreign state in India inter alia. A substantive law on the topic does not exist.

As technically a person can sue a foreign sovereign in a court of law, the permission from the central government is quintessential. In the prominent case of *Mirza Ali Akbar Kashani v. United Arab Republic and Anr.*,[20] the Supreme Court held that the permission from central government ought to be taken at the earliest instance possible. In the case *Royal Nepal Airline Corporation v. Monorama*,[21] the suit was instituted without the approval from the central government. The government of Nepal through its Ministry of Transport and Communication owned the Royal Nepal Airline Corporation. Chief Justice of Calcutta High Court Bose C. J. held that the corporation was a department of government of Nepal prima facie from the proofs submitted and hence was entitled to jurisdictional immunity.[22] However, the determination of whether a claim for immunity may be granted or not should not be discussed while the proceedings of the court have started as it is not the judiciary's prerogative. If sovereign immunity is to be granted, it has to be allowed at the very onset. The permission to entertain a suit cannot be deterred until the disposal of the lawsuit but has to be sought ex-ante. Although administrative, the consent order under Section 86 ought "to follow the principles of natural justice as it decides the rights of the concerned parties."[23]

On a close examination of Section 86, it can be noted that the central government can grant the permission to sue and waive off immunity subject to the provisions made in clause 2 of the same section. Of the four subsequent paragraphs from 2(a) to 2(d), it is only in sub-section 2(b) and 2(c) that the central government is required to decide. In the other two sections, it is left to the foreign sovereign to decide whether to give in to the jurisdiction or not. An important aspect that is not deliberated upon in this section is 'contracts of employment'. Neither of the two subparagraphs 2(b) and 2(c) mention 'contracts of employment' as an exception to foreign state immunity, let alone its scope and applicability (Choudhary,

2010). It is ultimately left to the executive to conclude whether to treat this as a valid exception to foreign state immunity or not. Hence, only subsection 2(b) and 2(c) empower the government to decide if a suit is permissible or the nature of the activity is sovereign function.

Several pre-independence[24] and post-independence[25] case judgments have deliberated upon the dissimilarity between sovereign and commercial activities. Taxation, police functions, eminent domain, preservation of law and order etc. are considered as the sovereign functions of the state. Sovereign functions essentially are those functions the execution of which cannot be delegated to any private agency or person. The Supreme Court has unambiguously stated "Act done in the course of employment but not in connection with sovereign powers of the state, State like any other employer is vicariously liable."[26] However, while executing sovereign functions the state enjoys immunity. This indicates a departure from the feudalistic notion of sovereign immunity.

With the rising trend of public-private partnerships and neoliberal public administration, it becomes ambiguous as to what tests distinguish the sovereign function from non- sovereign. Post 1970s, there has been a move towards the restrictive interpretation of what constitutes sovereign function. In cases *Union of India v. Miss Savita Sharma*,[27] *Mrs. Pushpa v. State of Jammu & Kashmir*,[28] and *Fatima Begum v. State of Jammu & Kashmir*,[29] it was held that drivers driving army/government vehicles "do not always constitute an act in exercise of sovereign power." Further, sovereign immunity is not applicable in cases under Motor Vehicles Act 1988; when right to life guaranteed under Article 21 is in question[30]; and in cases in the public domain under Article 32 and Article 226.[31]

There are three prominent inadequacies while resorting to Section 86 for deciding about sovereign immunity. Firstly, the permission to sue a sovereign is left to the discretion of the central government categorically. The grant of approval is not premised upon rule of law but political and diplomatic considerations which make it ambiguous. There is an absence of any explicit directive as to what reasons factor in while granting permission to sue. It has been observed in several cases that neither the CPC nor any other legal instrument stipulates procedure to be followed by the Central government while granting or refusing the requisite permission (Sen, 1965). The very basis of suing a foreign state becomes a political rather than rule-based system.

Secondly, the process followed in India may turn contrary to international law as when the central government gives such consent, the foreign state cannot rely upon rules of international law pertaining to jurisdictional immunity of states (Choudhary, 2010). Thus, it is alleged that Section 86 exclusively empowers the Ccentral government to determine the competency of suits against a foreign state in India.[32] Also, it supplants the relevant principles of international law governing sovereign immunity (Sen, 1965).

Thirdly, the scope of immunity remains indeterminate as Section 86 does not enlist which state entities or instrumentalities may claim state immunity in India. Presently, India endorses a restrictive approach towards sovereign immunity and accords immunity to a foreign state and its instrumentalities which constitute a part of the sovereign's *jure imperii*. However, Section 86 fails to delimit the scope, extent and degree of immunity.

Neither section 86 nor any other rules or practice establish legal clarity on the determination of degree, scope and extent of state immunity or the difference between *jure imperii* and *jure gestionis*. A need is felt to ordain an Indian Foreign State Immunity Act which reflects the Indian legal position on state immunity at national and international levels (Choudhary, 2010). An India-specific comprehensive immunity code is long overdue. Time and again, several scholars and judges have expressed a desperate need for a legislative act exclusively dealing with the concept of sovereign immunity to avoid misuse of this doctrine (Krishna, 2012). As the ancient conception of unrestricted sovereign immunity has no space in the contemporary transnational trade relations (Schmitthoff and Wooldridge, 1972), the requisite domestic code on sovereign immunity should be such that it is coherent with the UN convention and facilitates the development international trade while upholding the rule of law simultaneously. The growing concerns oblige that each state must tailor a statute to its unique legal setting (Davis, 1970).

Conclusion

To be forewarned the rise in FDI has to be coupled with a corresponding evolution of legislature and jurisprudence balancing the rights of citizens and foreign sovereign. Drawing from the jurisprudence, it is amply clear that the doctrine of absolute sovereign immunity grounded in archaic colonial jurisprudence does not befit modern Indian jurisprudence. Not only in India but in a majority of developing countries it is gradually realized that the concept of sovereign immunity is anachronistic. It is an outdated justification in a republican nation which guarantees life and liberty as well as the rule of law (Garje, 2009). Despite the contemporary developments in trade, legislation and jurisprudence, Indian position on foreign state immunity remains unsettled.

As is clear from the preceding discussion, neither Section 86 nor any other rules or practice establish legal clarity on the determination of degree, scope and extent of state immunity or the difference between *acts iure imperii* and *acts iure gestionis*. A need is felt to ordain an Indian Foreign State Immunity Act which reflects Indian legal position on state immunity at national and international levels (Choudhary, 2010). Time and again, several scholars and judges have expressed a desperate need for a legislative act exclusively dealing with the concept of sovereign immunity in order to avoid misuse of this doctrine (Krishna, 2012). As the ancient conception of unrestricted sovereign immunity has no room in the international trade relations of the modern world (Schmitthoff and Wooldridge, 1972), the requisite domestic code on sovereign immunity should be such that it is coherent with the UN Convention on Jurisdictional Immunities of States and their Properties and at the same time does not freeze the useful development of law and international trade. The growing concerns oblige that each state must tailor a statute to its unique legal setting (Davis, 1970). An India-specific comprehensive immunity code is long overdue.

Notes

1 This chapter was originally presented in the panel of "Interface of Law and Public Policy" during the third international conference of Public Policy 28–30 June 2017 at Lee Kuan Yew School of Public Policy, Singapore. The author has benefited from comments during the conference presentation and from reviewer comments at different stages of publication.
2 Mexico defaulted again in 1995.
3 Spain, Portugal, Greece, Ireland, Iceland.
4 Debt Relief for Poverty Reduction: The Role of the Enhanced HIPC Initiative. (2001, August 2), available at: www.imf.org/external/pubs/ft/exrp/debt/eng/
5 Norway is an exemplary in extending bilateral debt relief.
6 Intergovernmental Group of Twenty-Four on International Monetary Affairs and Development Communiqué. (2012, April 19), available at: www.imf.org/external/np/cm/2012/041912.htm
7 Sovereign debt workouts: Going forward roadmap and guide (2013). (2016, July 17), available at: http://unctad.org/en/PublicationsLibrary/gdsddf2015misc1_en.pdf
8 Often used interchangeably, there is a difference between State immunity and sovereign immunity. When immunity is granted against litigation in foreign courts it is termed as State immunity whereas immunity in domestic courts amounts to sovereign immunity.
9 [2007] EWHC 197 (Comm.).
10 Based in the U.S., NML Capital Ltd. is a subsidiary of Elliot Capital Mgmt. An ardent sponsor to the U.S. Republican Party campaigns, its public face is Paul Singer (Rossi, 2016).
11 Seized Argentinian sailing ship leaves Ghana (2016, July 10), available at: www.theguardian.com/world/2012/dec/20/argentina-sailing-ship-ghana-release
12 Section 87A CPC defines *foreign State* as "any State outside India that is recognized by the Central Government."
13 This maxim translates to "one sovereign State is not subject to jurisdiction of another State." See Y.V. Chandrachud, The Law Lexicon 21 (1st ed., Wadhwa and Company 1997).
14 It is remarkable to note here that most of the developing countries that face an unsustainable debt situation have been colonies. The main reason for over indebtedness can be easily traced back to the violative practice by colonial masters. When the colonies gained independence, huge piles of debt were handed down to the nascent domestic governments which did not have any experience or expertise in handling macroeconomic problems like external debt in a globalizing international world order. As a consequence, these governments soon fell into debt traps. Catching up with the industrialization process was also difficult for most and they were directly dependent on the same colonial masters for acquisition of the needed machinery and technology. These problems in addition to several other difficulties like civil unrest, lack of education etc. accentuated the pace at which foreign exchange reserves depleted. It is beyond the purview of this dissertation to give a detailed analysis as to how variable factors which are beyond a State's control can increase the debt pile. The point being made is the interconnection between colonization and excessive external debt.
15 First Report of the Law Commission of India, Liability of the State in Tort 1950.
16 Submitted to the Asian-African Legal Consultative Committee (AALCC), 1960.
17 India signed the UN convention in 2007.
18 With the consent of the central government.
19 Section 86, the Code of Civil Procedure, India.
20 (1966) 1 SCR 319 Suit against the United Arab Republic and the Republic of Egypt Ministry of Economy, Supplies, Importation Department.
21 A.I.R. 1966 Cal. 319.
22 *Bidhusbhusan Prasad v. Royal Nepal Film Corporation*, A.I.R. 1983 NOC 75 (Cal.).
23 *Shanti Prasad Agarwalla & Others v. Union of India and Others*, A.I.R. 1991 SC 814.

24 *P. & O. Steam Navigation Co. v. Secretary of State.*
25 *State of Rajasthan v. Mst. Vidyawati,* (A.I.R. 1962 SC 933); *Kasturi Lal Ralia Ram v. State of UP,* (A.I.R. 1965SC1039); *Satyawati v. Union of India,* (A.I.R. 1957 Delhi 98); *Union of India v. Smt. Jasso,* (A.I.R. 1962 Punj 315 FB); *Union of India v. Sugrabai* (A.I.R. 1969 Bom 13).
26 *P. & O. Steam Navigation Co. v. Secretary of State.*
27 1979 ACJ.
28 1977 ACJ 375.
29 1976 ACJ 194.
30 *Challa Ramkonda Reddy v. State of AP,* (A.I.R. 1989 AP 235).
31 *State of A.P. v. Chella Ramakrishna Reddy* (A.I.R. 2000 SC 2083).
32 *Ali Akbar v. United Arab Republic,* (A.I.R. 1966 S.C. 230).

References

Ashe, L.V. (1992) "The flexible approach to the foreign sovereign Argentina", *Inter- American Law Review,* 23(2), 465–491.

Blackman, J. I. and Mukhi, R. (2010) "The evolution of modern sovereign debt litigation: Vultures, alter egos, and other legal fauna", *Law and Contemporary Problems,* 73(4), 47–62.

Brownlie, I. (2003) *Principles of public international law.* 6th ed. Oxford: Oxford University Press.

Buchheit, L. C. (1999) "Sovereign debt litigation", *Memorandum for the International Monetary Fund,* 4.

Calitz, J. (2012) "An overview of certain aspects regarding the regulation of sovereign insolvency law", *De Jure,* 45(2), 329–347.

Choudhary, V. (2010) "Jurisdictional immunity of foreign trading state enterprises in India and international law", *SSRN 1669519.*

Das, U. S., Papaioannou, M. G. and Trebesch, C. (2013) *Restructuring Sovereign debt: Lessons from recent history, financial crises, consequences, and policy responses.* Washington, DC: International Monetary Fund. Available at: https://www.imf.org/external/np/seminars/eng/2012/fincrises/pdf/ch19.pdf (Accessed 13 September 2019).

Davis, K. C. (1970) "Sovereign immunity must go", *Administrative Law Review,* 383–405.

Dodd, R. (2002) "Sovereign debt restructuring", *The Financier,* 9, 1–6.

Drudi, F. and Giordano, R. (2000) "Default risk and optimal debt management", *Journal of Banking & Finance,* 24(6), 861–891.

Eurodad. (2014) "Conditionality yours: An analysis of the policy conditions attached to IMF loans". Available at: http://www.eurodad.org/files/pdf/53466a66139aa.pdf (Accessed 7 July 2016).

Feibelman, A. (2010) "Ecuador's Sovereign default: A Pyrrhic victory for Odious debt?", *Journal of International Banking Law and Regulation,* Forthcoming (2019, July 10). Available at: SSRN: https://ssrn.com/abstract=1560722

Finke, J. (2010) "Sovereign immunity: Rule, comity or something else?", *European Journal of International Law,* 21(4), 853–881. https://doi.org/10.1093/ejil/chq068

Foakes, J. and Wilmshurst, E. (2005) "State immunity: The United Nations convention and its effect", *Transnational Dispute Management,* 2(5), 0–18.

Garje, A. (2009) "Sovereign immunity: No defense in private law", *SSRN,* 1347948. https://doi.org/10.2139

Gelpern, A. (2005) "After Argentina", *Policy Briefs in International Economics, PB05–2.*

Ghosal, S. and Miller, M. (2003) "Co-ordination failure, moral hazard and sovereign bank-ruptcy procedures", *Economic Journal*, 113(487), 276–304. https://doi.org/10.1111/1468-0297.00125

Goldmann, M. (2012) "Sovereign debt crises as threats to the peace: Restructuring under chapter VII of the UN charter? Table of contents", *Goettingen Journal of International Law*, 4, 153–175. https://doi.org/10.3249/1868-1581-4-1-goldmann

Guder, L. F. (2008) *The administration of debt relief by the international financial institutions: A legal reconstruction of the HIPC Initiative*. Vol. 202. Berlin: Springer Science & Business Media.

G8, Shah, A. (2005, July 10) "G8 summit 2005". Available at: http://www.globalissues.org/article/541/g8-summit-2005

Herman, B. (2010) "Why the code of conduct for resolving sovereign debt crises falls short." In Barry Herman, Jose Antonio Ocampo, and Shari Spiegel (Eds.), *Overcoming developing country debt crises*, (pp. 389–427). New York: Oxford University Press.

Hatchondo, J. C., Martinez, L. and Sapriza, H. (2007) "The economics of sovereign defaults", *Economic Quarterly (10697225)*, 93(2), 163–187.

HIPC (2016, April 8) "Factsheet debt relief under the Heavily Indebted Poor Countries (HIPC) initiative". Available at: https://www.imf.org/external/np/exr/facts/hipc.htm

Khor, M. (2015, February 12) "Battle hots up to curb 'vulture funds", *South Bulletin*, No. 83. Available at: http://www.southcentre.int/question/battle-hots-up-to-curb-vulture-funds/

Krishna, K. (2012) "Development of the doctrine of sovereign immunity in England and India", *SSRN 2402176*.

Krueger, A. O. (2002) "A new approach to sovereign debt restructuring". Available at: https://doi.org/10.5089/9781589061217.054 (Accessed 10 July 2019).

Kupelian, R. and Rivas, M. S. (2014) "Vulture funds-the lawsuit against Argentina and the challenge they pose to the world economy (February) the state capitalist". Available at: https://statecapitalist.wordpress.com/2014/08/05/kupelian-sol-rivas-vulture-funds-the-lawsuit-against-argentina-and-the-challenge-they-pose-to-the-world-economy/ (Accessed 13 September 2019).

Lumina, C. (2011) Sovereign debt and human rights. *Realising the Right to Development*.

Martinez, J. V. and Sandleris, G. (2011) "Is it punishment? Sovereign defaults and the decline in trade", *Journal of International Money and Finance*, 30(6), 909–930.

MDRI: International Development Association & International Monetary Fund (2009, September 15) Heavily Indebted Poor Countries (HIPC) Initiative and Multilateral Debt Relief Initiative (MDRI)—Status of Implementation 19 N.30.

Paliouras, V. (2017) "The right to restructure sovereign debt", *Journal of International Economic Law*, 20(1), 115–136. Available at: https://doi.org/10.1093/jiel/jgx005 (Accessed 10 July 2019).

Panizza, U., Sturzenegger, F. and Zettelmeyer, J. (2009) "The economics and law of sovereign debt and default", *Journal of Economic Literature*, 47(3), 651–698. Available at: https://doi.org/10.1257/jel.47.3.651 (Accessed 10 July 2019).

Paris Club Initiative (1956) "Publication of the first annual report of the Paris Club". Available at: http://www.clubdeparis.org/en/communications/press-release/publication-of-the-first-annual-report-of-the-paris-club-11-06-2008 (Accessed 11 June 2008).

Paris Club Initiative (2007) "Publication of the first annual report of the Paris Club". Available at: http://www.clubdeparis.org/en/communications/press-release/publication-of-the-first-annual-report-of-the-paris-club-11-06-2008 (Accessed 11 June 2008).

Porzecanski, A. C. (2010) "When bad things happen to good sovereign debt contracts: The case of Ecuador", *Law and Contemporary Problems*, 73(25), 251–271.

Reddy, Y. V., Valluri, N. and Ray, P. (2014) *Financial and fiscal policies: Crises and new realties*. India: Oxford University Press.

Rogoff, K. and Zettelmeyer, J. (2002) "Bankruptcy proceedings for sovereigns: A history of ideas, 1976–2001", *IMF Staff Papers*, 470–507.

Rossi, J. (2016) "Sovereign debt restructuring, national development and human rights", *Sur International Journal on Human Rights*, 13(23), 185–196. Available at: https://search.proquest.com/docview/1857448107?accountid=26662%5Cnhttp://link.periodicos.capes.gov.br/sfxlcl41?url_ver=Z39.88-2004&rft_val_fmt=info:ofi/fmt:kev:mtx:journal&genre=article&sid=ProQ:ProQ%3Asocabs&atitle=SOVEREIGN+DEBT+RESTRUCTURING%2C+NATIONA (Accessed 10 July 2019).

Schadler, S. (2012) *Sovereign debtors in distress: Are our institutions up to the challenge?* Waterloo, ON: Centre for international Governance Innovation.

Schmitthoff, C. M. and Wooldridge, F. (1972) "The nineteenth century doctrine of sovereign immunity and the importance of the growth of state trading", *Journal of International Law and Policy*, 2(1959).

Sen, B. (1965) *A diplomat's handbook of international law and practice,* ed. G. Fitzmaurice. The Hague, Netherlands: Martinus Nijhoff.

Sharan, S. (2016) "India: Suing a foreign state in India: Piercing the veil of sovereign immunity". Available at: http://www.mondaq.com/india/x/500590/trials+appeals+compensation/Suing+A+Foreign+State+In+India+Piercing+The+Veil+Of+Sovereign+Immunity (Accessed 14 June 2016).

Stichelmans, B. T. (2015) Why a United Nations sovereign debt restructuring framework is key to implementing the post-2015 sustainable development agenda By Tiago Stichelmans, (May), 16.

Sookun, D. (2010) *Stop vulture fund lawsuits: A handbook,* ed. C. Atthill. London, United Kingdom: Commonwealth Secretariat.

Waibel, M. (2007) "Opening pandora's box: Sovereign bonds in international arbitration", *American Journal of International Law,* 2000(2001), 711–759.

Wright, M. L. J. (2012) "Sovereign debt restructuring: Problems and prospects", *Harvard Business Law Review,* 2, 153–197.

Wright, M. L. J. and Pitchford, R. (2011) "Holdouts in sovereign debt restructuring: A theory of negotiation in a weak contractual environment", *The Review of Economic Studies Working Paper*, 1–38.

5

THE LEGAL AND POLICY QUESTIONS IN FOREIGN DIRECT INVESTMENT

An assessment using Indian case[1]

Priya Misra and Praveen Tripathi

Introduction

One of the important aspects of India's economic policy relates to Foreign Direct Investment (FDI). Since the advent of economic liberalization, the entry of foreign capital is welcome as long as it fits in with the general plan for economic development. The use of foreign capital is a costly method of financing economic development insofar as profits and dividends are earned by foreigners and are likely to flow out of the country. Such profits are deductions from the national income that the investment yields.

However, reliance on foreign capital is not always a matter of choice. When the supply of domestic capital is short and the need for economic growth is urgent, recourse to foreign capital becomes a necessity. In the present climate of international investment, the question is not whether foreign capital should be allowed to come or not; the question is whether investors would like it or not. Governments are competing to attract foreign capital. Two bodies of literature hold different opinions about this competition. The first sees such competition as harmful. Many scholars argue that the fear of capital outflows restricts governments from providing welfare services, environmental regulations and non-productive public goods that the citizens value. Capital mobility prompts a 'race to the bottom' in social and environmental policy, both among subnational governments within decentralized states and among countries competing in world markets (Keen and Marchand, 1997; Rom et al., 1998; Rodrik, 1997). By contrast, the second body of literature views such competition as salutary. The competition for capital motivates governments to reduce their corruption, waste and inefficiency, and to provide more growth-promoting infrastructure (Qian and Roland, 1998; Montinola et al., 1996; Obstfeld, 1998; Stiglitz, 2000).

Where there is an intense 'global race' for FDI, how important is FDI is to a country's economic growth? It is certainly a difficult task to separate and quantify the complex package of resources that FDI confers on the host country. According to economic theory, the three principal contributions of FDI to a host country are: a) the financial capital invested by foreign firms, b) the export market access provided by them, and c) the faster technology development that is expected to occur through technology transfer as part of the FDI package (UNCTAD, 2006).

There are various macro studies conducted to determine the nexus between FDI and growth. A review of these studies points out a number of apprehensions in the assumptions of causality: does FDI lead to greater productivity and overall economic growth, or are these pre-requisites for attracting FDI? Critiques believe that increased economic activity expands the market size, offering greater opportunities for foreign investors to reap economies of scale in a large market economy like India. Thus it is not *FDI led growth*, rather it is more in the nature of *growth led FDI* (Athreye and Kapur, 2001). Apparently developing countries need to have reached a certain level of education, technological and infrastructure development before being able to benefit from the foreign presence in their markets. An additional factor that may prevent a country from reaping the full benefits of FDI is imperfect and underdeveloped financial markets. FDI also appears less effective in least developed economies, suggesting existence of threshold level development (Blomstrom and Kokko, 2003).

In this context, it is important to note that the theory of *Comparative Advantage* plays the most prominent role in the development of foreign investment phenomenon. It made a vital contribution to the economic thought that attracts foreign investment.[2] The earlier logic of free trade could be advantageous for the countries based on the concept of the *Absolute Advantage*,[3] which is practically a one-sided advantage to a country in supplying of goods and services. It may have negative impact on the other country which is in a disadvantageous position. But in certain situations, one country may make a specialized good with lower cost and the other country may make a different good with another type of specialization with low cost expenditure. *Comparative Advantage theory* refers to where both countries may have a beneficial edge in the global trade.

India, with its relatively well-developed financial sector, strong industrial base and critical mass of well-educated workers appears to be well placed to reap the benefits of FDI due to comparative advantage. In view of this, it is appropriate that Indian policymakers continue to make concerted efforts to make India an attractive destination for FDI.

Legality of FDI framework in India

Statutorily, FDI means investment by non-resident entity/person resident outside India in the capital of an Indian company under Schedule 1 of the Foreign Exchange Management (Transfer or Issue of Security by a Person Resident

Outside India) Regulations, 2000.[4] FDI refers to an investment made to acquire lasting interest in enterprises operating outside of the economy of the investor. Further, in cases of FDI, the investor's purpose is to gain an effective voice in the management of the enterprise. The foreign entity or group of associated entities that makes the investment is termed as a 'direct investor'. The unincorporated or incorporated enterprise receiving the investment is referred to as a 'direct investment enterprise.'[5]

The primary drivers of FDI in India are human capital, quality of infrastructure, economic stability and political stability. All of them are to an extent influenced by public policy. For instance, human capital, if not backed by public policy, will fail to provide the efficiency, encouragement and security that the human resource needs. Several departments in the government of India decided to take up a series of initiatives utilizing the opportunity of FDI availability. For instance, the Department of Industrial Policy and Promotion (DIPP) as per the Allocation of Business Rules, 1961 was allocated the subject of "Direct foreign and non-resident investment in industrial and service projects, excluding functions entrusted to the Ministry of Overseas Indian Affairs." As per the policy suggested by DIPP, relevant amendments were made by RBI in[6] its regulations.

Over the past two decades, India has progressively liberalized its FDI policy. Consequently, in most sectors foreign investors can hold 100% of the equity in firms registered in India. Restrictions on foreign ownership are imposed in two ways. Firstly, foreign investors are not allowed to invest in 11 sectors,[7] and secondly, some sectors (mostly in services)[8] are subject to ceilings on FDI and/or specific government approval. The justification for this is dependent on the sector (Table 5.1). Notable among the areas subject to caps are defence industries, insurance, civil aviation, print media, broadcasting, telecommunication, banking etc. In order to prevent foreign investors from breaching the ceilings by investing through other Indian companies which they either "own" or "control", the government has spelt out the methodology for calculating direct and indirect foreign equity in Indian companies.[9]

Though these broad guidelines of cap are rationalized, some distortions which are present in the FDI policy are as follows:

1   Special rights can change the relationship in favour of the minority shareholders irrespective of the extent of their voting rights. These rights are often given to institutional investors or promoters of a company;
2   Another manner in which the aforesaid percentages can lose their significance is the deployment of differential voting rights. For example, where a person holds 10% shares with differential voting rights which allow him to exercise votes amounting to 30% voting rights;
3   The situation would also depend on the distribution of remaining shareholding. This is more so in case of listed companies where the shares are so scattered that a person holding 3% may be a majority shareholder because no other has a higher accumulated shareholding in the company.

TABLE 5.1 Sectoral caps usually observed in FDI policy

Share in equity (%)	Significance/implications
10 (print media till 2010)	Usually taken as the minimum share capital required to exercise control/ influence. Identification of FDI relationship is based on this perception. Under Sections 241 and 242 of the Indian Companies Act, 2013, those holding a minimum of 10% share capital (alone or together with others) can approach the tribunal against oppression of minority shareholders and mismanagement. The 10% shareholding is also significant from the point of suggesting scheme of merger with other company/ies. (Section 230–232 of the Companies Act, 2013) Regulation 21(7), SEBI (FPI) Regulations 2014, imposes restrictions at this level by a single portfolio investor.
20 (e.g. public sector banking)	International Accounting Standard 28 assumes that the investor exerts significant influence if it holds, directly or indirectly, 20% or more of the voting power at stake. A similar position is also reflected in Companies Act, 2013 in the definition of 'associate company" wherein this percentage reflects "significant influence."[1]
25 (e.g. terrestrial broadcasting FM till 2014)	Securities and Exchange Board of India (SEBI) (Substantial Acquisition of shares and Takeover) Regulations, 2011 applies when this percentage of voting rights is reached by the acquirer. Based on the shareholding pattern of listed Indian companies, the Achutan Committee felt that 25% is the level at which promoters would be capable of exercising **de facto** control.
26 (e.g. insurance sector till 2014, print media)	Most often used FDI cap starts from this figure. The minimum shareholding required to get special resolutions passed at a company's general meetings being 75%, those controlling 26% shareholding can block any special resolution, if they so desire. This is also called 'negative control' which may not help the owner of those voting rights to get a resolution passed independently but such person can prevent any significant decision from being taken.
49 (e.g. civil aviation sector since January 2018, petroleum etc.)	Another important cap on FDI in certain restricted sectors. The objective is to have majority shares (51%) in Indian hands.
51 (e.g. multi-brand retail trading)	Minimum government shareholding required under the Companies Act, 2013 to be classified as a government company.[2] In other cases, such percentage of shareholding implies that the person has majority control over the company and if the owner of such shares is a company, the company is called a holding company and is imposed with certain responsibilities with regard to its subsidiary company.[3]

(Continued)

96 Priya Misra and Praveen Tripathi

TABLE 5.1 Continued

Share in equity (%)	Significance/implications
74 (e.g. private security agencies, private sector banking)	This is the upper limit allowed where 100% FDI is not permitted. This is the counterpart of 26%. Indian shareholders with 26% shareholding will be in a position, if they so desire, to block special resolutions.
100 (e.g. single-brand retail sector, agriculture etc.)	This implies that the Indian company can be wholly owned by the foreign enterprise and therefore all control lies with the latter.

[1] Section 2(6) of the Companies Act, 2013.
[2] Section 2(45) of the Companies Act, 2013.
[3] For example, see Section 129(3), wherein a holding company must consolidate the accounts of all its subsidiary companies and show the accounts of all as if it were a 'single economic entity'

Source: Annexure 5 FDI Master Circular 2016 [notified through Press Note No 2 (2009 Series); sectoral examples and explanation added by authors

Role of judiciary in policy pertaining to inflow of foreign investment

The judiciary has been reluctant in deliberating on the issue of public policy generally, especially when it is specific to FDI. Some of the landmark judgments have been summarized in Table 5.2 to give a glimpse of the nature of approach taken by the judiciary.

The views on the efficacy of a government policy and the objectives such policy seeks to achieve may differ but in any case are beyond the clutches of the judicial review. The counterview(s) may have some merit but under the Constitution, the executive has been accorded primary responsibility of formulating governmental policy. The executive function comprises both the determination of policy as well as carrying it into execution. If the government of the day after due reflection, consideration and deliberation feels that by allowing FDI in a particular sector will help grow the economy and facilitate better access to the market for the producer of goods and enhance employment potential, then it is not open for the court to go into merits and demerits of such policy, as has been enunciated in the aforementioned cases. However, such restriction has its pros and cons. For instance, when courts refuse to interfere to assess if a particular public policy of the executive is wise and acceptable, the ultimate (but remote) consequence of which may violate an individual's right to equality under Article 14 of the Constitution of India, would it not be prudent on the part of the judiciary to be pro-active and prevent violations by looking into the policy beforehand, instead of later when it is challenged post-violation of a right? It is true that the court should refrain, but to what extent is a big question.

TABLE 5.2 Landmark judgements on FDI

S. No	Parties	Facts	Year of decision	Key decision
1	R.K. Garg etc. v. Union of India & Ors	Petition filed to declare Special Bearer Bonds (Immunities and Exemptions) Ordinance, 1981unconstitutional as it could be used as a vehicle to convert black money into white.	Supreme Court (1982) S.C.R. 347	"The court should feel more inclined to give judicial deference to legislature judgment in the field of economic regulation than in other areas where fundamental human rights are involved."
2	Premium Granites v. State of T.N	Petition to prevent the State government from giving a license to another by framing a rule deviating from the Mineral Concession Rules already made in exercise of the powers conferred under Section 15(1) of the Mines and Minerals (Regulation and Development) Act, 1957 and the rule framed thereunder had conferred arbitrary, uncanalized and unguided power on the executive, thereby offending Article 14 of the Constitution of India.	Supreme Court 1994 AIR 2233	"it is not the domain of the Court to embark upon unchartered ocean of public policy in an exercise to consider as to whether a particular public policy is wise or a better public policy can be evolved. Such exercise must, be left to the discretion of the Executive and Legislative authorities as the case may be."
3	Delhi Sci. Forum v. Union of India	Petition alleging that the then existing Telecom Policy was a threat to the national security of the country.	Supreme Court (1996) 2 S.C.R. 767	"No direction can be given or is expected from the courts unless while implementing such policies, there is violation or infringement of any of the Constitutional or statutory provision. . . . This Court cannot review and examine as to whether said policy should have been adopted. Of course, whether there is any legal or Constitutional bar in adopting such policy can certainly be examined by the court."

(Continued)

TABLE 5.2 Continued

S. No	Parties	Facts	Year of decision	Key decision
4	Balco Employees Union v. Union of India and others	Validity of Union of India's decision to disinvest and transfer 51% shares of M/s Bharat Aluminium Company Limited ('BALCO') was questioned.	Supreme Court 2002 (2) SCC 333	"The process of disinvestment is a policy decision involving complex economic factors. The Courts have consistently refrained from interfering with economic decisions as it has been recognized that economic expediencies lack adjudicative disposition and unless the economic decision, based on economic expediencies, is demonstrated to be so violative of constitutional or legal limits on power or so abhorrent to reason, that the Courts would decline to interfere. In matters relating to economic issues, the Government has, while taking a decision, right to "trial and error" as long as both trial and error are bona fide and within limits of authority."
5	Government of Andhra Pradesh and others v. A Hanumantha Rao	Petitioner challenged the Excise Policy of the Andhra Pradesh State Government w.r.t. the grant of liquor licenses.	Andhra Pradesh High Court 2005(2) ALD 780	"A policy refers to a tendency of probable effect with respect to the social or political well-being of a State, where court cannot not exercise its power of judicial review that amounts to questioning the wisdom of executive behind the policy decision."
6	Manohar Lal Sharma v. Union of India and Anr.,	Petition challenged the Press Notes of 2012 wherein the policy of Foreign Direct Investment (FDI) in Single-Brand Product Retail Trading, Multi-Brand Retail Trading, Air Transport Services, Broadcasting Carriage Services and Power Exchanges was reviewed.	Supreme Court (2013) 6 SCC 616	"On matters affecting policy, this Court does not interfere unless the policy is unconstitutional or contrary to the statutory provisions or arbitrary or irrational or in abuse of power."

Source: Authors

Case study of FDI policy in four sectors

So far we have dealt with the legal and policy questions in FDI in a generic manner. However, the issues are specific to each sector, and jurisprudential development has to be understood in this light. In this section, we are examining the developments in the sectors of banking, aviation, defence and pharmaceuticals. The public interest question in each of these sectors is different. In the banking sector the profit motives of banks (to satisfy the investors) conflicts with that of priority sector lending. With FDI policy in place, whether all types of banks (public, private and foreign) should have similar norms is a question in this context. In the case of civil aviation, the economic viability in remote and lean sectors with limited connectivity is the question. In the defence sector, apart from national security question, how the growth of medium and small industries which are domestic comes into picture when FDI is allowed. Finally, in the pharmaceutical sector the affordability of drug prices and capacity building through research investments become the public interest question. We will see in detail how these issues are addressed.

Banking sector

By nature, banking companies' shareholding pattern suggests that the owners or shareholders of the banks have only a minor stake and considering the leveraging capacity of banks (more than ten to one), it puts them in control of very large volume of public funds of which their own stake is miniscule. Investors/depositors in a developing economy have less tolerance for downside risk, many of whom place their life savings in the banks. Stable and continuing operations depend on the public confidence in individual banks and in the banking system. In a sense, therefore, shareholders of a banking company act as trustees and as such must be fit and proper for the deployment of funds entrusted to them; at the same time they have self-interest in profit maximization.

Under FEMA's regulatory framework, the banking sector was originally kept under a 100% investment with approval route. However, this figure was diluted twice in 2002 and 2004. And per the Consolidated FDI policy of 2017, the cap on foreign direct investment (FDI) in private and public sector banks, was set at 74% and 20% respectively.[10] Further, to regulate the foreign investment and control in banking sector, Section 12 (2) of the Banking Regulation Act, 1949 provided that in the case of private banks the maximum voting rights per shareholder will be 10% of the total voting rights. This helped in diversification of ownership which is desirable as is also ensuring fit and proper status of such owners and directors. In addition to this FDI Guidelines had declared that no *single* foreign entity or group could hold more than 10%. There was also a 10% limit set for individual Foreign Institutional Investors (FIIs) and an aggregate of 24% for all FIIs, with a provision that this can be raised to 49% with the approval of the Board of Directors and General Body of the company. There is also a limit of 5% for individual NRI portfolio investors with an aggregate cap for NRIs of 10%, which can be raised to 24% with board approval. In keeping with this more cautious policy, the RBI decided to retain the stipulation under the Banking Regulation Act, Section 12 (2), that in the case of private banks the maximum voting rights per shareholder will be 10% of the total voting rights (1% for public banks). These rules specifically dilute the concentrated shareholding in banks controlling a substantial amount of public funds, which poses a threat to corporate governance. Diversified ownership is a means to achieving balanced stakes. Further, the present does not create an ecosystem which discourages foreign investment; rather the purpose of these rules is clearly to avoid those investors who have the intent of controlling the banking business.

Other implication of entry of foreign banks or foreign investment was fear of shareholders' self-interest in avoiding regulatory norms focussed on public policy. To start with, even with the diluted regulation that is currently in place, the private banks in general and foreign banks have been lax in meeting the regulatory norms. The implication of this for the priority sectors, especially agriculture, was predicted to be quite damaging, however the following figures show a completely different picture. RBI Annual Report 2015–16 suggests following figures in priority sector lending wherein the regulatory requirement is 40% of adjusted net bank credit or credit equivalent amount of off-balance sheet exposure, whichever is higher. As of end-March 2016, bank-group wise achievement of priority sector target shows that even public sector banks are not able to match the regulatory requirements. Secondly, the expansion in foreign bank presence will expose public sector banks to unfair comparisons about 'profitability' and 'efficiency', and this would force these banks to change their lending practices as well. But, if we analyze this from efficiency in the banking sector, such competition will be healthy as the consumer will benefit from this competition. Further, RBI is keeping strict vigil on the performance of banks on various guidelines and through its regulatory tool it is in position to prevent any sort of market failure in banking sector. In this scenario it will be more appropriate to increase the FDI caps for public sector banks as well for not just bringing in monetary investment but also technology, modernization and healthy management practices.

Civil aviation

The civil aviation sector has a multiplier effect on the economy.[11] Government has proposed to take flying to the masses by making it affordable and convenient.[12] The "Open Skies Policy" and "UDAN" scheme initiated by the government of India led to a spurt of airlines which have since catered to the growing passenger traffic. According to the International Air Transport Association, growth in India is being propelled by a comparatively strong economic backdrop as well as by a substantial increase in service frequencies (Sanjai, 2016). The Indian civil aviation market is on an unprecedented rise with passenger traffic with almost 15–20% annual growth.[13] This growth has put a lot of pressure in the allied infrastructure including airports, ground handling, maintenance repair & overhaul (MRO) etc.

Thus, keeping all these factors in consideration, India had a very liberal foreign investment regime in the civil aviation sector, which is a huge capital-intensive

Foreign Direct Investment **101**

sector, and was nationalized until 1994[14] as the need was felt to infuse foreign capital in the civil aviation sector. Initially, as except the case of scheduled commercial airlines/domestic air transport, FDI was allowed through automatic route up to 100% in the civil aviation sector. Even in remaining areas FDI is allowed up to 100% subject to approval from Ministry of Civil Aviation. The Indian civil aviation sector has seen a lot of growth since the early 2000s. For non-resident Indians (NRIs), 100% FDI will continue to be allowed under the automatic route while the foreign airlines which are keen to have a 100% stake in Indian airlines have unfortunately been explicitly barred.

The primary benefit of this liberal FDI policy is that airport development has now been opened to further investment and the same is reflected on various airports. As we have seen from the experiences of Delhi, Hyderabad, Mumbai, Bengaluru and Kochi, privatization has certainly resulted in improved service standards as these airports have only served to enhance passenger experience. The Indian aviation market also witnessed affluence wherein passenger traffic is increasing at a healthy rate (Mishra, 2018). However, this development is not seen in Tier II and Tier III cities, even though there is demand. Airlines are reluctant to operate in these areas, as the demand is not sufficient to cover operational cost and without economies of scale. In a case pending before the Supreme Court, Justice T.S. Thakur has also conveyed his disappointment and criticized the attitude of the ministry for neglecting the uneconomic route, specifically hilly areas. This observation of the Supreme Court is in the larger public interest and in tune with the civil aviation policy for providing air services to more people, however foreign investors might not be happy to operate their airlines on uneconomic routes.

Further, the problem gets compounded by reducing incentive for foreign airlines investors due to restrictive clause in FDI Policy on 'substantial ownership and effective control' (SOEC) under FDI Policy. The SOEC Clause creates a two-way problem; first the quantitative in terms of substantial ownership by limiting the share held by foreigners, and second qualitative that focusses in 'who controls' national air carriers. Investors in the sectors believe that the ability to provide strong oversight through equity ownership would be very important and involvement in decisions like fleet, network product etc. is important to an experienced airline investor.[15] However, the effective control requirement discourages FDI in air transport, which is an important aspect to achieve connectivity between remote areas as per National Civil Aviation Policy, 2016 and thus FDI rules will have an adversely impact to it. In addition to this, for airlines operating in India, several restrictions are imposed through Director General of Civil Aviation by mandating majority control, board seats etc. of any airline wanting to fly in India resting with Indians.[16] This discourages foreign investment in transport services of the civil aviation sector.

Defence sector

After independence defence was kept under central control as it was directly linked to sovereignty of the state and national security.[17] India restricted FDI in the sector for a long period of time, i.e. till June 2016. Initially, India was purchasing most of the modern developed planes and other defence weapons and equipment from outside because though India had a production facility, it lacked the technology to produce them cost effectively. Further, if India bought such weapons from a foreign country, the country would only sell the product, not the technology. For instance, India bought fighter planes 'Sukhoi' from Russia and Hindustan Aeronautics Limited does provide maintenance support, yet, India is heavily dependent on Russia (Peri, 2017). Due to this deprivation of technology, India had 'state of the art' products, but no technology to improvise or build further. Further, the defence manufacturing remains highly capital intensive with huge amount of cost on Research and Development and limited buyers. The risk levels for investors remain quite high as the ultimate payoff is unpredictable (Sujatha, 2016). Therefore such opening of the sector will not ensure heavy flow of funds *per se*, despite an effort made by present government to fill the gap in the defence technologies by opening up the sector and promoting 'Make in India'.

Now, the defence sector is open for foreign investment up to 100% through the approval route instead of the previous 49% automatic route.[18] This implies that the original equipment manufacturers can now independently set up their businesses in India unlike before wherein they had to establish a joint venture with an Indian counterpart (who would hold a controlling stake in the business) to be able to transact with the government of India. However, a restriction that has been injected is that the technology being provided by the foreign manufacturer should not be available in India though the requirement of 'state of the art' technology is now replaced with 'modern technology'. This gives more flexibility to committee in deciding the approvals of the proposal for FDI in Defence Sector. The thrust of FDI reform in the defence sector is not on the funds, but access to the latest technologies and a foreign partner with long-term stake and investment will be appropriate to bridge the present gap in technology. Further, the argument of compromising the sovereignty and national security is misconceived, as between the choice of importing a final product and manufacturing the product in India, the latter will augment the technological standards in the defence sector and consequently national security.

This move of the government is in consonance of its policy to foster competition in the market and to ensure a level playing field wherein foreign manufacturers can now bid and compete in defence procurement space (Sanjai and Mohile, 2016).[19] Other policy considerations for such relaxation were, the policy of 'Make in India', which has been aggressively implemented in all sectors and employment generation. However, in doing so government has also kept in mind interest of indigenous manufacturers and suppliers by making a reservation regarding medium and small size enterprises (MSMEs) wherein the central government has mandated that Indian MSMEs should be preferred if they and another company stand at the same pedestal in terms of eligibility.[20] This public policy of the government provides a differential and protective treatment towards indigenous companies, thereby encouraging their growth in the face of open gates to FDI in this sector. However,

Foreign Direct Investment **103**

as previously noted, because the defence sector is capital intensive no MSMEs in India may be eligible to compete and invest the huge amount in research and development activity.

Pharmaceutical sector

The pharmaceutical sector, specifically research and development of drugs, require huge capital for a long period of time to produce a drug that is commercially viable. Keeping in view the cost of production in the sector and slow growth of innovation in drugs, this sector has recently been opened to up to 100% through the automatic route since the year 2015 and has come a long way since its drug policy of 1978 wherein it resolved to achieve self-reliance.[21] Such relaxation is in view of the current government's target called "Pharma Vision 2020", a policy which intends to transform India into a world leader in the area of end-to-end manufacturing of drugs. The opening of the market is to relieve itself from dependence on China for active pharmaceutical ingredients[22] apart from emphasizing on the 'Make in India' programme. The move to open the economy to foreign investment in this field is also to balance the withdrawal of government funds from the pharmaceutical industry, thereby starving the public sector research institutions that could not support the industry with innovative technology sans foreign investment.

The Indian pharmaceutical market is dominated by the branded generics which account for almost 70–80% of the retail market.[23] Investment in greenfield projects was always welcomed and India adopted an open policy in new pharmaceutical manufacturing plants. However, with respect to acquisition and merger with local generics ("brownfield" FDI) India adopted a cautious approach. The Planning Commission in its 110th Report highlighted a few of the concerns as follows, and also observed that

> FDI has failed to bring about any real change in the existing pharma R&D environment as domestic pharma companies are still to gain the competence and capacity to achieve cutting edge drug innovation by carrying a new compound through all stages of research up to marketing.[24]

However, the present regulation facilitates the investment in brownfield projects and thus acquiring space in the generic drugs market in India. In the face of denial of support by public policy, the Indian generic companies that were challenging the transnational corporations of US and EU before, were later forced to change their strategy to collaborate.(Sengupta, 2016).

However, the strong policy of the Indian government regarding compulsory licensing and strong control on the prices of life-saving drugs restricts foreign investors from investing in India. Three years ago, Novartis faced a grave defeat for its cancer drug patent application which was denied by the Supreme Court of India stating that the updated drug could not fulfil the criteria of 'inventiveness', an essential for the grant of patent.[25] A noteworthy point here is that the judiciary gave public interest and public health primacy over the FDI in the pharmaceutical sector. This has made multi-national corporations to adopt a more cautious approach towards patenting and commercialization of pharmaceutical products in India.

Another way in which FDI in this sector has been hindered, though for a good cause, is the prohibition on clinical trials by the Supreme Court. In a public interest litigation filed by an NGO,[26] the regulatory framework of clinical trials in India was found to be flawed. As a result of this petition, clinical trials were halted for a period of two months, causing inconvenience to the foreign investors. Because of the judgment of the apex court, the Ministry of Health and Family Welfare issued three parameters that every global clinical trial must report to be able to conduct trials, all of which pointed to larger public interest.[27]

Further, making availability of drugs at affordable prices through the Drug Price Control Order and the National Pharmaceutical Pricing Authority is a public policy concern protected by the government, but this concerns foreign pharma companies who wish to establish their business in India. The price control policy mandates that the price of a drug should be determined based on its cost. Recently, the policy was changed to a 'market based' mechanism, which has resulted in public interest litigation and the matter is pending before the Supreme Court of India. While 'market driven' pricing is ideal for foreign investors, it may not necessarily be in the interest of the public.

Impact of global outlook on Indian soil

Historically, at its inception, investment law was principally considered to be "a vehicle for controlling through legal means resistance emanating from capital-importing states" (Miles, 2013: 8). The primary vehicle for negotiations among different countries has been international investment agreements (IIA) but they have their limitations because like most other treaties, IIAs are a product of the time when they were negotiated and concluded "in a specific historic, economic and social context and respond to the then-existing needs and challenges" (UNCTAD, 2015) and therefore may not have contemporary relevance.

Even if the investment agreements hold that value in the present time, few scholars believe that the endeavour of countries should be towards removing all barriers of investment and trade because

> free markets and free trade will free the creative potential and the entrepreneurial spirit which is built into the spontaneous order of any human society, and thereby lead to more individual liberty and well-being, and a more efficient allocation of resources.
>
> *(Thorsen, 2008)*

International institutions such as International Monetary Fund (IMF) and the World Bank have played a very significant role in disseminating and promoting these neoliberal ideas of free trade through the conditions of credits and aid (e.g.

aid to India from 1971 to 1975)[28] and the adoption of certain domestic changes in law and policies. These conditions were widely incorporated into structural adjustment programmes, including obligations to liberalize markets, impose fiscal austerity, promote foreign investments etc. as fundamental to economic development (Robinson, 2002). The opinion may have altered, such as how Stiglitz, a winner of Economics Nobel Prize puts it:

> Founded on the belief that there is a need for international pressure on countries to have more expansionary economic policies such as increasing expenditures, reducing taxes or lowering interest rates to stimulate economy, today the IMF typically provides funds only if countries engage in policies like cutting deficits or raising interest rates that lead to a contraction of the economy.
>
> *(Stiglitz, 2008: 15)*

Stiglitz also criticized the working of IMF for serving the needs of the group of seven developed countries (G-7) and for failing to promote global economic stability for which it was set up.[29]

Given the conditions that IMF could impose, India took measures to make itself capital self-sufficient by slowly opening the gates of FDI in strategically important sectors discussed in this chapter. This was done because IMF's lending came with clauses that were onerous for the borrowing countries and led to their further downfall.[30] Recently, the IMF has itself advised India to rely on FDI for financing its current account deficit instead of relying generally on global financial markets.[31]

At the international level, public policy has been recognized as a caveat to the free flow of trade. As per the UNCTAD Investment Report of 2018, "Concerns about a shift toward protectionist policies could have a negative impact on FDI." Whenever countries impose tariffs, it affects the trade and global value chain in the concerned sector, which ultimately affects the FDI, which in turn becomes inefficient (UNCTAD, 2018).

Of late, various countries are interested in investing in the defence sector of India, given its requirements (India is the biggest arms importer in the world and has the world's second largest military force) and its scope of growth. Multi-national companies such as Dassault & Thales and entities such as the governments of Israel and the US have shown great interest in this area.

A global criticism that India receives in terms of policy structure is the need for labour reforms. The IMF has remarked that India needs to catch up with the other developed countries in terms of its labour regulation.[32] The manufacturing sector in India generally, and specifically in the pharmaceutical sector, benefits from availability of cheap labour. This availability usually entails lower threshold of wages and compromised working conditions in the factories. For a long time, the world has been watching India progress since its liberalization but its laws, unfortunately, have remained archaic. Most of the labour laws that prevail in India are of pre-liberalization era.[33] The World Trade Organization and its members insist on having human resource laws at par with developed countries but for India it may result in increase of cost of production and the resultant reflection on the final prices. In this regard India has been voicing the concerns of the developing countries by resisting the inclusion of matters of labour and environment issues and other non-tariff barriers into the policies of WTO. However, from the public policy perspective, this global pressure is justified because it brings about better living standards and health for the labour force of India.

Another area wherein IMF has suggested reforms for India is infrastructure. This is specifically true for the civil aviation sector wherein the infrastructure is not supportive of development in the sector so far. The domestic airlines suffered due to lack of investment from the homefront and it's only recently that foreign investors have started pitching in more finances. From airports to aircraft quality regulation to air pollution control, a lot needs to be done in this crucial sector.

With regard to the banking sector, IMF reflects that India needs to buckle up in order to strengthen the governance over its public-sector banks in order to be at par with international standards. One of the ways it is possible is to open the sector for investment which will lead to the ingress of private sector banks operating elsewhere in the world, but India is still reluctant, given the volatile nature of the sector and its public policy. India is protecting its domestic banks from being exposed to the fluctuations of the international market because these public-sector banks have deposits from different strata of the society and any strong international activity can cripple these banks severely.

IIAs can also influence public policy in India through clauses of expropriation etc, especially when it comes to investor protection. Some of these investors' rights can actually affect issues of public interest such as health, labour conditions, food security, environment etc. India, in turn, has either resisted the change or absorbed it to suit its public policy concern with regard to capital inflow from foreign lands.

Conclusion

India has a unique standing in the world, having surpassed the GDP growth of most of the developing nations but is still to catch up with the developed countries. So, one can imply that India is the super-developing economy for which development at an accelerated pace is crucial. Given this mandate, India needs to maintain the sensitive balance between an attractive destination for investment while not compromising on its constitutional goals; otherwise economic development focussed only on industries without factoring public policy is nothing but a 'race to the bottom'. This balance is being sought through the implementation of dynamic public policies of the government and at the same time limiting and restricting the ownership and access of Indian land for businesses affecting public and national interest.

Through this chapter, we analyzed what goes into the decision-making process with regard to capital inflow in certain crucial sectors of the Indian economy and how the government and legislature balance the need for investment with the need to protect the industry from financial shocks. The new government has implemented many reformative measures and smoothened the road for foreign

Foreign Direct Investment **107**

investment by harmonizing the laws concerning the sectors as well. However, the judiciary, as is our finding through the aforesaid analysis, has been reluctant to delve into the scrutiny of the policies, except in the cases of blatant disregard to principles of natural justice. In this regard, we submit that the judiciary should actively participate in the judicial review of these policies even if it is not a patent violation of the laws of the land. What is desired from them is examination through the lens of constitution without assessing whether the policy is going to succeed or not, similar to how judiciary has struck a beautiful balance in corporate law wherein it does not scrutinize the business judgment (because that is not the area of expertise of the judges) but whether it was taken *bona fide* or otherwise. The judiciary can also deliberate on a policy matter which may have a remote consequence of violation of constitutional mandates because after all, the three pillars of governance i must act in unison to make the country economically more viable and financially more tenable through foreign investment.

Notes

1 This chapter was originally presented in the panel of "Interface of Law and Public Policy" during the Third International Conference of Public Policy 28–30 June 2017 at Lee Kuan Yew School of Public Policy, Singapore. The author has benefited from comments during the conference presentation and from reviewer comments at different stages of publication.
2 David Ricardo opined that countries should specialize in what they are best or most efficient at, and then exchange these products, so that every country would flourish. For details, see Rothbard (2006).
3 Adam Smith propounded the theory in *Wealth of the Nations* in which he highlighted that the "If a foreign country can supply us with a commodity cheaper than we ourselves can make it, better buy it of them with some part of the produce of our own industry, employed in a way in which we have some advantage." (Book IV, Section ii, 12).
4 SEBI (Foreign Portfolio Investors) Regulations, 2014 prescribe 10% as the limit of indirect investment for foreign portfolio investor on stock exchange; Foreign Exchange and Regulation Act (FERA), 1974 stipulated foreign firms to have equity holding only up to 40%, exemptions were at the government's discretion. Setting up of branch plants was usually disallowed; foreign subsidiaries were induced to gradually dilute their equity holding to less than 40% in the domestic capital market. The law also prohibited the use of foreign brands but promoted hybrid domestic brands (e.g. Hero-Honda, for instance).
   Section 6 of the Foreign Exchange Management Act (FEMA), 1999 enumerates the capital account convertibility clause and prohibits transactions done under capital account transaction head. Said provision provides that, central bank of India (Reserve Bank of India – RBI) to prescribe the conditions for debt instrument in capital account transactions and Central Government to prescribe the non-debt instrument. Both central government and RBI may consult each other in discharging these functions.
5 IMF, Balance of Payments Manual (5th edition 1993).
6 All press notes are forwarded to RBI to incorporate necessary amendments in the Regulations.
7 Lottery business including government/ private lottery, online lotteries etc.; gambling and betting including casinos etc.; chit funds; Nidhi Company; trading in transferable development rights; real estate business or constructions of farmhouses; manufacturing of cigars, cheroots cigarillos and cigarettes of tobacco or of tobacco substitutes; atomic energy; railways.
8 Financial services and information services.

9 See, Annexure 5 to FDI Master Circular 2016 [notified through Press Note No 2 (2009 Series)].
10 See, Master Circular of Foreign Direct Investment, 2016.
11 National Aviation Policy, 2016 para 1.2 (As per an International Civil Aviation Organisation (ICAO) study, the output multiplier and employment multiplier are 3.25 and 6.10 respectively).
12 The National Civil Aviation Policy (NCAP 2016) Para 2: to create an ecosystem to make flying affordable for the masses and to enable 30 crores domestic ticketing by 2022 and 50 crores by 2027, and international ticketing to increase to 20 crores by 2027. Similarly, cargo volumes should increase to 10 million tonnes by 2027. Policy available at http://www.civilaviation.gov.in/sites/default/files/Final_NCAP_2016_15-06-2016-2_1.pdf (accessed 15 July 2019).
13 IATA, India's Air Transport Sector, 2018, available at: www.iata.org/publications/economics/Reports/India-aviation-summit-Aug18.pdf (accessed 10 July 2019).
14 In March 1994, the Indian Government first opened Indian skies for private and foreign investment by repealing the Air Corporation Act, 1953.
15 Tarun Shukla, Will foreign airlines fly into India, 2016, available at: www.livemint.com/Companies/ZgSMp1012FBFMt3udUXP9J/Will-foreign-airlines-fly-into-India.html (accessed 1 April 2018).
16 Clause 3, Minimum Requirements for the Grant of Permit to operate Scheduled Passenger Air Transport Services, 1994.
17 Historically during the British rule, kings used to have agreement called a subsidiary alliance wherein the defence services were outsourced to East India Company for payment and if kings fail to pay, East India Co. could acquire a portion of land in lieu of the payment. This led to a gradual increase in power of the company (see also Barnett, 1980).
18 Cumulative data on Foreign Direct Investment from 2000 to 2018 ranks the defence sector at 61 out of 63 items. See DIPP, Factsheet on Foreign Direct Investment, available at: https://dipp.gov.in/sites/default/files/FDI_FactSheet_29June2018.pdf (accessed 11 March 2019).
19 Also note the comment of the official spokesperson for Tata Motors Ltd, a leading car manufacturer in India, who observed that

> A 100% FDI in defence will create a win-win situation for the country's defence forces, local industries and international OEMs. It will ensure availability of cutting edge technologies for the defence forces, boost local manufacturing in India and provide assured returns for international OEMs. The move will also enhance overall R&D to develop and deploy solutions catering specifically to the country's security needs.

See P. R. Sanjai, Shally Seth Mohile, What does 100% FDI in defence mean? *Livemint*, 22 June 2016, available at: www.livemint.com/Industry/MqTrPlsdKy1D0YUGnVfygI/What-does-100-FDI-in-defence-mean.html (accessed 19 April 2018).
20 See, Defence Procurement Procedures, 2016 (Capital Procurement).
21 Drug Policy of India, 1978 introduced by Hathi Committee (see more in Badiger, 2006).
22 At present, India's need for active pharmaceutical ingredients is satisfied by China to the extent of 85%.
23 Mckinsey, India Pharma 2020 Propelling access and acceptance, realising true potential, available at: www.mckinsey.com/~/media/mckinsey/dotcom/client_service/Pharma%20and%20Medical%20Products/PMP%20NEW/PDFs/778886_India_Pharma_2020_Propelling_Access_and_Acceptance_Realising_True_Potential.ashx (accessed 19 April 2018).
24 Rajya Sabha, One Hundred and Tenth Report on FDI in Pharmaceutical Sector, 2013, available at: http://164.100.47.5/newcommittee/reports/EnglishCommittees/Committee%20on%20Commerce/110.pdf (accessed 11 March 2019).
25 Novartis AG v. Union of India, Civil Appeal Nos. 2706–2716 of 2013 dated April 1, 2013.

Foreign Direct Investment **109**

26 Swasthya Adhikar Manch, Indore & Anr vs. Min. of Health and Family Welf. &Ors, W. P. No. 33 of 2012, Supreme Court.
27 The three parameters are: a) assessment of risk versus benefit to the patients, b) innovation vis-à-vis existing therapeutic option, and c) unmet medical need in the country.
28 Through mechanisms such as stand-by agreements and extended fund facility that are complemented with certain conditions that the borrowing country must adhere to, including lowering down the tariffs and removing restrictions on FDI.
29 In fact, Stiglitz points out that IMF's policies that it imposed on the developing countries for premature capital market liberalization had such adverse effect that it led to global instability.
30 Certain scholars (see Padel and Das, 2010) have observed that the public policies and legal measures adopted by the local and national governments in alliance with the multi-national companies and supported by international economic institutions (World Bank and IMF) made, of course, in the name of development, had actually impoverished the communities and driven them away from their lands, resources and social networks.
31 IMF wants India to focus on FDI, cautions against relying on global markets, 25 July, 2018, Business Standard, available at www.business-standard.com/article/economy-policy/imf-wants-india-to-focus-on-fdi-cautions-against-relying-on-global-markets-118072401449_1.html (accessed 11 March, 2019).
32 IMF, India's Strong Economy Continues to Lead Global Growth August 8, 2018, available at: www.imf.org/en/News/Articles/2018/08/07/NA080818-India-Strong-Economy-Continues-to-Lead-Global-Growth (accessed 19 April 2019).
33 Such as Factories Act of 1948 and Industrial Disputes Act of 1947.

References

Athreye, S. and Kapur, S. (2001) "Private foreign investment in India: Pain or Panacea?", *The World Economy*, 24, 399–424.
Badiger, A. et al. (2006) Economic reforms and drug policy: Economic reforms and drug policy: Economic reforms and drug policy: A micro level analysis, 2006. Available at: www.iipa.org.in/common/pdf/PAPER%202_Economic%20Reforms%20and% 20Drug%20Policy.pdf (Accessed 10 April 2018).
Barnett, R. B. (1980) *North India between empires: Awadh, the Mughals, and the British, 1720–1801.* Berkeley, Los Angeles, London: University of California Press, p. 151.
Blomstrom, M. and Kokko, A. (2003) The economics of foreign direct investment incentives, Working Paper 168, Stockholm, Sweden.
Keen, M. and Marchand, M. (1997) "Fiscal competition and the pattern of public spending", *Journal of Public Economics*, 66(1), 33–53.
Miles, K. (2013) *The origins of international investment law: Empire, environment, and the safeguarding of capital.* Cambridge: Cambridge University Press.
Mishra, M. (2018) Domestic air passenger traffic crosses 100mn mark in 2017. Available at: https://economictimes.indiatimes.com/industry/transportation/airlines-/-aviation/domestic-air-passenger-traffic-crosses-100-mn-mark-in-2017/articleshow/63119685.cms (Accessed 10 April 2018).
Montinola, G., Qian, Y. and Weingast, B. R. (1996) "Federalism, Chinese style: The political basis for economic success", *World Politics*, 48(1), 50–81.
NCAP (2016) "National civil aviation policy 2016". Available at: http://www.civilaviation.gov.in/sites/default/files/Final_NCAP_2016_15-06-2016-2_1.pdf (Accessed 15 July 2019).
Obstfeld, M. (1998) "The global capital market: Benefactor or menace?" *Journal of Economic Perspectives*, 12(4), 9–30.

Rothbard, M. N. (1995) *Classical economics*. 2006 ed. Cheltenham: Edward Elgar Publishing, pp. 94–98.

Qian, Y. and Roland, G. (1998) "Federalism and the soft budget constraint", *American Economic Review,* 88(5), 1143–1162.

Padel, F. and Das, S. (2010) *Out of this earth: East India Adivasis and Aluminium Cartel*. New Delhi: Orient Blackswan.

Peri, D. (2017) "Long-term supply pact for Sukhoi jets inked", 17 March 2017. Available at: www.thehindu.com/news/national/long-term-supply-pact-for-sukhoi-jets-inked/article17523088.ece (Accessed 11 March 2019).

Robinson, W. (2002) "Capitalist globalisation and the transnationalization of the state", in M. Rupert and H. Smith (eds.), *Historical materialism and globalisation: Essays on continuity and change*. New York: Routledge, 201–215.

Rodrik, Dani (1997) "Has globalization gone too far?" Institute for International Economics, Washington, D.C.

Rom, M. C., Peterson, P. E. and Scheve, K. F. Jr. (1998) "Interstate competition and welfare policy", *Publius,* 28(3), 7–27.

Sanjai, P. (2016) "What does 100% FDI in aviation mean?" Available at: www.livemint.com/Politics/qXiX9p9ViAPzupDjqsnlWN/What-does-100-FDI-in-aviation-mean.html (Accessed 20 August 2016).

Sanjai, P. and Mohile, S. S. (2016) "What does 100% FDI in defence mean?" Available at: www.livemint.com/Industry/MqTrPlsdKy1D0YUGnVfygI/What-does-100-FDI-in-defence-mean.html (Accessed 22 June 2016).

Sengupta, A. (2016) "FDI in pharmaceuticals why hand over a national asset to foreign MNCs?" Available at: http://peoplesdemocracy.in/2016/0703_pd/fdi-pharmaceuticals-why-hand-over-national-asset-foreign-mncs

Stiglitz, J. (2000) "Capital market liberalization, economic growth, and instability", *World Development,* 28(6), 1075–1086.

———. (2008) *Globalization and its discontents*. New York: Penguin Publications.

Sujatha, "100% FDI in defence: What it means". Available at: www.mapsofindia.com/my-india/india/100-fdi-in-defence-what-it-means (Accessed 27 June 2017).

Thorsen, D. (2008) "What is neoliberalism?" University of Oslo. Available at: http://folk.uio.no/daget/neoliberalism.pdf (Accessed 27 June 2017).

UNCTAD (2006) *World Investment Report, FDI from developing and transition economies: Implications for development*. Geneva: UNCTAD.

——— (2015) *World Investment Report 2015: Reforming international investment governance*. Geneva: UNCTAD.

——— (2018) *World Investment Report, FDI from developing and transition economies: Implications for development*. Geneva: UNCTAD.

6

POLITICS OF MAKING AND UNMAKING OF THE INDIAN PLANNING COMMISSION

Destiny of non-statutory institutions in a democracy[1]

Sony Pellissery, Sharada Srinivasan and Anusha Chaitanya

Introduction

Is the idea of Planning Commission aligned with the aims and objectives of the constitution? This question was asked earlier (Rao, 1953; Paranjpe, 1964) and is still relevant today in light of recent changes in its form and function. Ambedkar's ideas on the constitution have been used in support of the Planning Commission (Paranjpe, 1964), in support of NITI Aayog (Times, 2015), as well as those who have questioned the legitimacy of the Planning Commission in terms of its extra-constitutional nature (Rao, 1953; Kamath, 1994; Rao, 1986).[2] While legitimacy is one aspect, the fact that the planning exercise has now had a few decades of history, lets us also ask, what interests are being served through the planning exercise? Answers to these questions are at the heart of the politics of planning. An attempt is made in this chapter to answer these broad questions, not philosophically, but through the empirical case of dismantling the Planning Commission and contentions and agreements around the same. This chapter analyzes the discourses, how these discourses were divided and then converged in the journey towards the institutionalization of NITI Aayog in 2014.

Then Prime Minister Nehru created a non-statutory body through a cabinet resolution,[3] which set up the Planning Commission in March 1950. There was wide agreement that since there was no constitutional provision for it, the Planning Commission was an extra-constitutional body (Rao, 1986). The politics of the making of the Planning Commission, and particularly the absence of constitutional legitimacy, has been documented by many researchers (Frankel, 2005; Chatterjee, 2001; Guha, 2008). While the politics of making the Planning Commission is overshadowed by de-politicization of development (giving a prominent hand for technocracy over ideological debates), the politics of unmaking of the Planning Commission is primarily led by decreased space for politics in the context of

112 Sony Pellissery et al.

economic liberalization. Both types of politics have been an axe on the transformative constitution that was envisioned by its founding fathers.

The rest of the chapter is organized in two broad sections. The first part will show how the depoliticization of development took place through the planning process. Then, in the second part, we will show how neoliberal developments across the world and its waves in India decreased the space for politics, necessitating an epitaph for the Planning Commission.

Transformative constitution and deformative planning[4]

At the heart of the transformative constitutional vision is an aim to break away with "old forms of state, society, and culture (social formations) and inaugurating a new order of things" (Baxi 2008). This was the dream of the founding fathers of the nation-state of India. The first prime minister of the country, Jawaharlal Nehru, viewed the objective of the Constitution as "the removal of all invidious social and customary barriers which come in the way of the full development of the individual as well as of any group."[5] On the other hand, the architect of the Indian Constitution, Dr B.R. Ambedkar, viewed the Constitution of India as a tryst with destiny to live with contradictions:

> On the 26th of January 1950, we are going to enter into a life of contradictions. In politics we will have equality and in social and economic life we will have inequality. In politics we will be recognizing the principle of one man one vote and one vote one value. In our social and economic life, we shall, by reason of our social and economic structure, continue to deny the principle of one man one value. How long shall we continue to live this life of contradictions? How long shall we continue to deny equality in our social and economic life? If we continue to deny it for long, we will do so only by putting our political democracy in peril. We must remove this contradiction at the earliest possible moment or else those who suffer from inequality will blow up the structure of political democracy which this Assembly has so laboriously built up.[6]

Dr. B.R. Ambedkar was acutely aware of these contradictions and was worried that as long as the governing class of dominant castes continued to hold strategic positions of power as they had historically done by excluding others, and the working class constituting the oppressed castes continued to be marginalized, the Constitution may not be put to practice in spirit (Ambedkar, 1946). Hence, he also built in mechanisms of reservations although not to the extent that he deemed necessary (see Poona Pact) due to opposition, to ensure inclusive representation of the oppressed classes. Administrative arrangements, including planning, without adequate representation continued to create an imbalanced society; repercussions of the same were reflected through forms of violence. Hence, Kannabiran (2003) argued that Maoist violence was one of the reactions to the failure of achieving constitutional vision. Planning exercises, however, continued to take place without constitutional legitimacy or a legal form, while subject to changes based on the shifting governing class interests.

The Constitution of India provided a legal basis for coordinated planning for the country as a whole by including 'Economic and Social Planning' in the concurrent legislative list. However, in the context of the Indian state being formed from erstwhile regional states, the Constituent Assembly did not endorse the idea of a 'centralised' planning body as part of the constitutional structure.[7] On 3rd September 1949, the response of Dr B. R. Ambedkar in the Constituent Assembly to the questions of planning power by the states is important to consider. With reference to the subject matter of planning, he said "What the State would not be entitled to plan would be 'religion'; everything else would be open to the State."[8] On the one hand, with reference to who should do planning, he emphasized the active role for the regional state governments:

> the State also would have the freedom to do its own planning in its own way. It is only when the Centre begins to have a plan and if that plan conflicts with the plan prepared by the State that the plan prepared by the State will have to give way and this is in no sense an encroachment upon the planning power of the State.

Because of this demand for autonomy by the regional states, the Constitution did not adopt centralized planning as a principle.

It is important to recognize the deep and obviously clear connections between five-year plans prepared by the Planning Commission and the interests of the industrialist class along with the ruling class. Eight very powerful industrialists had prepared what is known as the Bombay Plan in 1944, most of them associated with Tata and Birla. The Bombay Plan charted a roadmap of state intervention once the British left the country. There were two key objectives to the Bombay Plan. Firstly, the two-fold growth of agriculture as well as a five-fold growth of the industrial sector. Secondly, the industrial class from the country should be protected from competition with foreign capital. The eight industrialists who were the architects of the Bombay Plan had strong connections both within the country as well as internationally.[9] G.D. Birla was especially close to M.K. Gandhi and the congress (Sanyal, 2010: 23). However, the links between the origins of the Planning Commission and the Bombay Plan are not emphasized enough and only very limited analysis is available (Lokanathan, 1945; Chibber, 2003; Sanyal, 2010; Kudaisya, 2014). Sanyal (2010) argues that the Bombay Plan is embarrassing to the congress and the left political parties. Congress was embarrassed about its direct links with the business class. Left parties, particularly CPI, though opposed to the Bombay Plan supported the first few five-year plans which had much in common with the Bombay Plan. He also describes briefly the position of the right-wing (though not a political party at that time, some members in congress or the Hindu Mahasabha) as those who wanted a free hand for the business class without any government influence, though they did not take an explicit stand on the Bombay plan. However, analysis from an Ambedkarite perspective on planning seems to be lacking, given that the congress, the CPI and the right can be understood to be mostly constitutive of the governing class belonging to the dominant castes. Further analysis from an Ambedkarite perspective on planning by understanding caste-based representation in the Planning Commission bodies along with their political party affiliation since 1950 and the selection mechanism of these members might be useful. In fact, the Independent Evaluations Office's (2014) report on reforming the PC acknowledged arbitrariness in selection processes, and its direct accountability to the Prime Minister as problematic for democracy. This unrepresentative (and less inclusive) body defining and carrying out a central role of planning is at the heart of deformative planning.

The illness of deformative planning[10] is not the result of the Constitution. Dr Bhim Rao Ambedkar, architect of the Indian Constitution, during his speech on November 4, 1948, delivered in the Constituent Assembly in the process of drafting the constitution for modern India said:

> The form of the administration must be appropriate to and in the same sense as the form of the Constitution.... [It] is perfectly possible to pervert the Constitution, without changing its form by merely changing the form of the administration and to make it inconsistent and opposed to the spirit of the Constitution.... Constitutional morality is not a natural sentiment. It has to be cultivated. We must realise that our people have yet to learn it.[11]

Ambedkar says that constitutional morality is not a natural sentiment given huge social inequalities (e.g. caste-based hierarchy) preventing the spirit of equality as envisioned in the Constitution. As a result, the Planning Commission as an administrative arrangement, to change the substantive value system in the country, was bound to deliver deformative planning because of the absence of an inclusively designed membership of the top planning body.

Planning in less-legitimate states

When the state, as a social construct, is defined by the dominant forces in the society (or market forces), the prospect of upholding planning with a 'public purpose' aim gets vitiated. In the context of many Asian countries, state could be termed as what Reno (1995) called the corrupt state of Sierra Leone: the 'shadow state'. As the state's arms are unable to control social and cultural forces, regulation becomes near impossibility. It is the private contracts (often exploitative) and social identities that regulate this sector. Thus, there is hardly any distinction between the state and the market here.

> When we look at the local state, the actually existing state below the levels of state capital, as we follow policies down the hierarchy of levels, we soon find ourselves in an economy that is on the edge of – or frankly outside – the

Politics of the Indian Planning Commission **115**

ambit of state regulation (despite what is laid down in official statements of intention, and in legislation and orders and institutions); that is, in the informal economy.

(Harris-White, 2003: 74)

A host of new actors emerge here. Private armies (*goondas*) to enforce illegal contracts, fixers, intermediaries, gatekeepers etc. are some of the numerous people who actually carry out the daily routines of the 'shadow state'. This political and economic disorder is deliberately used to enable collective and highly-organized economic abuses and misappropriation of state's assets by the local elites and leaders.[12] Here, the state exists, but in such a way that the authority and legitimacy reside in the private social status of the individuals since following the rules of the shadow state is the route to get things done (Corbridge and Harriss, 2000: 168). Values of the dominant social forces become values of the state. As a result, the boundary between state and society is blurred (see also Appadurai, 1996). In this blurred-boundary situation the winners are the leaders or local elites since they are able to reduce the power of the bureaucrats, and to accumulate that power as their personal power. Partly, this is due to the post-colonial nation-state making, where "merging of State and Society as common expressions of a set of shared values did not take place" (Clapham, 1985: 12) in the Global South.

The issue becomes complex in 'prismatic societies' (Riggs, 1964) where opposing values (modern and traditional) are simultaneously in the operation of administration and state. Contestation about the nature of development planning is very high in prismatic societies, particularly in the Global South due to different value orientations. Thus, development against development is possible. In other words, what is considered as development for one group is considered as disadvantage for another group. This dilemma has been beautifully captured by Myrdal (1968) in his theory of cumulative circular causation, which emphasizes the limitations of economic planning in countries in Asia. Without some intervention in the cultural sphere, economic intervention seems to be adversely affecting the culture. Without such intervention (in cultural arenas), social and cultural forces continue to determine economic policies.

What is at question is the knowledge used in planning stages as technocratic understanding. This deception, that knowledge transcends diverse value systems and cultural conditionings, makes it attractive to a planner. Through these, the costs that different people bear are brought to a comparable level. Thus, a planner fails to see how "relationships and values are converted into figures and charts" (Shore and Wright, 1997: 32) following the logic of frames.

A number of anthropological works have challenged developmental projects in the spirit of *Seeing Like a State* (Scott, 1998). How policies imbibed the values of the state, and how society's aspirations were disconnected from such policies were successfully demonstrated by a number of anthropologists. Illustrative is the following example: the works of Indian planners such as Sukhomoy Chakravarti and Yoginder Alagh (both extensively shaping various five-year plans through their work in the

Planning Commission), who have applied econometric tools to the problem solving or designing of mega projects (in the case of Yoginder Alagh, the key contributions to Sardar Sarovar Project in Gujarat), have been criticized as 'technocrats' by scholars from the discipline of social anthropology (Aandahl, 2010) meaning that application of econometrics in solving human problems is insensitive, devoid and irresponsive to social stimuli.[13]

Esha Shah (2011) has demonstrated, studying the field of bio-technology and genetic seeds, how such 'rational' decisions by state actors often were influenced by business interests. Similarly, Myron Weiner (1991) has shown how India's policies arose from fundamental beliefs, embedded in the culture, rather than from economic conditions. Identifying the specific values that elsewhere led educators, social activists, religious leaders, trade unionists, military officers and government bureaucrats to make education compulsory and to end child labour, he explains why similar groups in India do not play the same role.

Unlike Western countries, the issue of development, particularly low productivity (Kalecki, 1976: 23), was "related to the social structure and the attitudes supported by that structure, the widespread existence of absentee land ownership and tenancy being of particular importance" (Myrdal, 1968: 1546). However, the Planning Commission, because of less inclusive nature in its membership, as explained in the previous section, was unable to take on such social structure, and rather be content with dominant models of planning. Yet, what is saddening is the fact that a radical planning by which society controls and directs itself (Friedman, 1987; Healey, 1997) is not what demolished the Planning Commission in 2014.

Moving from planning to policy

One important discourse that usurped during the controversy of dismantling of the Planning Commission was the functional differentiation between planning and policymaking. It was argued that earlier both the functions were vested with the Planning Commission. The critiques of the Planning Commission always argued that planning for a country as diverse as India would not be possible in a centralized fashion (Pellissery, 2010). Thus, in the proposal to dismantle the Planning Commission, it was argued (IEO, 2014) that the function of planning is best left to the states and policymaking may be the focus of the Planning Commission. In this section, we will argue that while the Planning Commission was dismantled, there was little space left for planning, since global models of policies had appropriated the planning capacities at nation-state level without a proper analysis of the socio-economic factors characteristic of India such as caste or other societal forces.

As early as 1968, the Administrative Reforms Commission's study team on the 'Machinery of the Government of India and its Procedures of Work' suggested the creation of an "office of planning & policy" in each ministry for the purposes of overall planning and also as the unit for formulation of policy in the ministry in the strategic field.[14] This suggestion was given in the context of creating an organ for detailed, interdisciplinary study necessary for policymaking. It was also suggested that specialized personnel should be hired for such research and analysis work. The Second Administrative Reforms Commission (2009) directly invoked measures of Citizen Centric Governance through Public Policy approach.[15] It also argued for separation of policymaking and implementation through institutional changes.[16]

These recommendations of the Administrative Reform Commissions were indications of how the planning model was evaporating as India embraced globalization and a neoliberal mode of governance since 1991 through a range of economic reforms. Impact of the same on governance is seen through institutionalization of a range of regulatory institutions (in the place of tribunals), application of information-based management systems to government programmes, public management approach to administration, public-private partnership in social sector investments etc.

While these developments took place in the sphere of the reorganization of the state, complementary changes took place in the sphere of civil society organizations and the market. Among civil society organizations, a number of 'policy think tanks' emerged (e.g. Centre for Policy Research, Delhi).[17] These think tanks acted as a voice to provide policy advice to government on sectoral issues. Among market players, significant development took place where consultancy firms made policy advice part of their core business. Most of the consultancy firms such as KPMG, Ernst and Young, Deloitte andPricewaterhouseCoopers have specialized wings to work with governments to provide policy advice.[18] Many bureaucrats have established 'working relationships' with the heads of such private firms. Some bureaucrats were entrepreneurial in setting up such think tanks after their retirement, since their established contacts within the government ensured successful tender bids.

What is important to take note of is the fact that these changes are largely driven by the political economy external to the country. We need to take note of the developments elsewhere to establish this point. Study of the changes to five-year plans across the world can illuminate us. Five-year plans (FYPs) were centralized and integrated national economic programmes. Joseph Stalin implemented the first FYP in the Soviet Union in the late 1920s. Most communist states and several capitalist countries subsequently adopted them. India launched its First FYP in 1951, and China began its plan in 1953. Both countries are now in their Twelfth FYP. Just like the changes towards policymaking, as we noted earlier in this section, China renamed its Eleventh FYP (2006–2010), a *guideline* (*guihua*), rather than a *plan* (*jihua*), to signify the central government's more hands-off approach to development (Geall and Pellissery, 2012).

Both planning and policy deal with the 'value' question. However, the way value is dealt is different in both planning and policy. "Plan is a political program" (Myrdal, 1968: 1888) since the agency of planning is "a government bent on development and thus also on changing the valuation in the country" (Myrdal, 1968: 1881). Compared to this, disagreement on 'value' is institutionally allowed within policy models. In the post-liberalization period, the government is reduced to one of the players in the governance process, and value imposition without negotiation with other players is impossible. Policy scientists tend to agree with

118 Sony Pellissery et al.

Sen (2009) on the limited use of transcendental institutionalism or the project of creating perfectly just institutions. Policy views that different valuations emerge from different interests, and a negotiation of actors is an essential component of policy process. In this sense, policy opens up a new "government by discussion" through a public exchange of reasons and "open impartiality" (Sen, 2009: 321–54). However, in a pragmatic sense, such negotiations with 'open value' systems are hugely skewed towards the gravity of power. It is in this sense, the Planning Commission was being used for the aims of neoliberal goals since early 1990s (Patnaik, 2014). The Planning Commission's inability to rise above political subjugation was merely a signal of how it succumbed to social forces, rather than its ability to act as a catalyst for social transformation through a model of social learning in the planning process.[19]

Views of chief ministers on dismantling the Planning Commission

The Constitution of India provided a legal basis for coordinated planning for the country as a whole by including "Economic and Social Planning" in the concurrent legislative list. In addition to the Planning Commission at the union level, there were planning boards at state level. While until 1964, the arrangement seemed to work fine because of the same party at the centre and most of the states, after 1964 there seemed to be friction between the centre and state relations as the political parties were different (Paranjape, 1990). In this section, the responses from Chief Ministers expressed on 7 December 2014 at the gathering at the Prime Minister's office, on the dismantling of Planning Commission is analyzed through categorizing the responses by party affiliations.[20]

Four types of party affiliations are visible. First, the chief minister of the state belongs to BJP, i.e. the ruling party of the central government when the Planning Commission was dismantled in 2014. Secondly, the chief minister of the state belongs to congress, i.e. the major opposition party in the parliament. Thirdly, the chief minister of the state belongs to regional party and supports BJP. Fourth, the chief minister of the state belongs to the regional party and opposes BJP, the ruling party of the central government. The views are summarized in Table 6.1.

In South India, the chief ministers of Kerala and Karnataka (both states ruled by the congress) strongly opposed the dissolution of the Planning Commission. Kerala's Chief Minister Oommen Chandy called the proposal "half-baked, unwarranted, and ignores the need of planned development." He also expressed his fear of the loss of perspective and a long-term outlook to development when NITI Aayog replaces the Planning Commission (The Statesman, 2014). Karnataka's Chief Minister Siddaramaiah, too, questioned the rationale behind replacing the Planning Commission, calling it a time-tested entity. These two views from the chief ministers belonging to the congress party were in stark contrast, however, to the neighbouring states of Tamil Nadu and Andhra Pradesh. The newly formed state of Telangana (needing support from the central government in the form of financial

TABLE 6.1 Views of chief ministers on dismantling planning commission

Political party	Name	Allegiance to NDA (Ruling Coalition)	Category (special or non-special)	Chief Minister	Should the PC be dissolved?
BJP	Rajasthan	Yes	Non-Special	Vasundhara Raje	Yes
BJP	Chhattisgarh	Yes	Non-Special	Raman Singh	Yes
BJP	Goa	Yes	Non-Special	Laximikant Parsekar	Yes
BJP	Gujarat	Yes	Non-Special	Anandiben Patel	Yes
BJP	Maharashtra	Yes	Non-Special	Devendra Fadnavis	Yes
BJP	Madhya Pradesh	Yes	Non-Special	Shivraj Singh Chauhan	Yes
BJP	Haryana	Yes	Non-Special	Manohar Lal Khattar	Yes
SAD	Punjab	Yes	Non-Special	Parkash Singh Badal	Yes
NPF	Nagaland	Yes	Special Category	TR Zeliang	Yes
TDS	Andhra Pradesh	Yes	Non-Special	Chandrababu Naidu	Yes
TRS	Telangana	No	Non-Special	K Chandrashekar Rao	Yes
AIADMK	Tamil Nadu	No	Non-Special	O Paneerselvam	Yes
TC	West Bengal	No	Non-Special	Mamata Banerjee	Yes
BJD	Odisha	No	Non-Special	Naveen Patnaik	Yes
SP	Uttar Pradesh	No	Non-Special	Akhilesh Yadav	Yes
J D (U)	Bihar	No	Non-Special	Nitish Kumar	No
JMM	Jharkhand	No	Non-Special	Hemant Soren	No
J&KNC	Jammu and Kashmir	No	Special Category	Omar Abdullah	No
SDF	Sikkim	No	Special Category	Pawan Kumar Chamling	No
CPI(M)	Tripura	No	Special Category	Manik Sarkar	No
INC	Arunachal Pradesh	No	Special Category	Nabam Tuki	No
INC	Assam	No	Special Category	Tarun Kumar Gogoi	No
INC	Manipur	No	Special Category	Okram Ibobi Singh	No
INC	Meghalaya	No	Special Category	Mukul Sangma	No
INC	Mizoram	No	Special Category	Lal Thanhawla	No
INC	Uttarakhand	No	Special Category	Harish Rawat	No
INC	Himachal Pradesh	No	Special Category	Virbhadra Singh	No
INC	Karnataka	No	Non-Special	Siddaramaiah	No
INC	Kerala	No	Non-Special	Oommen Chandy	No

Source: Compiled by authors from press releases after chief ministers' meeting on 7 December 2014

120 Sony Pellissery et al.

assistance) expressed a confidence that NITI Aayog would give a democratic approach to planning, replacing the existing bureaucratic approach of the Planning Commission. He diametrically countered Oommen Chandy's allegation and said NITI Aayong would bring perspective and strategic planning while conceding the mandate of rationale behind funds allocation to the Finance Commission (Mission Telangana, 2014). It is useful to note that both the supporting view from Telangana and opposing view from Kerala are mere assertions and hope, rather than based on any evidence as to whether perspective planning was possible or within the mandate of NITI Aayog. Tamil Nadu was ruled by a regional party, which was supporting BJP in the central government. Its chief minister, O Paneerselvam[21] stressed the need for participation by states in the planning process, as opposed to the current status quo where the states were at the mercy of ministers at the centre (The Economic Times, 2014).

This trend of speaking in unison is observable in Table 6.1 where the views of chief ministers are summarized. Invariably seven chief ministers belonging to BJP supported the proposition to dismantle PC, while at the bottom of the table, we find chief ministers from nine states ruled by congress unanimously opposing the proposal.

During the chief ministers' meeting, 15 out of the 29 states favoured dissolving the Planning Commission. Out of this, 14 were non-special category states, with Nagaland being the sole special category state in favour of the proposition. Seven of these 15 were BJP-led states, with three others (Punjab, Nagaland, Andhra Pradesh) being NDA allies. As it can be observed, there is unanimity among all NDA states and allies to the proposal being made to dissolve the Planning Commission, with all congress-led states and allies in opposition. Trinamool Congress was an interesting anomaly, as it supported the proposal despite not being strongly in favour of the ruling party in power.

These polarized views on party lines do not help us in the analysis as to whether some evidence is overruled because of party affiliations. It is here the socio-economic variable of the state will become helpful. (We will undertake a detailed analysis in the next section on this). Most of the special category states were ruled by the congress in 2014. Since they are opposing the proposal of dismantling PC, we cannot conclusively argue whether this is due to party affiliation or status of the state (as special or non-special). However, there are no special category states which are ruled by BJP. So, we have no evidence there. There are four special category states (Tripura, Sikkim, Jammu and Kashmir, and Nagaland) which are neither ruled by BJP or congress. Out of these, except Nagaland, the remaining three are ruled by parties which are allies to the congress or opposing NDA. Therefore, naturally, the response from the chief ministers of these three states to oppose the proposal of dismantling the PC is on expected lines. The case of Nagaland is crucial. In Nagaland, congress is the main opposition party. Yet, despite being a special category state its chief minister supports the dismantling of PC from which it receives support from the existence of Planning Commission. In the next section, we will examine this evidence.

Socio-economic basis that shaped the politics of NITI Aayog

Articles 36–51 of the Constitution (Part IV) give a direction to the content of state policies. This part, compared to Part III which is about fundamental rights of citizens, is about the collective goals for the state. The key collective goal of "the welfare of the people" (Article 38[1]) was set to be achieved as articulated in Article 38 (2):

> The State, shall in particular, strive to minimize the inequalities in income, and endeavour to eliminate inequalities in status, facilities and opportunities, not only amongst individuals but also amongst groups of people residing in different areas or engaged in different vocations.[22]

India being a federation of regional states and central government, the Constitution has clearly divided the responsibilities into state list, central list and concurrent list. Important welfare activities such as health, education and employment are the responsibility of regional state governments. However, resource raising capacity to fund such welfare activities are very limited for the regional state government. Therefore, assistance from the central government becomes hugely important to deliver the development goals of the regional states. One of the key functions of the Planning Commission was to derive a mechanism of allocating central assistance to reduce regional disparity.

For the purpose of reducing regional inequality, the Planning Commission was mandated to devise a formula for allocation of funds to state governments. This is legitimized through Finance Commission transfers (Articles 275–280) to bring equitable public services across the country. A formula, popularly known as Gadgil formula, was used since 1980. Later, this was revised in 1991 and was known as Gadgil-Mukherjee formula. This formula considered four dimensions: population (60% weight), per capita income (25%), fiscal management (7.5%) and special problems (7.5%). Using this formula, special category states were identified and significant portions of central plan allocation were made available to these special category states. In Table 6.1, the special category states refer to such states. It is in this context that the differences of views between special category states and ordinary states become important.

The Planning Commission model directly allocated funds to centrally sponsored schemes, which accounted for where the money was being spent. The new model looks at a system where money is devolved to ministries instead, which does not have the same guarantee that the money so devolved will be used for the purposes of development.

While the debate in the mainstream media has broadly focussed on the political contours of opposition to the idea of dissolution of the Planning Commission, the analysis in the previous section clearly indicates that the responses from respective ruling parties of those states have strong association with the current socio-economic conditions prevalent in those states. There were two dimensions to this. Firstly, the ambition for special category status, with reference to the political economy that prevailed in the particular state due to economic growth. Secondly, increased centralization by downplaying the autonomy of the states.

The absence of the Planning Commission's ability to influence plan expenditure and central assistance as per the Gadgil-Mukherjee formula will impact the current special category states adversely, a sentiment that was echoed by the chief ministers of almost all special category states.[23] The first point of divergence is in terms of viewpoints towards development – while most small states and special category states viewed development as inherently a process aided by the centre due to the unique characteristics and disadvantages, larger states placed a higher value on the ability to compete for resources with other states, as they claim that there exists the scope for competitive federalism. The absence of resource allocation by the Planning Commission would lead to a more competitive environment in terms of states vying for resources, which will impact smaller states differentially than the bigger ones. It is likely that regional disparities will increase, at least in the short term, since certain regions like the states in the north-east do not share the same competencies or the same starting point as other regions. Southern states and large states that are already more advanced are likely to be able to work in a competitive environment. A key consensus that emerged was in terms of flexibility that states requested in terms of untied funds to pursue their own developmental agendas.

The second point to note is the degree of centralization that this new system would bring against the autonomy of the regional state governments. In fact, federal structure of a healthy relationship between the state government and the union government is one of the basic features of the Indian Constitution.[24] Therefore, it is important to balance these relationships through the institutional spaces. The critics of the Planning Commission argue that a 'Delhi-centric' model of development is unsuited to specific states' needs, but this argument fails to see the comparative framework in which the political economy of planning operates. While planning functions may have been devolved to the states, and policymaking will be aided by NITI Aayog, the functions of resource allocation are now in the hands of the Finance Ministry. This increases the scope for political battles over expenditure, especially in states that have opposition parties in power that do not have the support of the centre. Another thing to note about the new model is the absence of transparency on a relative metric. The Planning Commission model directly allocated funds to centrally sponsored schemes, which accounted for where the money was being spent. The new model looks at a system where money is devolved to ministries instead, which does not have the same guarantee that the money so devolved will be used for the purposes of development.

Conclusion

This chapter has examined how far the institution of the Planning Commission has served the constitutional vision of India. On the one hand, the contradictions of the value systems of society and state in the making of India, did not allow planning to function in the true sense of the term planning. This was to be expected in society where 'public' had not emerged through its natural historical process (Pellissery and Zhao, 2016). While the moral legitimacy of the Planning Commission was lost through its inherent inability to function in a complex society as India, its formal significance was lost through the process of economic liberalization where politics was subsumed to economic decisions led by market processes. In the words of Patnaik (2014), it is a political agreement of the nation-state that the objectives of the national economy are same as that of global corporate capital. Agility of the human mind and its collective aspirations will need to invent institutions which are appropriate to deal with the fragile but connected existence.

Notes

1 An earlier version of this chapter has been submitted to *Madhya Pradesh Journal of Social Sciences*.
2 Note that we are talking about the existence of a centralized planning institution as extra-constitutional. Many of the constitutionally existing bodies engage in unconstitutional activities is a different matter. For instance, Finance Commission, though is a constitutional body was engaged in a unconstitutional act of curtailing the powers of the regional states to advance neoliberal agenda, against which one of the Finance Commission members dissented as noticed in the 13th Finance Commission report.
3 This cabinet resolution clearly identifies two earlier precedents: a) The National Planning Committee constituted by Indian National Congress in 1935, and b) establishment of separate Department of Planning and Development by government of India in 1944.
4 We are very grateful to Prof. Babu Mathew for his insightful lectures at National Law School of India University, Bangalore on Constitutional assembly debates.
5 Refer Baxi (2013: 22).
6 Ambedkar, B. R. (1948) 'Draft Constitution' a speech delivered in the Constitutional Assembly, *The Constitution and the Constituent Assembly Debates*. Lok Sabha Secretariat, Delhi, 1990, pp. 107–131, 171–183.
7 This unconstitutionality has been acknowledge by Independent Evaluation Office's (2014) recommendation on reforming the Planning Commission.
8 Ambedkar's comments came in response to why "Economic and Social Planning" was sufficient and no additional adjectives such as 'educational' to planning was not required. This is adopted in the concurrent legislative list.
9 The eight industrialists who gave shape to the Bombay Plan are: Jehangir Ratanji Dadabhoy Tata, Ghanshyam Das Birla, Ardeshir Dalal, Sri Ram, Kasturbhai Lalbhai, Ardeshir Darabshaw Shroff, Sir Purshottamdas Thakurdas and John Mathai. Ardeshir Shroff had attended United Nations Bretton Woods Conference. What is most interesting is the case of John Mathai. He went on to become the second Finance Minister of India (1949–1950), and eventually resigned in protest at the growing power of the Planning Commission. The press statement issued by John Mathai read:

> I consider the Planning Commission not merely ill-timed but in its working and general set-up ill-conceived. The Planning Commission was tending to become a

124 Sony Pellissery et al.

parallel cabinet ... it would weaken the authority of the Finance Ministry and gradually reduce the Cabinet to practically a registering authority. The Planning Commission was totally unnecessary and in fact hardly qualified for its work ... there was a general tendency amongst the various Ministries to disregard the authority of the Standing Finance Committee and that some of the greatest offenders were the Ministers directly under the control of the Prime Minister. When departures from accepted practice were approved by the Prime Minister, it has a demoralizing effect on other departments of Government.

(Quote reproduced from Mathai's resignation letter as
printed in Chakraborty, 2014)

10 Planning as an ideal to achieve required the state to be in command of the social forces. However, in Riggsian primastic society, this was nearly impossible (1964). Deformative planning took place when social forces reversed the planning ideals for strengthening same forces. For a balanced view on how state is influencing social forces and how social forces mould the state, read Migdal et al. 1994.

11 Ambedkar was referring to George Grote's (1794–1871) concept of constitutional morality. Ambedkar paraphrases Grote in his speech:

Constitutional morality means a paramount reverence for the forms of the constitution, enforcing obedience to authority and acting under and within these forms, yet combined with the habit of open speech, of action subject only to definite legal control, and unrestrained censure of those very authorities as to all their public acts combined, too with a perfect confidence in the bosom of every citizen amidst the bitterness of party contest that the forms of constitution will not be less sacred in the eyes of his opponents than his own.

12 For an empirical exposition of such developments, refer Pellissery et al. (2016).

13 For detailed account on depoliticized approach to development planning, refer Ferguson (1994). See Pellissery (2014) for an overview of anthropology's contributions to public policymaking in India.

14 Report of the Study Team on the Machinery of Government of India and Procedures of its work, Vol.1, Part II, 1968.

15 'Citizen Centric Administration', 12th report of Second Administrative Reforms Commission (2009).

16 'State and District Administration', 15th report of Second Administrative Reforms Commission (2009).

17 It is important to note that during 2008–2019 IDRC Canada invested to develop 43 think tanks in 20 developing countries out of which 14 were in South Asia. More details could be found here: www.idrc.ca/EN/Programs/Think_Tank_Initiative/Pages/default.aspx

18 The consultancy services provided range from preparing a vision document for government to undertaking detailed planning. The consultancy firms often pick up a policy advice provided to another country and repackage to provide to another country. At the global level, new service has emerged when another government provides services to a different government. In such cases, policy transfer is called 'government to government' trade (The Economist, 2014). "Westphalian" notion of sovereign state and its ability to plan its own affairs becomes impossible with such arrangements.

19 On the other hand, note that such process was possible at regional level through decentralized planning. For instance, Kerala Decentralised Planning model, and to date Planning Department of Kerala is most functional in the country (see Iyer and Pellissery, 2016).

20 It is important to recognize these are responses from chief ministers, and not respective state. This raises the question of the legitimacy of elections, and right of the democratically elected representative to voice the views on behalf of the state. Particularly in

Politics of the Indian Planning Commission **125**

societies where ideological polarizations exist, these questions are important. However, we will not be able to delve on this issue in this chapter.
21 He was asked to step into the shoe of chief minister when Jayalalita had to resign due to judgement on a corruption case; she came back to the position of chief minister when the Supreme Court reversed the high court decision.
22 Note that Cabinet Resolution dated 15 March 1950 which sets up the Planning Commission quotes this directive principle to argue the mandate for Planning Commission.
23 In the new fund allocation based on Goods and Service Tax (GST) is based on the voice you could raise in GST Council in which states have representation. However, voices from small states have high possibility to be marginalized.
24 In the case of *Kesavananda Bharati vs State of Kerala* (1973) the Supreme Court stated that basic features of the Constitution cannot be altered by the legislature.

References

Aandahl, G. (2010) "Technocratic dreams and troublesome beneficiaries". The Sardar Sarovar (Narmada) Project in Gujarat. Dissertation submitted for the Ph.D. degree, University of Oslo.

Ambedkar, B. R. (1946) *What Congress and Gandhi have done to the untouchables.* 2nd ed. Bombay: Thacker & Co., Ltd.

———. (1948) Constitutional Assembly Debates (8 November).

Appadurai, A. (1996) *Modernity at large: Cultural dimensions of globalization.* Minneapolis: University of Minnesota Press.

Baxi, U. (2008) "Outline of a theory of practice of Indian Constitutionalism", in R. Bhargava (ed.), *Politics and ethics of the Indian Constitution.* New Delhi: Oxford University Press.

Baxi, U. (2013) "Preliminary notes on transformative constitutionalism", in O. Vilhena, U. Baxi and F. Viljoen (eds.), *Transformative constitutionalism: Comparing the Apex courts of Brazil, India and South Africa.* Pretoria: Pretoria University Law Press, pp. 19–47.

Chakraborty, P. (2014) "The complete truth about how Jawaharlal Nehru forced John Mathai to resign". Available at: www.Indiafacts.org (Accessed 10 June 2016).

Chatterjee, Partha. (2001) "Development planning and the Indian state", in P. Chatterjee (ed.), *State and politics in India.* New Delhi, India: Oxford University Press, pp. 271–297.

Chibber, V. (2003) *Locked in place: State-building and late industrialization in India.* Princeton: Princeton University Press.

Clapham, C. (1985) *Third world politics.* London: Groom Helhim.

Corbridge, S. and Harriss, J. (2000) *Reinventing India.* Cambridge.: Cambridge University Press.

Ferguson, J. (1994) *Anti-politics machine.* Minnesota: University of Minnesota Press.

Frankel, F. R. (2005) *India's political economy: The gradual revolution (1947–2004).* Oxford: Oxford University Press.

Friedmann, J. (1987) *Planning in the public domain: From knowledge to action.* Princeton, NJ: Princeton University Press.

Geall, S. and Pellissery, S. (2012) "Five-year plans", *Encyclopedia of Sustainability*, 7, 453–455.

Guha, R. (2008, February 2) "Autonomy and ideology", *Economic and Political Weekly*, 43(5), 33–35.

Harriss-White, B. (2003) *India working.* Cambridge: Cambridge University Press.

Healey, P. (1997) *Collaborative planning: Shaping places in fragmented societies.* London: Macmillan.

Independent Evaluation Office (2014) *Reforming the planning commission: An assessment by independent evaluation office.* New Delhi: Government of India.

Iyer, D. K. and Pellissery, S. (2016) "Local planning as social technology to achieve justice: A study of planning boards in India", Paper prepared for KILA's 5th international conference series to be held during 19–22 November 2016 at Thrissur, Kerala.

Kalecki, M. (1976) *Essays on developing economies*. Hassocks, UK: Harvester Press.

Kamath, S. J. (1994) "The failure of development planning in India", in P. J. Boettke (ed.), *Collapse of development planning*. New York: New York University Press, pp. 90–145.

Kannabiran, K. G. (2003) *Wages of impunity: Power, justice and human rights*. New Delhi: Orient Blackswan.

Kudaisya, M. (2014) "'The promise of partnership': Indian business, the state, and the Bombay plan of 1944", *Business History Review* (Harvard Business School), 88(01) (Spring), 97–131.

Lokanathan, P. S. (1945) "The Bombay plan", *Foreign Affairs*, 23(4), 680–686.

Migdal, J., Kohli, A. and Shue, V. (1994) *State power and social forces*. Cambridge: Cambridge University Press.

Mission Telangana (2014) "On changes in planning commission", News items on the website. Available at: http://missiontelangana.com/ (Accessed 12 October 2015).

Myrdal, G. (1968) *Asian drama*. Delhi: Kalyani Publishers.

Paranjpe, H. K. (1964) *The Planning Commission: A descriptive account*. New Delhi: The Indian Institute of Public Administration.

———. (1990) "Planning commission as a constitutional body", *Economic and Political Weekly*, November 1(November 10), 2479–2482.

Patnaik, P. (2014) "End of the planning commission", *Economic and Political Weekly*, 49(29).

Pellissery, S. (2010) "Central agency in plural democracy", *The India Economy Review*, 7(4), 12–15.

———. (2014) "Anthropology's contributions to public policy", *Indian Anthropologist*, 44(1), 1–20.

Pellissery, S. and Zhao, F. (2016) "Borrower and follower in knowledge domain: Challenges in teaching public policy in China and India", Paper presented during HKU-USC-IPPA Conference on Public Policy during 10–11 June 2016.

Pellissery, S., Chakradhar, A., Kylasam Iyer, D., Lahiri, M., Ram, N., Mallick, N., Kumar, N. and Harish, P. (2016) "Regulation in crony capitalist state: The case of planning laws in Bangalore", *Public Sector*, 42(1), 110–126.

Rao, K.V. (1953) "Centre-state relations in theory and practice", *Indian Political Science Association*, 14(4), 347–355.

Rao, V. B. (1986) "Planning and centre-state relations in India", *Indian Political Science Association*, 47(2), 214–228.

Reno, W. (1995) *Corruption and state politics in Sierra Leone*. Cambridge: Cambridge University Press.

Riggs, F. W. (1964) *Administration in developing countries: Theory of prismatic societies*. London: Houghton Mifflin.

Sanyal, A. (2010) "The curious case of the Bombay plan", *Contemporary Issues and Ideas in Social Sciences* (June), 1–31.

Scott, J. C. (1998) *Seeing Like a State: How certain schemes to improve the human condition have failed*. New Heaven: Yale University Press.

Sen, A. (2009) *The idea of justice*. Harvard: Harvard University Press.

Shah, E. (2011) "Science in the risk politics of Brinjal", *Economic and Political Weekly*, 56(31), 34–56.

Shore, S. and Wright, S. (1997) "Policy: A new field of anthropology", in S. Shore and S. Wright (eds.), *Anthropology of policy*. London: Routledge, pp. 1–37.

The Economist (2014) "Unbundling the nation state" (February 8–14), 48–49.

The Statesman (2014) "On planning commission" dated 15 December 2015 (Kolkata Edition).

Times, T. E. (2015) "January 1. PM to chair 'Niti Aayog': Here's what the revamped Planning Commission aims to do Planning A Will Project Management New Women Grant Apps", *The Economic Times*. Available at: http://articles.economictimes.indiatimes.com/2015-01-01/news/57581386_1_new-india-prime-minister-narendra-modi-planning-com mission (Accessed 15 June 2019).

Weiner, M. (1991) *The child and the state in India*. Princeton: Princeton University Press.

7

CONSTITUTIONAL PROMISES VS PRACTICES OF PARTICIPATION AND REPRESENTATION OF MINORITIES IN SOUTH ASIA[1]

Mushtaq Ahmad Malla

Introduction

South Asia, which comprises of India, Pakistan, Bangladesh, Nepal, Sri Lanka, Bhutan, Maldives and Afghanistan, has a unique place in global development and security. It hosts one fifth of the world's population and is the home of a large number of minorities, divided into numerous crosscutting and overlapping identities on the basis of religion, language, ethnicity, caste and region. Theorists have argued that greater heterogeneity (minority groups) in a particular society increases the chances of horizontal inequality thereby becoming a serious threat to national development and human security. Reducing this inequality and associated threats demands adherence to the principles and values of democracy, in theory and in practice. While there are various elements of transformative justice in a democracy – right to life and security, culture and identity, socio-economic development and participation, this chapter is more interested in the right to participation and the representation of minorities. The main reason is that ensuring each group's desired participation in the political and public arena and access to power is very critical for the realization and enhancement of their other rights, as well as sustaining peace, security and development in the country (Stewart et al., 2008; Jacob, 2014). Any such exclusion is more likely to alienate group leaders to mobilize people along group lines and wage a war against the state. The issues of minority political integration gaining wider currency (Jacob, 2014) is an outcome of the fact that never before have this many minorities in the world turned into armed groups and become a threat to the national, sub-continental and global security and development. Cases are widespread across post-colonial Asian, African and Latin American democracies and recently turned democracies of Middle East. In the case of South Asia, the creation of Pakistan out of British India and then Bangladesh out of Pakistan are two unique and early cases of non-accommodation of minorities resulting in the creation of a separate nation-state.

In every nation power is located at many levels – legislature, executive, judiciary, police and army and the centre, provincial/state and local governments. In both democratic and non-democratic societies, opening the doors for political and public participation to minorities doesn't happen automatically; it has to be built through formal and/or informal processes (Stewart et al., 2008). Most of the countries in South Asia emerged from long discriminatory colonization. In the post-colonization period, while all inherited most of the political, electoral and institutional features of colonizers, they did so by embracing democratic polity. Because of this commitment to the basic values and principles of democracy, they all reflect some form of individual and/or group constitutional guarantees of accommodation and inclusiveness. However, after more than 60 years of decolonization, minorities continue to struggle for basic access and participation. While some bloody wars, with roots in horizontal inequality have broken out in the past, some are on the verge of exposure.

Considering this backdrop, this chapter maps and compares the constitutional promises of Participation and Representation (PR) with their practical outcomes and suggests a possible future constitutional and policy framework. It does so by using a case study of four of the oldest democracies of the sub-continent – India, Pakistan, Sri Lanka and Bangladesh. The chapter is one of the initial such efforts at the sub-continental level. The methodology adopted is a critical analysis approach based on an extensive literature review.

The chapter uses participation and representation as two different concepts with different meaning and weightage. By participation it refers to the numerical presence of minorities in political and public domains of a state, and by representation it means the power of minorities in the decision-making process in the political and public domains. The rest of the chapter is divided into three sections – firstly, country case studies; secondly, emerging typology of TCPRM; and thirdly, pathways to overcoming hurdles to minority PR in South Asia.

Transformative provisions and outcomes – country cases

India

Constitutional promises

India consists of six major religions, six ethnic groups, 52 major tribes and 6400 castes and sub-castes. When it comes to minorities, for practical usefulness, four major minorities are debated – linguistic, religious, caste and tribal (Weiner, 1989). Scheduled Castes (SCs) constitute 16.2%, Scheduled Tribes (STs) 8.2% and religious minorities 19% (with 12.4% Muslims) (Census, 2011). The genesis of transformative constitutionalism dates back to the 1909 colonial question of minority safeguards, when the colonial state set provisions for their special representation in legislature and public employment (Bajpai, 2011). This created a space for long constituent assembly debates and the emergence of one of the most comprehensive constitutions in South Asia.

The transformative nature of the Indian constitution starts in its preamble, which refers to Bharat (India) as a sovereign, socialist, secular and democratic republic, with social and political justice and equality of opportunity. It recognizes minorities in Article 29 – citizens with a distinct language, script and culture. In Article 30, religious and linguistic differences; and the National Commission for Minorities Act recognizes Muslims, Christians, Sikhs, Buddhists, Parsis and Jains as minorities. Further, the constitution refers to oppressed groups under Schedule 4 and 5 as SCs and STs.

As far as the promise of political and socio-economic PR of minorities is concerned, it presents two domains. Firstly, general domain/indirect measures. Part III guarantees Fundamental Rights (FR) to all citizens of equality before the law (Article 14), the prohibition of discrimination on grounds of religion, ethnicity, caste, gender and place of birth (Article 15), political rights without discrimination (Articles 14 and 15A), equality of opportunity in matters of employment and appointment in public offices (Article 16), freedom of conscience (Article 25), freedom of expression and association (Article 19). Part IV, Directive Principles of State Policy, provides for the elimination of all forms of inequalities. Part XV provides the right to vote and to contest elections, and Article 324 an independent Election Commission. Moreover, there is also no restriction on access to the posts of prime minister (PM) and president.

Secondly, separate domain/direct measures are provided for the advancement of so-called traditionally socially and educationally excluded classes – SCs and STs (Hassan, 2016). Though the Indian electoral system is based on the First Past the Post System (FPPS), Article 330 provides proportional reservation of seats for SCs and STs in parliament, state assemblies, municipalities and panchayats.[2] Further, Articles 15(4) and 16(4) stipulate affirmative action for them in education and public employment to overcome a history of social injustice. To safeguard these guarantees, Article 338 provides for the setting up of a National Commission for SCs and STs (Khan and Rahman, 2009). For linguistic minorities, Article 350 provides for the appointment of a special officer. Article 224 and the Manipur (Hill Areas) District Act 1971 provide some degree of self-governance to certain geographically aggregated tribal groups by establishing Tribal Advisory Groups, and Autonomous Regions and Districts.

Outcomes

Looking at the application of promise, a good starting point is that the Indian Constitution recognizes most of the minorities. However, it is not comprehensive when it comes to defining minorities. In Articles 29 and 30 it refers to language, religious and cultural minorities, but doesn't define oppressed castes and tribes as minorities. However, when it comes to direct constitutional measures for PRPEL, SCs and STs are included but not religious minorities (Ibid. 2009). These PPEP reservations have led to an immeasurable change compared to pre-independent India. Similarly, the provision of federalism, decentralization and the creation of autonomous tribal councils have brought a considerable change in political autonomy for ethnolinguistic minorities (Lokniti, 2008). Overall, notwithstanding some lacunas, these direct measures present a good example of the successful transformation of constitutional guarantees to minorities.

While the Constitution preaches secularism and no other forms of restrictions, when it comes to the religious minorities (particularly Muslims), there are strong, what can be called *de facto* restrictions on access. Their status as minorities in 1906 – with political reservations and affirmative action policies (Adeney, 2015) – became the victim of a majoritarian agenda in independent India's Constitution. While in the first constitutional draft of 1948, they were guaranteed group-specific entitlements, in the final draft they saw a complete reversal (Bajpai, 2000). This resulted in an equally backward, but culturally different group being excluded. The reasons being that the majoritarian Indian National Congress tagged Muslims representing communal interests, and lack of powerful Muslim conciliates to resist. Due to a lack of direct promises, their right to equality of opportunity and PRPEL is not explicit and doesn't have any enforceable legislative backing (Hassan, 2016). As a consequence, their PRPEL of the state has been historically disproportional and under-represented, compared to SCs and STs (Adeney, 2015).

Politically, the FPPS with a single electorate system encourages the winner to take all. Further, being accompanied by majoritarian politics, communal polarization and Hindu backlashes has made it difficult for geographically dispersed Muslims to gain a fair share in elected bodies (Ibid. 2016). Fielding minority candidates, by the majoritarian parties, as a means for greater minority PR is rarely seen as incentivizing (Hassan and Khair, 2016). This is more prominent in the current regime with almost complete exclusion of Muslims (Hassan, 2014). Against their 14.2% population, their participation score in the Lok Sabha is −19.16% (2.42% seats), compared to −1.01% Christians, −0.25% Buddhists, −0.22% Jains, and 0.31% Sikhs (Livemint, 2014).[3] Also for the first time since independence, the ruling BJP doesn't have a single Muslim MP in the Lok Sabha, and in the most Muslim populated state, Uttar Pradesh. Part of the issue also arises from the violation of Muslims' right to vote (large numbers of eligible Muslims are not included on the voter list), and to nominate their own members in elections (most of the Muslim dominated constituencies are reserved for SCs and STs) (Sachar, 2006). Similar is the case of their representation in decision making. The present cabinet has four members from religious minorities – one Muslim, two Sikhs and one Zoroastrian – but none of them holds a senior position. Also the Muslim member – the Minister for Minority Affairs – is from the upper house (Adeney, 2015). This issue of Lok Sabha representation is long-standing; during Nehru's time also Muslims didn't have any senior cabinet positions (Wilkinson, 2000). The periodic appointment of Muslims to positions of visibility – president, vice-president and chief justice – have always been used as tactical political strategies to give an impression of equality of Muslim representation in public life (Ansari, 1997). In reality they are just 'political delegates' rather than 'representatives' (Pellissery, 2016).

132 Mushtaq Ahmad Malla

As far as issues of Muslims' participation in public employment are concerned, two widely recognized reports are of the government's Gopal Singh Committee Report (1983) and Sachar Committee Report (2006). The Singh report in 1983 highlighted that Muslims are the poorest of the poor in the country, and their representation in the Indian Administrative Services (IAS) is only 3.2% and in the Indian Police Services (IPS) 2.6%. Later in 2006 SCR reported an unchanged situation with only 3% in IAS, 4% in IPS, 1.8% in Indian Foreign Services, and 4.9% in central and state governments – mostly concentrated in lower level jobs. The report also found gross violation rights of citizenship in the form of procedural discrimination (unhelpful eligibility criteria), practical discrimination (underrepresentative selection boards) and general discrimination (a general sense of discrimination in the selection processes). The report recommended various policy measures, including the constitutionally guaranteed quotas and affirmative action policies. However, not all the policies are accepted, and/or implemented, especially the long-standing demand of all religious minorities – giving benefits of affirmative action as stipulated in Articles 15 and 16 of the Constitution, because of the consistent refusal of the Indian state on the grounds that it would be divisive (Weiner, 1989). Instead, an informal arrangement was made by encouraging the government department to give special focus to the inclusion of minorities, especially Muslims. However, the Amithab Kundu Committee in 2011, while examining the impact of the SCR recommendation, found a fall in minority recruitment in public sector from 6.39% to 6.24%, and a reversal in police and security forces recruitment from 8.39% to 6.52% between 2006 to 2011 (GoI, 2014, 123). More importantly, even these informal arrangements were attacked by the current regime, which rolled back a lot of policies of the previous government, reportedly the ones which were related to the Muslims (Heptulla, 2014).

Pakistan

Constitutional promises

Pakistan has three main minority groups. Religious – Christians, Hindus, Ahmadis, Parsis, Buddhists and Sikhs, constituting about 3.72% of its population; and Ethnic and Linguistic – Sindis, Pakhtuns and Baluches, constituting about 30% of its population (Khan and Rahman, 2009; Weiner and Banuazizi, 1986). The constitutional journey of Pakistan with regard to the PR of religious minorities has remained dramatic. At its birth assuring security and freedom to the religious minorities was a great concern, against which the father of the nation, Quaid-e-Azam, during his first Legislative Assembly speech on 11th August, proclaimed all minorities as equal citizens and wished to declare August 11th as a minority day. However, the path thereafter faced complex modifications, making the constitution less accommodative.

The first Objective Resolution 1949 made the nation an Islamic state exercising authority within the limit of Almighty God. The preamble of the first constitution in 1956 named the nation the Islamic Republic of Pakistan where principles of freedom, equality, tolerance and social justice, as enunciated by Islam, would be fully observed (Zia, 2010). In Part III it guaranteed FR of equality and equal protection (Article 25). Non-discrimination in access to public places, services and appointments on the grounds of religion, race, caste, sex, residence (Articles 26 and 27). Discouraged racial, sectarian and provincial prejudices (Article 33). Also assured due representation of minorities in federal and provincial services (Article 36). Notwithstanding, the same constitution also restricted non-Muslims from holding apex state offices (president, PM and governor) (Article 41 and 91). In successive constitutions, while the FR and liberties were retained, a parallel set of reforms was also brought in, which skewed the space for minorities. The third constitution in 1975 made Islam the state religion (Article 2), declared Ahmadis as non-Muslims and included them in the minority list (Article 260), followed by the Anti Ahmadi Ordinance 1983.

Arrangements for political participation began with the colonial system of FPPS, with a separate electorate for religious minorities (Lijphart, 1977), but after the first general election in 1956, it was changed to joint electorate. In the 1975 constitution, they were given reservation of nine seats – four in the provincial and six in the national assembly. In 1977 the electoral system was reserved to separate the electorate. After 22 years, in 2000 it was again changed to proportional representation under the Devolution of Power Plan. The number of minority seats was also increased to 33 – 10 in the national and 23 in provincial assemblies. They were to be filled by political parties' nomination, and were also given freedom to contest non-reserved seats (Khan and Rahman, 2009; Jacob, 2014). In 2012 another constitutional amendment was proposed to increase minority seats as a proportion of their population (26 seats increase) (Tribune, 2012).[4]

In public employment, while they are not given any constitutional group reservations, in 2009 through a government notification they were given 5% quota in federal jobs (Jacob, 2014). To protect their rights, the Ministry of Minority Affaires (MOMA) was also established in 2004.

In the case of ethno-linguistic minorities' recognition, participation and autonomy, a single constitutional measure is the 18th CA 2010, which recognized the Pakhtuns' long-standing demand of being called Khyper Pakhtunkhwa, instead of North West Frontier Province, and promised devolution of greater provincial control over their natural resources revenue (Adeney, 2012).

Outcomes

A good starting point is that in South Asia, Pakistan reflects a higher degree of awareness of religious minority rights, enshrined in law and institutions (Castellino and Redondo, 2006). All of them are constitutionally recognized as minorities (Khaliq and Aslam, 2016). In political participation, the separate electoral system had limited their choice and excluded them from mainstream politics. This was overcome by a new reservation policy of 2002, which gave them a reserved seat quota (in parliament, provincial and local bodies), as well as an equal standing to their vote in the general elections (they can also contest on general seats) (Jacob, 2014; HRCP, 2015). This system has secured and enlarged their participation in the democratic process, encouraged their members to join ranks in mainstream political parties and opened up space for their bargaining. In the 2013 general elections, five Hindus, three Christians, one Parsi and one minority woman were nominated for parliament (PCP, 2013). Moreover, about 60 years after Quaid-e-Azam's promise, the country also gave official recognition of 11th August as minority day (Khaliq and Aslam, 2016).

Apart from these special domains for religious minorities, the other side of the Constitution continues to reflect a closed space (Hassan, 2016) and barriers to their complete political integration, with majoritarian Islamist parties pushing more Islamic content through objective resolutions (Shahla, 2010). Besides constitutional restrictions on holding apex public offices, they also lack representation in other forms of political decision making, namely cabinets, because such arrangements are non-statutory (Jacob, 2014). The majoritarian parties – the Pakistan Peoples' Party (PPP) and the Pakistan Muslim League (PML) – do not ensure their adequate representation (UPI, 2013 in Adeney, 2015). While six of the ten current minority parliament members belong to the ruling party PML-Nawaz, with the exception of the Minister of Minorities, none of them is in the cabinet. This leaves them neither equipped nor empowered to negotiate for their socio-economic rights and personal security. Besides job quotas, they have not been able to achieve any significant legislation. Consequently, their political reservation is viewed more as a concession rather than a genuine integrative measure (Jacob, 2014). A certain degree of this challenge also arises from their small numerical strength. Since 1985 while the general category seats have increased by 31% in the national and 7%, in provincial assemblies, in minority-reserved seats the increase had been marginal. Moreover, constraints are also posed by disenfranchisement of Ahmadis who do not register themselves as non-Muslims.

In the case of public employment, while things are changing, there are still many gaps to be filled. The Christian representation in the Pakistan army was always there, whereas Hindus and Sikhs were invisible (Riaz, 2015). In 1983 there were 1.15% Christians in civil and army services, whereas the Hindus constituted only 0.2% (Singh, 2007). The recent quota policy in mainstream services, especially judiciary, civil services and army are considered very good and politically significant steps of accommodation (Jacob, 2011). While initial evidence suggests that a few Hindus being enrolled in the Navy, and one Sikh in the Army (Riaz, 2015). Some also reflect an increasing pessimism about its effectiveness because of poor regulatory and monitoring mechanisms (Jacob, 2011). The MOMA is largely ineffective and confined to giving awards to members of the minority community (Khaliq and Aslam, 2016). The local bodies are dysfunctional due to a delay in the implementation of the 18th CA (Jacob, 2014). The overall case of religious minorities in Pakistan, tells us that a space has been opened up, but it is still limited, with their marginal control on decision making, and minuscule presence in public employment (Riaz, 2015).

The current status of ethno-linguistic minorities presents a fair case of provincial federalism, decentralized governance (Lokniti, 2008), and signs of accommodation under the 18th CA. Although it came out of desperation to quell internal conflict, which broke out in 2000, it was welcomed, especially for the political and economic inclusion of historically excluded Khyper Pakhtunkhwa. Notwithstanding these progressive steps, these minorities continue to face some basic issues, such as unlike religious minorities they are not constitutionally recognized and defined (Khan and Rahman, 2009). Also they are not given an equal share in political and public life. Historically such has proven disastrous for the country. Firstly, the refusal to accept the legitimacy of linguistic claims resulted in a delay in the national election. Once elections were held after 23 years of independence, the refusal by the Western wing to recognize the legitimacy of the Eastern wing led to a secessionist movement, followed by a bloody war and the creation of Bangladesh. Secondly, the remaining ethno-linguistic minorities also continued to hold a very limited space (non-recognition and inadequate representation) which turned into a hot bed and fueled back increased violence and internal conflict. The recent rise of the Pakistan Taliban is partly an outcome of these non-accommodative practices. While the majority of the ruling parties in South Asia are personalistic and dynastic, Pakistan reflects a more open version of it (Adeney, 2015). About 44% of the seats in the outgoing 2013 national and provincial assemblies were occupied by individuals or their relatives who had occupied seats in the previous assemblies (Kohari, 2013). In 2013, 31 cabinet members were Punjabis (Adeney, 2015), and the positions given to non-Punjabis were mostly less important and insignificant (Hassan, 2014). Due to this Punjabi dominance, the current parliament is called the evil Punjabi empire, which is even argued to be hindering the implementation of the recent 18th CA, by curtailing the promised control of the Khyper Pakhtunkhwa over their natural resource revenues (Adeney, 2012).

Sri Lanka

Constitutional promises

Compared to the rest of South Asia, the Sri Lankan population demonstrates less diversity in terms of ethnicity, religion and language, and higher intersectionality across these groups. Tamils are predominantly Hindu constituting 15.2%, Sinhalese Buddhists constituting 74.9% and Moor Muslims constituting 9.2% of the population. Linguistically Sinhala is spoken by 68%, Tamil by 9% and English by 7% of the population. Hindus, Muslims and Christians constitute religious minorities with, 12.6%, 9.7% and 7.4% of the population, respectively (Census, 2012).

The Constitution of Sri Lanka is the oldest in the sub-continent. It defines itself as secular. Part III guarantees FR of equality and non-discrimination (Article 12), and equal protection and non-discrimination on the grounds of race, religion, language, caste, sex, political opinion and place of birth (Article 21). Part IV promotes co-operation, mutual confidence, equality of opportunity, political opinion and occupation among all sections of society (Article 27). However, in Article 9, the same constitution gives foremost place to Buddhism and duty to the state to protect and foster Buddha Sasana. The first constitution proclaimed the official language being Sinhala and Tamil, with English as a link language (Article 18). However, the Official Languages Act of 1956 replaced English and gave no status to Tamil. The political pressure brought in the Tamil Language (Special Provisions) Act in 1958, and its implementation in the North and East in 1966. Later in 1991 Tamil was re-recognized as one of the national official languages.

The electoral system of the country started with the FPPS, which was replaced by proportional representation, along with preferential voting in 1978 (Uyangoda, 2015). Later in 1987, the 13th CA was also made to create some autonomy in the nine provinces of the country (Fonseka, 2016).

Outcomes

Constitutionalism and minority rights in Sri Lanka are marked by minority anxieties regarding majority dominance through representative democracy, and the majority community's absolute lack of sympathy or sensitivity towards such anxieties (Haniffa, 2010). A starting point is that minorities are not constitutionally defined. Further, while the constitution preaches secularism, in practice the state gives prominence to majoritarian religion – Buddhism (Perera, 1999). Also, even after being the oldest consistent democracy in South Asia, it has never allowed a non-majoritarian candidate to hold apex offices. The United National Party and Sri Lankan Freedom Party, with roots in Sinhalese/Buddhist ethnicity, have always played unevenly in the country's democratic development (Adeney, 2015), leaving Tamils and Muslims frozen out of power.

The two constitutional measures – devolution of powers and a proportional representation system – were felt to have been brought to create an atmosphere of equality in participation and power distribution, considering that minority rights issues in the country are mainly related to access and the sharing of state power. However, they turned out to be instruments to quell secessionism, self-determination and autonomy claims of minorities (Uyangoda, 2010).[5] The 13th CA, a post-conflict strategy, is widely seen as an unsuccessful attempt which made Muslims and Tamils frustrated, instead of giving autonomy, especially in the North and East where it was needed the most, due to excessive central control through dissolution of the elected provincial council in 1990 and running provincial administration through a governor appointed by the president; and the Supreme Court's decision in 2006 to separate the two provinces, against the wishes of Tamils (Ibid. 2010). Also, after the defeat of the LTTE in 2009, the nature and the terms of a political solution to the ethnic conflict are being altered.

The proportional electoral system did create possibilities for Tamils and Muslims to maximize their seats at both provincial and parliament levels, which is even argued to have played a key role in the recent politics of the country, with minority parties being a key in making and breaking the governments (Hanifa, 2015). However, even under this system, minorities are argued to have been starved of decision-making power regarding their wellbeing and unmet demands, owing to lack of reservations (Haniffa, 2010). In Rajapaksa's parliament only one Tamil was included in the 67-member cabinet who held a small portfolio of Traditional Industries and Small Enterprises Development (Francis, 2013). In Sirisena's parliament, a shift is seen, but it is also partial – of about 25% minority, the representation is only 20%. Out of the 43-member cabinet, announced after the win, there were four Muslims and three Tamils with small portfolios.[6] Also there was no Tamil from the East or North appointed for the development of either of these two regions (Rajasingham, 2015).

Within minorities, Muslims in particular, being smaller in size, face double majoritarianism from both Sinhala and Tamil (Haniffa, 2010). The dominant country's debate on power sharing and federalism does not account for their rights, and Tamil nationalism no longer considers them as their part. The nationalist parties do not rely much on them, instead use them as fillers as and when needed. This often leads to representational deception – the positions promised are not given once won, thereby risking them to becoming more oppressed under territorial devolution.[7] The proposed 20th CA towards the strengthening of FPPS is seen as a new threat, especially for geographically dispersed Muslims, towards losing whatever political participation they had gained under the proportional system.

Coming to the PR in public employment, no constitutional group guarantees are provided to minorities. Since the 1980s, minorities, especially the Sri Lanka Muslim Congress, has been pushing for a reservation in the public sector, which is being struck down by the Supreme Court. As a consequence, both the Tamils and Muslims are facing a glass ceiling, and underrepresentation in all kinds of public employment, even in the areas of their concentration (Skanthakumar, 2011; Fonseka, 2016). Tamil representation in universities is 18% – almost proportional to their population, but only 6% in Tier 2, and 3% in Tier 1 public sector. The gap between Sinhala and Muslims is 8:1 in university admission, and 30:1 in both Tier 1 and 2 public sector (VR, 2013).[8]

In addition, there are several other restricting factors such as employment policies being very discriminatory, resulting in frustration and unrest in the North and the East (Thangarajah, 2002). Sinhala as the primary language in all government receipts and documents restricts access of linguistic minorities (Fonseka, 2016; Perera, 1999). Furthermore, after 25 years of ethnic conflict, the country still lacks equal opportunity legislation because of resistance from Sinhalese nationalist group, posing a serious challenge to the juridical redressing of the violation of rights to equality in public employment (Uyangoda, 2010). Overall in both political and public discourse and practice, the minority in Sri Lanka continues to be a complex analytical and non-neutral subject.

Bangladesh

Constitutional promises

Bangladesh has the highest percentage of social homogeneity in the world, spread across three major minorities – religious, ethnic and linguistic, consisting of 10.3%, 1.13% and 2% of its population, respectively (Khan and Rahman, 2009; Tripura, 2018). The first constitution (1972) was based on the principles of secularism, plural parliamentary democracy and equality. In Part III it guarantees FR of equality before the law (Article 27), non-discrimination on the grounds of religion, race, caste, sex or place of birth (Article 28), equality of opportunity in public employment (Article 29), and freedom of association (Article 38). Under Article 12 it also guarantees political status in favour of all religions and prohibits abuse of religion for political purposes. However, in 1977 CA, the provision of secularism was substituted with the principle of absolute trust and faith in Almighty Allah (Article 8). In 1988 CA, Islam was declared as the state religion, with additional guarantees for others (Article 2), Bengali as the national language (Article 3), all citizens be known as Bengalis (Article 6) and the state being unitary. In 2011 CA, while secularism was again brought in, Islam continued as the state religion. This amendment also referred to ethnic minorities as 'tribes', 'minor races', 'sects' and 'communities' (MRG, 2016).

Outcomes

A starting point in the case of Bangladesh is that there is a changing political and cultural conception of nation-state through constitutional tempering by self-interest–based regimes – both democratic and authoritarian, and the rise of the issues and identity of religious, ethnic and linguistic (Biharis) minorities (Mohsin, 1997; Ahmed, 1997). The country started with a secular and relatively accommodative constitution; however, over time it has turned into fundamentalism by moving from Bengali nationalism to Bangladeshi nationalism to Islamic nationalism. Recognizing Islam as the state religion has excluded about 10% of religious minorities, and Bengali as the national language about 45% of ethno-linguistically non-Bengalis. The legal challenges filed against it in 1988 and 2016 were rejected in March 2016 (MRG, 2016).

Also constitutionally no minority group is recognized, defined or provided with any group protection in political or public employment (Mandal, 2007; Amin et al., 2016).[9] Beyond the constitution, it recognizes the existence of religious minorities – Hindus, Buddhists and Christians – but not linguistic minorities, which mainly consists of Tribes of the Chittagong Hill Tracts (CHTs) and Biharis (Khan and Rahman, 2009).[10] While the 2011 CA has referred to ethnic minorities as 'minor races', it didn't include their actual demand of being known as indigenous people and a minority, which would strengthen their land rights (MRG, 2016).[11]

Constitutional promises vs practices **139**

Without group guarantees, the FPPS, along with a state of polarized politics, leaves marginal scope for a meaningful representation of minorities. FPPS requires only 30% to 35% votes to win a seat, and 40% of votes can easily translate into 50% to 60% of legislative seats. The religious minorities constitute only 11% of the electorate and are in the majority in only 20% of the parliamentary constituencies. While these 20% constituencies are potentials for creating a representative system where minorities could exercise their rights, due to the lack of a formal arrangement, this electoral democracy has become an instrument of oppression for them. As in other countries, the majoritarian parties do not find it incentivizing to take on the cause of minorities (Shaha, 1998, in Samad, 1998). They are just looked at as numbers, a vote bank, instead of human beings. Consequently, throughout the history their participation in Parliament has remained far below their share. In 1973 – 3.8%; 1979 – 2.48%; 1986 – 2.18%; 1988 – 1.28%; 1991 – 3.38%; 1996 – 1.28%; 2001 – 2.67%; and 2008 – 4.67%. Currently there are 14 Hindus, one Christian and two Buddhists, which is the highest (4%) in the history of Bangladesh (Ferdous, 2016). The case of representation in cabinets has been much worse. In 1991 – 1 of 48; 1996 – 3 of 51; 2001 – 2 of 63; and 2009 – 3 of 35. Moreover, no person other than a Bengali majoritarian party Muslim (Bangladesh Nationalist Party or Bangladesh Awami League) has ever become a head of the state.

In public employment, religious minorities' difficulty in securing justice and equal participation (MRG, 2016) is reflected by their reverse trend compared to the British period (Dasgupta et al., 2011). This limiting space is an outcome of silent discrimination with lock offs starting at the entry level, which includes no provisions for minority representation in the selection boards (Amin et al., 2016); non-Muslim candidates facing uncomfortable questions and rude behaviour; their personal integrity and sense of patriotism being challenged; unwritten laws and a customary practice of not giving sensitive positions – head of state, chief of the armed forces, governor of the Bangladesh Bank, Home Affairs, Foreign Affairs and Finance – to minorities (Shaha, 1998, in Samad, 1998).

Due to the lack of reliable and updated data, their exact current strength in public employment is difficult to gauge (Islam, 2006). However, in 1993 they represented 5.3% in government officers, 1.62% in defence service and 2.5% in police service (BHBCUC 1993a in Dasgupta et al., 2011). In BCS 2008, only 68 (65 Hindus and three Buddhists) of 940 general cadre seats, and 90 (81 Hindus, three Christians and six Buddhists) of 1477 health cardre seats were held by religious minorities. Further, the executive order of 40% 4th class jobs reservation for Dalits acts more as an unfavourable inclusion, because it reinforces the caste-based shame. In so-called sensitive assignments, a 1970s Para-Military group (Jatiyo Rakkhi Bahini) with a substantial number of Hindus was dismantled in 1975. Moreover, a recent study showed only two in the Foreign Service, and a few lower rank commanders in the army from religious minority (Amin et al., 2016).

While the ethnic (CHTs) and linguistic (Bihari) minorities are victims of similar discriminatory policies (Islam, 2006), the practice of exclusion is little different. CHT's long-standing issue has been the erosion of their administrative autonomy given in 1881 and strengthened in 1900 under the Chittagong Hill Tracts Regulation (Khan and Rahman, 2009). The first president's rejection of the request for the re-establishing of special autonomy (own legislature, continuation the of Tribal Chiefs Office and a ban on the influx of non-tribal into the area) by a delegation led by Monobendra Narayan Larma (the only MP from CHTs), forced Larma to form an agitation movement, which later turned into a full-fledged armed Maoist group – Shanti Bahini (Nandy, 1983). The state responded through military action and forced settlement, which widened divides and violence. After several negotiations, the CHT Regional Council was promised a central role in general administration, law and order and the development of the region under the Chittagong Hill Tracts Peace Accord 1997 (Khan and Rahman, 2009). However, when the Accord led to the disarmament of the Shanti Bahini (Ferdous, 2016), the Chittagong Hill Tracts Regional Council Act 1998 was passed, which curtailed many aspects of earlier promised autonomy (Khan and Rahman, 2009). After more than 18 years, no progress is achieved in tribal control over their governance, land and other indigenous rights (KFO, 2015). Their negotiation power also continues to be weak due to marginal representation in Parliament (currently one representative); consequently, the violence, and threat of reverting conflict continues (Khan and Rahman, 2009).

Biharis are facing a continued victimization of political persecution, on charges of their anti-liberation role. Until recent times, most of them didn't have citizenship rights. Presently, while they are constitutionally recognized as citizens, they continue to face victimization through discrimination in every aspect of life – education, employment, business, development and access to justice.

With this theory and practice of fundamentalism, Bangladesh is actually reproducing majoritarianism, of which it was a victim, and against which it fought the liberation war.

Emerging typologies of transformative constitutionalism

From the preceding discussion what we take away is a four-pronged typology of TCPRM in South Asia, each having relatively different consequences (Table 7.1). An 'ideal type model' is one in which a state's constitution recognizes and defines all its minorities and guarantees individual and group-specific transformative provisions for their PRPEL. Then, in practice, shows political will and commitment in transforming those constitutional guarantees into action so that minorities feel fully wedded into national life, and there are no signs of their exclusion and threat to the national development and security.

While all countries in South Asia are far from this ideal type, the closest one appears to be India. As shown earlier, the constitution recognizes and defines all its minorities (though not under a single provision), but it is partially transformative. It guarantees individual rights to all its citizens; however, the group guarantees for participation are given only to SCs and STs, and some geographically concentrated ethno-linguistic minorities. These protections have made India considerably

Constitutional promises vs practices **141**

TABLE 7.1 Typology of the transformative constitutionalism vis-à-vis the participation of minorities in South Asian states

Country	Constitutional promise	Practice	Consequence
India	Recognitive-cum-partially transformative	Considerably accommodative	Selective exclusion
Pakistan	Partially recognitive-cum-partially transformative	Partially accommodative	Widespread exclusion
Sri Lanka	Narrowly recognitive-cum-partially transformative	Narrowly accommodative	Widespread exclusion
Bangladesh	Narrowly recognitive-cum-narrowly transformative	Non accommodative	Complete exclusion

Source: Author

accommodative, with SC and STs getting proportional participation at all levels of politics and public employment and most of the geographically concentrated ethno-linguistic minorities getting their demand of right to autonomy partially fulfilled (through autonomous districts, regional councils and the formation of separate states).[12] This consequently eliminated their threat to national security and development to a considerable extent. Not having similar group guarantees for religious minorities is a hindrance to its complete accommodation of minorities. As a consequence, these minorities, especially Muslims, are continually pushed towards what can be called 'selective exclusion' from PRPEL.

The second type is Pakistan, which highlights that partially recognitive and partially transformative constitution can, in practice, lead to partial accommodation and create possibilities of widespread exclusion. Constitutionally, only religious minorities are recognized and defined, whiles ethno-linguistic minorities are seen as a homogeneous group. Further, while it guarantees individual rights of equal participation to all its citizens, it rejects non-Muslims from holding the office of president and PM. Furthermore, while it guarantees group rights of political reservation and affirmative action for religious minorities, the ethno-linguistic minorities are distant from it. This theory has made Pakistan's constitution partially transformative, and its practice partially accommodative. The claims and rights, in particular of ethno-linguistic minorities, have been consistently ignored, leading to their widespread exclusion and turning them into a great threat to national and sub-continental security and development (in 1971 through Bangladesh war, and since 2000 with the rise of Pakistan Taliban). Also, even after various forms of reservations the full accommodation of religious minorities is still dicey.

The third type, close to Pakistan, is Sri Lanka, which highlights that a narrowly recognitive, and partially transformative constitution, in practice, can lead to the narrow accommodation of minorities and create possibilities of widespread exclusion. Narrow recognition emerges from the constitution not classifying any ethnic and religious groups, with the exception of referring to Tamil as an official language at one place. Partial transformativeness comes from the fact that while it provides a proportional electoral system and devolution of power, it does not guarantee any group-specific protections to Tamils, Muslims and Christians. Narrow accommodativeness emerges from the practice of centralized control over both these transformative measures, and their failure in meeting the wishes and claims of minorities. Further, the lack of other measures to bring equal minority leadership in decision making in central and provincial cabinets, and public employment leaves the key demands (constitutional representational rights in all institutions of politics and governance) of minority groups almost unattended (Uyangoda, 2010). This has consequently led to a widespread minority exclusion thereby creating large-scale human development catastrophes – earlier by fuelling ethnic conflict, and later (post-war) by increasing civil unrest.

Finally, unlike other countries, Bangladesh shows that a constitution with a narrow definition and recognition of minorities, and narrow transformative nature in practice creates incentives for the majority for complete non-accommodation of minorities, and thereby possibilities of their complete exclusion from all domains of life. As shown earlier, besides some executive orders, there are no group-specific constitutional guarantees available to any minority. Their minuscule participation in political and public employment domains is *de facto* rather than *de jure*, or accidental instead of intentional. This consequently has created possibilities for the complete exclusion of minorities, not only from politics and public employment, but also from the country (evident through forced settlement policy in CHTs, and the intimidation of other minorities), which is feeding into more targeted violence, and possible re-emergence of rebel fighting.[13]

Pathways to overcome hurdles to minority participation

South Asia, unlike some other developing countries, has a basic commitment to the idea of democracy and democratic rights. There is also a constitutional definition, recognition, and transformative measures for some minorities (varying across countries) (Hassan, 2016). However, there is also a common gap (varying across countries), in translating the democratic commitments into a balanced and equitable PR of minorities (Adeney, 2015). To completely wed these heterogeneous minority groups in the national processes (Hassan, 2016), South Asian countries need to reach the 'ideal type model'. This demands a deepening of democracy – adherence to the democratic principles and constitutionality in the letter and spirit (Pellissery, 2016), compared to the western world, because it has an extremely heterogeneous nature of minorities.

Out of all the measures of integrating minorities in every aspect of public life, indirect and informal means are considered as the best, because they benefit without increasing the salience of a particular minority group (Stewart et al., 2008). However, in the case of South Asia, such measures as reflected previously, present largely a failure. Hence, there is a need for both indirect and direct constitutional measures. Firstly, by re-working around the practice of individual rights of

Constitutional promises vs practices **143**

citizenship and equality. Secondly, by widening the theory and practice of group guarantees. Thirdly, through setting up independent monitoring systems.

Re-working around the practice of individual rights

The individual FRs of the equality of citizenship and participation, as guaranteed by all countries, actually mean equal treatment for all individuals as members of different communities. However, this idea is going against the existing majoritarian idea and practice of nation-state. To overcome this, there is a need of mind-set change about what these individual transformative rights actually mean. The systems also need to be empowered in order to strengthen the rule of law and anti-discrimination differential treatments such as checking laws, entrenching an independent judiciary, and setting strong mechanisms of protecting human rights and promoting diversity and multiculturalism (Hassan, 2016).

Widening the theory and practice of group guarantees

As reflected in this chapter, individual rights under a weak rule of law and state of majoritarianism have not created much space for minorities. Hence, minority rights can no longer be framed entirely on the basis of individual or civil and political or language rights alone (Uyangoda, 2010). Instead, what has worked fairly well in such conditions is constitutionally guaranteed group rights alongside individual rights. Be it the case of SCs, STs and some linguistic minorities in North East India, religious minorities and to some extent Pashtus in Pakistan,[14] this makes a strong case for the provision of constitutional group guarantees for all minorities. However, extending group rights discourse demands a complex task of the radical restricting of the state. Owing to such complexity, a starting point could be constitutionally guaranteeing, or extending (where some minorities already have it) promotional policies of political reservation and affirmative action in public employment.

Political participation

The electoral system in a democracy is a skeleton on which the body of a society grows. Its nature, to a large extent, determines the inclusion of minorities in a particular polity, and the approach in which majority parties will appeal or mobilize minority voters and leaders (Reynolds, 2006). Unfortunately, the colonial-inherited FPPS has made democracy just a numbers game for most minorities in the subcontinent (Adeney, 2015), which instead of accommodation has led to their political marginalization (Reynolds, 2006). For such minorities, there is a definite need of overhauling the existing electoral system.

The first move towards this would be replicating the existing promotional policies to all minorities – a single electorate with proportional participation. This system has the potential of ensuring all groups' participation, broadly, in proportion to their population (Stewart et al., 2008) and would especially benefit disaggregated minorities – Indian and Sri Lankan Muslims, and Bangladeshi Hindus and tribes (Dasgupta et al., 2011).[15] This system has shown its merit in reducing minorities' exclusion from the provincial and state assemblies. However, it has not guaranteed them decision-making power due to non-power sharing at the executive level (Stewart et al., 2008). As mentioned earlier, Indian SCs and STs, Pakistani and Sri Lankan religious minorities enjoy some form of proportional political participation but have marginal representation in cabinets. This demands a second move, from the informal cabinet sharing system dictated by the mood of the ruling party, to a formal proportional cabinet sharing arrangement. An example of this is in Lebanon where the president's position is reserved for Christians, PM for Sunni and speaker for Shi'a Muslims. Such arrangements are crucial in developing countries like South Asia, where groups who dominate the executive largely tend to favour policies towards their own communities (Langer, 2005).

For geographically concentrated ethno-linguistic minority claims of self-rule, autonomy, or secessionism most of the countries have initiated some form of constitutional devolution of power. However, with the exception of India – where power devolution measures, to a considerable extent, have met the demands of Northeast's ethno-linguistic minorities – all other countries have either forged their promises (Sri Lanka and Bangladesh) or didn't meet most of the minority claims and/or are highly centralized (Sri Lanka, Bangladesh and Pakistan). Consequently, these regions are underdeveloped, and ethno- and/or linguistics regionalism continues to threaten nation-states (Lokniti, 2008). Overcoming these challenges demands addressing the normative and practical weaknesses of these models of devolution, by giving due consideration to the participation and power-sharing claims of these minorities.

Public employment

In countries like in South Asia, the government is still a large service provider, and the participation in bureaucracy and security (front line providers) is highly detrimental in determining the access to services and development. Hence, the question of power sharing beyond politics becomes equally crucial. As mentioned earlier, like political PR, the individual guarantees of accommodation in public employment have led to marginal outcomes for minorities due to lack of set measurement criteria (Adeney, 2015). Consequently, Muslims in India, ethno-linguistic minorities in Pakistan, and religious and ethno-linguistic minorities in Bangladesh and Sri Lanka are disproportionally underrepresented. To ensure these minorities equal and balanced PR in the public sector, a good starting point would be extending them existing promotional frameworks of proportional employment (Stewart et al., 2008). Such measures have led to instrumental distributional outcomes, which is evident in the case of SCs and STs in India, Muslims in few South Indian states (Tamil Nadu, Kerala and Telangana) and religious minorities in Pakistan (though not well documented yet).[16] The environment of discrimination by separating minorities as second-class citizens, which is argued to continue even after such measures (MRG, 2016), can be overcome by putting in place additional measures of educational and awareness campaigns, media initiatives and cultural platforms to celebrate the minorities' contribution to countries (Jacob, 2014).

Setting minority commissions and space for CSOs

A long-standing demand of South Asian minorities has been the setting up of minority commissions (Uyangoda, 2010; Sachar, 2006; Hassan, 2016). But this demand, though crucial for transforming their constitutional guarantees into practice and putting checks and balances on systems, has not been met. While some countries, as mentioned earlier, have MOMA or linguistic commissions at various levels, they lack transparency, accountability and inclusive consultation and are controlled by majoritarian politics. Hence, there is a serious need for setting up minority commissions as tribunals in accordance with the Paris principles at the central, provincial and local levels (Jacob, 2014). Being autonomous, inclusive and accountable bodies, they will safeguard the interests of minorities, particularly by monitoring the implementation of aforementioned constitutional guarantees, widening the non-constitutional measures, developing an equal opportunity index, facilitating independent research and up-to-date data, and systematic reporting on their PR. Also, the most prominent group of people, who risk their lives to work for the wellbeing of minorities and have a commitment to measuring their progress – activists, NGOs and lawyers – should be protected by states, allowed freedom to work and investigate without fear and intimidation or violence by extremists, and form vibrant organizations across the sub-continent (MRG, 2016).

On face value, and in the growing wave of majoritarianism, some of these measures might sound radical, too sensitive and unattainable, as reported by some research respondents in India (Salter, 2011). However, these challenges can be overcome through states changing their political attitudes towards minorities and having the political will to mobilize the public and come up with such reforms.

Conclusions

The theory of transformative constitutionalism in South Asia presents a fairly progressive promise towards minorities' participation and representation in political and public domains, through individual and/or group rights. However, its practice doesn't stand quite well and equitable with the promise. The translation of group rights into laws and concrete policies, their upholding by judiciary and their impact is significant. In countries where group guarantees are not promised to some or all minorities the quantum of individual transformative provisions, translating into laws and concrete policies, is abysmal, the role of the judiciary in upholding them is weak, and the impact vague and marginal. For example, emphasis through various reports over the last 70 years on upholding the rights of equal participation guaranteed under individual rights to Indian Muslims in order to overcome their plight of exclusion are not making any dent. The rule of law and the institutions

146 Mushtaq Ahmad Malla

of human rights are also unable to uphold the state accountable to such promises, compared to the same rights enjoyed by other equally culturally excluded minority groups such as ST and STs in the form of group rights. While such practices make the majoritarian state mightier, they also endanger national and sub-continental security and development with increasing inequalities.

While this takes the overall theory and practice of TCPRM in South Asia on a bumpy road, at the same time, it also reflects a hope, originating from the basic democratic principles and polity followed across the sub-continent. This hope allows us to think of a possible 'Ideal Type' of TCPRM, which can be realized in the sub-continent, by re-working around the individual rights through strengthening the discrimination checking laws, rule of law, empowering an independent judiciary and promoting diversity alongside individual rights, strengthening of group rights for all minorities, with a starting point being constitutional guarantees or an extension of existing promotional policies in political and public employment domains. Existing minority rights institutions should be made accountable and transparent. Independent minority commissions should be established as tribunals to safeguard minority rights, and creating a fertile space for civil society to support in translating constitutional promises into practice through comprehensive policymaking, and backing judiciary, state and other institutions in upholding and delivering on promises.

Notes

1 This chapter was originally presented in the panel of "Interface of Law and Public Policy" during the third international conference of Public Policy 28–30 June 2017 at Lee Kuan Yew School of Public Policy, Singapore. The author is grateful to Dr Sajjad Hassan for comments on the earlier version of this chapter. The author also has benefited from comments during the conference presentation and from reviewer comments at different stages of publication.

2 In the Lok Sabah 15.47% (84) seats are reserved for SCs and 8.66% (47) for ST/*adivasis*.

3 Interestingly, out of 282 MPs in the current ruling party BJP, no one is a Muslim. In the Lok Sabah there are 23 Muslim members out of 543, which is lower than 1957.

4 In addition, through government ordinance, reservations are also given in local bodies in 1979 and 2000. The court has also directed government to create institutions for enforcing and monitoring the minority protection laws – District Minority Advisory Councils 1980, Commission on Minorities 1993, and National Council for Minorities (Jacob, 2014).

5 The conditions that led to the emergence of these constitutional measures/amendments was to address the demands and aspirations of minorities in ethnic conflict during the 1980s and 1990s, when conflict was on peak. The language policy changes in 1960 and 1970, and the state-sponsored settlement policy of Sinhalese in Tamil areas was followed by the 1983 riots and killing of several hundred Tamils by Sinhalese. This broke into a conflict between Tamils, represented by the Liberation Tigers of Tamil Eelam (LTTE) and state-favoured Sinhalese (Serena, 1997). While the conflict claim was for federalism and autonomy, the conflict shifted discourse towards secession and self-determination, and also gave rise to multi-layered power sharing demands from minorities within minorities (Uyangoda, 2010). The conflict was over in 2009 through a massive army action of the Sri Lankan government.

6 Industry and Commerce, Urban Development & Water Supply, Public Enterprise Development, Postal Service & Muslim Affairs, Estate Infrastructure, Community Development, and National Dialogue.

7 For example, after the disarmament in the East, the government promised Muslims CM position, if they win in 2007 local elections. However, even after winning the largest number of seats, the position was given to the former LTTE based party – Tamil Makkal Viduthalai Paligal (Haniffa, 2010).
8 Means a Sinhala is three times more likely to climb to the top two tiers.
9 The exception is women, who have reservation of 45 of 300 parliament seats. However, their actual participation has been marginal – one in 1973, 1986, 1991 and 2008 and three in 1996 (Amin et al., 2016).
10 CHTs have different cultures and languages, and Biharis are migrants from India and Pakistan.
11 The government has even warned against using 'indigenous' to describe them (MRG, 2016).
12 While some tribes are not happy with these solutions and continue to fight for self-rule, overall these measures have brought a considerable amount of stability within these groups.
13 The majoritarian atrocities and fear are argued to have squeezed the religious minority population from 21% in 1971 to 10.3% in 2001, and the demands of United Council of Minorities for reservation as per 1971 population proportion are being continuously denied. In CHTs the non-tribal Bengalis population has increased from 10% in 1947 to 50% in 1991. Bangladesh also didn't observe UN declaration 1994, Year of Indigenous Peoples.
14 Beyond South Asia, such cases are also evident in post-colonial Malaysia, Indonesia and South Africa, and Lebanon (Stewart et al., 2008).
15 In 1954 Hindu leaders won 23% (72 of 309) of seats in East Pakistan under proportional reservation system. Since the launch of combined election for all they have remained marginalized (Kabir, 1980).
16 Outside South Asia, some minorities in post-colonial Nigeria, Ethiopia and Malaysia have also done fairly well with similar constitutional guarantees at all levels of government (Stewart et al., 2008).

References

Adeney, K. (2012) "A step towards inclusive federalism in Pakistan? The Politics of the 18th amendment", *Publius: The Journal of Federalism*, 42(4), 539–565.

———. (2015) "A move to majoritarian nationalism? Challenges of representation in South Asia", *Representation*, 51(1), 7–21.

Ahmed, I. (1997) "Indo-Bangladesh relations: Trapped in the nationalist discourse", in D. Barun and R. Samaddar (eds.), *State, development and political culture: Bangladesh and India*. New Delhi: Har Anand Publications.

Amin, A., Amin, M. and Hossain, Z. (2016) "Bangladesh; Paving the way to liberation", in ed. CES (ed.), *South Asia state of minorities report 2016*. Bangalore: ActionAid Enterprise.

Ansari, I. (1997) *Communal riots, the state & law in India*. New Delhi: Genuine Publications and Media Pvt. Ltd.

Bajpai, R. (2000) "Constituent assembly debates and minority rights", *Economic and Political Weekly*, 35(21/22).

———. (2011) *Debating difference: Group rights and liberal democracy in India*. New Delhi: Oxford University Press.

Castellino, J. and Redondo, E. (2006) *Minority rights in Asia: A comparative legal analysis*. New York: Oxford University Press.

Census (2011) *Census of India*. Ministry of Home Affairs, Government of India.

——— (2012) *Census of Sri Lanka*. Ministry of Home Affairs, Government of Sri Lanka.

Dasgupta, A., Togawa, M. and Barkat, A. (2011) *Minorities and the state: Changing political landscape of Bengal*. New Delhi: SAGE.

Ferdous, H. (2016) "Enabling minority voices", *Daily Star*, 11 April. Available at: www.thedai lystar.net/op-ed/politics/enabling-minority-voices-1207264 (Accessed 26 March 2017).

Fonseka, S. (2016) "Sri Lanka: A mosaic under stress", in CES (ed.), *South Asia state of minorities report – 2016*. Bangalore: ActionAid Enterprise.

Francis, K. (2013) "Sri Lanka turning authoritarian, says UN Human Rights Chief Navi Pillay", *The Independent*, 31 August. Available at: www.independent.co.uk/news/world/asia/sri-lanka-turning-authoritarian-says-un-human-rights-chief-navi-pillay-8792601.html (Accessed 26 March 2017).

GoI. (2014) *Post Sachar evaluation committee*. New Delhi: Ministry of Minority Affairs, Government of India.

Gopal Singh Committee Report. (1983) *Report on the condition of minorities, scheduled castes (SCs) and scheduled tribes (STs) and other weaker sections*. New Delhi: Ministry of Home Affairs, Government of India.

Haniffa, F. (2010) "Muslims in Sri Lanka: Political choices of a minority", in R. Manchanda (ed.), *States in conflict with their minorities: Challenges to minority rights in South Asia*. New Delhi: SAGE.

Hanifa, F. (2015) "Competing for victim status: Northern Muslims and the ironies of Sri Lanka's post-war transition", *Stability: International Journal of Security & Development*, 4(1), 1–18.

Hassan, J. (2014) "All the king's men!", *Dawn*, 27 December. Available at: www.dawn.com/news/1153465 (Accessed 21 July 2018).

Hassan, S. (2016) "Introduction: Minority rights in South Asia – rough road to citizenship", in CES (ed.), *South Asia state of minorities report – 2016*. Bangalore: ActionAid Enterprise.

Hassan, S. and Khair, N. (2016) "India: Is the idea unravelling?", in CES (ed.), *South Asia state of minorities report – 2014*. Bangalore: ActionAid Enterprise.

Heptulla, N. (2014) "Quota no solution to development issues of Muslims", *Economic Times*, 27 May. Available at: https://economictimes.indiatimes.com/news/politics-and-nation/quota-no-solution-to-development-issues-of-muslims-najma-heptulla/articleshow/35634478.cms (Accessed 15 May 2017).

HRCP. (2015) *State of human rights in 2014*. Lahore: Human Rights Commission of Pakistan.

Islam, F. (2006) "Ethnicity, ethnic conflict and discrimination against ethnic minorities of Bangladesh", *Journal of Ethnic Affairs*, 2, 27–31.

Jacob, P. (2011) "Mainstreaming minorities: Accumulated legal and other discriminations have made this year's experience for the minorities one of acute social and economic marginalization", *Daily Times*, 18 July. Available at: https://dailytimes.com.pk/111304/mainstreaming-minorities/ (Accessed 6 July 2017).

Jacob, P. (2014) *Political integration and affirmative legislation for minorities in Pakistan*. Policy Brief, Open Democracy Initiative, Jinnah Institute.

Kabir, M. G. (1980) *Minority politics in Bangladesh*. New Delhi: Vikas Publishing House.

KFO (2015) "Human rights report 2015 on indigenous peoples in Bangladesh". Available at: http://kapaeeng.org/kapaeeng-foundation-launches-human-rights-report-2015-on-indigenous-peoples-in-bangladesh (Accessed 23 April 2018).

Khaliq, B. and Aslam, K. (2016) "Pakistan: Need to go back to founding principles", in CES (ed.), *South Asia state of minorities report – 2016*. Bangalore: ActionAid Enterprise.

Khan, B. and Rahman, M. (2009) *Protection of minorities: A South Asian discourse*. Dhaka: EurasiaNet.

Kohari, A. (2013) "Herald exclusive: Political dynasties in Pakistan", *Dawn*, 9 May. Available at: https://www.dawn.com/news/1026679 (Accessed 21 July 2018).

Langer, A. (2005) "Horizontal inequalities and violent group mobilization in Côte d'Ivoire", *Oxford Development Studies*, 33(1), 25–45.

Lijphart, A. (1977) *Democracy in plural societies*. New Haven: Yale University Press.

Livemint (2014) "Minorities better represented in the Indian parliament than in US". Available at: www.livemint.com/Opinion/bKRhH5ST4fMV7TvcbRMVxO/Minori ties-better-represented-in-the-Indian-parliament-than.html (Accessed 21 May 207).

Lokniti (2008) *State of democracy in South Asia*. New Delhi: Oxford University Press.

Mandal, G. (2007) "Treatment of law to the minorities in Bangladesh: Rhetoric and reality", in M. Rahman (ed.), *Human rights & corruption*. Dhaka: Empowerment Through Law of the Common People, pp. 219–228.

Mohsin, A. (1997) *The politics of nationalism: The case of the Chittagong Hill tracts. Bangladesh*. Dhaka: University Press.

MRG (2016) *Under threat: The challenges facing religious minorities in Bangladesh*. Sweden: Minority Rights Group International.

Nandy, A. (1983) *The intimate enemy: Loss and recovery of self under colonialism*. Delhi: Oxford University Press.

PCP (2013) "The Christians of provinces of Sindh and KPK have no representation in national assembly of Pakistan in election 2013", *Pakistan Christian Post*, 28 May. Available at: www.pakistanchristianpost.com/news-details/1906 (Accessed 23 July 2018).

Pellissery, S. (2016) *Minorities, democracy and capitalism*. Bengaluru: CSSEIP, NLSIU.

Perera, J. (1999) "Minorities in Sri Lanka", in S. Banerjee (ed.), *Shrinking space: Minority rights in South Asia*. Kathmandu: South Asia Forum for Human Rights, pp. 68–71.

Rajasingham, K. (2015) A total of 42 New Cabinet Ministers Sworn in, but no One for North East Development. 5 September, *Asian Tribune*.

Reynolds, A. (2006) *Electoral systems and the protection and participation of minorities*. London: Minority Rights Group International.

Riaz, A. (2015) "Non-Muslims and défense of Pakistan", *LinkedIn*, 16 May. Available at: https://www.linkedin.com/pulse/non-muslims-defense-pakistan-ahmad-riaz (Accessed 4 May 2016).

Sachar Committee Report. (2006) *Social, economic and educational status of the Muslim community of India*. New Delhi: Ministry of Home Affairs, Government of India.

Salter, M. (2011) *Democracy for all? Minority rights and minorities' participation and representation in democratic politics*. Stockholm: International IDEA.

Samad, S. (1998) "State of minorities in Bangladesh: From secular to Islamic hegemony". Available at: https://mm-gold.azureedge.net/Articles/saleem/secular_to_islamic.html (Accessed 3 August 2018).

Serena, T. (1997) "Newspaper nationalism: Sinhala identity as historical discourse", in S. Jonathan (ed.), *Sri Lanka – History and the roots of conflict*. London: Routledge.

Shahla, Z. (2010) "Discrimination in Pakistan against religious minorities: Constitutional aspects", in R. Manchanda (ed.), *States in conflict with their minorities: Challenges to minority rights in South Asia*. New Delhi: SAGE, pp. 143–172.

Singh, S. K. (2007) *Human rights in Pakistan: From Zulfkar Ali Bhutto to Musharraf*. Delhi: Pentagon Press.

Skanthakumar, B. (2011) "Sri Lanka: Implementation of the international covenant on economic, social and cultural rights", in *Status of economic, social and cultural rights in Sri Lanka*. Colombo: Law & Society Trust.

Stewart, F., Brown, G. and Langer, A. (2008) "Policies towards horizontal inequalities", CRISE Working Paper No. 42.

Thangarajah, C. Y. (2002) "Youth, conflict and social transformation in Sri Lanka", in S. T. Hettige and M. Mayer (eds.), *Sri Lankan youth: Challenges and responses*. Colombo: Friedrich-Ebert-Stiftung, pp. 172–207.

Tribune (2012) "Parliamentary representation: New bill on the cards for increased minority seats", *The Express Tribune – Pakistan,* 31 August. Available at: https://tribune.com.pk/story/428889/parliamentary-representation-new-bill-on-the-cards-for-increased-minority-seats/ (Accessed 4 May 2018).

Tripura, P. (2018) "The denial of linguistic diversity in Bangladesh", *Tribune*, 27 February. Available at: https://www.dhakatribune.com/special-supplement/2018/02/21/denial-linguistic-diversity-bangladesh (Accessed 18 May 2018).

Uyangoda, J. (2010) "Sri Lanka: Recent shifts in the minority rights debate", in R. Manchanda (ed.), *States in conflict with their minorities: Challenges to minority rights in South Asia*. New Delhi: SAGE.

———. (2015) "Electoral reforms: Some critical reflections", *Daily News*, 6 April. Available at: http://www.onetext.org/electoral-reforms-some-critical-reflections/ (Accessed 18 April 2016).

Verite Research (VR). (2013) "Do women and minorities in Sri Lanka face glass ceilings in employment?" Available at: www.island.lk/ (Accessed 1 January 2018).

Weiner, M. (1989) *The Indian paradox: Essays in Indian politics*. New Delhi: SAGE.

Weiner, M. and Banuazizi, A. (1986) *The state, religion, and ethnic politics: Afghanistan, Iran, and Pakistan*. New York: Syracuse University Press.

Wilkinson, S. (2000) "India, consociational theory, and ethnic violence", *Asian Survey*, 40(5), 767–791.

Zia, S. (2010) "Discrimination in Pakistan against religious minorities: Constitutional aspects", in R. Manchanda (ed.), *States in conflict with their minorities: challenges to minority rights in South Asia*. New Delhi: SAGE.

8

GROWING UP IN FAMILIES WITH LOW INCOME

The state's legal obligation to recognize the child's right to adequate standard of living

Julia Köhler-Olsen

Introduction

This chapter discusses Norwegian social policy targeting the risk of poverty and child poverty in light of children's right to an adequate standard of living laid down in the UN Convention on the Rights of the Child (CRC) Article 27. The legal framework of Norway's obligation to combat child poverty is, beside the CRC, laid down in the UN Covenant on Economic, Social and Cultural Rights (ESCR) Article 11 and the Norwegian Constitution section 104 on the constitutional rights of the child. This Article presents an overview of Norway's legal obligation towards children living in poverty or at risk of poverty and gives account of the term poverty in a Norwegian context, as well as challenges linked to governmental strategies to reduce poverty or combat its negative effects. Finally, the article discusses policies targeted at improving households' income in light of CRC Article 27 and other relevant legal sources. The aim is to answer the main question, namely whether the Norwegian state by designing its social policy in this field is giving appropriate weight and consideration to the rights of the child.

Welfare policy and human rights obligation

Before analyzing some of the Norwegian state's policies regarding combatting child poverty, the relationship between legal rights, legal obligations and policy needs to be discussed in general. This discussion matters greatly, since it informs the scope of discretionary power a state may have when designing social policies, or putting it differently, it matters to know when a state can be held legally accountable for policy choices, for ways of implementation of policies or lack thereof.

Human rights are here understood as being legal rights which are enshrined in various binding international law instruments. Human rights as legally binding rights protect the individuals' basic interest against possible policy choices by their own state.

Several legal authors have argued that human rights which relate to human needs are not substantially different from other human rights. Langford (2008) as well as many other scholars have argued that it has not been possible to prove that economic, social and cultural rights (ESC rights) differ from civil and political rights. There is no specific reason to deny ESC rights judicial protection (Bilchitz, 2007; Fredman, 2008; Young, 2012).

Yet, Arosemena (2015) argues quite convincingly that some human rights, which he says put "welfare duties" on states, are not justiciable. He argues that the degree of costliness of welfare duties has implications for adjudication. For welfare duties, judges cannot simply adjudicate the duty and expect the state to absorb the cost in such a way that the rights of other persons need not be affected. By contrast, compliance with the rights of one person will typically detract from the possibility of complying with the welfare rights of others. Because of the high levels of costs attached to welfare duties, the state is faced with hard choices. Even though all rights may involve trade-offs, the state cannot simply catch up with the costs linked to the implementation of welfare rights due to the high level of costs attached to welfare duties. In that sense, conflicts in the sphere of welfare duties are endemic (Eddy, 2006): a demand for resources in a context of scarcity (Arosemena, 2015).

I question, however, the premise that ESC rights need to be justiciable in the meaning of case-to-case decisions on the distribution of welfare goods. Agreeable, justiciable rights leave more power to the right holder. However, welfare duties put in legal terms provide the right holder with arguments when hard choices must be made by policymakers. Policymakers do not only have to make choices between various welfare duties, but they also must make choices regarding the design of a certain policy. In that process human rights understood as legal rights can provide powerful arguments for how policy design should be, as opposed to, for example, solely based on economic arguments. Furthermore, human rights can serve as a benchmark for states' performance in fulfilling their welfare duties.

The South African Constitutional Court has developed a practice of reasonableness review which has a similar approach to the role of rights-based arguments regarding public welfare policies. The South African judicial practice reduces the role of the judge to one of determining whether, overall, governmental efforts in one area of welfare are reasonable or not (Arosemena, 2015). This practice of reasonable review is in line with the practice of the UN Committee on Economic, Social and Cultural Rights (UN ESC Committee) when supervising the implementation of ESC rights in member states of the UN Covenant on Economic, Social and Cultural Rights. The South African Constitutional Court and the UN ESC Committee monitor if unreasonable efforts are made, for example, by lack of adequate progression in social targets, unjustified retrogression, discriminatory policies or lack of concern with the worst off (UN ESC Committee General Comment no. 3, 1990). By doing so the state is held accountable without the judge being decisively active in distributing resources (Arosemena, 2015).

This said, the following analysis discusses the Norwegian state's policy in light of the state's human rights obligations and tries to answer the question of whether unreasonable efforts are made to eradicate, reduce and/or combat child poverty in Norway.

The child's right to an adequate standard of living

In this section, we will review different legal backing for child protection. The relevant legislation we review here are the UN convention on the rights of child, UN Covenant on Economic, Social and Cultural Rights, and the Constitution of Norway.

UN Convention on the Rights of the Child Article 27

Sections 1–3 of Article 27 of Child Rights Convention are relevant with reference to the main aim of this chapter. These sections show the state has a subsidiary responsibility to take appropriate measures regarding the child's right to an adequate standard of living. The appropriate measures are to assist parents and others responsible for the child to secure the condition of living necessary for the child's development.

The state must 'recognize' the child's right to an adequate standard of living ensuring its development to the maximum extent possible as laid down in Article 6 of the CRC. The ordinary meaning of 'to recognize a right' entails a rather weak obligation compared to, for example, 'to ensure a right' and might require even less active action than 'to respect a right'. To recognize something means to acknowledge the existence of it. States, thus, must acknowledge the existence, validity and legality of the right to an adequate standard of living of the child. However, acknowledging its existence does not necessarily mean that member states to the CRC must actively ensure the right to an adequate standard of living being fulfilled.

It is the parents or caretakers of the child who have the primary responsibility to secure the child's right to an adequate standard of living, as laid down in section 2. The state, having subsidiary responsibility, cannot, however, remain passive and just acknowledge the right of the child and the obligation of the parents though this might be the impression after having read the state's obligation to 'recognize' the child's right. In section 3 the wording establishes a concrete obligation for the state to take positive actions to assist parents to implement this right. Section 3 accentuates that the state has "to take appropriate measures" to assist parents in their implementation efforts. Furthermore, states must also provide material assistance and support programmes, particularly with regard to nutrition, clothing and housing, for those parents and caregivers who are in need of such support.

The scope of the state's obligation is limited by the national conditions and means. Though having all means available, it is on the one hand considered legitimate that wealthy states like Norway have sound economic and social policies. On the other hand, national economic and social policies need to consider the child's right to an adequate standard of living and contribute to realize appropriate measures to assist and support families.

The aim of the assistance and support of the parents or caregivers must be to secure for the child living conditions that are necessary for the child's development. The development of the child is understood broadly as can be read in section 1 of Article 27. The development of the child includes not only its physical development, but also its mental, spiritual, moral and social development. Read in conjunction with the CRC basic principle laid down in Article 6 no. 2, the state shall *ensure* to the maximum extent possible the development of the child. Parents and caregivers, as well as public institutions and authorities supporting families, must approach their support for the child broadly and thoroughly to the maximum extent possible.

The CRC Committee states in General Comment no. 7 on implementing child rights in early childhood (2005) in section 26 that growing up in relative poverty undermines children's wellbeing, social inclusion and self-esteem and reduces opportunities for learning and development. Correspondingly, the CRC Committee underlines that the impact of poverty has profound implications during adolescence, sometimes leading to extreme stress and insecurity and to social and political exclusion and reminds states of the obligation according to CRC Article 27 (General Comment no. 20 on the implementation of rights of the child during adolescence, 2016, section 66).

To support families with low income or in poverty, the state's obligation is twofold. One part relates to reducing poverty, and the other part is directed to combat poverty's negative effects on children's wellbeing. CRC Committee's General Comment no. 19 regards public budgeting for the realization of children's rights grounded in CRC Article 4 on state obligation. The Committee underlines that children's rights, and especially those of vulnerable children, must be safeguarded and realized in all economic priorities regarding children. "Vulnerable children" include children living in poverty, and as such, the Committee points out that they are particularly susceptible to violations of their rights (section 3). Rights that are knowingly affected by poverty and risk of poverty are the right to leisure, rest and activities and the right to education. Furthermore, the state is obliged to assess on a regular manner how budgets affect different groups of children and to ensure that their budget decisions lead to the best possible outcome for the largest number of children, paying special attention to children in vulnerable situations (section 59).

UN Covenant on Economic, Social and Cultural Rights Article 11

In addition to Norway's obligation following from CRC Article 27, the state is also obliged to fulfil Article 11 of ESCR. Article 11 no. 1 states the right of everyone to an adequate standard of living for himself and his family, including adequate food, clothing and housing, and to the continuous improvement of living conditions. The UN ESCR Committee, supervisory treaty body to the ESCR, submitted General Comment no. 3 on state obligation regarding economic, social and cultural rights in 1990. Because implementation of economic, social and cultural rights was considered to be highly dependent on the state's condition and means, the Committee stressed that this type of human rights not only require states to progressively realize their fulfilment, but also establishes immediate obligations regardless of the state's condition or means. This document, though part of the ESCR, is now considered to express state obligation related to economic, social and cultural rights in general.

One central and immediate obligation is to implement any economic, social or cultural right without any discrimination meaning that all citizens of the state need to have access to the same economic, social and cultural rights with the same standard of quality. A second central and immediate obligation for the state is to take appropriate and targeted steps towards progressively fulfilling the respective economic, social and cultural right. This means that Norway must implement its obligation to assist and support families to endeavour to secure the child's conditions of living necessary for the child's development without any discrimination and without any delay.

The Constitution of Norway section 104

The Norwegian Constitution was amended with a catalogue of human rights in 2014. In section 104, the Constitution states that children have the right to respect their human dignity. In addition, for actions and decisions that affect children, the best interests of the child shall be a fundamental consideration. Children are also ensured the right to be heard in questions that concern them and the state is obliged to facilitate the child's development, including ensuring that the child is provided with the necessary economic, social and health security, preferably within their own family.

Section 104 of the Norwegian Constitution entails in addition to the child's right to economic and social rights, also CRC Article 3 on the best interest of the child and CRC Article 12 on the right of the child to be heard in all actions and decisions concerning the child.

The Norwegian state has in other words not only an obligation to ensure children an adequate standard of living according to international legal obligations, but also according to the state's own constitution. Since children are dependent on their parents or guardians or caretakers, and since they do not themselves have the possibility to improve their socio-economic status, national and international obligations demand a positive effort to implement the child's right to an adequate standard of living. The social policies must assist parents and must simultaneously ensure that the best interest of the child is considered appropriately (CRC Article 3) as well as children being given the possibility to participate in policy development and implementation (CRC Article 12).

A political task or legal obligation?

To conclude this section, we ask ourselves the question as to whether Norwegian state's obligation on reducing, eradicating and combatting child poverty is a legal

156 Julia Köhler-Olsen

obligation or if it is all 'just politics'. Legal obligations in this field mean the state is accountable for its actions and must show constant awareness in its strategies to ensure each child an adequate standard of living. However, legal norms do not provide the full answer to what is considered to be an adequate standard of living for a child.

The CRC requires policymakers to ensure that the child's development is secured to the maximum extent possible according to CRC Article 6, that the child's best interest is a paramount consideration in policy development, CRC Article 3, that the child's rights and possible violation of them is taken into consideration and is considered, and that parents are supported to ensure the child a standard of living adequate for its physical, mental, spiritual, moral and social development (CRC Article 27). Last, but not least, social welfare policies supporting families with low-income must be designed in a non-discriminatory way (CRC Article 2). The rights of the child, in other words, must be considered when balancing various political interests designing social policy.

Child poverty in Norway

Before discussing the child's right to an adequate standard of living and some of Norwegian state's social policies affecting child poverty, it is necessary to clarify the terms 'low income' and 'poverty'.

Low income as measurement of poverty: In the latest report published by the Norwegian Labour and Welfare Administration (NAV) about the state of the public welfare spending (Norwegian Labour and Welfare Administration, 2017), it is explained that low-income households in Norway include approximately 98,000 children, which is about 10% of the population of children living in Norway. This number is based on the definition that "low income" is any income below 60% of the median income of a population such as a single household, or household consisting of two adults and three children. The number of children living in households with low income changes however when compared to previous and present living costs in Norway. Living costs have fallen quite significantly in the last decade. The Norwegian statistical office (SSB – Statistisk sentralbyrå) does therefore point out that if one starts at a fixed point of, for example, 2005, looking at what was then 60% of the median income and relates this income to living costs and then compares this with low income and living costs today, the number of children living in households with low income in Norway is about 38,000 children today (Lura et al., 2017).

Low income might not necessarily equate with poverty, because this equation does not consider free or subsidized public services in Norway such as child care, public education and health and social care (Aaberge et al., 2010). If one includes the value of public services in the calculation of a household's income, the result of income differences decreases and the share on low-income decreases. However, the population having a greater risk of poverty is the same, independent of whether one adds these values of services or not (Fløtten and Nielsen, 2015).

Poverty defined by poor living conditions: Low income does not necessarily mean that the families and children are poor. Poverty because of low income depends on the living and housing costs, debts, and how long a family might live on low income. One definition of who is poor is to look at the actual living conditions of the household, family or individual. The access or ownership of certain goods can provide some indicators if a household is poor, such as owning a washing machine, being able to travel for vacation, participation in spare time activities, or to participate in birthdays with a present (Fløtten and Pedersen, 2008).

Poverty defined by the question if people have the income to get access to these basic living conditions: The Consumption Research Norway Institute (SIFO) has developed a minimum budget including necessary items, goods and activities for an ordinary household in Norway, adjusted to various forms of household. The minimum budget shows the lowest consumption level which can be accepted by the Norwegian population. According to this budget, poverty is when one does not have sufficient means to cover basic consumer needs (Borgeraas, 2017).

Subjective experience of poverty: With and Thorsen (2018) have investigated poverty in Norway by asking the Norwegian population whether they experience not being able to afford certain material goods, participate in social arenas and whether they experience economic difficulties. The advantage of such research lays in linking poverty to the actual needs of people. Yet, a challenge is that one does not get accurate measures on the number of people living in poverty. Households can adjust to their income. One can neither state which or how many goods one must lack access to in order to be considered poor.

Due to these various definitions of how we can understand poverty, it is necessary to define the term for this chapter. Firstly, it will not be of paramount interest for the discussion on social policy related to the child's right to an adequate standard of living how many or few children in Norway grow up in households with long-term low income. Secondly, since social policy in Norway is aimed at raising the income of adults in households with low income to avoid poverty or the risk of poverty, this chapter will understand poverty as "low income with a risk of poverty" and by that especially include those families living on low income for a rather long period. Norwegian public reports and statistics consider three years of low income to be persistent in increasing the risk of poverty. This definition will be used as basis for this chapter as well. Thirdly, the terms "risk of poverty" and "poverty" are understood as households lacking income to fulfil their basic needs, lacking income which leads to exclusion from social arenas and lacking income which leads to mental and physical stress as well as economic difficulties.

Reasons for and implications of poverty

Notwithstanding, it is not doubted that the number of households in poverty or risk of poverty are low in international comparison, yet children in Norway have moved from having insignificant risk of experiencing poverty, to be overrepresented in low-income statistics (Epland et al., 2016).

The risk of poverty due to long-term low income represents a risk to the physical, mental, spiritual, moral and social development of the child. This has severe implications for the quality of life of each child living in poverty or risk of poverty. It also has implications for the lifecycle of the child, which again has implications for society. There are great costs when members of society fall out of education and the labour market.

There are mainly three central reasons for the increase of share of children growing up in families with persistent low-income in Norway. The first and most important reason is that the group of children in migrant families where parents have low education and weak labour market attachment has increased (Epland and Kirkeberg, 2017). The second reason is that families with children have had lower revenue during recent years compared to families without children (Epland and Kirkeberg, 2016). The third reason is that public money transfers have not increased in line with wage increase, meaning that income from paid work has become even more important for the economy of a family (Epland and Kirkeberg, 2016).

In the period of 2015–17 the Norwegian government had a strategy targeted at children living in poverty. At the end of this three-year period all seven involved governmental branches published a report titled "Children who live in poverty – report on the work with the governmental strategy 2015–2017" (The Norwegian Directorate for Children, Youth and Family Affairs et al., 2018). The strategy had the CRC as guideline, and the report summarizes the knowledge and experiences from the work on following up this strategy in three years. Much of the information regarding child poverty, risk of child poverty and existing measures to combat poverty is based on this governmental report. The report gives account of several various measures which in total counted 64 measures (see appendix I page 188–193, The Norwegian Directorate for Children, Youth and Family Affairs et al., 2018). One can therefore hardly argue that Norway is not doing enough. The question remains whether Norway is doing it right.

Some measures are not directly targeted at reducing or combatting poverty's negative effects on children but do have implications for households in poverty and their children. Other measures are more specifically targeted at child poverty.

Norwegian authorities define the work against child poverty and risk of child poverty as a "wicked problem." Such problems are characterized by concerning several sectors and that it is difficult to subdivide problems into concrete areas of responsibilities. The sectors involved have different understandings of and perspectives on the problem, and causality can be unclear and partly unknown (Agency for Public Management and eGovernment, 2014).

Not only are perspectives, understandings and responsibilities of large variety but relevant measures also cover a broad range of strategies. One type of measure can be defined and characterized by its target. Measures can be universal or selective. By universal measures one talks about public strategies which are directed towards all citizens without distinguishing between groups or individuals. In Norway's welfare system this might be both monetary transfers (e.g. child allowance) as well as public services (e.g. health stations for families with young children, elementary and secondary school). As a supplement, Norway's welfare system provides selective targeted measures for certain groups or individuals. Measures that target certain groups within child poverty are often directed at immigrant families, single parents and families with a weak connection to the labour market, the latter often overlapping with the two other categories. In addition, measures can be distinguished by their purpose and aim. Some measures are implemented to reduce or even eradicate poverty, others to combat the long-term effects of children and youth's living conditions, while others again are implemented to improve the living conditions of children and youth in short term. The various measures relate to various areas of society effecting groups' and individuals' living conditions, that is: housing, health, work, education, income security and participation and inclusion.

To add to the complexity, in Norway municipalities have autonomy regarding local concerns within the boundaries of the national law. That means that municipalities can decide if and how they want to work on reducing, eradicating and combatting poverty and the risk of poverty. The risk of local autonomy lies in the large variety of the scope of services and measures municipalities offer. The implementation of children's economic, social and cultural rights and the implementation of social policies may differ greatly from one municipality to another. This variety might lead to unequal treatment of citizens depending on which municipality they live in.

Child poverty and the risk of child poverty is not only difficult to define, it is also a wicked problem including the risk of the pulverization of responsibility. In addition, it is a highly politicized question on which type of measure is best suited to reduce child poverty and combat its negative effects on individual's lifecycle. In the remaining space of this chapter, the discussion revolves around measures regarding improvement of income for persistent low-income families in Norway in light of the child's right to an adequate standard of living as laid down in CRC Article 27.

Social policies targeted at "risk of poverty" in Norway

Social benefits as cash transfers

Social policy targeted at families is challenging because it must balance measures which secure the welfare of the child with supporting parents' participation in the labour market. Workfare policy is the basis of much of Norwegian policy designs, meaning that it must pay off to work. Simultaneously, transfers between groups and persons shall equalize the differences in income and standard of living (NOU, 2017: 6, white paper on public support for families).

Child poverty and the risk of poverty in Norway is linked to the fact that parents or caregivers in the household have no or only a weak attachment to the Norwegian labour market. According to the Norwegian Labour and Welfare Administration in 2017, the combination of a growing number of citizens living on low income and a growing number of citizens with high capital income increases inequality in Norway. Higher numbers on unemployment and immigration are factors enhancing this development. Immigrant workers, other immigrants and single parents have less working activity than other groups of Norwegian society. Single parents, families with migration background and claimants of social assistance are overrepresented in the group of citizens with persistent low-income (Norwegian Labour and Welfare Administration, 2017).

Thus, an obvious social policy aim for reducing or eradicating child poverty is to strengthen these parents' affiliation to and long-term inclusion in the labour market. One way of ensuring that these parents want to work is to make it pay off. Low social benefits may provide the necessary incentive for (re)entering the labour market (Kostøl and Mogstad, 2014; Fevang et al., 2017).

The performance of cash transfers by the Norwegian social welfare system are deliberately kept low. The argument by politicians, including those criticizing the Norwegian government for not doing enough to combat child poverty, is that by increasing the income through transfer of social benefits, people lack the incentive to enter the labour market (Lura et al., 2017). The Norwegian Labour and Welfare Administration (2017) describes that social benefits such as social assistance, but also certain social insurance benefits are beneath the poverty line of 50% or 60% of the median income in Norway.

The European Social Charter Article 13 on the right to social assistance includes the right for everybody to adequate social assistance. The European Committee on Social Rights, supervisory body to the European Social Charter, to which Norway is a state party, has concluded in 2013 that:"the level of social assistance [in Norway] is inadequate." It further stated that the level of social assistance benefits falls well below the poverty threshold defined as 50% of median equivalized income and as calculated based on the Eurostat at risk-of-poverty threshold (The European Committee on Social Rights, 2013).

As mentioned previously, the Consumption Research Norway Institute (SIFO) has developed a minimum budget including necessary items, goods and activities for an ordinary household in Norway adjusted to various forms of household. This minimum budget can be used to assess reasonableness of public social benefits and the level of social assistance. According to Borgeraas (2016) the government guidelines on the level of social assistance is lower than what is calculated as a necessary minimum budget, which implies that these guidelines are too low to maintain a reasonable living standard.

Acknowledging that low social benefits may prove to motivate parents to (re) enter the labour market, it is to question if Norway is fulfilling its obligation under CRC Article 27 no. 3 with such low social assistance benefits. The wording of the state obligation is to "assist parents . . . to implement this right" pointing to the child's right to a standard of living adequate for the child's physical, mental, spiritual, moral and social development.

These low social assistance benefits are in my opinion not in accordance with the state's obligation to assist parents in their responsibility to ensure the child living conditions necessary for the child's development. Keeping payments that low can barely be considered as "appropriate measure" according to CRC Article 27 no. 3. However, the Norwegian state does not only assist parents in their primary responsibility through pecuniary transfers. It would therefore be incorrect to consider Norwegian social policy in light of the rights of the child to an adequate standard of living by only looking at social assistance benefits.

In the following sections, other measures assisting parents with low income will be considered and discussed in light of the state's human rights obligation.

Activation policies

Workfare as a basis for social policy has played well for a large part of Norwegian society with high numbers of employed adults. But for some, the way into the Norwegian labour market is extremely long and hard, whether this is due to lack of skills, caring responsibilities or other reasons.

The recent studies regarded effects of compulsory activities for young people between 18 and 25. The elder studies looked at the entire population of social assistance recipients. Their results were more ambiguous and splayed. These ambiguous research results on activation policy in Norway allows one to question if social policies based on low levels of social assistance benefits and workfare programmes are appropriate measures for reducing or eradicating children's risk of growing up in poverty.

Families with low income in Norway have often migrated to Norway mainly from areas like Asia, Africa and Latin America, as well as Eastern Europe. This group makes up 53% of low income households. Another large group of families with low incomes are single parent households (Norwegian Labour and Welfare Administration, 2017).

Norwegian Labour and Welfare Administration offers three different programmes for immigrants called The Chance to Work, The Introduction programme (for refugees) and The Qualifying Programme. The content of these programmes is under constant evaluation and rather frequent changes. A recent evaluation calls for new measures that increase the participants' formal competence required by the Norwegian labour market (Djuve et al., 2017). The programme The Chance to Work shows success for migrant women with originally low attachment to the labour market, having started education or entered work. At the same time, those refugees graduating from the introduction programme have an income level below 60% of the entire income of the population between 20 and 50 years of age. The income gap does not decrease, even five years later. The dependence on public benefits decreases, but income stays (Blom and Enes, 2015).

The results by studies on effects of activation policies and programmes in Norway are ambiguous, vary and are somewhat uncertain. Based on this, combined with critically low social assistance benefits, it is reasonable to question if these parts of the Norwegian social policies on reduction or eradication of risk of poverty for children and their families represent "appropriate measures" as required by CRC Article 27 no. 3.

Universal social services

The term 'to assist' does not specify what type of assistance. Norwegian social welfare provides not only social benefits in pecuniary form, but also rather generous rights-based social services, either highly subsidized or for free. Thus, the Norwegian state's choice of social policy does assist all families universally by providing public services as a common good for all. These universal types of social benefits in the form of services enjoy high legitimacy in Norwegian society, and therefore people are willing to contribute to the welfare state through taxes (NOU, 2017: 6). It is argued that possible negative consequences for children's development due to low income and hard living conditions are compensated for by these types of social services.

A movement from pecuniary social benefits to social services has been a wanted and supported policy in Norway since the 1990s (Grødem, 2017). The Solberg government of 2013 then also officially followed this "social services policy line" as a strategy for combatting poverty's negative effects (The Norwegian Directorate for Children, Youth and Family Affairs et al., 2018). In the white paper NOU, 2017: 6 on public support for families with children, the expert panel underlines that an important consideration in family policy must be to ensure good living conditions for children independently of the parents' socio-economic status, including the parents' status in relation to the labour market. The experts also stressed that support for families can prevent negative consequences in the future and stop the cycle of inheritance of poverty. To do so the expert panel suggests that family policy must support services like early child care, school and afterschool activities which at least partly can compensate for social differences between families social and/or economic background (NOU, 2017: 6). By that, the expert panel supports the policy line of social services and argues that the Norwegian state rather should choose to invest in social services than social pecuniary benefits for families.

It is for the state to assess, evaluate and choose social policies that are "appropriate measures to assist parents" (CRC Article 27 no. 3). Investing in social services that are either accessible for free or highly subsidized for those with low income, seems to be an appropriate measure for assisting parents in their primary responsibility. The question remains, however, if this choice of assistance recognizes the right of the child to a standard of living adequate for its physical, mental, spiritual, moral and social development. Do these social services contribute well enough to the development of the child, so we can conclude that the state is fulfilling its obligation to assist in the parents' responsibility to achieve the best possible development? Grødem (2017) states that:

> We have little updated knowledge of how it is to grow up with low income in such a rich society as the Norwegian, and which role free social services play for low-income families' quality of life.

(p. 200)

Though we have little updated knowledge on children's experiences, we have some knowledge of the effect of early public childcare, and free primary and higher secondary education's significance for children's inclusion in society at present and in the future. According to Frønes (2017), a society requiring highly skilled and well-educated labour demands social skills in combination with professional skills. The education system in Norway is not characterized by exams and competition as compared to other parts of the world, e.g. parts of Asia, but also in Norway the educational system is an arena for selection as well as development of skills (Frønes, 2017). Those children coming from families with low socio-economic status have low IQ results over time and their behavioural problems easily become school problems, which again can lead to future problems related to entering the labour market. What is known is that children of families with migration backgrounds and/or low income enjoy less early childcare; there exist barriers to attend after-school activities; and differences exist regarding school results, wellbeing in school and dropping out (The Norwegian Directorate for Children, Youth and Family Affairs et al., 2018).

Since future problems are connected to trouble early in a person's lifecycle, early intervention in a child's life are necessary for interrupting reproduction of poverty in families. Frønes (2017) argues that early investment in the development of social and educational skills among the youngest children is paramount for combatting the risk of poverty. He states that:

> Early support is basic; in modern children's developmental and educational marathon the same rules apply as in other marathons; one should not loose contact to the main field. If one does, motivation busts as one must run faster.
>
> *(p. 60)*

He argues therefore that instead of distribution of social pecuniary benefits or other economic cash transfers, social policy should put its emphasis on factors relevant to children's skills development, especially early child care (Frønes, 2017). This will ensure the child not losing contact with the main field.

The suggestion of investment in early childhood is in line with the CRC Committee's General Comment no. 7 (2005) on implementing children's rights in early childhood. In addition, General Comment no. 19 (2016) on budgeting for the realization of children's rights underlines the vital importance of investment in early childhood development with positive impact on children's ability to exercise their rights, breaking poverty cycles and bringing high economic returns. The Committee (General Comment no. 19) points out that:

> Underinvestment in children in their early years can be detrimental to cognitive development and can reinforce existing deprivations, inequalities and intergenerational poverty.
>
> *(section 50)*

164 Julia Köhler-Olsen

Even though we know that such investment in early childhood and public child-care can have positive effects, we also need to acknowledge that children coming from families with low-economic status today in general have difficulties to benefit from the existing services within the educational system. As Frønes (2017) accentuates, the risk of poverty and child poverty is to be understood in the perspective of possibilities. Low-income and/or low conditions of living might prevent children from using the possibilities that ensure them a future.

Human rights-based approach on social policies against poverty

After the presentation of three central lines of social policy in Norway, relevant for the reduction or eradication of risk of poverty and child poverty, I conclude that the Norwegian welfare system might improve its international obligation to assist parents with appropriate measures to ensure the child adequate living conditions for its development. The Norwegian model is perfectly designed to ensure good distribution of conditions for and chances in life. However, it is not enough to do better than others (Fløtten, 2017). It is visible that differences between households are increasing, and political aims with well-founded policies are necessary to hinder further inequality in conditions in life.

I would like to put forward human rights-based arguments for including the perspective of *substantive equality* and *perspective of child participation* in the design and development of social policy combatting poverty or risk of poverty for children and their families.

Substantive equality and the right to non-discrimination

According to the CESCR Committee General Comment no. 3 of 1998, one central and immediate part of state obligation is to implement any economic and social right without any discrimination. The child's right to non-discrimination is furthermore laid down in CRC Article 2. Access to a standard of living adequate for the child's physical, mental, spiritual, moral and social development must be ensured without discrimination. Furthermore, the assistance provided for parents must be provided for without discrimination.

Another way of dismantling the right to non-discrimination is to analyze social policies in light of the theory of *substantive equality*. Legal theorists have developed the term "substantive equality" by analyzing legal practice on the right to non-discrimination.

Substantive equality is a multidimensional concept (Fredman, 2016). Instead of addressing one single objective, such as equality of opportunity, equality of results or dignity, substantive equality pursues four complementary and interrelated objectives (McCrudden, 2008). The four dimensions of substantive equality are: *redistributive dimension, recognition dimension, participatory dimension* and *transformative dimension* (Fredman, 2016).

Among these four dimensions, the participatory dimension deserves special attention in the context of child rights. This dimension refers to social exclusion, whether through age, poverty, disability or confinement in the private sphere of the family (Fredman, 2016). In relation to the child's right to a standard of living which is adequate for its development, this links closely to the child's right to participate and be heard as laid down in CRC Article 12.

The white paper on public support for families, NOU (2017: 6) does mention children's rights and the four principles of the CRC on one page out of a 280 page report. The rights of the child are shortly explained under the headline of "central terms." At no stage in any of the discussions in the white paper are the rights of the child included in the various analyses or discussions. The expert panel, thus, is an example of what itself is written in the report (NOU, 2017: 6):

> There has been criticism on unilaterally focus on social transfers without including the child as a competent actor. The child's and children's needs are not considered, and the child and children are conceived as indirect recipients of cash transfers and services through the unity of the family.
>
> *(p. 35)*

Children's experiences, their voices as competent actors not being included in policy design, is also criticized by the Norwegian Ombudsman for Children. In its last report to the UN Committee on the Rights of the Child in 2017, the Norwegian Ombudsman for Children (2017: 4) stated that: "Children in vulnerable situations are the ones facing the highest risk of breaches in the fulfilment of their rights."

Not being included with one's own experience in policy design and implementation is per se a violation of the child's right to participation according to CRC Article 12. By not listening to children's knowledge, experiences and suggestions, part of the decision making on what is best for children, as required by CRC Article 3, will lack an important piece of valuable information. Furthermore, not having the perspective of children themselves in social policy design and implementation can lead to the violation of CRC Article 27 on the right to a standard of living adequate for the child's development.

In the report on the governmental work on the strategy against child poverty from 2015–2017, one of the feedback from non-governmental, voluntary organizations is that it is vital that children participate, that the voices of children and youth are included and heard in the development and implementation of policies. The organizations underline that children's and youth's perspectives must be safeguarded (The Norwegian Directorate for Children, Youth and Family Affairs et al. (2018). In the evaluation of the strategy against child poverty with its 64 measures, it is paramount to ask children and youth if the measures are appropriate to the challenges they face.

Heimer and Palme (2016) highlight that child welfare thinking is often based on a "social investment approach," which is placing children at the centre regarding them as "becomings." Approaching child welfare thinking using children's right to

166 Julia Köhler-Olsen

participation as a basis would lead to placing children at the centre by regarding them as "beings." According to the authors:

> Thus, a reconceptualization of child welfare, in line with the CRC, suggests that children's right to participation makes up an integrated and a constitutive part of the concept of child welfare, in the sense that traditional dimensions of welfare are partially conditioned on the right to voice.
>
> *(p. 439)*

I agree with Heimer and Palme that child welfare must be conceptualized in a way that integrates the child's right to participation to detect what is a standard of living adequate for the child's physical, mental, spiritual, moral and social development, ref. CRC Article 27 no. 1. However, although I believe that the child's 'being' influences the development of the child, the CRC in this section of Article 27 is focussing on the child as a 'becoming' by using the term "development." Thus, one must argue that Article 27 no. 1 must be understood in light of Article 12 and Article 3 to highlight and put emphasis on the child's right to an adequate standard of living also in the situation and context the child is situated in as 'being' in its present life.

Furthermore, Heimer and Palme (2016) argue that children should be viewed as separate entities, not simply as indirect recipients of income or services through the family unit. However, the wording of the CRC Article 27 must then be read in a rather broad understanding. The member states to the CRC signed up for a wording, that explicitly points to the parents' primary responsibility "to secure, within their abilities and financial capacities, the conditions of living necessary for the child's development." In addition, the member states are obliged to assist the parents in their effort to implement the child's right to a standard of living adequate for its development, not to assist the child directly and as a separate entity. Article 27, thus, does in my point of view support the conception of children being indirect recipients of income or services through the family unit. That being said, one must be aware that the CRC establishes minimum rights for children. Member states can always ensure rights with a larger scope than those laid down in the Convention. It is therefore not in violation of the Convention if social policies are aimed directly at the children. In my point of view, however, the CRC does not require the approach of viewing children as separate entities related to social welfare policies.

Yet, Article 12 does require at the same time that children's views on their situation at present and for the future are vital and central perspectives in the design of social policies in general, as well as in concrete decisions regarding assistance to its parents or other caretakers.

Conclusions

A discussion of some of the main Norwegian social policies on the risk of poverty and child poverty in light of the child's right to a standard of living adequate for its development must start by presenting the Norwegian state's obligation according to CRC Article 27. The main feature is that the state has a subsidiary responsibility when it comes to ensuring that the child experiences an adequate standard of living; the parents or caretakers being primarily responsible. Furthermore, the wording of Article 27 no. 3 places responsibility on the state to assist parents. This implies indirect responsibility of the state towards the child, allowing the state to see the child's social welfare as part of a family unit. Though having a subsidiary and indirect responsibility, the Norwegian state is obligated to assist with appropriate measures in a non-discriminatory manner, taking immediate and targeted steps that assist parents in their efforts.

Acknowledging the continuous effort by the Norwegian state to reduce poverty and combat the negative effects of poverty, it is from a human rights-based perspective relevant to ask whether the measures chosen are appropriate. In this chapter, I have focussed on three main strains of social policy: social benefits cash transfers, workfare and universal social services.

The Norwegian state keeps social benefits as cash transfers deliberately on a low level to ensure motivation for those receiving these benefits to enter the labour market. Norway has been criticized for maintaining social assistance benefits being below the poverty income line. Knowing that those living with the risk of poverty or experiencing poverty are recipients of social assistance, this low level of cash transfer is not an appropriate measure to assist parents to secure the child living conditions necessary for its development.

If low levels of cash transfers would lead to access to the labour market, one might defend the levels of social benefits. However, activation policies targeted at those living on low income to support them in their effort to (re)enter the labour market show rather uncertain effects of success. This means that a family and the children in this family might need to live on too-low cash transfers for an extended period, longer than anticipated by the state.

Even though a child grows up in a household with low income, the child's development might be ensured by assistance, which is more directly targeted at the child, that being universal social services for children in the form of early child care, school or health care. What is known about these types of universal social services is that they manage to level out the playing field between children's various backgrounds only to a certain degree. Early intervention is necessary to prevent harm from growing up in a low-income household. That means that children from low-income families must spend their days in public childcare. At the moment, those children are among the fewest attending early childcare. When attending school, the differences between children based on socio-economic status already has consequences on how they can perform in the education system.

In conclusion, the Norwegian state needs to reconsider the level of social benefits as cash transfers, especially social assistance. It needs to consider if workfare with the distinct types of activating measures are appropriate for low-income households with children. Furthermore, the state must not only use the social policy of universal social services to combat child poverty. Children are not necessarily able to benefit from these universal social services due to their socio-economic background.

168 Julia Köhler-Olsen

One suggestion to design and implement social policies more in line with children's human right to an adequate standard of living is to apply a human-rights–based approach. One of the immediate state obligations, according to the CRC, is to implement human rights without discrimination. The perspective of substantive equality with the four highly relevant dimensions – the redistributive, the recognition, the participatory and the transformative dimension –can be of assistance for doing so. In addition, the child's and children's right to participation might lead to new and different insights on which types of social policies would best serve the interest of the child and children.

References

Aaberge, R., Bhuller, M., Langørgen, A. and Mostad, M. (2010) "The distributional impact of public services when needs differ", *Journal of Public Economics* [Online], 94(9–10), 549–562. Available at: doi.org/10.1016/j.jpubeco.2010.06.004 (Accessed 10 March 2018).

Agency for Public Management and eGovernment (2014) *Mot alle odds? Veier til samordning i norsk forvaltning.* [Online] Difi-rapport 2014:07. Available at: www.difi.no/rap port/2014/11/mot-alle-odds-veier-til-samordning-i-norsk-forvaltning (Accessed 4 July 2018).

Arosemena, G. (2015) "Retrieving the differences: The distinctiveness of the welfare aspect of human rights form the perspective of judicial protection", *Human Rights Review* [Online], 16(3), 239–255. Available at: doi-org.ezproxy.hioa.no/10.1007/s12142-014-0333-3 (Accessed 3 July 2015).

Bilchitz, D. (2007) *Poverty and fundamental rights: The justification and enforcement of socioeconomic rights.* Oxford: Oxford University Press.

Blom, S. and Enes, A. W. (2015) *Introduksjonsordningen – en resultatstudie.* Statistisk Sentralbyrå, Rapporter 2015/36 [Online]. Available at: www.ssb.no/utdanning/artikler-og-publikasjoner/_attachment/237747?_ts=14f68b95ab0 (Accessed 20 March 2018).

Borgeraas, E. (2016) "Minimumsbudsjett for forbruksutgifter. Et forbruksbasert fattigdomsmål. Oppdragsrapport no. 14–2016", *Forbruksforskningsinstituttet SIFO* [Online]. Available at: file:///C:/Users/juliak/Downloads/PN7–2017%20Forbrukstiln%C3%A6rming% 20til%20barnefattigdom%20%20(2).pdf (Accessed 10 March 2018).

———. (2017) "Forbruksbasert fattigdomsmål – forbrukstilnærming til barnefattigdom. Prosjektnotat no. 7–2017", *Forbruksforskningsinstituttet SIFO* [Online]. Available at: file:///C:/Users/juliak/Downloads/PN7–2017%20Forbrukstiln%C3%A6rming%20 til%20barnefattigdom%20%20(1).pdf (Accessed 10 March 2018).

Djuve, A. B., Kavli, H. C., Sterri, E. B. and Bråten, B. (2017) *Introduksjonsprogram og norskopplæring. Hva virker – for hvem?* Fafo-rapport 2017:31 [Online]. Available at: www.fafo.no/index.php/zoo-publikasjoner/fafo-rapporter/item/introduksjonsprogram-og-norskop plaering (Accessed 2 July 2018).

Eddy, K. (2006) "Welfare rights and conflicts of rights", *Res Publica* [Online], 12(4), 337–356. Available at: dx.doi.org/10.1007/s11158-006-9022-7 (Accessed 3 July 2018).

Epland, J. and Kirkeberg, M. I. (2016) *Barnefamilienes inntekter, formue og gjeld 2004–2014.* Rapporter 2016/11. Statistisk sentralbyrå [Online]. Available at: www.ssb.no/inntekt-og-for bruk/artikler-og-publikasjoner/barnefamilienes-inntekter-formue-og-gjeld-2004-2014 (Accessed 15 March 2018).

———. (2017) *Ett av ti barn tilhører en husholdning med vedvarende lavinntekt.* Statistisk sentralbyrå [Online]. Available at: www.ssb.no/inntekt-og-forbruk/artikler-og-publikasjoner/

ett-av- ti-barn-tilhorer-en-husholdning-med-vedvarende-lavinntekt (Accessed 15 March 2018).

Epland, J., Kirkeberg, M. I. and Revold, M. K. (2016) "Sosiale indikatorer for barn og barnefamilier", in E. L. Omholt (ed.), *Økonomi og levekår for ulike lavinntektsgrupper 2016*. Rapporter 2016/30. Statistisk sentralbyrå [Online]. Available at: www.ssb.no/inntekt-og-forbruk/artikler-og-publikasjoner/okonomi-og-levekar-for-ulike-lavinntektsgrup per-2016 (Accessed 15 March 2018).

European Committee on Social Rights (2013) *Conclusions 2013 – Norway – Article 13–1* [Online] ECSR Doc. 2013/def/NOR/13/1/EN. Available at: http://hudoc.esc.coe.int/eng?i=2013/def/NOR/13/1/EN (Accessed 15 March 2018).

Fevang, E., Hardoy, I. and Røed, K. (2017) "Temporary disability and economic incentives", *Economic Journal* [Online], 127(603), 1410–1432. Available at: doi.org/10.1111/ecoj.12345

Fløtten, T. (2017) "Den norske modellen i et oppvekstperspektiv", in Barne- ungdoms- og familiedirektoratet, *Oppvekstrapporten 2017* [Online]. Available at: www.bufdir.no/Page Files/32639/Oppvekstrapporten_2017.pdf (Accessed 1 March 2018).

Fløtten, T. and Nielsen, R. A. (2015) "Barnefattigdom – en kunnskapsoppsummering", in Barne-, likestillings- og inkluderingsdepartementet, Barn som lever i fattigdom. *Regjeringens strategi (2015–2017)* [Online]. Available at: www.regjeringen.no/no/dokumenter/barn-som-lever-i-fattigdom/id2410107/ (Accessed 1 March 2018).

Fløtten, T. and Pedersen, A. (2008) "Fattigdom som mangel på sosialt aksepterte levekår", in I. Harsløf and S. Seim (eds.), *Fattigdommens dynamikk. Perspektiver på marginalisering i det norske samfunnet*. 3rd ed. Oslo, Norway: Universitetsforlaget, pp. 34–61.

Fredman, S. (2008) *Human rights transformed: Positive rights and positive duties*. Oxford: Oxford University Press.

———. (2016) "Emerging from the shadows: Substantive equality and article 14 of the European convention on human rights", *Human Rights Law Review* [Online], 16(2), 273–301. Available at: doi.org/10.1093/hrlr/ngw001 (Accessed 4 March 2018).

Frønes, I. (2017) "Barnefattigdom i kompetansesamfunnet". In Barne- ungdoms- og familiedirektoratet, *Oppvekstrapporten 2017* [Online]. Available at: www.bufdir.no/Page Files/32639/Oppvekstrapporten_2017.pdf (Accessed 25 March 2018).

Grødem, A. S. (2017) "Farvel til den barnevennlige Velferdsstaten?" in Barne- ungdoms- og familiedirektoratet, *Oppvekstrapporten 2017* [Online]. Available at: www.bufdir.no/Page Files/32639/Oppvekstrapporten_2017.pdf (Accessed 26 March 2018).

Heimer, M. and Palme, J. (2016) "Rethinking child policy post-UN convention on the rights of the child: Vulnerable children's welfare in Sweden", *Journal on Social Policy* [Online], 45(3), 435–452. Available at: doi.org/10.1017/S0047279415000744 (Accessed 4 July 2018.

Kostøl, A. R. and Mogstad, M. (2014) "How financial incentives induce disability insurance recipients to return to work", *American Economic Review* [Online], 104(2), 624–655. Available at: www.aeaweb.org/articles?id=10.1257/aer.104.2.624 (Accessed 3 April 2018).

Langford, M. (2008) "The justiciability of social rights: From practice to theory", in M. Langford (ed.), *Social rights jurisprudence. Emerging trends in international and comparative law*. Cambridge: Cambridge University Press, pp. 3–45.

Lura et al. (2017) "Lysbakken sa at 98.000 barn lever i fattigdom. Stemmer det?" [Online]. Available at: www.nrk.no/norge/lysbakken-sa-at-98.000-barn-lever-i-fattigdom.-stemmer-det_-1.13460736 (Accessed 22 March 2018).

McCrudden, C. (2008) "Human dignitz and judicial interpretation of human rights", *European Journal of International Law* [Online], 19(4), 655–724. Available at: doi.org/10.1093/ejil/chn043

Norwegian Labour and Welfare Administration (2017) "Fattigdom og levekår i Norge", *Tilstand og utviklingstrekk – 2017*, NAV-rapport Nr. 4/2017. [Online]. Available at: www.nav.no/no/NAV+og+samfunn/Kunnskap/Analyser+fra+NAV/NAV+rapportserie/NAV+rapporter/fattigdom-og-levek%C3%A5r-i-norge.tilstand-og-utviklingstrekk-2017 (Accessed 1 March 2018).

NOU 2017:6. "White paper on public support for families" [Online]. Available at: www.regjeringen.no/no/dokumenter/nou-2017-6/id2540981/ (Accessed 4 March 2018).

The Norwegian Children Ombudsman (2017) "The UN Convention on the rights of the child – Supplementary report" [Online]. Available at: http://barneombudet.no/wp-content/uploads/2018/02/The-Ombudsman-for-Children-in-Norway-Supplementary-Report-to-UN-2017.pdf (Accessed 15 March 2018).

The Norwegian Directorate for Children, Youth and Family Affairs et al. (2018) "Barn som lever i fattigdom", *Rapport om arbeidet med regjeringens strategi 2015–2017* [Online]. Available at: www.bufdir.no/Bibliotek/Dokumentside/?docId=BUF00004373 (Accessed 1 March 2018).

UN Committee on Economic, Social and Cultural Rights (1998) "General Comment no. 3 on state obligation regarding economic, social and cultural rights" [Online]. Available at: https://tbinternet.ohchr.org/_layouts/treatybodyexternal/Download.aspx?symbolno=INT%2fCESCR%2fGEC%2f4758&Lang=en (Accessed 1 March 2018).

UN Committee on Economic, Social and Cultural Rights, Fifth session (1990) General Comment no. 3: The nature of states parties' obligations (art. 2, para. 1, of the Covenant).

UN Committee on the Rights of the Child (2005) General Comment no. 7 on implementing child rights in early childhood. UN Doc. CRC/C/GC/7/Rev.1 [Online]. Available at: https://tbinternet.ohchr.org/_layouts/treatybodyexternal/Download.aspx?symbolno=CRC%2fC%2fGC%2f7%2fRev.1&Lang=en (Accessed 1 March 2018).

———. (2016a) General Comment no. 19 on public budgeting for the realization of children's rights. UN Doc. CRC/C/GC/7/Rev.1 [Online]. Available at: https://tbinternet.ohchr.org/_layouts/treatybodyexternal/Download.aspx?symbolno=CRC%2fC%2fGC%2f19&Lang=en (Accessed 1 March 2018).

———. (2016b) General Comment no. 20 on the implementation of rights of children during adolescence. UN Doc. CRC/C/GC/20 [Online]. Available at: https://tbinternet.ohchr.org/_layouts/treatybodyexternal/Download.aspx?symbolno=CRC%2fC%2fGC%2f20&Lang=en (Accessed 1 March 2018).

UN Covenant on Economic, Social and Cultural Rights (1966) [Online] Available at: www.ohchr.org/EN/ProfessionalInterest/Pages/CESCR.aspx (Accessed 1 March 2018).

UN Convention on the Rights of the Child (1989) [Online] Available at: www.ohchr.org/EN/ProfessionalInterest/Pages/CRC.aspx (Accessed 1 March 2018).

With, M. L. and Thorsen, L. R. (2018) "Materielle og sosiale mangler i den norske befolkningen – Resultater fra Levekårsundersøkelsen EU-SILC", Statistisk sentralbyrå, 2018/7 [Online]. Available at: www.ssb.no/inntekt-og-forbruk/artikler-og-publikasjoner/_attachment/339727?_ts=161bdb9a620 (Accessed 3 March 2018).

Young, K. (2012) *Constituting economic and social rights*. Oxford: Oxford University Press.

9

IMPLEMENTERS OF LAW OR POLICYMAKERS TOO?

A study of street-level bureaucracy in India

Amrutha Jose Pampackal

Introduction

"We do everything as per the law (*niyamam*). Government issues orders and we do everything by following those." This was the response of a bureaucrat at a block-level Tribal Extension Office in Kerala, India, on being asked how he takes decisions on local issues on a day-to-day basis.[1] I was interacting with street-level bureaucrats as part of a study on the role of bureaucratic behaviour in determining policy direction. The particular case being evaluated was the Tribal Resettlement and Development Mission, a programme set up by the government of Kerala to distribute land to *adivasis* (indigenous/tribal peoples) and provide assistance for their development. The response by the street-level bureaucrat was just one of the many instances where bureaucrats talked of their reliance on law for decision making. The statement is at times in a tone of defence, trying to convey to a complainant that the bureaucrat is not acting according to his or her wishes, but simply following what he or she is expected to under the law.

Interestingly, the Malayalam term *niyamam* used to refer to 'law' also translates to 'rule'. This widens the scope of the term to include aspects of public policy that might normally be distinguished from law. In my interactions, street-level bureaucrats were found to use the term colloquially to loosely refer to legislation, government circulars as well as other forms of written instructions and rules issued by the government. Seeking the support of *niyamam* (be it in any of the previously mentioned varieties) to back their actions helps street-level bureaucrats to justify their choices and even claim objectivity, even if that claim might not be entirely in sync with the subjective discretion exercised by them in everyday decision making.

The perception of bureaucrats as mere followers and implementers of existing laws is rooted in some of the earlier notions that treat bureaucracy as "not an autonomous brain in its own right but rather the neutral executer of plans made by others" (Sayre, 1964: 224). Such notions are in sync with the common understanding of separation of powers within a government where the legislative branch is responsible for the making of laws, the executive is responsible for administration of the laws enacted by the legislature and the judiciary is vested with the responsibility of interpreting laws and applying those to resolve controversies. Such a division recognizes formulation of legislation and policies as the core responsibility of the legislature and the political executive, while the permanent executive (bureaucracy) and the courts are expected to play an active role in the implementation phase. However, commencing with Barclay and Birkland (1998), there has emerged a body of literature that persuades public policy scholars to recognize the role of "courts as policymakers" and thereby try developing a more holistic picture of the policy process. In the Indian context too, there has been an increase in literature on judicial activism (Birchfield and Corsi, 2010; Bhagwati, 1985; Dam, 2005; Verma, 2001), particularly around public interest litigations and specifically the case of 'PUCL vs Union of India and others' (2001), which has helped in showing the policymaking possibilities of the judiciary.[2] However, the literature on public policy and bureaucracy in India still tends to view street-level bureaucrats as mere policy implementers, without much recognition of their potential to contribute to development of laws and policies.[3] There is some recognition of the contribution of higher levels of bureaucracy to policymaking, may be because they often play a direct role in policymaking by scripting policies and laws. Development of subordinate laws, where the executive branch is delegated the task of framing rules/orders/schemes to supplement a primary legislation, is an important avenue for upper echelons of bureaucracy to contribute to law making. Since TRDM, the programme that will be studied in this chapter, is not backed by legislation, we do not get to see this aspect of bureaucracy's role in law making. However, we are still able to witness another crucial role played by bureaucracy which, in the words of R.B Jain (1987: 34), occurs when "the top echelons of bureaucracy conceive and formulate recommendations in respect of policy decisions that the government may announce." Thus, while it is easy to identify instances where higher levels of bureaucracy participate in different stages of policymaking, this chapter recognizes that increased attention is needed to understand the role of street-level bureaucracy in the process. One has to understand what the task of doing "everything as per the law" entails and evaluate if, in doing so, a street-level bureaucrat has the potential to co-create public policy and laws, and not just follow them.

In the light of the need to answer such questions, this chapter attempts to analyze the day-to-day practices of street-level bureaucrats to explore how they contribute to policymaking, even while performing their commonly recognized duty of implementing policies at the local level. This exploration is being undertaken by using the case of Tribal Resettlement and Development Mission (TRDM), a developmental policy for *adivasis*, to conduct an in-depth study of behaviour of local-level bureaucracy. Such a case study is relevant due to various reasons.

Firstly, understanding the practices of street-level bureaucrats can throw light on the dynamics of state-society interaction at the local level. This is because they are the representatives of the state who directly interact with citizens and form the first point of contact within the state for common man (Gupta, 2012; Lipsky, 1980). However, there is a dearth of studies in the context of developing countries that examine street-level bureaucracy with an intention to understand how their practices are shaped by interaction with the policy text as well as the local environment. While there is a rich canvass of literature in the western context that analyzes behaviour of street-level bureaucrats (Brodkin, 1997; Evans and Harris, 2004; Kelly, 1994; Lipsky, 1980; Meyers and Vorsanger, 2007; Prottas, 1979; Schaffer, 1973; Self, 2009), it is only of limited relevance for developing countries like India where the nature of state-society interactions is more complex. The penetration of social forces into the formal structures of the state makes the boundary between the state and society blurred (Fuller and Harris, 2001; Gupta, 1995; Harris-White, 1991) in such contexts. This difference in nature of the state, in turn, gives way to difference in the drivers of bureaucratic discretion between the two contexts. Hence, it is important to add to the limited literature on street-level bureaucracy that exists in contexts like India (Crook and Ayee, 2006; Gupta, 2012; Mathur, 1970; Riggs, 1961).

Secondly, considering the emphasis given by street-level bureaucrats to 'law' (such as legislation, rules, policies, government orders, administrative guidelines etc.) in defending their actions, this study will focus on the street-level bureaucrats' understanding of government orders on TRDM that they help execute. This helps to fill the gap in existing studies on street-level bureaucracy in India, which do not provide enough analysis of policy text. The existing narratives are centred on particular themes such as "the structural violence" committed on the poor through bureaucratic actions (Gupta, 2012) or the socio-environmental factors that shape bureaucratic behaviour (Mathur, 1970).

Thirdly, the case of TRDM gives an avenue for exploring *adivasis'* experience of the state through local bureaucracy. *Adivasis* are one of the most marginalized of the social sections in India and are therefore, the intended beneficiaries of a large number of social policies. Capturing their experience of the state is crucial in understanding if the policy process and public service delivery systems are equipped to capture the needs of such *adivasis* and respond to them. While capturing *adivasis'* experience of the state is not the central focus of this chapter, it nevertheless offers insights on the topic by presenting various dimensions of their interactions with the local-level TRDM officials and their perceptions about the officials.

Finally, by raising questions on the role of street-level bureaucrats in policymaking, this study tries to re-evaluate some of the prominent notions on the separation of powers within government and the various stages constituting the policy process.

Understanding the context: locating TRDM within the history of land policies in Kerala

The Tribal Resettlement and Development Mission is a government programme that came into being in 2001 as the culmination of decades of struggle by *adivasis*

174 Amrutha Jose Pampackal

in the state of Kerala, India for land. Since the time of British rule in India, *adivasis* have faced the brunt of land alienation, having to flee the forestlands that they had full control over for centuries. While the Constitution of India adopted in 1950 recognized 'right to property' as a fundamental right, it was later deleted to facilitate equitable land distribution. Since land was defined as a 'state subject', individual state governments formed after Indian independence tried implementing their own versions of land reforms.[4] While Kerala is one of the very few states hailed for its successful land reforms (Isaac and Tharakan, 1995; Mannathukkaren, 2011), *adivasis* in the state did not benefit from many of the reforms, and alienation of tribal land continued even after independence (Bijoy, 1999). In the 1990s, when there was a spike in atrocities against *adivasis* in Kerala, the social movements for *adivasi* land struggle strengthened, resulting in 48 days of continuous protest in front of the secretariat of the state government in 2001 (Sreerekha, 2010). As a result, the government of Kerala signed an agreement in October 2001 promising one to five acres of land to *adivasis* who were landless or had only small land holdings. The Tribal Resettlement and Development Mission (TRDM) was set up to implement the provisions of this agreement. In addition to the goal of land distribution, the mission also had the stated goal of catering to "overall welfare" of the *adivasis* (SCSTDD, 2001).

Despite the lofty goals of TRDM, the progress of its implementation has been tardy and discreditable. While the mission had identified 53,472 eligible families in 2001 itself, land has been distributed to only 7,033 families as of March 2016. Even in the cases where families were allotted land and resettled, issues of poor quality of land, inadequate housing and insensitivity to tribal community practices are ample (George and Pampackal, 2017).

Bureaucratic system for TRDM implementation: the importance of street-level bureaucracy

In order to understand the role played by the street-level bureaucracy, it is important to understand the bureaucratic machinery for administration of TRDM. The bureaucratic structure for TRDM consists of two sets of bureaucratic arrangements: a) inter-departmental committees constituted for approving projects and overseeing implementation, and b) individual bureaucrats within the Scheduled Tribes Development Department (STDD) of the government of Kerala, which is the nodal ministry in charge of TRDM implementation. The inter-departmental committees include

1   an Empowered Mission Committee which looks at the policy matters related to functioning of TRDM, approves projects and suggests solutions to problems faced by the Mission on field;
2   a State Mission constituted to implement the decisions of Empowered Mission Committee and bring in regulations necessary for smooth functioning of TRDM on field; and

3 a District Mission under the chairmanship of district collector to oversee and take decisions on district-level implementation of TRDM.

All the three committees are groups that meet only couple of times a year and are composed of bureaucrats from various departments whose services for TRDM are available for only a few days a year. Hence, most of the day-to-day implementation is managed by bureaucrats within the STDD. The structure of TRDM bureaucracy within the STDD is depicted in Figure 9.1 and explained in the following.

Since the focus of this chapter is on understanding the practices of street-level bureaucracy, only limited description is being provided about the state-level and district-level bureaucracy. The important point to note about the higher levels of bureaucracy represented in Figure 9.1 is that there are very few officials, other than clerks, who are allocated full-time responsibility for TRDM implementation. When data was collected for this study in 2015–16, even the TRDM chief who is chairman of the state-level mission had many responsibilities outside of TRDM administration.

At the local level, it is the TRDM site manager who is in charge of every single matter related to TRDM. Site managers are placed only in areas where there are many TRDM settlements and therefore, there are only four such positions in the entire state. The area under a site manager is vast and each of the four site managers have to oversee at least 600 families spread across multiple settlements in one or more administrative blocks in their respective districts. In areas where there are no TRDM site managers, it is the project officer who supervises TRDM affairs along with his or her other duties.

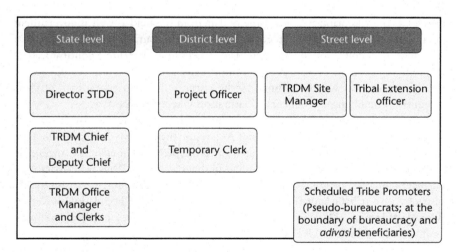

FIGURE 9.1 Bureaucratic structure for TRDM implementation within STDD

Source: Author's depiction based on information collected from STDD head office

176 Amrutha Jose Pampackal

A Tribal Extension Officer (TEO) is placed at the block-level. At times there is more than one TEO in a block if the population of *adivasis* in the block is very high. TRDM site managers and TEOs are officers of equal ranking in the bureaucratic hierarchy. The difference however is that while the TRDM site manager is responsible for TRDM alone, the TEO is in charge of all matters related to *adivasi* welfare and therefore has both TRDM beneficiaries and other *adivasi* families under the purview of his work. Even though a TEO is not assigned explicit responsibilities related to TRDM, it is he who is present at the local office and hence becomes the nearest point of contact for *adivasis*. Since a TRDM site manager has to travel to multiple sites each day, in many cases, it is the TEO who is immediately approached by the TRDM beneficiaries for most of their TRDM related needs.

The site manager is assisted in site-level management of TRDM by Scheduled Tribe (ST) promoters, a set of educated *adivasis* who have been appointed by the STDD to act as an effective link between the government and the *adivasis*. They are selected after an interview in order to "function as *facilitators* [italics mine] in tribal areas for channelizing and extending the benefits of tribal development schemes to the STs" (STDD, 2014). They are appointed on the basis of renewable one-year contracts and are paid honorarium, not salary, and cannot strictly be considered government bureaucrats.

The preceding presentation of bureaucratic hierarchy shows that the tasks at the hand of a street-level bureaucrat like TRDM manager is huge as, apart from temporary clerks, he is the only official in the current administrative system who is fully in charge of TRDM.

Methods

Both primary and secondary data were collected for the study.[5] However, the main source of data was primary, comprising of data from the field as well as government documents. There were four categories of people who came under the purview of field-level data collection: bureaucrats, *adivasis*, *adivasi* leaders/local political leaders and representatives of NGOs/people's movements. Sample size for various categories of interviewees was determined by the purpose of interviewing each of these categories, employing the concept of saturation wherever necessary.

To ensure that the findings of the study are reliable, it was decided that fieldwork should not be limited to a single district. As a result, the top two districts in the state in terms of ST population were selected since the presence of *adivasis* is negligible in most of the other districts. This resulted in the selection of Wayanad district with a tribal population of 151,443 (31.2% of total ST population in Kerala) and Idukki district with a tribal population of 55,815 (11.5% of total ST population in Kerala) (Census of India, 2011). Within each district, the gram panchayat where maximum land was allotted under TRDM was selected.[6]

To study the role of policy text in shaping bureaucratic behaviour, two sources were relied upon: policy text and bureaucrats. The process involved referring to policy text and interacting with bureaucrats in a cyclical manner to understand how the bureaucrats interpret the text and how their actions were being guided by the various guidelines specified in government orders. For this study, policy text is primarily composed of the government orders that have been issued by STDD between November 09, 2001 when TRDM was constituted and November 30, 2015 which marks the beginning of the fieldwork for this study. Since TRDM is a policy not backed by a legislation, it is the government orders that form the text of the policy. However, other written documents like circulars, file notings and official letters by senior bureaucrats and Minister for Tribal Welfare also form part of the written text that guides the functioning of lower level bureaucracy and were referred to as part of the study wherever available.

Understanding the local ecological factors that shape bureaucratic behaviour involved in-depth interviews with bureaucrats and observation of their working patterns while situating them in the local socio-political and cultural setting. Data was collected from different levels of bureaucrats ranging from street-level bureaucrats to officials at the state head office. More data was collected from the street-level bureaucrats as they are the primary subjects of the study. Data was also obtained from *adivasis*, their leaders and local NGOs to understand their perceptions of bureaucratic behaviour as shaped by their interactions with the street-level TRDM bureaucrats. Apart from various categories of people, file notings made by the bureaucrats were studied as they are sources that throw light on the process through which opinions are given by bureaucrats and decisions are made.[7] File notings also threw light on the time taken for each level of decision making as all recordings are accompanied by date stamps.

Throughout the period of study, observations were made of both the participants and the setting. It supported the interview process as contextual questions could be framed based on what was observed on ground. The chief advantage of observation was that it helped in ensuring that inferences are not drawn from interview responses alone. Considering the busy schedule of street-level bureaucrats who could not be expected to spare enough time to interact with, observation came in as a handy tool to study the practices of street-level bureaucrats as I was given permission to spend time at the local office to observe the daily routine and attend various meetings, both internal and with the *adivasi* beneficiaries. Doing so provided the opportunity to witness live the interaction between different tiers of bureaucracy and the communications between street-level bureaucrats and *adivasi* beneficiaries. It also exposed me to local gossip about bureaucrats and some of the unexpected scenarios that bureaucrats had to face on ground.

Policy text and its multiple interpretations: the scope for exercise of discretion by street-level bureaucrats

In this section, I first try to illustrate how the policy text pertaining to TRDM, that is the various forms of official documents that govern TRDM, are very weak in content and filled with ambiguities, omissions and contradictions. I argue that this weakness in content accentuates the importance of street-level bureaucratic

178 Amrutha Jose Pampackal

practices in determining policy direction as the gaps in the policy text are left for the street-level bureaucrats to fill. If the policy text is clear on what the bureaucrat is expected to do, the scope for exercise of bureaucratic discretion may largely be constrained even if it cannot fully be eliminated. While there are various ways in which a street-level bureaucrat can easily subvert even well-defined, clearly outlined policies by ignoring or violating the guidelines or rules it entails, the weakness in policy text lets him or her exercise discretion without being 'lawless'. The purpose of this section is to demonstrate how the intentional or unintentional interpretations of policy text by street-level bureaucrats interact with the sociopolitical and administrative environment he is immersed in to shape the direction that policy takes on ground. I attempt to do so by identifying at least some kinds of ambiguities that are present in the policy text on TRDM and analyzing how these ambiguous spaces shape bureaucratic decision making.

Ambiguity in policy goals

In any central legislation of the government of India, it is easy to locate the intended goals of the Act as there is a section titled 'Statement of Objects and Reasons'. Unlike a policy that is implemented in accordance with the clauses of an act passed by the legislative wing of the government, TRDM was not conceived as part of any particular legislation. It is a programme that is governed by administrative orders issued by the executive at the state level. These orders do not clearly convey the intended goals or the reason for adopting the policy. The order issued by the Scheduled Castes and Scheduled Tribes Development Department (SCSTDD, 2001) which instituted TRDM states that the aim of the programme is to provide land to landless *adivasis* and *adivasis* with little land, ensuring that at least one acre of land is given to each family for resettlement and activities for their overall welfare are undertaken. In areas where more land is available, up to five acres of land may also be given. The rest of the order deals with the nature of the committees constituted for the purpose. There is no statement provided in the text of the 2001 order or any of the subsequent orders on why it is important to give one to five acres of land to *adivasis* or what purpose this initiative will serve. Even while the policy is titled "Tribal Resettlement and Development Mission," the development goals it seeks to achieve are not mentioned. The order states 'overall welfare' as an intended goal of the policy, but it is hard to define what constitutes overall welfare of *adivasis*. What a bureaucrat perceives as welfare might be different from an *adivasi*'s conception of his or her welfare.

Because of the ambiguity in government orders regarding the goals of the policy, the bureaucrats too are not clear about what the policy seeks to achieve. For instance, one senior bureaucrat at the state-level office of STDD recollects that the original aim of the policy was to distribute land to 'landless' *adivasi* families alone and it is because of later "interpretations and reinterpretations" that land started being given to not just landless families, but ones with less land as well. The understanding of the policy by the bureaucrat is evidently flawed with respect to the policy text, as the very first order on TRDM itself (SCSTDD, 2001) clearly states that it is not limited to landless *adivasis* alone. Moreover, despite having been involved in implementation of TRDM since its inception in 2001, never during the 45 minutes of my interaction with the official about the goals of TRDM and its progress over time did he mention what the policy seeks to do for the "overall welfare" of *adivasis* beyond allotment of land. According to a street-level bureaucrat, the aim of the policy is to resettle *adivasi* families to the allotted land and create an enabling environment for them to practice agriculture. His is definitely a better capturing of the goal of TRDM in comparison to that of the senior bureaucrat in the sense that it goes beyond land allocation. While the policy texts do not explicitly state agricultural development as a purpose to be achieved by land allocation, the street-level bureaucrat says it is evident as nothing else can one expect to be done in the land allotted. But he says enabling agriculture is not a primary concern for him and that he can call the policy a success if all the families who have been allotted land start living there. While supporting agriculture might not be of much importance to the bureaucrat, its importance to the *adivasi* beneficiaries was evident during data collection when it was found out that many *adivasis* who were allotted land refused to relocate to those plots because of the uncultivable nature of the land given. Thus, a street-level bureaucrat who does not think agricultural feasibility is important to facilitate resettlement bases his actions on his own perceptions about *adivasi* land needs and policy goals. In the light of lack of clarity among various levels of bureaucracy about policy goals, what street-level bureaucrats rely on are various approximations of what they consider the goal to be.

Ambiguity in guidelines for implementation

The main ambiguity in the guidelines for TRDM implementation is regarding beneficiary selection, a probable reason for which is the lack of clarity in the policy goal itself. As mentioned in the previous section, the initial order on TRDM (SCSTDD, 2001) stated that it is for both landless *adivasis* and *adivasis* with less land. But the concept of 'less land' is not quantified and different bureaucrats interpret it differently. One local bureaucrat said that eligibility condition might vary from one district to another. Another bureaucrat expressed that it really does not matter since priority in land distribution has to be given to landless people. Since there are many landless families who are yet to receive land, he feels that he need not worry about the lack of clarity in defining people with less land.

While a single government order itself can be vague, researchers working on bureaucratic behaviour in other contexts have shown that the presence of multiple orders – at times, conflicting orders – leads to increased vagueness and exercise of bureaucratic discretion (Lipsky, 1980; Evans and Harris, 2004). This is applicable to the case of beneficiary selection in TRDM as well where the government orders issued from time to time increased the ambiguity in many cases. According to a government order issued in 2010, land is to be distributed under TRDM 'only' to those families who do not have any land under the name of husband or wife and have less than 30,000 rupees as annual income (SCSTDD, 2010). However, while this is stated as an eligibility condition in the government order, the reply given on the topic by the Minister for Tribal Welfare (Government of Kerala, 2013) in the legislative assembly states that the people who meet these conditions will be given "priority." While this implies that others are not fully excluded, the words used in the government order convey the criteria as a necessary eligibility condition which needs to be satisfied for securing land. This discrepancy led to implementing officers, who followed the 2010 order for two years, freezing the transfer of land to many *adivasis* in Aralam Farm in Kannur District who were otherwise eligible for land as per the 2001 government order. Following the demands raised by *adivasis* of Aralam, government issued another order in 2012 exempting *adivasis* of Aralam alone from the 2010 order (SCSTDD, 2012).

There are other ambiguities too regarding land allotment. The government orders are unclear about the quality of land to be awarded to *adivasis* or the manner in which it has to be allocated to eligible recipients. As a result, in many areas, it is uncultivable and uninhabitable land that has been distributed (George and Pampackal, 2017). In some instances, land has been distributed to people from multiple communities in the same area by random selection of occupants using a lottery system. This affects the practising of traditions by each tribal community and at times leads to disharmony within the settlement. Also, extended families who were previously living together have been split across different settlements as a result of random allocation. Such occurrences show the lack of effort on the side of some officers who implement the policy to cater to the cultural needs of tribal communities while allotting land. Many a time, the officers do the bare minimum that is prescribed to them via official orders, not taking the extra effort required to ensure that *adivasis*' cultural needs associated with land are met. However, there also exist bureaucrats who are more responsive to the needs of the people. According to a clerk, "it all depends on the personal charisma of the local officer."

In the absence of clear guidelines, there are various administrative and socio-economic factors that determine what direction a street-level bureaucrat adopts. Let us consider the appointment of ST promoters as an example to illustrate this since they are the most vital links between the street-level bureaucrats and the local people. The guidelines on selection of ST promoters are very vague, leaving a lot to the discretion of the appointment committee usually chaired by local bureaucrats and politicians. As a result, what we witness in one of the research sites is the appointment of all ST promoters for the year 2015–16 on the basis of political recommendation. This has been confirmed by multiple political and bureaucratic sources, including the local politician who made the recommendation. The result is that, while there are ten different *adivasi* communities dwelling in the panchayat, four out of the eight ST promoters are from the same tribal community as that of the politician. NGO workers in the locality feel this also gives space for preferential treatment of this particular community by the promoters. In another site, an ST promoter who has been suspended for poor performance and not following bureaucratic instructions got re-appointed after two years based on political recommendation. Such occurrences reveal to the street-level bureaucrat that it is hard to take any action against these politically backed ST promoters. These findings echo what was previously noted by Akhil Gupta (2012: 187) in another rural Indian setting when he wrote about how "bureaucrats complained that they had been reduced to becoming servants of politicians . . . who forced them to indulge in corrupt actions."

However, in another scenario, a man – who was part of a group of people who had come to the Tribal Extension Office to raise their complaint regarding exercise of bureaucratic bias – pointed his fingers at the Tribal Extension Officer saying, "It is only since this man took charge that things have become this bad. He thinks that he is the Minister [for Tribal Welfare]'s relative and can do anything. He is selectively targeting those from other [political] parties." In this case, the street-level bureaucrat was perceived not as a forced 'servant' of a politician, but someone who wilfully acts as a political representative for his personal gains or because of his personal background.

The nature of work to be handled by street-level bureaucrats requires that the agency grants them a certain level of discretion in responding to cases of rule-breaking (Lipsky, 1980). Just like a traffic police officer cannot be expected to identify every single traffic violation in his area, there is no clearly stated official expectation from TEO to respond to all cases of violation. A bureaucrat working within various constraints might not be aware of all violations occurring around him or her. While it is thus possible that specific actions or inactions by a street-level bureaucrat are results of constraints such as lack of information, heavy workload or political pressure, it can also be the result of his personal preferences that he tries to exercise with or without being lawless.

Ambiguity in responsibilities of bureaucrats

One day at a Tribal Extension Office in one of the research sites, a group of 14 men came to meet the TEO and the TRDM site manager to raise a grievance that one of them, Madhavan, had regarding the land allocated to him under TRDM. Once they entered the office, TEO took the lead in explaining the issue to all. He said,

> The problem is that Madhavan is saying that the land he has received is uninhabitable. He is currently staying in a plot that falls within the 40 acres of land that has been set aside by the government for public purposes after distributing individual plots to *adivasis*. Not just him, others too are plucking coffee from there. First of all, his land is not uninhabitable. Even if it is, he should file a written complaint and convince the concerned authorities. . . . That's what needs to be done instead of stealing government assets.

One person angrily asked the TEO who it is that gave him this responsibility of intervening in this issue. The TEO replied that it is "The Tribal Welfare and Development Department [*sic*]." Upon this, the man questioned if welfare includes only taking care of coffee and land, possibly hinting that TEO seems to be not concerned of the welfare of the people, to which the TEO replied, "All of us here are responsible for the betterment of life of all the people here and we are trying to do that. The Site Manager cannot be here every day. But I am here every day and I cannot close my eyes to the wrongdoings happening in front of my eyes." On hearing that all the officers are responsible for everything related to tribal welfare, he aggressively pointed out the faults of the local bureaucrats, "Sir, you should not say so. On the top of that hill, an old couple has been bed ridden and there has been nobody to even feed their grandchild. Did either of you two from here bother to look at their problems? I am not talking about the coffee and pepper that you see in front of your eyes but of the problems faced by the people here." As things got worse, the TRDM site manager said they will see what can be done in Madhavan's case "as per the law" and if he has done nothing wrong, then he need not be scared. The people said they will also see what they can do legally, and the assembly dispersed.

In the preceding scene, it seems that the *adivasis* are not fully aware of the exact responsibilities of each street-level bureaucrat. When individually targeted by the people, TEO immediately invokes a collective identity for the bureaucrats and says, "all of us" are responsible for "all the people here." While this might be used by him to convey that all bureaucrats are really working hard towards *adivasi* welfare, the actual implications of having no delineation of responsibilities are quite different.

As mentioned in the section on bureaucratic structure for TRDM implementation, while the TRDM site manager is the only street-level officer fully dedicated to looking after TRDM implementation, the TEO also supports the implementation as he is the one present at the local office on a daily basis. In the incident narrated previously, we can see that it is not the TRDM site manager but the TEO who is leading the discussion to which the people respond by asking who gave him the responsibility to do so.

While TEOs thus play a role in local level administration of TRDM, some *adivasi* beneficiaries report that when they go to the Tribal Extension Office to raise their complaints, they are told to come later when the site manager is present as it is his responsibility. At the same time, if one of the bureaucrats is targeted by a beneficiary, the bureaucrats define themselves as a collective unit. This might be, among other things, a function of the workload to be handled by the TEOs and site managers that prevent them from responding to all issues. A TRDM site manager reported that he has not been able to visit the settlement that is farthest from his office even once in the last two months. A TEO in Wayanad finds the responsibilities so much to handle that he lives in the office building itself, going home only on holidays. In a recent petition submitted by the TEOs of the state to the government, they explain the drastic increase in responsibilities of a TEO from 1980–81 to 2014–15 because of non-creation of more TEO positions, combined with the increase in *adivasi* population and number of government schemes for *adivasis* (see Table 9.1).

Thus, in the light of various ambiguously delineated responsibilities and unmanageable workload, street-level bureaucrats define their responsibilities in different

Implementers of law or policymakers too? **183**

TABLE 9.1 Increase in responsibilities of TEOs in Kerala from 1980–81 to 2013–14

	1980–81	2013–14	Increase from 1980–81 to 2013–14
No. of TEOs	48	48	0
ST Population in Kerala	2.61 lakh	4.31 lakh	1.7 times
No. of schemes for ST	7	49	7 times
Money allotted for ST	75 lakh INR	700 crore INR	933 times

Source: A written petition submitted by TEOs to the state government (2015)

manners in different situations, in ways that are favourable to them. For an *adivasi* beneficiary who is not aware of the officially envisioned division of duties among the street-level bureaucrats, a bureaucrat's duty is what he says it is. This diffusion of responsibilities does not allow beneficiaries to pin down accountability to individual bureaucrats.

Non-specification of penalty in government orders

The government orders on TRDM do not attach any specific penalty to the bureaucrats who fail to adhere to them. Though the impracticality of imposing penalty on every kind of violation is understandable considering all bureaucrats are subject to administrative laws of the country, it is quite revealing to see that penalty clauses are absent even in contracts for outsourcing specific project implementation components. For instance, District Nirmithi Kendra of Idukki district, a government agency, was awarded the contract for laying down water pipelines in a tribal settlement. As per the agreement signed in 2002, District Nirmithi Kendra was expected to finish the project in 90 days, with extensions allowed for valid reasons. However, a look at the various files on the issue and the notings on them shows numerous discussions on the issue and how the agency has repeatedly been granted so many extensions to the extent that the project is incomplete even today. Lower level bureaucrats at STDD pointed out that the reason is bureaucratic itself. The District Collector who is the Chairman of District-level TRDM is also the Chairman of District Nirmithi Kendra, as a result of which he has not initiated any action against the Kendra. Nirmithi Kendra being a government agency, other senior bureaucrats too have been hesitant to take action, resulting in many years of misery to the *adivasis* of the concerned settlement who did not have proper access to water. This finding challenges the argument made by some researchers that higher the scope for exercising discretion, higher is the bureaucrat's willingness to implement a policy (Sandfort, 2000) or make it more meaningful for clients (Palumbo et al., 1984). This need not be so in all cases. Willingness to interpret and implement a policy in a manner that is meaningful for beneficiaries is dependent on various factors mentioned earlier such as personal charisma, political pressure, presence of organized *adivasi* groups, workload, etc. One street-level bureaucrat said

184 Amrutha Jose Pampackal

that he is "not motivated to work hard" because of low salary, high work pressure and various financial constraints within the department.

Conclusions and scope for further research

While the chapter has been able to outline several key patterns of bureaucratic behaviour and its importance to the policy process, it does not claim to be comprehensive in scope as it is too ambitious to expect all possible patterns of bureaucratic behaviour to be unveiled during the short span of data collection. But it does throw light on how bureaucratic behaviour at the street-level is a function of bureaucratic interpretation of policy text in the context of the local socio-political and administrative environment. The chapter shows that the policy text pertaining to TRDM is filled with ambiguities about policy goals, implementation guidelines, division of responsibilities and penalties, thus leaving a lot be interpreted by individual street-level bureaucrats. The interpretation of policy text is found to be influenced by at least few factors such as the personal and political preferences of a street-level bureaucrat, political pressure, presence of organized *adivasi* groups and various administrative constraints such as heavy workload, inadequate number of street-level bureaucrats, low salary and lack of financial resources within the government department. Since the contextual factors that influence a local bureaucrat have been studied by various other scholars in the context of developing countries (Riggs, 1961, 1964; Gupta, 1995, 2012; Mathur, 1970), I would like to take more effort in developing insights about the less-discussed aspect of bureaucratic interpretation of policy text.

Based on field-level observations presented in this chapter, I argue that it is important to study factors shaping bureaucratic behaviour at the local level, especially in settings such as that of TRDM settlements which involve illiterate and marginalized communities, as for the local people who are not familiar with the written text of a policy, the policy mostly is what the local bureaucrat says it is. If a TEO or TRDM site manager says that he is not responsible for a particular aspect of policy implementation or declares that an *adivasi* is not eligible for land, it might many a times go unchallenged due to the ambiguous nature of policy text and the lack of familiarity of *adivasis* with administrative jargon and the complicated systems of policy implementation. Thus, the way a beneficiary experiences a policy is largely determined by the street-level bureaucrat with whom he or she interacts. This crucial role played by street-level bureaucrats in representing the state at the local level and re-presenting policy to beneficiaries shows that policymaking role of bureaucracy is not restricted to instances when rule-making powers under delegated legislation are provided to bureaucrats or when they advise the political executive in policymaking. Even street-level bureaucrats, who are in the lower rung of the official bureaucratic hierarchy, act as policymakers in the way they interpret policies and present them to the beneficiaries.

To develop a better understanding of the way a street-level bureaucrat acts as a policymaker or a co-creator of policies, it might be useful to draw from certain ideas on authorship presented in the field of literary theory, particularly by Roland Barthes. Barthes, in his essay "The Death of the Author" ([1964] 1989), celebrates the reader as the producer of a literary work since he feels the text does not function as lines that release a single message from the 'Author-God' and it is the job of the reader to create meanings. Thus, the author does not have ultimate authority over the text. Unlike in fiction where ambiguity can be accommodated, the purpose with which laws and policies are scripted is to serve as the definite authority that drives implementation. That's why the Tribal Extension Officer is expected to "do everything as per the laws." However, Barthes' argument on the reader's role in creating meanings is relevant to our discussion on street-level bureaucrat as a reader, interpreter and producer of policies. The discussion in this chapter about the content and language of TRDM orders and the way they are interpreted by individual bureaucrats shows that it is not a single message that emanates from the written policies and that a street-level bureaucrat ends up being a co-creator of policies through the act of reading where he or she interprets the text and imaginatively fills the gaps. Thus, when a TEO says he implements a policy by doing everything "as per the law" he does it as per the way he reads and interprets the official text, not necessarily what was intended by those who made the decision or those who scripted it. It forces us to think of the importance of policies as read and re-presented by the street-level bureaucrats, as it is they who present it to the local community. I therefore argue for a larger understanding of policymaking that gives space for acknowledging the role played by street-level bureaucrats in the process.

The study also makes us rethink our understanding of the different stages of policy process. While many researchers of the policy process tend to separate the stage of implementation from that of formulation (DeLeon, 1999) and separate the role of bureaucrats from that of political executive and the legislature, the findings of the study show how the two stages of formulation and implantation continuously overlap with each other. Bureaucratic interpretation of policy text is a continuous process within policy implementation. Each time there occurs differences in the way different bureaucrats interpret a policy text, a policy is getting reformulated in different ways. The vaguer a text, greater is the scope for bureaucratic interpretations and more are the differences in implementation of the policy by different bureaucrats. While some interpretations might be favourable to the spirit of a policy's intended goals, others might not be, leading to undesirable manners of policy implementation. This in turn may lead to revision of policy text, which in the case of TRDM is witnessed in the form of corrective government orders issued from time to time, as discussed earlier in the context of ambiguous guidelines on beneficiary selection. In short, one can observe that the day-to-day interpretation of policy text by the bureaucrat as well as the revision of policy text on the basis of bureaucratic learnings from the ground are a part of policy formulation and not just implementation. This continuous cycle of interpretation and revision of policy text makes it hard to identify the point of completion of policy formulation and beginning of implementation. While the simplistic categorization of policy implementation as a separate stage in the policy cycle that follows policy formulation might be useful for some kinds of analyses, this chapter, through its study of bureaucratic practices, urges everyone to recognize the entangled nature of formulation and implementation processes and the role of the street-level bureaucrat in them.

Notes

1 Block or Community Development Block is a sub-district level administrative unit in India.
2 *PUCL vs Union of India* and others, also popularly known as the 'right to food' case is a public interest litigation filed in 2001 by the People's Union for Civil Liberties (PUCL) in the light of the prevailing hunger situation in the country despite having high stock of food grain stocks. Through the interim orders passed in this case, the Supreme Court played an active role in formulation of the National Food Security Act of 2013 by issuing policy directions to the central and state governments for ensuring right to food.
3 While this chapter, at times, uses law and policy as interchangeable terms because of their highly overlapping nature and the broad way the term 'law' is used by local bureaucrats, it does concur with Kreis and Christensen (2013) in recognizing that "not all policy is law and not all laws are policy". It recognizes that both policies and the legal instruments through which policy options are enacted are important in addressing policy problems, and that it is important to analyze them holistically.
4 The history of land reforms in India is complex, involving many legal battles and constitutional amendments around the right to property. Land being a 'state subject' adds to the complexity as there is a huge variation in the trajectory of land reforms from state to state. While a discussion of the rich history of land reforms is outside the scope of this chapter, various scholars have already undertaken the task. See Pellissery et al. (2017) on the history and challenges of land policies in India, Appu (1997) on post-independence land reforms and Kohli (1987) on the politics of land redistribution.
5 This chapter is based on a section of the author's graduate thesis written under the guidance of Dr. Sony Pellissery. However, the methods described here pertain only to the sections of the study that are relevant to this chapter.
6 Gram panchayat or village council is the basic level of the three-tier system of local self-governance in India.
7 The Chief Information Commission of India in a decision dated 31 January 2006 has explained 'file notings' as follows: "Most of the discussions on the subject/matter are recorded in the note sheets and decisions are mostly based on the recording in the note sheets and even the decisions are recorded on the note sheets. These recordings are generally known as 'file notings'."

References

Appu, P. S. (1997) *Land reforms in India: A survey of policy, legislation and implementation.* New Delhi: Vikas Publishing House.
Barclay, S. and Birkland, T. (1998) "Law, policymaking, and the policy process: Closing the gaps", *Policy Studies Journal*, 26(2), 227–243.
Barthes, R. [1964] (1989) "The death of the author". In *The rustle of language*, trans. R. Howard. Berkely and Los Angeles: University of California Press, pp. 49–55.
Bhagwati, P. N. (1985) "Judicial activism and public interest litigation", *Columbia Journal of Transnational Law*, 23(3), 561–578.
Bijoy, C. R. (1999) "Adivasis betrayed: Adivasi land rights in Kerala", *Economic and Political Weekly*, 34(22), 1329–1335.
Birchfield, L. and Corsi, J. (2010) "The right to life is the right to food: People's Union for Civil Liberties v. Union of India & others", *Human Rights Brief*, 17(3), 15–18.

Brodkin, E. Z. (1997) "Inside the welfare contract: Discretion and accountability in state welfare administration", *Social Service Review*, 71(1), 1–33.

Census of India. (2011) "Scheduled castes and scheduled tribes". Available at: http://census india.gov.in/Census_And_You/scheduled_castes_and_sceduled_tribes.aspx (Accessed 23 February 2015).

Crook, R. and Ayee, J. (2006) "Urban service partnerships, 'street-level bureaucrats' and environmental sanitation in Kumasi and Accra, Ghana: Coping with organisational change in the public bureaucracy", *Development Policy Review*, 24, 51–73.

Dam, S. (2005) "Lawmaking beyond lawmakers: Understanding the little right and the great wrong (analyzing the legitimacy of the nature of judicial lawmaking in India's constitutional dynamic)", *Tulane Journal of International and Comparative Law*, 13, 109–140.

DeLeon, P. (1999) "The stages approach to the policy process: What has it done? Where is it going?", *Theories of the Policy Process*, 1(19), 19–32.

Evans, T. and Harris, J. (2004) "Street-level bureaucracy, social work and the (exaggerated) death of discretion", *The British Journal of Social Work*, 34(6), 871–895.

Fuller, C. J. and Harris, J. (2001) "For an anthropology of the modern state", in C. J. Fuller and V. Bénéï (eds.), *The everyday state and society in modern India*. London: C Hurst and Co Publishers Ltd.

George, K. and Pampackal, A. J. (2017) "Question of land, livelihood and development: Tribal resettlement and development mission, Kerala", *Economic and Political Weekly*, 52(7), 99–106.

Government of Kerala. (2013) Reply to 13th Kerala legislative assembly unstarred question no. 927.

Gupta, A. (1995) "Blurred boundaries: The discourse of corruption, the culture of politics, and the imagined state", *American Ethnologist*, 22(2), 375–402.

———. (2012) *Red tape: Bureaucracy, structural violence, and poverty in India*. Durham, NC: Duke University Press.

Harris-White, Barbara. (1991) *Informal Economic Order and the Shadow State in India*. QEH Working Paper Series QEHWPS06.

Isaac, T. M. T. and Tharakan, P. K. M. (1995) "Kerala: Towards a new agenda", *Economic and Political Weekly*, 30(31–32), 1993–2004.

Jain, R. B. (1987) "The role of bureaucracy in policy development and implementation in India", *Southeast Asian Journal of Social Science*, 15(2), 20–39.

Kelly, M. (1994) "Theories of justice and street level discretion", *Journal of Public Administration Research and Theory*, 4, 119–140.

Kohli, A. (1987) *The state and poverty in India: The politics of reform*. Cambridge University Press.

Kreis, A. M. and Christensen, R. K. (2013) "Law and public policy", *Policy Studies Journal*, 41, S38–S52.

Lipsky, M. (1980) *Street-level bureaucracy: Dilemmas of the individual in public services*. New York: Russell Sage Foundation.

Mannathukkaren, N. (2011) "Redistribution and recognition: Land reforms in Kerala and the limits of culturalism", *The Journal of Peasant Studies*, 38(2), 379–411.

Mathur, K. (1970) *Bureaucratic thinking: A study of block development officers of Rajasthan and Uttar Pradesh in India*. Michigan: University of Hawaii. Available at: http://scholar space. manoa.hawaii.edu/bitstream/handle/10125/11849/uhm_phd_7112209_r.pdf? sequence=1 (Accessed 23 August 2015).

Meyers, M. K. and Vorsanger, S. (2007) "Street-level bureaucrats and the implementation of public policy", in *The handbook of public administration*. London: SAGE Publications Ltd, pp. 153–163.

Palumbo, D. J., Maynard-Moody, S. and Wright, P. (1984) "Measuring degrees of successful implementation", *Evaluation Review*, 8(1), 45–74.

Pellissery, S., Davy, B. and Jacobs, H. M. (eds.) (2017) *Land policies in India: Promises, practices and challenges*. Singapore: Springer.

Prottas, J. M. (1979) *People processing: The street-level bureaucrat in public service bureaucracies*. Lexington, MA: Lexington Books.

Riggs, F. W. (1961) *The ecology of public administration*. Bombay: Asia Publishing House.

———. (1964) *Administration in developing countries: The theory of prismatic society*. Boston: Houghton Mifflin.

Sandfort, J. R. (2000) "Moving beyond discretion and outcomes: Examining public management from the front lines of the welfare system", *Journal of Public Administration Research and Theory*, 10(4), 729–756.

Sayre, W. S. (1964) "Bureaucracies: Some contrasts in systems", *Indian Journal of Public Administration*, 10(2), 219–229.

Schaffer, B. (1973) *The administrative factor: Papers in organization, politics and development*. London: Frank Cass.

SCSTDD. 2001 G.O(P) No. 53/2001/SCSTDD dated 09.11.2001.

———. (2010) G.O(P):23/2010/SCSTDD dated 24.02.2010.

———. (2012) G.O(P):81/2012/SCSTDD dated 13.06. 2012.

Self, P. (2009) *Political theories of modern government: Its role and reform*. na: Routledge Revivals.

Sreerekha, M. S. (2010) "Challenges before Kerala's landless: The story of Aralam farm", *Economic & Political Weekly*, 45(21), 55–62.

STDD. (2014) "Plan schemes". Available at: www.stdd.kerala.gov.in/plan_schemes.htm (Accessed 17 February 2015).

Verma, Arvind. (2001) "Taking justice outside the courts: Judicial activism in India", *The Howard Journal of Crime and Justice*, 40(2), 148–165.

10

PRODUCTION OF SPACE IN URBAN INDIA

Legal and policy challenges to land assembly

Varun Panickar

Introduction

The Census of India, 2011 revealed a strong emerging trend in the population demographics of the country. It suggested that at least 31% of the population of the country lived in urban areas (Sreevatsan, 2017). While it may strike many as a surprisingly high figure for a country which has been typified by the predominance of rural themes in its development narrative, the trend of booming population growth across urban centres in the country has been on the rise over the last two decades. In fact, the figures being put forth by the census are considered to be far too conservative based on the indices the census utilizes in the determination of 'urban areas', and other studies (see Sreevatsan, 2017; United Nations, 2018) project a much higher figure for urban populations in India. The Union Ministry of Housing and Urban Affairs predicts that India will add up to 165 million people to its current urban base of 377 million by 2030. Some of these numbers will surely be added from the 180 million rural people living close to 70 of India's largest urban centres (Ministry of Housing and Urban Affairs, 2018). Naturally the expectation is that there will be an increasing pressure on the demand for land in urban centres. In a best-case scenario where the state is able to effectively plan and regulate the growth of cities, the requirement for urban land in India in 2050 is projected to be 54.8 million hectares, which is 31 million hectares more than the quantum of urban land in the country in 2010 (Hoda, 2018: 19).

'Urban land' alludes to a particular kind of space, which presupposes the existence of certain conditions (see Qadeer, 1981). This chapter attempts to look pointedly at the capacity for establishing property rights, as a basic tool to be utilized in the production of urban land. Henri Lefebvre (1991: 85) explains the centrality of property relations, especially the ownership of land, in the forces of production of space which impose forms on the land in his seminal work 'The Production of

Space'.[1] This central status given to property rights does not lend itself to a linear discourse on the production of spaces, but is instead a part of a policy subsystem that is dictated by multifarious actors, pressures and strategies (Lefebvre, 1991: 73). This chapter seeks to extend this line of thinking in trying to understand the spiralling of policy strategies that attempt to address the need to produce urban spaces, which all retain the formal capacity to establish property rights at the core of their strategy.

These policy strategies essentially express themselves as strategies of land assembly and development. Ranging from strategies deployed by individual citizens working in their limited capacities to state-led efforts stemming from the state's exercise of eminent domain and ideas of top-down town planning, these strategies have to overcome the challenges posed by the lack of a functioning formal system of property rights in urban India. The idea of dictating land development by the dint of legislation is a practice that has been in place since the colonial times in India and continues to this day. The modes of land assembly and development employed in urban India are also shaped by legislation. But the manner in which these laws are interpreted and finally implemented is a matter of public policy. The influence of public policy in the development of urban land is especially important because the workings of a formal system determined entirely by legislation is compromised by the absence of a strong repository of property records.

Land records in urban India

In India the colloquial use of the term 'land records' generally pertains to the system of land records which are prevalent in rural areas. These 'land records' are actually records of land revenue and trace their origins back to records of agricultural land revenue that were conceived in the empires of the medieval rulers in the country (Raychaudhuri, 2008). These records were inherited by the British, who retained their form and function[2] (Dutt, 1902) while introducing incremental improvements in the technology employed to survey lands and the methodologies of recording property rights (Michael, 2007). The idea that land records only covered agricultural lands was also retained by the British. This was only because India was, for the most part, an agricultural economy during these periods and these regimes were focussed on recording only those aspects which were productive and hence of extractive benefit to them. The settlement area in villages was usually designated as a single survey number, demarcated only for the purposes of distinguishing it from the agricultural land holdings (Dutt, 1902).

Eventually it was the settlement areas of villages which expanded their boundaries as villages transformed to towns and then cities. When India achieved its independence, the land records systems were continued as they were inherited from the British. The lack of records for settlement areas became an apparent inadequacy in the land administration machinery as the number of towns and cities grew, expanding from their limited extents as settlement areas in villages. The matter took on an increased urgency as cities became hubs of economic activity and the value of

Production of space in urban India **191**

land increased, making the recording of land parcels in urban settlement areas a crucial factor for the maintenance of formal land markets (Anderson, 1918). It is not that there are no instances of land records for urban areas in India. The states of Maharashtra and Gujarat do have property cards (textual records) and city survey sheets (spatial records), which are the land records for urban areas in these states. These property cards were devised by the British for the Bombay Presidency, which covered extents that are a part of both these present-day states ("Maharashtra State Gazetteers: Greater Bombay District", n.d.). The British expected the need for land records in urban areas to arise as they had already come across some of the issues that came to light much later in the rest of the country, in their governing of the city of Bombay – a burgeoning metropolis in the early 1900s itself (Anderson, 1918). But the property cards in Maharashtra and Gujarat remain an isolated instance of land records for urban areas in India. There have been efforts made in Karnataka to issue property records in urban areas, but these have stalled (Krishna Kumar, 2017).[3]

Without any land records to ascertain property rights in urban areas, other forms of certification and evidencing of property transactions have assumed the role of legitimizing claims on property. The property tax records are the most prominent example of these emergent forms of property rights certification. But this substitute for formal land records has not managed to completely fill the gap. Firstly the coverage of properties by the property tax records is poor (Govinda Rao, 2013) and secondly the form of the property tax records does not support efforts to establish property rights since that is not their intended use. Similar to the property tax records are substitutes like receipts for the payment of utilities. Often times, these substitutes are used in conjunction to convey a higher degree of security of the claimants right over the property.

Individual-led forms of producing spaces

Property rights and their representation as property records along with other factors like land values are the building blocks on which decisions and strategies of the production of space are based. The first response to the unavailability of a formal system of certifying and verifying property rights is exhibited by the individual citizens. Establishing secure tenurial rights over immoveable property is one of the foremost requirements to be met for individuals to be accommodated in the economic activities of cities (De Soto, 2000). Individuals are the first respondents to the crisis of non-availability of formal property records because their engagement with the land markets is much greater than that of the abstract state.

Teresa Caldeira (2016) characterizes the individual's modes of producing space in the global South as peripheral urbanization. Her description of peripheral urbanization consists of a set of interrelated processes which

> (a) operate with a specific form of agency and temporality, (b) engage transversally with official logics, (c) generate new modes of politics through

practices that produce new kinds of citizens, claims, circuits and contestations, and (d) create highly unequal and heterogenous cities.

(Caldeira, 2016: 2)

Her idea of peripheral urbanization does not refer to the spatial location of the production of space but rather to a way of producing space in the city.

The absence of a formal system for establishing property rights in the cities along with having to confront top-down, rent-seeking urban local governance authorities forces a large extent of people living in Indian cities to take peripheral urbanization as a mode to produce spaces for themselves. The substitutes for formal land records that have emerged as a matter of practice in Indian cities are born out of the citizen's need to approach official logic of having formal property rights, transversally at least (Caldeira, 2016). In the absence of land records in urban areas, the official logic itself is not challenged but inferior substitutes are sought to somehow tide over the gap. The acceptance in practice of these substitutes then opens the gates to several combinations of substitutes credited to various levels on the ladder of establishing formal property rights; with land records granting guaranteed, conclusive titles being at the very top of the ladder. Typically access to higher combinations of substitute records are indicative of the superior socio-economic status of individuals with access to relatively more formalized land markets (Zimmer, 2012). Over long periods of time peripheral spaces that have been around for a relatively longer period of time acquire legitimacy as a matter of practice or through the retrospective legitimization of these spaces and the substitute records that were used to create and develop these spaces (Caldeira, 2016).

The 'GPA sale'[4] is a typical example of substitutes taking the place for formal records in the face of adverse official logic. The 'GPA sale' emerged as a practice in the land market of the Delhi-National Capital Region. The term 'GPA sale' pertains to the combined use of an agreement to sell, a general power of attorney and a will; all executed in favour of the buyer, to transfer property in the Delhi-NCR. This practice evolved as a way for people who had been allotted tenements built by the Delhi Development Authority (DDA) to transfer their tenements in the land market (*Suraj Lamp and Industries Pvt. Ltd. v State of Haryana and Ors*, 2009). The DDA, which has been the main provider of housing in the Delhi-NCR since 1967, only allotted housing tenements to people on a leasehold basis till 1992. The official logic that informed this policy decision of the DDA was that it was providing housing to the people of Delhi at nominal rates to meet the objectives of affordable housing and hence it was only proper that the person receiving housing through such a policy must not unfairly benefit from it by selling that property in the market. Accordingly the DDA made it mandatory for those intending to transfer their DDA-allotted tenements to seek prior approval of the DDA and pay to the DDA the unearned increase in the value of the property in the property market, in relation to the rate at which the DDA had given it to the individual (Maitra, 1991). This created a strong disincentive for the tenement holders to go through the legal channels of transferring DDA properties and the 'GPA sale' was invented as a way of avoiding both the payment of the unearned increase on the property to the DDA and the payment of the requisite stamp duty on the transfer of the property. The avoidance of stamp duty created an added incentive for the use of 'GPA sales' for the transfer of properties which were not DDA tenements as well (*Suraj Lamp and Industries Pvt. Ltd. v State of Haryana and Ors*, 2011a). Over time this practice became so prevalent across the Delhi–NCR that the documents used in 'GPA sales' came to be considered the foremost form of establishing property rights (Zimmer, 2012). Even the Delhi High Court recognized these 'GPA sales' as a mode of transferring property (*Asha M. Jain v Canara Bank*, 2001). The DDA which had switched to giving its housing developments on a freehold basis since 1992 had initiated several leasehold to freehold conversion drives which accepted requests for conversion from people who had acquired their property through 'GPA sales', thus legitimizing this practice ("DDA allows conversion of select flats to freehold, with riders", 2013). It was only in 2011 that the Supreme Court eventually declared the 'GPA sale' as an illegal mode of transacting in property (*Suraj Lamp and Industries Pvt. Ltd. v State of Haryana*, 2011b). Despite this judgement, the prevalence of its use and the acceptance of the 'GPA sale' in leasehold conversion drives has ensured that the 'GPA sale' imports a perceived legality.

In comparison to the perceived legitimacy of the 'GPA sale' are the property transfers that are carried out in poorer informal settlements where the documentation evidencing claims on the property may be flimsier, reflecting in the precarity of the occupiers of these settlements. Caldeira posits that over long periods of time older peripheral spaces acquire an air of legitimacy and become a part of the formal land market. This evolution pushes the land values higher in these spaces and people seeking avenues of affordable housing will be forced to seek newer peripheral spaces where this transition has not been completed (Caldeira, 2016: 4).

While the description of peripheral urbanization processes may suggest that it thrives in circumstances of complete chaos and unplanned growth, that is not necessarily the reality of this form of producing urban spaces. Since the evolution of these spaces is dictated by the need to at least transversally meet the official logic, these spaces are conceived and developed within the frames of legislation and state-led planning, but their execution does not follow the diktats of these frames (Caldeira, 2016: 5). Despite the advantages of affordability and easier access that peripheral urbanization affords individuals, it is at best only an alternative way for individuals to overcome the gaps in the formal structures. Also, as Caldeira explains, peripheral spaces eventually transform into heterogenous urban spaces which bar access to those seeking more affordable properties.

The longer-term solution to produce urban spaces must then come from the state-led modes of assembling and developing land to meet the needs of these fast-growing cities of India.

State-led modes of producing urban spaces

The state-led modes of producing urban spaces can be categorized according to their approach to the matter of land assembly and development. Typically, these modes have been characterized by a heavy-handed approach from the state looking to exert its powers of eminent domain.[5] Legislation was the primary tool used not only to legitimize the state's actions but also determine the course of its actions. While the framework for land assembly and development in India continues to be set by legislation, it is the extent to which public policy considerations in the form of feedback loops influence the interpretation and implementation of these laws that set these modes apart from each other.

Presently the Right to Fair Compensation and Transparency in Land Acquisition, Rehabilitation and Resettlement (LARR) Act, 2013 is the main legislation which encapsulates the state's approach to land assembly by compulsory acquisition. The Act was conceived in response to the violent protests at Singur and Nandigram against the processes of compulsory acquisition under the older Land Acquisition Act, 1894 (Roy et al., 2018). The LARR Act sought to rectify the shortcomings and unfair manipulations of the provisions of the earlier act by increasing compensation for compulsory acquisition and making resettlement and rehabilitation a mandatory requirement to be complied with as part of the processes of acquisition. The Act included specifically urbanization as an objective for which compulsory acquisition may be exercised, but does not actually define what urbanization may entail. Despite the provisions of the Act accounting for the value of potentially urban land by assigning a sliding scale of compensation based on the distance of the rural land being acquired from an urban area, the lack of a clear definition of urbanization and the absence of clear guidelines for designing the scale of compensation have resulted in conflicts. State governments which had been tasked with designing the sliding scale of compensation have resorted to a flat structure of paying four times the average market value as compensation. The state governments have responded in this manner to quell the protests and legal challenges they have been faced with (Roy et al., 2018). But such quick-fix solutions have introduced an absurd logic where the Act had called for the establishment of a sliding scale of compensation to mimic the working of the land market. The introduction of a flat rate of compensation has made it practically impossible to acquire land in the peripheries of urban areas since the land prices in these areas have become almost twice as much as land prices in the heart of these urban areas (Chakravorty, 2013).

While the Act has faced several roadblocks in its implementation on other counts as well, the stupendously high rates of compensation that the state governments are being forced to pay in peri-urban areas is a specific issue in these areas. A telling example of the difficulties in meeting the compensation requirements of compulsory acquisition, is the delayed Mumbai-Nagpur expressway in Maharashtra. As farmers along the route of the proposed highway protested the compulsory acquisition of their lands, the state government was forced to increase the rates of compensation to be awarded. Consequently, the project has witnessed the grant of the highest ever compensation to acquire land in the state. At an average of rupees 87 lakhs per hectare, the compensation awarded in most cases in the project is about five times the going market rate in those areas. The compensations are even higher for lands in or near urban areas. In the urban districts of Thane, Nashik and Nagpur the average compensation awarded was rupees 1.63 crores per hectare. The highest individual compensation awarded was rupees 5.17 crores in Thane district. These compensation figures are higher than the compensations awarded as part of the Mumbai-Goa highway project which had been initiated a little earlier than this project (Gangan, 2018). This reflects a trend of very high compensation being awarded as a part of compulsory land acquisition making this form of land assembly virtually untenable.

In this context, a study carried out by geographer Sanjoy Chakravorty (2013) on the rise in urban land prices in India is especially relevant to an investigation of the sustainability of compulsory land acquisition as mode for producing urban spaces. This study revealed that there had been a five-fold increase in the price of urban land from 2001 to 2011 and that the land prices in urban India ranged from rupees 1.4 to 253 crores per acre. In this same period, the prices of land in rural areas had also increased by five to ten times. A counter argument to the questioning of the sustainability of the land acquisition approach in the face of high compensation costs is the fact that traditionally governments do not actually pay the high compensation requirements imposed on them by the law and they utilize lower valuation standards like circle rates to determine compensation figures (Wahi et al., 2017). But as the example from Maharashtra suggests, the compensation awards being granted under the LARR Act are significantly higher than even the market value of the lands being acquired. This is definitely the case in urban and peri-urban areas and may result in the costs of acquisition in these areas outstripping the actual costs of meeting the public purpose requirement for which the acquisition was carried out. These high compensation awards are of course being granted as a result of the state government looking to avoid the opposition to acquisition, put forth in the form of protests and litigation. But it is the make of the LARR Act, 2013 which has prompted a narrative which empowers the land losers to demand what they deem to be justified compensation for their land. The Act which was drafted in response to the rural backlash against the misuse of the earlier compulsory acquisition law has kept the interests of the land loser as the focus of the legislation. Thereby increased compensation, increased consent requirements, mandatory social impact assessments, mandatory resettlement and rehabilitation are the cornerstones of the current acquisition law.

These amendments introduced by the LARR Act are in fact a measure of the inputs the legislation has incorporated from the civil society groups that sought a repeal of the previous land acquisition law (Wahi et al., 2017). However, the mounting problems facing the implementation of the LARR Act suggest an inflexibility on the part of the state to customize a more purposive understanding of its provisions. The legal requirements placed by the Act on the state are considered to be onerous and there is an active attempt to subvert the aims of the legislation (Panagriya, 2015).[6]

This is of course not all of the legislation's doing; as indicated earlier, factors like high land prices in urban areas in India contribute to the difficulties in using this mode. The difficulties in carrying out compulsory land acquisition do not however reflect on the apparent advantages that this state-led mode of producing spaces has on other modes like peripheral urbanization which must eventually succumb to the need for regularization of the peripheral spaces. In the context of the gaps exposed by the lack of a land records system in urban areas in India, acquisition of land by the state presents some sort of panacea to the issues associated with no formal property records. Acquisition by the state at once extinguishes all other private claims over the land and the land then reassigned for meeting some public purpose is free from all claims and encumbrances which were previously extended to it.

The idea then would be to combine the state's capacity for producing spaces and its concomitant advantages of bestowing formal property rights with what is perceived to be a more 'balanced' approach to land assembly and development. This seems to be the apparent logic that has led to the emergence of town planning schemes as the newly heralded, preferred mode for the state to produce spaces in urban areas (see Chakravartty, 2017; Ministry of Housing and Urban Affairs, 2018). In fact the Ministry of Housing and Urban Affairs (2018) has backed this mode of producing spaces to meet the requirements of the growing populations in Indian cities. The emergence of this mode of producing spaces in urban areas has been welcomed in the light of the perceived failure of the compulsory land acquisition legislation in meeting these ends.

Town Planning Schemes are essentially "a hybrid form of land readjustment whereby agricultural landowners on the urban fringe are required to give up part of their land . . . to the government in exchange for compensation" (Sanyal and Deuskar, 2012: 151). Since the schemes are directed towards the development of planned spaces, the acquired land is utilized by the government for laying roads and civic amenities. Additionally, a portion of the land is retained by the government for it to sell at an auction in order to raise funds for infrastructure provisioning. The remaining land is returned to the landowners in the form of serviced plots. The landowners are free to transfer the serviced plots at their increased values or can develop the plots on their own. The landowners are only required to pay half of the increase in the value of their plots to the government as a betterment charge and they can retain the other half of the increase in their plot values (Mahadevia, Pai and Mahendra, 2018).

The apparent advantages that this mode holds over compulsory land acquisition is that it purportedly takes a market-based win–win approach to acquiring privately held lands. The idea that landowners are not subject to a complete taking of their holdings and also gain the profits from the escalated land values of the reconstituted, serviced plots is the 'win' for the landowners. The state 'wins' because it does not have to pay for gaining access to privately owned land and neither does it have to pay for the infrastructure costs since those are covered by the levy of betterment charges.

This is the form of the Town Planning Scheme as it exists in the state of Gujarat. The Town Planning Scheme is a physical planning provision contained in the Gujarat Town Planning and Urban Development Act, 1976. While Town Planning Schemes are available in largely the same form in Maharashtra as well, their form, function and implementation in Gujarat is what has led to these schemes being touted as a silver bullet solution to the difficulties of producing spaces in urban areas. The success of the Town Planning Schemes in acting as a force of urban transformation in urban areas of Gujarat, especially in Ahmedabad, is what has made this model a best practice (Mahadevia, Pai and Mahendra, 2018).

The town planning scheme is closely interconnected with the Development Plan. The Development Plan is a long-term plan which identifies areas for growth of the city and plans for city-level infrastructure. The Town Planning Schemes are to be devised and implemented in accordance with this development plan. These schemes are to be carried out in three phases under the stewardship of a town planning officer. The town planning officer is afforded considerable discretion in drawing up the plans for the scheme and carrying out the negotiations with the landowners. While the Town Planning Scheme is also couched in legislation, the discretion given to the town planning officer in implementing the scheme is to enable the customization of the scheme according to the prevailing circumstances (Sanyal and Deuskar, 2012). This is an important element in explaining the preference for Town Planning Schemes in developing urban spaces. This ensures that the implementation of the scheme is always dictated by the feedback received from its policy subsystem in an active manner.

Studies have shown the positive impacts of Town Planning Schemes across Gujarat (see Ballaney et al., 2013), which apart from the production of planned urban spaces of growth have helped improve other social parameters like equitable land allocation amongst competing considerations of urban planning. In Ahmedabad, for instance, the prevalence of Town Planning Schemes in the greenfield belts in peri-urban areas has enabled the development authorities to reserve a fair share of land for public purposes like roads, social housing and green spaces. The town planning mechanism has enabled Ahmedabad to build an excellent road network with a well-defined road hierarchy. The land made available through Town Planning Schemes has been used for the construction of 80,000 units under various social housing schemes (Mahadevia et al., 2018).

While the Town Planning Scheme has seen some success in Gujarat, developments like the amendment made to the Gujarat Town Planning and Urban Development Act in 1999 pose a risk to the 'balanced' nature of this mode of producing urban space. The amendment stated that upon the sanctioning of the draft plan of the Town Planning Scheme (i.e. the first step of a Town Planning Scheme) all lands required by the appropriating authority for the purposes of providing roads, drainage and sewerage, lighting and water supply will vest absolutely in the development authority free from all encumbrances (Mahadevia et al., 2018). While this amendment did kickstart a spate of new Town Planning Schemes in the state, the underlying logic contains the seed of potential opposition to the town planning mechanism. The vesting of the land in the control of the development authorities on the sanctioning of the draft plan itself greatly reduces the bargaining powers of the landowners. With their lands already ceded for the laying of trunk infrastructure, the landowners would have little option but to extend their consent to the terms of the Town Planning Scheme. Of course, the provisions of the Gujarat Town

198 Varun Panickar

Planning and Urban Development Act itself only require the development authorities to 'consult' with the landowners on the form and nature of the proposed Town Planning Scheme.

The suggestions put forth by the landowners create no binding impositions on the development authority to make them a part of the Town Planning Scheme. In the absence of a significant profit accruing to the landowner on account of the upgrading of their greenfield plot to a serviced plot, the prescribed conditions of functioning of the Town Planning Scheme may be perceived to be grossly unfair. It is with this note of caution that the Town Planning Scheme must be accepted as a solution to this problem of producing spaces in urban areas across the country.

Conclusion

While aspects of public involvement through consultation or mandatory consent-requirement clauses are a part of the legislative makeup of most modes of land assembly and development, it is their implementation as a matter of public policy which determines their acceptability as modes for producing spaces. The emergence of Town Planning Schemes as the preferred mode for land assembly and development in urban centres in India is down to the practice of implementing Town Planning Schemes in Gujarat. The Gujarat Town Planning and Urban Development Act only requires the state authorities to carry out a 'public consultation' exercise with the landowners while implementing a scheme and there is no mandatory consent requirement. Even a straightforward implementation of the Act would likely run into public opposition on account of the involuntariness of the entire exercise. However, the implementation of the Act in Gujarat has been such that these schemes are widely regarded as best practices in land assembly and development. In contrast there is stiff opposition to the use of compulsory land acquisition as per the LARR Act, 2013 both from the state as well as the landowners. This is because the implementation of land acquisition legislation has been found to be wanting in terms of incorporating the policy inputs provided from the state's acquiring agencies as well as the land losers. The high degree of public participation in the implementation of the Town Planning schemes is a response by the state authorities anticipating heavy public opposition in the absence of any public participation in the scheme (Mahadevia, Pai and Mahendra, 2018: 13).

It is especially important to strike a balance between the implementation of laws and the practice of public policy in the sphere of land governance. This is primarily because laws tend to be static and their provisions do not provide adequate solutions to problems as they evolve in practice. The outcome in such circumstances is, as described by the practice of peripheral urbanization, people tend to engage with the law only obliquely since it does not provide them with adequate solutions to their problems. Since the demand for producing urban spaces is high, it is unlikely that the development of cities will halt long enough to comply with the demands of unwieldy regulation by legislation. The onus is then on the public policy approach adopted, to be understanding enough to accommodate the needs

Production of space in urban India **199**

of people and respond accordingly. As the example of the GPA sales in Delhi-NCR shows, merely declaring a practice to be illegal does not stop its use and it is important to take a more considered approach to these matters.

Notes

1 I would like to extend my gratitude towards Sony Pellissery for introducing me to this seminal work by Henri Lefebvre.

2 When the British took over land administration functions from the Mughals and other regional princely states their approach was to continue the systems as they were. So the ryots, or the cultivating farmers were given pattadar (lease-holder) rights in regions where the ryotwari settlement was prevalent, the zamindari was given legitimacy where the zamindari settlement was in force and similarly the estates were regarded as units for revenue collection where the mahalwari system was in place. The land relations were secondary considerations for the British administration, which focussed its energies on increasing revenue collections. These intentions of the British demanded that they have more information of the territories they were administering. The search for more information led to the most telling contribution of the British administration to the land records of India – the cadastral surveys (see Dutt, 1902). This discussion needs to be placed within the historical context of evolution of property rights in India (see for example Mitra, 2017).

3 The Karnataka government launched the Urban Property Records Ownership (UPOR) project as a pilot in Mysuru in 2010. The project has since failed to take off across urban centres in the state, only making some headway in Mysuru and Shivamogga. In 2011, the Ministry of Rural Development released a Model Land Titling Bill on its website. The bill was drawn up as a template to be used by the states in enacting legislation facilitating conclusive titling. The bill introduced a new administrative framework helmed by a land titling authority which would comprise of a combination of the existing Survey, Revenue and Registration Departments in the state governments. The entire framework was based on the registration of title system and even suggested a new format for the land records which would grant title to the holder. While the bill did not at the time have many takers at the state level, the bill has since come to be a predecessor to the Rajasthan Urban Land (Certification of Titles) Act, 2016. In Maharashtra a Centre for Land Titling was established in 2018.

4 The 'GPA sale' is a colloquial term used in the Delhi-National Capital Region (NCR) to denote sales of immoveable property by using the modality of a general power of attorney + an Agreement to Sell + a will. This combination may not always consist of these three components and often may include only a general power of attorney and an Agreement to Sell drawn in favour of the buyer. The GPA sale evolved as a way of enabling persons holding DDA properties on a leasehold basis to sell their properties without paying the requisite unearned increment to the DDA as well as avoid paying the stamp duty which would have been applied had an instrument which transferred the property been utilized. Although the GPA sale does not amount to a legal transfer of immoveable property, the prevalence of its use has accorded it a semi-legal status.

5 The origins of the exercise of the power of eminent domain in India are associated with the period of colonial rule in the country. This is primarily because during the medieval period the concept of private property itself was not fully realized. The king or the ruler was the de facto and de jure owner of all the land; others may enjoy certain privileges by decree of the king or the ruler. It is only with the advent of the idea of land belonging to private individuals that the concept of eminent domain emerged. The Bengal Regulation I of 1824 was the first legislation to enable the state to compulsorily acquire land required for roads, canals or other public purposes at a fair valuation. After a few more versions, the Land Acquisition Act of 1894 came to be the definitive legislation governing compulsory

land acquisition by the state for the next 119 years before it was replaced by the Right to Fair Compensation, Transparency in Land Acquisition, Rehabilitation and Resettlement Act (LARR), 2013. Although the 1894 Act was subject to amendments to render a fairer application of the law for those who had to give up their land, its application was marked by several instances of the abuse of the state's power to compulsorily acquire land for a public purpose. The LARR Act has attempted to put paid to the rampant abuse of the powers of eminent domain by introducing several protective provisions like social impact assessments, mandatory rehabilitation and resettlement of the land losers.

6 The LARR Ordinance, 2014 exempted five categories of projects from meeting the mandatory consent and social impact assessment provisions under the Act. The ordinance was later put into the LARR (Amendment) Bill, 2015 which has been referred to a Joint Parliamentary Committee. The states of Gujarat, Telangana, Tamil Nadu, Jharkhand and Andhra Pradesh have made state amendments to the LARR Act, 2013 which exempted several categories of projects from meeting the consent and social impact assessment requirements and also diluted the provisions mandating the return of unutilized acquired land.

References

Anderson, F. G. H. (1918) *City survey manual: With chapters on plane table and minor triangulation.* Poona: Yerwada Prison Press.

Ballaney, S., Bertaud, M., Clarke Annez, P., Koshy, C. K., Nair, B., Patel, B., Phatak, V. and Thawakar, V. (2013) *Inventory of public land in Ahmedabad, Gujarat, India.* Policy Research Working Paper; No. 6664. Washington, DC: World Bank. Available at: https://open knowledge.worldbank.org/handle/10986/16878 (Accessed 3 February 2019).

Caldeira, T. (2016a) "Peripheral urbanization: Autoconstruction, transversal logics, and politics in cities of the global south", *Society and Space*, 1–18.

Chakravartty, A. (2017, February 2) "Does government favour land pooling over land acquisition?", *Down to Earth.* Available at: www.downtoearth.org.in/news/governance/ does-government-favour-land-pooling-over-land-acquisition – 56943.

Chakravorty, S. (2013) "A new price regime: Land markets in urban and rural India", *Economic and Political Weekly*, 48(17), 45–54.

DDA allows conversion of select flats to freehold, with riders. (2013, April 2) *Hindustan Times.* Available at: www.hindustantimes.com/delhi-news/dda-allows-conversion-of-select-flats-to-freehold-with-riders/story-AHxGCDssHfK873Nq3sjlSO.html.

De Soto, H. (2000) *The mystery of capital: Why capitalism triumphs in the west and fails everywhere else?* London: Transworld Publishers.

Dutt, R. (1902) *The economic history of India: Under early British rule.* Vol. 1. London: Kegan Paul, Trench & Tribuner, pp. 81–96.

Gangan, S. (2018, June 21) "Mumbai-Nagpur Expressway: State pays farmers up to Rupees 5 crore for land to get project going", *Hindustan Times.* Available at: www.hindustantimes. com/mumbai-news/mumbai-nagpur-expressway-state-pays-farmers-up-to-5-crore-for-land-to-get-project-going/story-JcZQa2F1BGq1w0l66sj94L.html.

Govinda Rao, M. (2013) *Property tax system in India: Problems and prospects of reform* (Working Paper No. 2013–114). New Delhi, India: National Institute of Public Finance and Policy, p. 9.

Hoda, A. (2018) *Land use and land acquisition laws in India* (Working Paper No. 361). New Delhi: Indian Council for Research on International Economic Relations, p. 19.

Krishna Kumar, P. (2017, May 22). "Future of UPOR in limbo", *The Hindu.* Available at: www. thehindu.com/news/national/karnataka/future-of-upor-in-limbo/article18526051.ece.

Lefebvre, H. (1991) *The production of space,* ed. D. Nicholson-Smith. Malden, MA: Blackwell Publishing, p. 73.

Mahadevia, D., Pai, M. and Mahendra, A. (2018) *Ahmedabad: Town planning schemes for equitable development – glass half full or half empty?* World Resources Report Case Study. Washington, D.C.: World Resources Institute. Available at: www.citiesforall.org.

Maharashtra State Gazetteers: Greater Bombay District. (n.d.) Available at: https://cultural. maharashtra.gov.in/english/gazetteer/greater_bombay/revenueadmin.html (Accessed 11 May 2017).

Maitra, S. (1991) "Housing in Delhi: DDA's controversial role", *Economic and Political Weekly*, 26(7), 344–346.

Michael, B. (2007) "Making territory visible: The revenue surveys of colonial South Asia", *Imago Mundi*, 59(1), 82.

Ministry of Housing and Urban Affairs. (2018) *Pilot on formation of Local Area Plan (LAP) and Town Planning Scheme (TPS) for selected cities.*

Mitra, M. D. (2017) "Evolution of property rights in India", in S. Pellissery, B. Davy, and H. Jacobs (eds.), *Land policies in India.* Singapore: Springer.

Panagriya, A. (2015, September 10) "Land Act bit draconian, frame own laws: Arvind Panagriya to States", *The Economic Times.* Available at: https://economictimes.indiatimes. com/news/economy/policy/land-act-bit-draconian-frame-own-laws-arvind-panagariya-to-states/articleshow/48901548.cms.

Qadeer, M. A. (1981) "Nature of urban land", *The American Journal of Economics and Sociology*, 40(2), 165–182.

Raychaudhuri, T. (2008) "The mid-eighteenth century background", in D. Kumar and M. Desai (eds.), *The Cambridge economic history of India.* Vol. 2. Cambridge: Cambridge University Press, pp. 3–36.

Roy, T., Jayaraj, R. and Kumar, A. (2018) "Amendment to the LARR Act, 2013 and the aspirations of the rural youth of India", *Economic and Political Weekly*, 53(32), 40.

Sanyal, B. and Deuskar, C. (2012) "A better way to grow? Town planning schemes as a hyper land readjustment process in Ahmedabad, India", in G. Ingram and Y. H. Hong (eds.), *Value capture and land policies.* Cambridge, MA: Lincoln Institute of Land Policy, pp. 149–183.

Sreevatsan, A. (2017, September 16). "How much of India is actually urban?", *Livemint.* Available at: www.livemint.com/Politics/4UjtdRPRikhpo8vAE0V4hK/How-much-of-India-is-actually-urban.html.

Suraj Lamp and Industries Pvt. Ltd. v State of Haryana and Ors., AIR 2009 SC 3077 (2009).

———, AIR 2012 SC 206 (2011a).

———, AIR 2012 SC 206 (2011b).

United Nations. (2018) "2018 Revision of world urbanization prospects". Available at: www.un.org/development/desa/publications/2018-revision-of-world-urbanization-prospects.html.

Wahi, N., Bhatia, A., Shukla, P., Gandhi, D., Jain, S. and Chauhan, U. (2017) *Land acquisition in India: A review of supreme court cases 1950–2016.* New Delhi, India: Centre for Policy Research.

Zimmer, A. (2012) "Enumerating the semi-visible: The politics of regularising Delhi's unauthorised colonies", *Economic and Political Weekly*, 47(30), 92–93.

11

RAWLS, NOZICK AND DWORKIN IN AN INDIAN VILLAGE

Land alienation and multiple versions of distributive justice

Naivedya Parakkal, Sony Pellissery and Rajesh Sampath

Introduction

Distributive justice concepts have been ingrained in us unconsciously or consciously from a very young age. There cannot be one amongst us who have not said things like, "That is not fair!" or "I think I deserve more than this" or "Why did that person get more than me?" Each individual has his or her own perception about fair distribution of resources, what he or she deserves in life and who gets how much of what. The question that has been baffling distributive justice philosophers, governments, decision makers and common people is, given how societies have limited resources and wealth, how we can decide on a distribution pattern which will have everyone convinced that they have got their fair share?

The objective of this study was to find out how people unknowingly apply the various theories of distributive justice including John Rawls' *Justice as Fairness*, Robert Nozick's entitlement theory and Ronald Dworkin's equality of resources in their daily lives and how it affects their perception of what is fair and what they deserve. Beyond academic significance of finding the convergence between the understanding of philosophers and common people, the recognition of convergence provides scope for social policy theorization and from a practice vantage point. It is important to understand people's perceptions about what they consider to be a fair distribution since the application of different distributive theories would result in different social outcomes, which could influence the wellbeing of each individual. A sense of injustice is aroused when individuals believe that their outcome is not proportional to the outcomes of other people of similar circumstances in the same society and this can lead to social unrest and instability.

Theories of distributive justice

Distributive justice principles are concerned with the division of goods within the society. These primary goods can include income, wealth, opportunities, liberties and rights. The most pressing question for all distributive justice theories is how to divide these goods in a manner that everyone receives their fair share. Different principles will determine how the goods are distributed. For example, egalitarian principles will result in all people getting an equal share of the goods. However due to a difference in the levels of needs of people, this might not result in equal outcomes in terms of possession of primary goods. On the other hand, welfare-based principles focus on maximizing the utility of an individual.[1] This can also lead to an unequal outcome as maximizing the welfare of the maximum number of people can still lead to many people living in a highly impoverished state. In this chapter, emphasis is given on the distributive justice principles of three philosophers[2]: John Rawls, Robert Nozick and Ronald Dworkin all of whom have attempted to move away from welfare-based principles and utilitarianism.

John Rawls – *Justice as Fairness*

Rawls described his theory of distributive justice through two classical works – *A theory of Justice* (1971) and *Justice as Fairness* (2001). He said that principles of justice must be chosen by individuals in the "original position." In the original position, they are placed behind a "veil of ignorance" where each individual is unaware of his or her position in the social hierarchy in terms of gender, class, race, natural talents etc. He asks us to imagine that we have to design a social order, and we do not know whether we are going to turn out to be rich or poor, male or female, one race or another, gifted or limited in any way. The rules of the social engagement and transaction will be made while we are ignorant about particular facts about ourselves. We will only know general things from the social and natural sciences about human beings and their preferences – for example, it's a world of moderate scarcity and that people behave out of self-interest. In particular we will not have information that will help us to bias things in our favour, hence the necessity of the veil of ignorance. Rawls is seeking impartiality in the attempt to derive principles of justice to which all free and equal rational persons would agree once they enter the social contract.

Rawls claims that if you don't have knowledge of what kind of person you are going to turn out to be in terms of class, gender, caste, economic position etc., you will have to think about the social rules for people regardless of who they turn out to be. To demonstrate the validity of this, Rawls gives the example of two people sharing a cake. If there is a piece of cake that two people want to eat, both desire the cake equally and want the larger share. To overcome this problem, they decide that one will cut the cake while the other will choose the piece. This guarantees that the cake would be shared fairly, leading to the concept of justice as fairness. Rawls

204 Naivedya Parakkal et al.

reaches the principle of maximin – which helps a person not to end up as worst off when deciding to go for the most.

The idea of the original position compels us to think about society as a whole even when we know that we are self-interested (Freeman, 2002). We would want principles of justice that will fairly distribute certain goods that everyone values, what Rawls refers to as primary social goods which include income, wealth, liberties, rights and self-respect. As we get more information later, as the veil of ignorance lifts, we cannot undo choices that were made earlier. Rawls is advancing the idea of social contract to a higher stage by incorporating egalitarianism and values of political liberal society. While cognizant of socio-economic inequalities, Rawls is finding an arrangement to empower the lowest class in the society in the process of distribution.

For Rawls, there are two basic principles of social co-operation which must be chosen under the veil of ignorance. According to the "basic liberty principle", each member of the society must have an equal guarantee to as many liberties (which include political liberty, freedom of speech, thought, expression association etc.) as can be guaranteed to every member of the society. In other words, whatever bundle of civil and political liberties and rights that one individual has must be available to all other individuals, and liberty can only be constrained to the protection of the whole. The second principle of social co-operation, the "principle of democratic equality" has two aspects. One is the "fair equality of opportunity", whereby regardless of levels of talent or accident of birth, a person should not be unfairly advantaged over others in their pursuit of primary social goods.[3] Another important aspect is the "difference principle" according to which an equal distribution is preferred unless an unequal distribution makes every member of the society better off.

Robert Nozick – entitlement theory

Nozick's entitlement theory (1974) is a historical concept of distributive justice as opposed to Rawl's theory of justice which is a patterned/end state concept. A patterned theory aims at achieving certain patterns such as equality or distribution according to need or merit. A historical concept such as Nozick's claims that whether a person is entitled to the wealth that he or she acquired depends on the process that was followed for acquiring the wealth. Nozick argues that people's property rights would ensure that they can keep their possessions as long *as they were attained fairly* – without violating other people's rights, harming others or cheating them. Nozick's theory has three basic principles:

1   Acquisition Principle: A person who acquires a holding which was initially acquired in a just way is entitled to that holding and the resulting distribution is just;
2   Transfer Principle: A person is entitled to a holding if he or she acquires a holding from a just transfer from someone else that was initially entitled to that holding and the resulting distribution is just;

3   Rectification Principle: No one is entitled to a holding except by applications of 1 and 2. Past injustice can be rectified by the application of the 1st and 2nd principles.

Nozick argues for his theory of justice through an experiment called the "Wilt Chamberlain example." He tells us to imagine that the great basketball player, Wilt Chamberlain, agrees to play for a team by getting 25 cents for each ticket that is sold. Now, every spectator was entitled to their money and they have the right to spend the extra 25 cents on Wilt Chamberlain. The 25 cents add up and Wilt Chamberlain ends up being a millionaire in a few years. Nozick argues that Wilt Chamberlain is entitled to the money given to him (even though it is against egalitarian principles) as the initial conditions were just and there were voluntary transfers and so then the outcome must be considered just.

Therefore, an unequal, albeit just system for wealth may actually result from what was originally a just system. This is how liberty upsets patterns of egalitarian distribution. Nozick argues that it is unnecessary to focus only on the initial condition, because you can pick them whether it is egalitarianism or merit-based and sometime later you end up with an unjust system. Then the only way it can be fixed is through coercion. This would result in the excess money being taken away from Chamberlain in the form of taxes and giving it back to the people in the form of transfer payment. However, Nozick would argue that this violates his freedom whereby the 'minimum state' is the maximum and vice-versa.

Nozick also claims that the rectification principle should be enacted to compensate rather than through redistribution. Compensation is better that redistribution because it does not require us to agree on a pattern (what kind of outcome is just). It is easier to deal with compensation because in a society where there are different people who have different opinions about what is just, it is much easier to decide how to compensate an individual to undo the particular harm that was done to them, so that we do not have to worry about what the just distribution of wealth in the entire society is.

Ronald Dworkin – equality of resources

Dworkin's concept of equality of resources tries to overcome the shortcomings of Rawls and Nozick's theories. Dworkin's conception of equality of resources (1986; 1996) assumes that liberty plays a central role in understanding economic justice and endorses private ownership in the means of production and personal property, which is similar to Nozick's view. However, unlike Nozick, Dworkin is strongly in favour of Rawls when it comes to rejecting the conclusion that liberty requires us to abandon or restrict the pursuit of economic equality.

Dworkin says that whether a distribution of privately owned resources is just depends on the distribution emerging from a particular type of market process.

He takes the envy test as a criterion of just distribution. He says that a distribution is just only if after the distribution no person envies another based on the bundle of resources that he or she has received. He illustrates this by asking us to imagine a group of castaways faced with the task of distributing private ownership rights in a desert island. This is done by a hypothetical auction where everyone gets the same initial amount of money and then has to bid for the resources that are available to the particular society. This means that the person has to part with more of his or her initial resources to get something which is more popular in the community.[4]

Elimination of envy is best secured when each bidder has the same purchasing power and lots are continuously divided until the market clears and no bidder wants to repeat the process. Dworkin also says that the envy test is valid only if there is not much difference between the people in terms of natural abilities and talents. Dworkin focusses on the need for endowment insensitivity and ambition sensitivity. Here, he introduces the concept of brute luck and option luck. Brute luck refers to inequalities that arise as a result of the natural lottery which is out of an individual's personal control, such as a physical disability. Option luck refers to inequalities that arise as a result of a fair lottery in which everyone had an opportunity to participate. According to Dworkin the victims of brute luck must be duly compensated by progressive taxation.

Having reviewed the ideas of distributive justice in the works of three philosophers, we move to examine how ordinary people sided with any one of these positions in a given problem context. In the next section, we introduce the study area and the problem of land alienation that required people to position through one of the lenses just described.

Geographical area of study

The study was conducted in one of the wards of Attapady block of Palakkad District (the ward is kept anonymous to protect the participants) in Kerala. Attapady is one of seven *adivasi* blocks in Kerala. Like all other wards in Attapady, the selected ward has people who migrated from the plains in south and central Kerala (known as settlers), mostly living near the road, while the *adivasis* (categorized as scheduled *adivasis* with constitutional protection in India)[5] mostly live in hamlets uphill known as *ooru* (hamlet). The area of study had two such *ooru* – Osathiyoor and Kollamkadavu. To understand the relevance of the chosen theme to explore the theories of justice in Attapady and to understand the ongoing conflicts in the area of study, it is important to understand the history of the Attapady valley.

History of attapady

Attapady was the *jenmam* (freehold property) of the Samoodhiri of Calicut which later became *jenmam* (property) of three *jenmis* (owners) who ruled Attapady from the late eighteenth century until the formation of the state of Kerala in 1956. Nearly 70% of Attapady was given to Kochunni Moopil Nair and he was entrusted with the administration of the area along with two other *jenmis*, Elarpad Raja and Palat Menon. This effectively made the *adivasis*, who were the original inhabitants of Attapady, the tenants of the *jenmis*, requiring them to give land revenue and forest produce in return for the right to own and cultivate their own land. In the late 1920s settler communities from the plains, mainly from the districts of Kottayam, Palakkad and Thrissur started coming into Attapady. They leased out land from Moopil Nair and started cash crop cultivation. After the formation of Kerala in 1956, by an act of law, the tenants became the owners of the land that was leased out by the *jenmis*.

The land alienation issue is one of the most important human rights issues in Kerala. The government is caught in the middle of two arguments. The *adivasis* claim that since they are the original inhabitants of the area, the land collectively belongs to them and so cannot be legally sold to the settlers.[6] The settlers (who are the migrants who came from the plains) claim that they have tenancy rights and ownership rights to the land.[7]

Recognizing the issue of land alienation, a range of measures were undertaken by the government of Kerala. The Kerala Scheduled Tribes (Restriction on Transfer of Land and restoration of Alienated Lands) Bill, 1975, states that land which was bought from the *adivasis* after 1960 has to be returned back to them. Successive governments requested repeated extensions to delay the implementation of the 1975 act and in 1996, the bill was amended and all transactions between 1960 and 1986 were made legal. In 2000, the Kerala High Court rejected the 1996 amendment. The case is still pending in the Supreme Court[8] with the *adivasis* of Attapady headed by the Girijan Seva Samithy, an association of the Attapady *adivasis* demanding the implementation of the original Kerala Scheduled Tribes Bill (Restriction on Transfer of Land and restoration of Alienated Lands), 1975.

The frame of study and fieldwork

Distributive justice theories are relevant in all social contexts. In Attapady, land alienation issues have been a cause for friction between the settlers and the *adivasis*. Also, the settlers are disgruntled about the perceived bias to the *adivasis* in the allocation of government benefits. This has affected the social dynamics of the area. Understanding the people's perceptions about just allocation of these resources could be instrumental in finding solutions for the long-standing friction between the two sections.

The main objective of the study was to find how complex theories of distributive justice were internalized and applied by the people of Attapady in their daily life. We seek to analyze to what extent theories of distributive justice are relevant for social science research that have policy implications. Differences on views emerge on the basis of caste, age, economic status, education as well as gender, and the aim of the chapter is to see if any generalizations can be made based on these criteria. The axis of the study was the question of land alienation. However, we also examined the issue of access to development programmes, addressing the question of historical injustice. Therefore, a conceptual map (Figure 11.1) is useful to find out people's perception about how the resources are distributed and about what they think would be the right way to distribute.

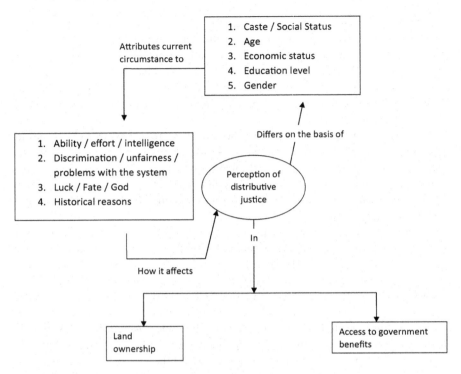

FIGURE 11.1 Concept map of causal relations to deprivation

Source: Author

The fieldwork to gather data was conducted during October–December 2012. The first three weeks of the field work were spent in building a rapport with the people, familiarizing ourselves with their routine, customs and traditions and understanding the social, political and economic aspects of their lives. Attappady is a region with a long history of non-*adivasi* scholars conducting research in *adivasi* communities, and we were not entirely welcome in the hamlets. We found that the settlers were friendlier initially when compared with the *adivasis*, so we sought the help of key informants from the hamlets to build a rapport with the *adivasis*.

After studying the social and political dynamics of the area, it was decided that the questions of the interview would revolve around the following areas of focus:

1   Aspects to which social and economic differences are attributed to.

   Questions asked: "Why do you think some people are rich and some people are poor?"; "Are you happy with your current lifestyle and financial status?"; Do you think you deserve more?"

2 Primary goods identification.

Questions asked: "What in your opinion does every person need to live a decent and comfortable life?"; "What should be done about people who are unable to get their share of primary goods?"

3 Opinion about land ownership, distribution and redistribution with emphasis on the land alienation issue. This was a very relevant area because of the frequent problems that arise in Attapady due to the way in which land was distributed and the differences and friction between the *adivasis* and the settlers regarding this issue.

Questions asked: "What is your opinion about the land ownership issue in Attapady?"; "What is your opinion about the law which states that land bought from *adivasis* after 1986 has to be returned?"[9]

4 Opinion about access to government benefits (who should get how much of what). Attapady block is one of only seven *adivasi* blocks in Kerala and ST population receives many government benefits through the Tribal Sub-Plan (TSP) fund. However, there is some friction between the settlers and the *adivasis* regarding the quantity of benefits received.

Questions asked: "What is your opinion about the government benefits that are available to you?"; "How do you think the government benefits should be allocated? Should it be given equally or on some other basis?"

Since the response to the questions had to be candid and in detail, we purposively searched for interviewees who were willing to provide time and engage in long conversations. Our selection of interviewees was primarily to get a mix of settlers and *adivasis*, whom we knew held different views on the question of land alienation. We also sought for variation in age, gender, educational qualifications and exposure to urban life, which made differences to the formation of views on justice. A summary of their characteristics is presented in Table 11.1.[10]

It was difficult to identify the interviewee's economic status as having a terrace house or land was not indicative of their financial condition. All the interviewees who had terraced houses acquired it through a government housing scheme. All the interviewees who owned land engaged in less agriculture and resorted to daily wage labour, construction work or food for work programmes for additional income.

Except for four interviews, all were conducted in the interviewee's house. After identifying the interviewees, their houses and places of work were visited several times before scheduling an interview to develop a rapport with them.

The recorded interviews were transcribed verbatim in Malayalam and translated into English, before discourse analysis was conducted. Views on four categories of

210 Naivedya Parakkal et al.

TABLE 11.1 Profiles of 12 interviewees

Name	Adivasi/settler	Age (approx.)	Education	Gender	Exposure to urban life
Ramaswamy	Settler	57	2nd standard	Male	Yes
John	Settler	40	5th standard	Male	No
Velan	Adivasi	55	5th standard	Male	No
Malayan	Adivasi	75	2nd standard	Male	No
Elamma	Adivasi	35	10th standard	Female	No
Kunjipennu	Adivasi	70	No formal education	Female	No
Ponnamma	Adivasi	28	Plus 2 (12th standard)	Female	No
Varghese	Settler	47	7th standard	Male	Yes
Gita	Settler	42	7th standard	Female	Yes
Abdur	Settler	50	10th standard	Male	Yes
Rosy	Settler	34	Plus 2 (12th standard)	Female	Yes
Thomas	Settler	71	5th standard	Male	Yes

Source: Author

issues (discussed earlier) attributed by settlers and *adivasis* were segregated. The findings pertaining to each of these categories are presented in the rest of the chapter before drawing conclusions on them.

Primary goods identification

Rawls identifies primary goods as the "things that every rational man is presumed to want." The primary goods are

- Basic rights and liberties.
- Freedom of movement and free choice among a wide range of occupations.
- Income and wealth.
- The social bases of self-respect: the recognition by social institutions that gives citizens a sense of self-worth and confidence to carry out their plans.
- The powers of office and positions of responsibility.

It was necessary to know what the interviewees considered to be primary goods because even though it was an idea introduced by Rawls, the means of distribution of these primary goods was a common base for Nozick and Dworkin. It was also important to identify what they assumed to be their most basic needs in order to further enquire about economic and social differences.

We found that there was not much difference in what people considered to be the primary goods, irrespective of age, gender or whether they were *adivasi* or a settler.

Social primary goods of income and wealth such as land, agriculture and cash were the first response for most of the interviewees.

Thomas (settler) said,

> you need at least 1 acre of land, then a house, some animals like cow or hens as that will supplement our income. Then some agriculture should be there. Then if we have land, then we can get a loan also and with that we can do lots of things and live comfortably. So we should have multiple income sources.

Many were of the opinion that even if land, cash and agriculture were available, health and intelligence were essential to ensure that the other social primary goods are sustained.[11]

Ramaswamy (settler) said,

> Land and agriculture alone is not enough . . . we have to be educated, that is very important . . . so it is not just education that you need. You also need to be smart. If you are smart, then you can live anywhere.

Abdur (settler) complemented this:

> So even if you get cash, you need to have the sense to use it properly.

Elamma (*adivasi*) said,

> We would need a certain sum of money, because without money we cannot live. Then we need the means to make that money. . . . If we are healthy then we would have the energy to do any work and earn some money.

No one spoke about rights, liberties or self-respect. However, it is evident from these voices that the Rawlsian 'moral powers', which explains the conception of the good and the sense of justice that is encapsulated within ideas of freedom, are embedded within *adivasis*' and settlers' references to the links between an autonomous individual and notions of smartness or intelligence.

Reasons for economic and social differences

One of the aims of this study was to find out what the interviewees attributed the economic and social differences of their current situation to, and how it affected their perception about distributive justice. Differences were attributed to a) variations in holding of primary goods, b) luck or divine intervention, and c) discrimination and corruption. Those who attributed variation in some primary goods referred to intelligence, inherited wealth, merit, opportunity and hard work.

Thomas (settler) said,

> then another aspect is that man should go about his life intelligently. See if I run short of money, I will take a loan or sell some land and try to move ahead.

Varghese (settler) said,

> I will tell you one thing. If one does not have inherited wealth then it is very difficult to come up in life. If you have something then you can work on it and make something out of it.

Elamma (*adivasi*) said,

> Then there are some people who have the sense to think about tomorrow and save accordingly, while some people don't do that.

Malayan (*adivasi*) said,

> like I went in the morning to the field to work right, we have to work hard. Some lazy people will sit simply and not do any work. How will they make any money? See in your house, if no one does for work and sits simple at home then that family becomes poor right. That is the reason why some people are poor. To make money we have to go to the fields are work hard. People without land, what can they do? They will go for work in someone else's fields. Sometimes the modalali (owner) will not be at home, that day is gone right?

Rosy (settler) said,

> I think that difference comes mainly because of their upbringing and how their parents were.

Few interviewees claimed that the difference was because of luck or because of divine intervention.

Velan (*adivasi*) said,

> So god is right above my head and guiding me. Till today, I have not had any shortage for food or anything. I don't know how it happens, but god always provides for me.

Rosy (settler) said,

> It is just my luck that things turned out in such a bad way. When we were in Perunthalmana [small town in northern Kerala], I used to work as a receptionist in a small company. My children also had a good life; they would go to school by bus only. But my husband ruined everything by drinking.

Only two interviewees attributed the differences partly to discrimination and corruption.

Abdur (settler) said,

> We cannot say that there is someone who is really rich in Attapady. Then if
> we talk about the *adivasis*, like I told you the other day, even though the gov-
> ernment gives all these schemes, their real motive is to make sure that they do
> not progress. Only then can they keep getting funds on their behalf.

Varghese (settler) said,

> These officials favour the *adivasis* because all sorts of funds come for them and
> three-quarters of it is used by these officials only.

To understand how these attributions affect their perception about distributive
justice, the interviewees were probed about whether these differences need to be
rectified and if yes, then how it should be done.

Only two interviewees, both settlers, were of the view that if a person was poor
or did not get opportunities because of a genuine inability to work or because of
some circumstances that was beyond their personal control, then they should be
helped. The help according to them should be from the government in the form of
pensions or schemes. This is clearly a Dworkinian position where victims of brute
luck should be helped by others (through the government in this case) through
progressive taxation.

Thomas (settler) said,

> the government helps them right. There are so many schemes for the poor.
> Even if you are disabled you get some pension. That is why the *adivasis* are
> being given so many free things. They get rice for Re. 1, if an *adivasi* goes
> to the hospital, they just have to say that they are an *adivasi* and they will be
> completely taken care of.

Ramaswamy (settler) said,

> in that case, they will have to be given extra help. The government might not
> be able to help everyone. If we are in a position where we can help, then we
> should also do something.

A majority of the interviewees were of the opinion that these differences were
either due to the incompetence of a person, their bad luck or fate. They believed
that irrespective of how bad one's condition, the individual must try to allevi-
ate their own condition. Many were of the opinion that such individuals may be
helped voluntarily, but did not agree to redistribute or compensate the individuals.
This is a Nozickian position, where the interviewees feel that since the primary
goods that they had acquired were through just principles, they were not obliged
to part with it.

Rosy (settler) said,

> Such people can be helped by people who have the ability to help, or maybe the government should do something. But there are some people who have all these problems and still work very hard and come up in life. So it all depends on one's fate. I will tell you one thing, how much ever others help us and give us things we will not be satisfied. We can only be happy with the things that God gives us.

Velan (*adivasi*) said,

> God will give people according to the work they do. There is no point in getting jealous about it . . . if their condition does not improve what can we do about such people?

Attributes to God need not be confused with fatalist rationality (Davy, 2012). Careful interpretation of the statements shows that this is reinforcing the Weberian Protestant ethics (1905) of individualistic logic of hard work. Some interviewees are of the opinion that people should be capable of converting their brute luck condition if they are given some initial resources, by choosing the correct options. They take after Dworkin's view that if they are unable to improve their condition because of their ambition insensitivity, then there is no reason to give them additional resources.

John (settler) said,

> we might think that if we help them to start something and give them the entire initial set up, then they will do something, but that won't happen. They will think, what the use of doing all this [work], and they will not continue whatever was started.

Ponnamma (*adivasi*) said,

> some people remain poor even if they are given benefits and they work hard. If they are not capable of handling money, then what can be done?

Opinion about land ownership and allocation

There is an underlying friction between the settlers and the *adivasis* regarding the long-pending land alienation issue. General enquiry about the land issues in Attapady brought out the differences between the settlers and *adivasis*.

Original owners of land in Attapady

There is a difference in the way the settlers and the *adivasis* interpret the original ownership issue of the land in Attapady (see Table 11.2). They both agree that the

Rawls, Nozick and Dworkin in an Indian village **215**

TABLE 11.2 Contrasting views on land ownership from settlers and *adivasis*

Settlers	Adivasis
Abdur said, *"Initially all this land was under Moopil Nair. The* adivasis *got their land measured and got a receipt made for it and they had to pay a small amount to the Moopil Nair so that they can live and farm on that piece of land. Then, when they have lived there for so many years, the land becomes their own."*	Malayan said, *"The other 4–5 acres is up in the mountains. No one owned all that land before. I cleared the land there and made the documents for it. . . . After we clear the forest; the survey people will come, put stones in the four corners and demarcate the land. Then it will become our own."*
Varghese said, *"actually the* adivasis *were slaves of the King in Madurai. They ran away from there and came here. In those days, it was just dense forests here. They cleared how much ever forest they could clear and made the land their own and started agriculture. They had to give a small tax to Moopil Nair. Then when the government came, they surveyed the land and made documents for them. That is how the* adivasis *came to own the land. They did not give money and buy it or anything. This was under the Zamorin of Calicut and he gave the land from Mannarkad to Anakkatti to Moopil Nair for free. That is why this place is god forsaken."*	Elamma said, *"You see those forests on the mountains there. It is all owned by the forest department. But there are people here who have original documents showing their ownership of that land for which they have paid tax, including us. We only cleared the land and got it demarcated as our own. Now they closed off that land as their own. There are about 20 to 30 people's land there. This puliyan moopan's land is also there. He got that land back by almost fighting with the officials. Can the poor do the same?"*

Source: Author

adivasis came to own that land by virtue of clearing as much forest as they can and demarcating it as their own. The *adivasis* believe that this is just as they seem to have a Lockean view about ownership. The Lockean right (1698) to property can be interpreted as:

a   People own themselves and so their labour.
b   By working on common or unowned resources, people turn it into their own property because they own their own labour.

Note that Nozick is adopting this view of property from Locke in his framework.

The settlers however seem to hint that the entire transaction is unjust because the *adivasis* received the land from the Moopil Nair who himself had got the land for free.

About how the settlers came to own the land

Some of the settlers' views on land ownership aligned with Nozick's transfer principle. They believed that since the land was given to them voluntarily by the *adivasis*, the transaction will be just even if the final outcome might be unequal. Also, when it comes to land owned by them, some of them are of the opinion that since the

216 Naivedya Parakkal et al.

land was initially unproductive and unused and they used their labour to transform it, they can rightly claim ownership.

John (settler) said,

> That kind of talk will always be there. See years back, some of our people [he means Christians] bought land here. Now some *adivasis* are saying that it is actually their land. That time they had no problem giving it to us. They say that it was bought on lease 50 years back. Now according to the law, if the land was owned by us in lease for 20 years, then it becomes our own.

Gita (settler) said,

> When the settlers bought the land, they must have given some money for it. But these *adivasis* will never admit to it. The land here was all forest. The settlers will come and clear the forest. That takes so much effort.

The worldview of *adivasis* for preservation of forest (without doing anything on it) is colliding with productivist worldview of settlers (in the process owning the same through Lockean labour). However, some settlers seem to hint that the transaction between some settlers and *adivasis* might have been unjust as the *adivasis'* ignorance might have been taken advantage of, though they do not say it explicitly, in which case Nozick's transfer principle cannot be applied.

Abdur (settler) said,

> what many of them have done is, they would approach the *adivasi* and ask them to give some land on lease for a year and pay them Rs. 500. Since the *adivasi* anyway does not to do anything on the land they give it away. Then the *adivasis* will ask for Rs. 500 advance for some emergency and give the settler permission to use the land for another year. After a while the settler would tell the *adivasi* to just transfer the land in his name and give some more money. That is how now most of the *adivasi's* land is with the settlers today.

Ramaswamy (settler) said,

> so during that time, the vandevasi [settler], who can be a malayalee, gounder or Christian or anyone, they would come and buy land for cash. There were no laws for buying/selling land. So they might have given just Rs.5 or Rs.10 and bought land.

The *adivasis* feel that the land was taken away from them by unjust means as they were unaware of the laws, uneducated, and did not know the real value of their land, and therefore they believe that it needs to be returned back to them. This would be on the lines of Nozick's third principle, according to which, a past injustice must be rectified. The *adivasis* seemed to be hinting that they were not able to get access to education that might have prevented all these problems and that was their brute luck. In lines with Dworkin's theory, they want to be compensated. Kunjipennu (*adivasi*) said,

> see I have lost 5 acres like that. We had about 10 acres of land there [points to a mountain]. I only cleared the land when I was younger. It was so difficult you know. But my sister, she has studied till 5th standard. She married a Gounter boy [dominant caste] and they got that land surveyed and made documents in her name. I am not educated at all right, so I could not do anything. Now he has claimed the land to be his own. I complained in the village office but no one came to check.

Ponnamma (*adivasi*) said,

> this is what I have heard from my parents ok. . . . Chettiyaar came here [Osathiyoor in 1970s] and spoke to the moopan. They spoke to Chelly's family because they have a lot of land and got some land on lease from her father and now he [the Chettiyar] claims to own it. . . . We are suffering now for the mistakes that we did then. Especially in our ooru there are many people who have lost acres and acres of land.

About the restoration of alienated land to adivasis

There are mixed opinions about compensation among the *adivasis* (see Table 11.3). Few of them stick to their stand that the land has to be returned because of the violation of Nozick's transfer principle (involuntary transaction) and rectification of past injustice has to be done. They are also of the opinion that any productivity that was brought about in the land by the settlers should not be returned back to them or compensated for, as the initial transaction itself was unjust.

However, some *adivasis* say that even though they might not have received a just price for the land, it was their choice to give the land to the settlers at that price and so they did not deserve to receive the land back. Hence as victims of option luck, according to Dworkin's theory, they did not want to be compensated.

What is important for this study is to observe the consistency in the logic for compensation between different actors with different positionalities. For instance, Kunjipennu's position on Nozick's principle of compensation clearly emerges from her earlier view that she was cheated in the transaction of land. Similarly, Malayan and Velan (both *adivasis*) who blamed themselves for their poor options had different views on compensation (compared to other *adivasis*).

Allocation of government benefits

Being an *adivasi* block, the people of Attapady, especially the scheduled tribes, receive benefits from the government through many schemes. This includes money

218 Naivedya Parakkal et al.

TABLE 11.3 Contrasting views among *adivasis* on compensation

Nozickian unjust transfer argument	*Dworkean option luck argument*
Kunjipennu: *"When the government is asking him to give it back then he has to give everything. It was our land; right? Who asked him to make all that there?"*	Malayan: *"How can I take the land back? I bought food for my children with the money I got for selling the land. So I wrote back saying that even if it is only Rs. 10, I used it for myself and so did not want the land back . . . but what to do, I already gave it to them; no?"*
Ponnamma: *"I have heard of some people who got their land back after some adalat [court order]. But what I heard happens is that, suppose somebody bought the land in say in the year 2000. They must have planted some coconut trees or arecanut trees which would have started to give produce. So those people who planted all that will have to be compensated by us. Now do we have enough money to give like that?"*	Velan: *"Here if the settlers have bought land, they have given a good price also. If I sold my land and I took money for it, then is it right to say later that I was cheated and to take the land back?'*

Source: Author

for construction of houses under IAY (Indira Awas Yojana) and AHADS (Attapady Hills Area Development Society) projects, money for buying livestock and building sheds under the Santhwanam scheme, along with subsidies in food through the Public Distribution System.

All the settlers except one (Rosy) are unanimously of the opinion that resources granted in the form of benefits should be distributed equally to everyone and then it would be up to the individual to use the resources appropriately. They feel that the *adivasis* are being given more share of benefits from government development programmes and this is making them lazy,[12] which is why their condition has not improved significantly over the past years. The settlers' views adheres to Dworkin's equality of resources theory, where after being given equal resources, people would succeed or lose based on their option luck, and goods should be distributed accordingly to hedge against the risks of unforeseen misfortunes. However, the settlers feel that *adivasis* are getting undue advantage because of the government's policy, which assumes that members of the *adivasi community* in Attapady are worse off than the settlers.

Gita (settler) said,

> They should understand that in a place like Attapady, everybody is almost in the same bad condition. In fact, I think we are worse off that some *adivasis*. Then there is no use giving them so much when they do not make proper use of what they get?

Thomas (settler) said,

> No, they should not discriminate right? If they are giving something then it must be given equally. But the problem is that when the government is allocating these benefits they are assuming that the settlers are more knowledgeable than the *adivasis*. Today, even though there are doctors, government officials and police men who are *adivasis*, they traditionally do not have the knowledge that the settlers have. It is not about education, it is the things that you learn about the world because of the kind of upbringing that you have.

Ramaswamy (settler) said,

> I was sanctioned 75,000 rupees to build this house. Out of that I got 70,000 rupees. For this house, I spent nearly 5 lakh rupees. The rest of the money, we have to give from our own hands. For *adivasis* it is not like that. For them they will be given 2 lakh rupees for a house with tile roofing and 400 sq. ft area. They won't use the money completely. They will waste it on unnecessary things. There are houses which have been incomplete for so many years. Then what is the point of the government giving more money then?

The *adivasis* on the other hand feel that the resources should be allocated based on who deserves more. They are of the opinion that because they are traditionally "backward",[13] they need to be compensated for their brute luck. However, they do hint that it is up to them to ensure that the benefits that are allocated be used resourcefully to improve their condition.

Elamma (*adivasi*) said,

> when it comes to giving goats or loan, there should be an enquiry into whether they are finding a livelihood with that benefit. That is why the benefits should be based on who deserves more and then they should be given the right direction. Otherwise giving these benefits is like drawing a line in water.

Ponnamma (*adivasi*) said,

> people in the 'others'[non-*adivasi*] category can pay the rest of the amount themselves. We are not capable of that. They already have money before. We only have enough to live on a daily basis. So they won't give it equally.

Except for two, all the settlers believe that the government should allocate resources equally and then let the individual's option luck decide the final outcome. However, the *adivasis* believe that since they are victims of brute luck, they should be compensated, primarily through unequal allocation of resources.

It is clear that these views are going beyond the frameworks of the three philosophers we have discussed in this chapter. Miller's want principles (1999) come up primarily in these voices.

It is interesting to note the discrepancy in the responses related to the rectification of economic and social differences and the redistribution of wealth, income and property. In questions related to how the differences in economic and social status may be rectified, Varghese, Rosy, Velan and Kunjipennu were of the opinion that such differences can only be attributed to fate and bad luck and were of Nozick's view that no one should be coerced to part with their wealth to help the underprivileged. However, when asked about tax payment and excess land distribution, which are two ways in which redistribution of wealth to rectify economic differences occurs in India, only Kunjipennu stuck to the Nozickian view. Varghese, Velan and Rosy said that tax payment and excess land distribution were necessary to reduce differences. This could be attributed the fact that none of the interviewees pay tax or have parted with excess land and therefore feel no obligation to be part of the process of redistribution.

Conclusion

This study did not aim to find a solution for the vexed problem of land alienation in Attapady (Kerala). Following the *'nilp samaram'* (protest by standing where people took a pledge not to sit down until their demands are met; this was called off after 162 days) in December 2014, the Government of Kerala decided to redistribute over 3,000 hectares of vested forest land to land-alienated scheduled tribe members in Attapady. As of now, the settlers will be allowed to keep the land that they acquired from *adivasis*. The study aimed to ask whether this solution (or any other solution) is in sync with the justice notions that settlers and *adivasis* held.

Our analysis found justice discourses definitely influenced by the positionalities of people (in this case settler or *adivasis*). Yet, there were clear differences within these groups, indicating a transcendental view of justice beyond positionality. These notions are internalized in people's minds. The way these theories are held and sorted by the people, can influence the social dynamics in a community. This is evident from the friction that exists between the settlers and the *adivasis* due to the difference in the way they perceive the just distribution of land and government benefits.

Adivasis traditionally held a view of trusteeship of land, rather than private ownership. However, they learned a lesson in hard ways that settlers, who preferred private ownership, were able to alienate them from the land. Law-backed justice provided a framework for this. During our interviews, it was observed that, today, when it comes to land ownership and allocation issues, the people of Attapady (both settlers and *adivasis*) are in favour of private ownership and everyone ascribes to various dimensions of Nozick and Dworkin's philosophies. There is a clear difference between the settlers and *adivasis* when it comes to opinions about land ownership and transaction. The settlers believe that the land transactions are just and that any differences should be attributed to the *adivasis'* option luck. The *adivasis* believe that the land transactions are unjust and that they deserve compensation according to the rectification principle.

In the case of allocation of government benefits, there again is a clear distinction between the settlers and *adivasis'* perceptions. All the settlers believe that the government should allocate resources equally and then let the individual's option luck decide the final outcome. However, the *adivasis* believe that since they are victims of brute luck, they should be compensated.

When it comes to redistribution of income and wealth, the interviewees, irrespective of whether they were an *adivasi* or settler, believed that the redistribution of wealth in the form of tax payment and allocation of excess land was just even though it resulted in unequal distribution because it is a way to make sure that everyone in the society is better off. This is clearly a Rawlsian position of difference principle. An exception to this view was just one *adivasi* who felt that if she had acquired the wealth by just means, she was not obliged to part with it. This is what Nozick would say as he would believe that coerced redistribution of justly acquired wealth is a violation of rights.

It clearly emerges in this study that legal solutions are far too simplistic to incorporate the complexities that people are articulating. People's voices in the study are also indicative of how powerful stakeholders within society used law to appropriate land titles and to continue the oppression of historically marginalized groups. Policy solutions must consider a wider axis and multiple frameworks through which the complexities of people's lived experiences can be addressed.

Notes

1 See Sen (1982) for the summary of limitations of welfare consequentialism and constraint-based deontological frameworks, which have the models of received wisdom in the tradition of distributive justice.

2 While there are several philosophers of theories of justice, we have selected these three philosophers for a specific reason. Our aim is not to be comprehensive in exploring different versions of theories of justice. Rather, we are looking for the ability of theories to be distinctly distinguishable on policy responsiveness.

3 When we move to understand the views of Nozick we will see he finds wealth and property acquired through talent can be justified.

4 His model is based on the hypothetical insurance markets. We all get a certain amount to work with as young adults before we enter the market and start our careers. We are responsible for the business decisions we make and must live with the ensuing economic inequalities that result. However, if one of us meets some kind of misfortune, say an accident, that cuts off our ability to grow our wealth in the market, then we must be compensated for it. Hence the notion of insurance or the equality of resources.

5 In the international context, they are identified as indigenous population. However, Indian government has not recognized any population as 'indigenous' in the context of UN's special rights for indigenous people.

6 Similar land struggles exist in several locations in India, particularly among *adivasi* communities. Most famous is the struggle between the government and *adivasis* of Niyamgiri, which is one of largest deposits of bauxite (Padel and Das, 2010; Pellissery and Biswas, 2012). In several places, *adivasi* culture and beliefs are tied to land. Therefore, land

value calculation from a purely economic sense misplaces the polyrationality at work (Davy, 2017).

7 Note that the Forest Rights Act, enacted in 2005, is not strictly applicable here, since land alienation took place much earlier. Yet, around the region, some reserve forest land is used by STs, for instance, the Sri Malleswara mountain peak during the Sivarathri festival.

8 The state *scheduled tribe development* department is considering people who have lost their land after 1986 for the allocation of redistributed vested forest land.

9 The local expression we used was *nyayapurnamaya vitharanam*, i.e. a justice driven distribution of land.

10 Pseudonyms were used to protect the identities of the research participants.

11 It is interesting at this stage to note that Sen's (2009) ideas of justice are finding a natural home to expand the concept of primary goods here. See also Nussbaum (1995, 2007).

12 This argument of meritocracy is common in the welfare state literature. Often, this argument is used to deny rights within the welfare state framework. It is also used as a mechanism of social control (Gubrium et al., 2013).

13 The people are not using a formal definition of 'backward'. Popular usage is through an expression of '*nyangal pavangalannu*' or '*pinnotta vibhagakaar*' which indicates less powerful, less wealth and less formal education.

References

Davy, B. (2012) *Land policy*. London: Ashgate.

———. (2017) "Human rights and property in land – A human rights approach", in S. Pellissery, B. Davy, and H. Jacobs (eds.), *Land policies in India*. Singapore: Springer.

Dworkin, R. (1986) *Law's empire*. Harvard: Harvard University Press.

——— (1996) *Freedom's law: The moral reading of the American Constitution*. Oxford: Oxford University Press.

Freeman, S. (2002) *Cambridge companion to Rawls*. Cambridge: Cambridge University Press.

Gubrium, E., Pellissery, S. and Lodemel, I. (2013) *Shame of it: Global perspectives on anti-poverty policy*. Bristol: Policy Press.

Locke, J. (1698/1991) *Two treatise of government*, ed. Peter Laslett. Cambridge: Cambridge University Press.

Miller, D. (1999) *Principles of social justice*. Harvard: Harvard University Press.

Nozick, R. (1974) *Anarchy, state, and utopia*. New York: Basic Books.

Nussbaum, M. C. (1995) *The quality of life*. Oxford: Clarendon Press.

———. (2007) *Frontiers of justice: Disability, nationality, species membership*. Harvard: Harvard University Press.

Padel, F. and Das, S. (2010) *Out of this earth: East India Adivasis and Aluminium Cartel*. New Delhi: Orient Blackswan.

Pellissery, S. and Biswas, S. (2012) "Emerging property regimes in India: What it holds for the future of socio-economic rights?" IRMA Working Paper No. 234.

Rawls, J. (1971) *A theory of justice*. Harvard: The Belknap Press.

———. (2001) *Justice as fairness*. Harvard: Harvard University Press.

Sen, A. (1982) "Rights and agency", *Philosophy and Public Affairs,* 11(1), 3–39.

———. (2009) *The idea of justice*. London: Penguin Books.

Weber, M. (1905) *The protestant ethic and spirit of capitalism*. London: Merchant Books.

12

CONCLUDING REFLECTIONS

Transformative constitutionalism as a framework for law and policy integration in the Global South

Avinash Govindjee

Introduction

'Policy' is a relevant recent concept focussed on the material welfare of large numbers of people in society (Clune, 1993: 1). Most law in modern states responds to the needs and consequences of "vast, dynamic and autonomous economic infrastructures and systems" and law and public policy

> seems built upon a series of tensions and contradictions: central steering through decentralised action; the melding of the public and private sectors; the focus of policy on future consequences coupled with the law's reference to historical text; sophisticated social engineering lacking adequate means to deal with elusive human behaviours; fine-tuned policies emerging from a disorderly political system and disturbed by a sense of crisis, contradiction and disorder; and a proliferation of disciplinary accretions and interdisciplinary activities without a clear paradigm for research. Yet for all these conflicting trends a common theme also exists: the emergence of empowerment as a model for designing policies in many different areas.
>
> *(Clune, 1993: 1–2)*

For Clune, the terminology at play is problematic, given that all law is public policy (in that it is the collective will of a society expressed in binding norms) and all public policy is law (in that it depends on laws and law-making institutions for at least some aspect of its existence). But, however defined, can law and policy intertwine properly, bringing together the executive, legislature and judiciary (in democratic forms of government), as well as other state and non-state actors, in order to utilize both policy and law as instruments for social change?

This concluding contribution supports literature that suggests that there is an advantage to adopting a transformative approach to constitutionalism in order to address poverty in the developing world context. It argues that such an approach, which culminates in state policy being aligned with legislative frameworks, must be accompanied by multi-stakeholder commitment to the achievement of social justice, including participatory and deliberative dimensions of democracy, judicial and quasi-judicial support, enforcement of human rights through non-judicial state institutions and private sector backing (Liebenberg and Quinot, 2012: 100). It is submitted that developing world countries with constitutions that lack justiciable socio-economic rights have a more difficult task, and that legal and policy alignment in these jurisdictions may require more activist forms of judicial intervention.

Addressing poverty through South-South co-operation – a global imperative

The Sustainable Development Goals (or Global Goals) are a universal call to action to end poverty, protect the planet and ensure that all people enjoy peace and prosperity (United Nations Development Programme, 2018). As countries seek to accentuate progress made in achieving the erstwhile Millennium Development Goals, agencies such as the United Nations aim to facilitate partnerships between governments, civil society, the private sector and citizens in order to achieve the desired outcomes (United Nations Development Programme, 2018). A 2017 review shows, however, that in many areas progress has been uneven and slower than what is needed to meet the set targets. The 2030 Agenda for Sustainable Development calls for partnerships (including North-South, South-South and triangular co-operation) and acknowledges the enormous potential of South-South co-operation to support accelerating progress towards achieving the goals (UN General Assembly, 2017: 2).

For countries in the Global South, the stakes are high. Although the global incidence of extreme poverty has decreased significantly during the past 100 years, a poverty rate of 10.7% suggests a total poverty headcount of 746 million people at present (Roser and Ortiz-Ospina, 2017). Unsurprisingly, Africa is the continent with the largest number of people living in extreme poverty (383 million people) followed by Asia (327 million) and South America (19 million) (Roser and Ortiz-Ospina, 2017). India is the country with the largest number of people living in extreme poverty (218 million people) with Nigeria and the Congo (DRC) following with 86 and 55 million people, respectively (Roser and Ortiz-Ospina, 2017). The consequences of this state of affairs have been felt in different ways. For example, migration for work has become an increasingly popular way to attempt to break out of extreme poverty and offshoring of low-skilled jobs has become increasingly prevalent. From a policy perspective, targeted cash transfer programmes are also in vogue in an attempt to reduce poverty in low-income countries. According to recent research, 119 developing countries have implemented at least one type of unconditional cash assistance programme, and 52 countries have conditional cash transfer programmes for poor households (Roser and Ortiz-Ospina, 2017).

Since the mid-1980s, the IMF and World Bank have generally promoted and supported structural adjustments of developing world economies in a manner which favours poverty relief through the trickledown of growth. Poverty reduction, so the argument went, belonged to the future with the 'market' expected to be more effective than state interventions and social programmes for poverty reduction (Townsend and Gordon, 2002). In many countries there are also concerns that the sheer aggregate amount of expenditure on existing social protection programmes is too high to be economically sustainable (Scholz et al., 2000).

There is renewed evidence, however, that economic success cannot be maintained over long periods if it is not supported by secure social protection systems which redistribute a meaningful amount of the nationally produced income (Scholz et al., 2000). The Indian government's national five-year plans from 1961–1966 onwards have indicated an awareness that poverty cannot be remedied by economic growth governed only by market considerations, but by "redistribution with growth" (Townsend and Gordon, 2002: 366). For the same reason Sen, in his seminal work *Development as Freedom*, concludes that the impact of economic growth depends mainly on how the fruits of economic growth are used (Sen, 1999). Sen distinguishes between "growth-mediated" and "support-led" processes. The former process works through fast economic growth, and its success depends on the growth process being wide-based and economically broad. In contrast, the support-led process does not operate through fast economic growth, but works through a programme of skilful social support of health care, education and other relevant social arrangements (Sen, 1999). The success of the support-led process in parts of India does indicate that a country does not have to wait until it is much richer before embarking on rapid expansion of basic education and health care and that the quality of life can be vastly raised, despite low incomes, through an adequate programme of social services:.

> The support-led process is a recipe for rapid achievement of higher quality of life, and this has great policy importance, but there remains an excellent case for moving on from there to broader achievements that include economic growth as well as the raising of the standard features of quality of life.
>
> *(Sen, 1999: 49)*

It must also be understood that the traditional North-South development paradigm (reinforced by the development paradigm of the Bretton Woods Institutions and the consequent structural adjustment programmes of the World Bank and the International Monetary Fund) is now giving way to a South-South model of cooperation that complements and positions countries from the Global South, and Africa in particular, on the centre stage (Modi, 2011).[1] According to the United

226 Avinash Govindjee

Nations, the increasing momentum of South-South co-operation needs to be supported by strengthened institutionalization of collaborative efforts. This includes

- The development of formal rules, informal norms and dedicated organizations, which have moved South-South co-operation increasingly into the mainstream of policymaking at the national level. A growing number of countries have created dedicated agencies for South-South co-operation,[2] or have enhanced the co-operation capacities of institutions;[3]
- An ongoing expansion of the number of actors engaging in South-South co-operation, including subnational entities such as municipal and provincial governments and non-state actors such as private firms, civil society, volunteer groups and academic and research institutions;
- A new wave of multilateral institutions devoted to South-South co-operation, including the Asian Infrastructure Investment Bank (AIIB) and the New Development Bank (United Nations, 2017: 2).

Such global responses to developmental challenges need to be complemented by strong regional and national legal frameworks to ensure that there is alignment between law and governmental policy directed towards poverty alleviation.

The promise of a transformative constitutional approach to poverty alleviation

> Transformation is not a temporary phenomenon that ends when we all have equal access to resources and basic services and when lawyers and judges embrace a culture of justification. Transformation is a permanent ideal, a way of looking at the world that creates a space in which dialogue and contestation are truly possible, in which new ways of being are constantly explored and created, accepted and rejected and in which change is unpredictable but the idea of change is constant. This is perhaps the ultimate vision of a transformative, rather than a transitional Constitution. This is the perspective that sees the Constitution as not transformative because of its peculiar historical position or its particular socio-economic goals but because it envisions a society that will always be open to change and contestation, a society that will always be defined by transformation.
> *(Langa, 2006: 354)*

It has been suggested that the "transformative" dimension of constitutionalizing social rights encompasses

> [A] long-term project of constitutional enactment, interpretation and enforcement committed (not in isolation, of course, but in a historical context of conducive political developments) to transforming a country's political and social institutions and power relationships in a democratic, participatory and egalitarian direction. Transformative constitutionalism connotes an enterprise

of inducing large-scale social change through non-violent political processes grounded in law.

(Klare, 1998: 146)

The South African experience provides a useful case study of a country approach that facilitates the alignment of legislative and policy direction courtesy of a supreme constitution that includes a slew of justiciable fundamental human rights. The dawn of the post-apartheid era in South Africa was characterized by the transition to a democratic legal system based on the supremacy of the Constitution of the Republic of South Africa, 1996 and the rule of law, supported by various values, including human dignity, the achievement of (substantive) equality and the advancement of human rights and freedoms (Section 1 of the Constitution of the Republic of South Africa, 1996 ("the Constitution")).[4] As the supreme law of the country, any law or conduct inconsistent with the Constitution is invalid, and the obligations imposed by the Constitution must be fulfilled (Section 2 of the Constitution).

Crucially, the drafters of the Constitution resisted the temptation to separate and distinguish between civil and political rights, on the one hand, and socio-economic rights, on the other. Recognizing that these groups of rights are inherently linked and mutually supportive, the Constitution provides for an expansive range of socio-economic rights as part of the Bill of Rights. Such rights are justiciable in South Africa, despite having been challenged, at the time of their inclusion, as being rights that have not been universally accepted as fundamental and because of their perceived inconsistency with the notion of separation of powers (Certification of the Constitution of the Republic of South Africa, 1996: 77). In particular, objectors argued that inclusion of socio-economic rights as justiciable rights in the Constitution would result in the courts dictating to government how the budget should be allocated. In rejecting such assertions, the Constitutional Court held as follows in the *Certification* judgment:

> It is true that the inclusion of socio-economic rights may result in courts making orders which have direct implications for budgetary matters. However, even when a court enforces civil and political rights such as equality, freedom of speech and the right to a fair trial, the order it makes will often have such implications. A court may require the provision of legal aid, or the extension of state benefits to a class of people who formerly were not beneficiaries of such benefits. In our view it cannot be said that by including socio-economic rights within a bill of rights, a task is conferred upon the courts so different from that ordinarily conferred upon them by a bill of rights, that it results in a breach of the separation of powers . . . we are of the view that these rights are, at least to some extent, justiciable.
>
> *(Certification of the Constitution of the Republic of South Africa, 1996: 77)*

The Constitutional Court accordingly concluded that the fact that socio-economic rights would almost inevitably give rise to budgetary implications was not a bar to their justiciability. At the very least, according to the Court, socio-economic rights could be negatively protected from improper invasion (Certification of the Constitution of the Republic of South Africa, 1996: 77). The effect of the decision in the *Certification* judgment was that socio-economic rights to education (section 29 of the Constitution), access to land and housing (section 25 and 26 of the Constitution), health care, food, water and social security, including, if people are unable to support themselves and their dependents, appropriate social assistance (section 27 of the Constitution), were interspersed with other (civil and political) rights in the Bill of Rights.

This landmark inclusion of socio-economic rights as justiciable "fundamental" rights was not without limitation. With a few notable exceptions, the state was only directed to take reasonable legislative and other measures, within its available resources, to achieve the progressive realization of these socio-economic rights.[5] In addition, the general limitations clause of the constitution confirms that

> The rights in the Bill of Rights may be limited only in terms of law of general application to the extent that the limitation is reasonable and justifiable in an open and democratic society based on human dignity, equality and freedom, taking into account all relevant factors.
>
> *(section 7(3) and 36 of the Constitution)*[6]

Beyond such limitations, the legislature, executive, judiciary and all organs of state are bound by the Bill of Rights, which applies to all law (section 2 of the Constitution),[7] and the state must respect, protect, promote and fulfil the rights in the Bill of Rights (section 7(2) and 8(1) of the Constitution).[8]

These advancements must, however, be contextualized against the backdrop of the reality of the situation in the country. South Africa, like a number of others on the African continent, is beset by fundamental challenges of under-development, unemployment, poverty and inequality. As a result, and despite the seemingly impressive constitutional framework described earlier, South Africa has been criticized for making slow progress in terms of addressing these challenges. People in South Africa who are unable to support themselves or their dependents (or other interested parties/classes of people) have increasingly turned to the courts in the hope that the various socio-economic rights contained in the Constitution may be interpreted in a fashion that will benefit the marginalized.

The views expressed in the key South African cases decided over the past 20 years generally indicate a problem faced by other developing societies as well, namely that courts are loathe to consider the appropriateness of fiscal policy choices (Chetty, 2002). Courts commonly argue that they do not have the capacity to make judgments on overall budgetary allocations and the division of revenue given the "clear" separation of roles when examining policies that influence the overall resource availability (Chetty, 2002; Minister of Health v Treatment Action Campaign, 2002). Similarly, courts have typically refrained from examining the efficacy of state policies to raise additional resources to address socio-economic problems in developing societies. Vulnerable individuals who are unemployed and destitute but uncovered by the social assistance system should, for example, be able to approach a court and claim that the state is not taking reasonable steps, within its available resources, to provide the social assistance level *which it is able to provide* at the time of the application. Such arguments will inevitably be met with the defence that the state lacks the resources to provide relief. In order for the applicant to be successful, courts should ideally be able to assess budgetary allocations for constitutional compliance. This is understandably more palatable in cases where there is explicit constitutional support for the justiciability of socio-economic rights.

Two extreme scenarios assist this argument. While the current environment for increasing the application of socio-economic rights may be favourable in countries which have enjoyed some level of economic growth, a new political regime may have different priorities (such as nuclear armament) and reduce socio-economic expenditure rapidly and completely. On the other end of the spectrum, there are certain things that a government cannot do in order to fulfil a single constitutional duty. Fabre (2000: 150) cites the example of a government decision to stop the provision of housing altogether in order to provide greater education. In both instances, the ability of an appropriate court to make an order that the state cannot fulfil its duty in such a fashion has obvious importance. Courts should ideally be supported by constitutional instruments so as to be able to order the government to raise standards of provision in a certain domain of welfare without cutting down on the existing provision in other domains of welfare, as long as it is possible to raise money by other means. The government thus chooses these other means, whatever they are, thereby maintaining a balance of power with the judiciary (Fabre, 2000).[9]

While states naturally enjoy a wide measure of discretion in their choice of policy and in the allocation of resources for giving effect to socio-economic rights, it must be accepted that courts can intervene to vindicate the right where the state's allocations are unreasonable (and therefore unconstitutional). This is completely consistent with the adage that determinations of reasonableness may have budgetary implications but are not themselves directed at re-arranging budgets. According to Sen (1999), the pragmatic and open-minded scrutiny of rival claims (such as increasing the defence budget) rectifies the risk of use of public resources for purposes where the social benefits are uncertain. Courts could also, in the name of constitutional review, ask government to justify a specific policy, budget or legislation in relation to socio-economic rights, not in order to choose between different policies but to make government explain how it envisages, for example, eradicating poverty. By doing this, the court would be reviewing policy choices without making them, again maintaining the balance of power (Yigen, 2000).

The court could at the very least argue that a piece of legislation and the resources it requires that the government use are not proportional to the end stated in the constitution, and that insofar as countries with similar economies and a comparable level of socio-economic development are doing better, the government should redraft the law and/or increase resources in fulfilment of the constitution (Fabre, 2000). To this end it must be accepted that courts are not precluded from

230 Avinash Govindjee

making orders that have some impact on policy (Minister of Health vs Treatment Action Campaign, 2002). If the courts find that states have failed to give effect to their constitutional obligations when formulating and implementing policies that are subsequently challenged as being inconsistent with a supreme constitution, they ought to be constitutionally bound to say so (Minister of Health vs Treatment Action Campaign, 2002).

This should not mean that groups of destitute people are automatically entitled to socio-economic rights. In some cases the court might legitimately find that the cost of providing assistance is so high, and the people who would benefit so few, that the resources in question would better be spent elsewhere when the government makes out a case in terms of the standard of reasonableness. In other cases, however, the court might be convinced that the costs of *not* providing assistance to the group concerned would be so devastating that they have legitimately established a claim to public resources.[10]

Judicial assessment of budgetary allocations therefore holds two potential advantages. Firstly, by acting as a check to government conduct, the court can ensure that the state is prioritizing social expenditure to the levels implicit in the wording of the constitution. By doing so it is likely that the government will be under greater pressure to make certain that it is devoting as much state resources as it can towards the goal of social justice (Bilchitz, 2003). Secondly, increased public interest litigation is bound to meet the defence that the state lacks resources to increase the actual provision of socio-economic rights. Judicial assessment of government action has the added benefit of enabling countries to meet constitutional promises and to ensure that state actions, including their budgetary allocations, must comply with this and must be subject to scrutiny (Moseneke, 2002).[11] This approach certainly contributes to an in-principle enhanced form of alignment amongst the constitution, state policy direction, legislation and judicial interpretation.

The transformative constitutionalism approach is not, however, without limits. Part of the challenge pertains to the "political nature of the project", and the argument that transformative adjudication is a disguised form of politically progressive interpretation (Liebenberg and Quinot, 2012). Furthermore, in reality, there appears to have been a general failure of a progressive development-oriented (or transformative) constitutional culture – particularly on the African continent, but also in other parts of the developing world (Liebenberg and Quinot, 2012).

Constitutional interpretation and political boundaries

According to Klaaren (2003), legal interpreters would do well to explore far-reaching interpretive possibilities as part of realizing the transformative potential of a constitution. Such an innovative approach is justified as being part of the building of a human rights culture (Klaaren, 2003).

> Public policy is the art of the possible, and this is important to bear in mind in combining theoretical insights with realistic readings of practical feasibility
> *(Sen, 1999: 132).*

The way in which directive principles have been used in the context of public interest litigation via the right to life and the use of simple letters to judges to revolutionize the law of standing are examples of such innovative interpretations in India (Steiner and Alston, 2000). The challenge remains for courts, and other quasi-judicial actors and state bodies tasked with contributing to human rights realization, to assist those most in need while maintaining the fine separations of power with government, effectively navigating a careful balancing exercise (Govindjee, 2013). In cases where the constitutional text arguably fails to go far enough (at least in an explicit sense, for example by including socio-economic rights as "directive principles of state policy", as in India), it is understandable that judiciaries may be more inclined to adopt an activist approach to constitutional interpretation.

> The deepening of democracy required goes far beyond the protection of individual liberties. The rule of law it embraces in the public sphere is one of accountable, open and responsive government, and of judicial oversight of the government's obligation to fight poverty and provide social welfare. Even in the public sphere, it pulls the courts into much deeper social and political choice-making than the conventional wisdom ever countenanced. In the private sphere it requires the courts to do their bit in eradicating distorting patterns of interpersonal, social and economic domination. The conventional wisdom pretends that courts may not do that. So both in the so-called "vertical" (public) and "horizontal" (private) spheres, the conventional wisdom does not provide us with the means or tools to perform our constitutional duty. Something more, and different, is required.
>
> *(Osode and Clover, 2010: 67)*

It may be argued that the role which judges are required to play in exercising their law-making functions has now assumed political importance and that the reality is that judicial law making is now a widely accepted reality (Alston, 1999).

> The courts do not operate in a valueless vacuum – even when they are ostensibly only applying the existing law, there is considerable scope for judges' own preferences to affect the way they marshal precedents, and assess the competing arguments, when deciding a disputed point of law.
>
> *(Alston, 1999: 512)*

A conservative legal culture can completely undermine transformative constitutionalism, leaving only a system of liberal democratic constitutionalism which emphasizes procedural democracy:

> Put differently, shorn of its transformative potentialities through retrogressive interpretation, transformative constitutionalism offers precious little in the form of an armoury with which to continue the fight to . . . contribute to eradication of poverty.
>
> *(Liebenberg and Quinot, 2012: 52)*

232 Avinash Govindjee

What makes it more difficult for the judiciary to contribute positively towards change is that some states have already displayed the courage to restructure their budgetary priorities in favour of social redistribution (Fabre, 2000).[12] Any judgment or argument which requires a state to devote more money than it is willing to towards social spending will, therefore, be opposed on the grounds that the state is already taking reasonable measures within its available resources to progressively give content to the right. One way in which judiciaries in the developing world may legitimately challenge such an opposition is by means of an argument based upon the supremacy of the constitution. This is clearly more easily achievable in instances where the constitution contains a set of justiciable right directed towards social development. Any serious challenge will be faced with the added concern of a state which refuses to comply with an order of court based upon the constitution, thereby triggering a potential 'constitutional crisis'. Because of this, the realization of socio-economic rights as a profoundly political process assumes added significance (Pieterse and Van Donk, 2002).

The 'urgent' case conundrum[13]

The challenges of law and policy integration and judicial approaches to legal interpretation play out quite starkly in 'urgent' cases. It is these matters that often display severe policy and budgetary implications (and which, as a result, courts generally try to avoid where possible). Although courts may preach that they need to show restraint and deference to the other branches of government when faced with such matters, when appropriate they have taken up the practice of declaring law and conduct inconsistent with the constitution to be invalid, thereby facilitating the transformation of society. Predicting the boundary of this involvement requires answering the question as to precisely when a court should override the legislature and prevent them from pursuing the policy of their choice and when it cannot do so.

Will the twenty-first century be the one when the judiciary ensures that both the executive and parliament function within the parameters of basic constitutional values and norms? It can be argued that the reality is often that institutions of democracy don't serve the purposes for which they were created and that this results in courts having to make very difficult decisions which the legislature, for example, is unable to align with the constitution.

It must be appreciated that a determination as to whether a matter falls within the purview of the judiciary or not is a matter to be decided on a case-by-case basis without a 'theory of when'. To establish their legitimacy as a legal institution vis-à-vis the political authorities, courts have had to strike a balance – neither giving up on social rights nor meddling unduly in policy issues (Gloppen, 2005). It may appear that a court ruling in effect telling the state how to allocate its budget would intrude on the legislature's domain in an unacceptable way which threatened the separation of powers. But undue reliance on the doctrine of formal separation of powers is problematic when it comes to finding the balance amongst the rights of different groups:

> [I]t will be the democratic institutions that will try to achieve an appropriate balance. But frequently these institutions will exercise their powers in a disproportionate way, overbalancing towards the state and going well beyond what is necessary to serve a legitimate public interest. They will limit the fundamental rights of individuals and communities far more than good government and the public interest really require. In these cases the courts will intervene, not to prevent the democratic institutions from doing their constitutionally mandated work, but to ensure that they exercise their powers within the limits that the Constitution requires.
>
> *(Sachs, 2004: 207)*

But how should judges strike the appropriate balance in practice when faced with difficult and urgent cases? The availability of resources and the budgetary implications of an application pressing for the realization of socio-economic rights together with the desperateness or urgency of the applicants' position may assume greater importance in particular cases – especially if it is accepted that judges often do decide difficult issues with reference to their 'ultimate conviction of what is right'.

According to Bilchitz (2003), and based upon the simple premise that people who are desperately in trouble require assistance from the government as a matter of priority, preference should be given to those whose mere survival is threatened. Bilchitz (2003) uses 'urgency' as a method of differentiating between cases where a court should assist an applicant and cases where it cannot due to resource constraints. A paradigm developed by Bollyky may assist this argument. According to Bollyky (2002), if a remedy (R) requires extensive policy (P) and budgetary choices (B), the court will only make them for a constitutional violation (C) which is proportionately extensive – described algebraically as R if $C > P + B$. Similarly, it may be argued that courts are more likely to find legislative or other measures designed to give effect to socio-economic rights to be unreasonable if the desperateness of the situation faced by the applicants challenging these measures outweighs the budgetary implications of the remedy sought.

The importance of multi-stakeholder support for law and policy integration

It may be argued that state policy alignment with legislative frameworks must be accompanied by multi-stakeholder commitment to the achievement of social justice, including participatory and deliberative dimensions of democracy (Liebenberg and Quinot, 2012), judicial and quasi-judicial support, enforcement of human rights through non-judicial state institutions and private sector backing. This is irrespective of the form that the constitutional text takes, although it is arguable

234 Avinash Govindjee

that the role of actors other than the judiciary assumes even greater significance in instances where there is a lack of clear policy and legal trajectory towards achieving social justice.

Greater commitment needs to be made towards ensuring conceptions of constitutionalism encompass significant advances in "mass bottom-up truly participatory democracy in that it allows people to take an active part in the decision-making processes that concern them (Liebenberg and Quinot, 2012: 56)."

Botha too suggests that judgments that conceive of democracy in formal terms (as the capacity of duly elected legislatures to enact law within their constitutional area of competence) are impoverished. He argues that these judgments are loath to impose requirements that would guarantee the participatory nature of the law-making process, while approaches that conceive of democracy in "dialogic, participatory and pluralistic terms" are preferred (Liebenberg and Quinot, 2012: 79–99).

For Sen, the attainment of social justice without public reasoning based on participatory and deliberative democratic models, is impossible. Sen argues that the vital role of public reasoning in the practice of democracy makes the entire subject of democracy relate closely with notions of justice, and that (true) democracy involves political participation, dialogue and public interaction (Liebenberg and Quinot, 2012: 104).

> In order for socio-economic transformation to have a real impact on the lives of the poor and marginalised, meaningful participation in the development of law and policy as well as administrative decision-making, is required. Opportunities for informed participation can lead to transparent, accountable dialogue and debate on key policy choices to address the impact of poverty and inequality. This resonates with a participatory constitutional democracy, which requires decisions to be considered in the light of certain fundamental norms and values.
>
> *(Liebenberg and Quinot, 2012: 100)*

The type of democratic development state, underpinned by a transformative constitutional mindset, that is ideal is one involving political will and a long-term developmental vision based on broad national consensus among political parties, civil society, business and organized labour, and the collaborative implementation of an integrated long-term development plan based on a holistic vision. This must be coupled to a participatory approach, focussed on the socio-economic needs of a country's population and involving policy development aimed at addressing socio-economic imbalances (Liebenberg and Quinot, 2012). Such efforts would support, rather than undermine, any judicial, policy and legal initiatives directed towards positive social change.

Conclusion: towards an integrated and aligned approach

O'Regan J, speaking at a World Jurist Association conference in 1998, makes it clear that the law, and by implication the judiciary, can contribute to social change, but there are many other factors that also influence changes in society (O'Regan,

Concluding reflections 235

1998).[14] Every branch of government must do its fair share in honouring its constitutional obligations. In her own words

> [i]n recognising that the courts have the power to determine whether their [the legislature's and the executive's] actions are in breach of the Bill of Rights or not, sight must not be lost of the importance of members of the legislature and the executive honouring their own constitutional obligations with integrity. To focus entirely upon the courts' development of constitutional rights is to focus upon the pathology of constitutionalism. A sound constitutional state must be based upon a daily recognition of their constitutional commitments by all who exercise public power.
>
> *(O'Regan, 1998: 14)*

The implication is that meaningful change as envisaged in a constitution or by a legal system will only be effected if each branch of government complies with its constitutional commitments and obligations. This in itself will contribute to law and policy alignment, a healthier inter-relationship between the different arms of government and enhanced social cohesion. Although courts have an important role to play as agents of societal transformation, it is not their primary function. In the final analysis, what happens in the courts is ultimately not determinative of social reality (O'Regan, 1998). The involvement of all the other branches of government and all of society is necessary to effect the optimum kinds of changes that are required. The buck, ultimately, does not stop with the judiciary. The responsibility for the success of the constitutional experiment is, in the final analysis, a collaborative venture between the branches of government and society in general.

The crafting of a country's constitution is a key determinant of the ease with which such alignment and integration may be possible. Countries with modern constitutional texts, which create clear roles for the judiciary as well as other relevant actors (such as a Public Protector, Human Rights Commission, Commission for Gender Equality and the like) are at an advantage, allowing the constitution to serve almost like the centre-piece of a carousel, around which the various arms, layers and spheres of government, the legislature, the judiciary and other stakeholders (including civil society and the private sector) are able to link and pivot. The nature of such constitutions may obviate the need for activist judiciaries in order to give effect to socio-economic rights.

In the final analysis, the challenges associated with poverty and under-development clearly require an integrated and aligned approach in order for discernible progress to be made. As indicated at the outset, it also requires international and regional co-operation, particularly amongst countries in the Global South which typically experience deeper and more prevalent forms of social exclusion.

Notes

1 As Modi suggests, South-South co-operation (SSC) as a concept has its genesis in the post–World War II period when developing countries of Asia and Africa were liberated

from colonialism and began to confront an international system balanced unfavourably towards them. This developing co-operation builds on historical, pre-colonial "Indian Ocean world" links, the Non-Aligned Movement of the 1960s and the formation of the Group of 77 (G-77) nations.

2 Examples include the Indonesian Ministry of National Development Planning and the South African Development Partnership Agency.

3 This has occurred, for example, via increased financial allocations, development of policy and regulatory frameworks, appointment of specialized personnel and through administrative and methodological innovations.

4 The Constitution provides in section 7(1) that the Bill of Rights is a cornerstone of democracy in South Africa, given that it enshrines the rights of all people in the country and affirms the democratic values of human dignity, equality and freedom.

5 See, for example, the so-called internal limitations contained in ss 26(2) and 27(2) of the Constitution.

6 Relevant factors listed in s 36 include the nature of the right; the importance of the purpose of the limitation; the nature and extent of the limitation; the relation between the limitation and its purpose; and less restrictive means to achieve the purpose.

7 The Constitution itself proclaims that it is the supreme law of the Republic of South Africa, and that any law or conduct inconsistent with it is invalid.

8 See, in general, Govindjee (2013).

9 The role of the court would normally be limited to directing the executive to propose concrete but affordable measures which would address the problem identified. See Darrow and Alston "Bills of Rights in Comparative Perspective" in Alston *Promoting Human Rights through Bills of Rights* (1999) 465–506.

10 This argument is based on Wesson's argument with respect to the chronically ill in Wesson "Chronic Illness and the Right of Access to Health Care Services" in M. Du Plessis and S. Pete, *Constitutional Democracy in South Africa 1994–2004: Essays in Honour of the Howard College School of Law* (2004), 97–106.

11 As Moseneke has argued, in the South African context, "the judiciary is commanded to observe with unfailing fidelity the transformative mission of the Constitution."

12 This is in accordance with Fabre's contention that constitutional social rights are not the solution to poverty and that greater structural changes are needed in order to bring about social justice.

13 This section has been modified from Govindjee and Olivier (2007).

14 This paragraph is drawn from Govindjee and Olivier (2007).

References

Alston, P. (ed.) (1999) *Promoting human rights through bills of rights*. New York: Oxford University Press.

Bilchitz, D. (2003) "Towards a reasonable approach to the minimum core: Laying the foundations for future socio-economic rights jurisprudence", *SAJHR*, 19(1).

Bollyky, T. (2002) "R if C>P+B: A paradigm for judicial remedies of socio-economic rights violations", *SAJHR*, 18(2).

Certification of the Constitution of the Republic of South Africa, 1996 [1996] ZACC 26; 1996 (4) SA 744 (CC); 1996 (10) BCLR 1253 (CC).

Chetty, K. (2002) "The public finance implications of recent socio-economic rights judgments", *Law, Democracy and Development*, 6(2).

Clune, W. H. (1993) "Law and public policy: Map of an area", *2 South California Interdisciplinary Law Journal*, 1, 1.

Fabre, C. (2000) *Social rights under the constitution: Government and the decent life*. New York: Oxford University Press.

Govindjee, A. (2013) "Adjudication of socio-economic rights by the constitutional court of South Africa: Walking the tightrope between activism and deference", *National Law School of India Review*, 25(1).

Govindjee, A. and Olivier, M. (2007) "Finding the balance: The role of the courts in giving effect to socio-economic rights in South Africa", *Speculum Juris,* 21(2), 167–183.

Gloppen, S. (2005) "Social rights litigation as transformation: South African Perspectives", in P. Jones, and K. Stokke (eds.), *Democratising development: The politics of socio-economic rights in South Africa*. Leiden: Martinus Nijhoff Publishers.

Klaaren, J. (2003) "A remedial interpretation of the Treatment Action Campaign decision", *SAJHR*, 19(3).

Klare, K. (1998) "Legal culture and transformative constitutionalism", *SAJHR*, 14.

Langa, P. (2006) "Transformative Constitutionalism", *Stell LR*.

Liebenberg, S. and Quinot, G. (2012) *Law and poverty: Perspectives from South Africa and Beyond*. Gauteng: Juta & Co.

Minister of Health v Treatment Action Campaign 2002 SA (5) (CC).

Modi, R. (2011) *South-South cooperation: Africa on the centre stage*. Houndmills, Basingstoke, Hampshire [England]: Palgrave Macmillan.

Moseneke, D. (2002) "The fourth Bram Fischer memorial lecture: Transformative adjudication", *SAJHR*, 18.

O'Regan, K. (1998) "The enforcement and protection of human rights: The role of the Constitutional Court of South Africa", in B. Ajibola and D. van Zyl (eds.), *The Judiciary in Africa*. Juta.

Osode, P. and Glover, G. (eds.) (2010) *Law and transformative justice in post-apartheid South Africa*. Spekboom.

Pieterse, E. and Van Donk, M. (2002) "Incomplete ruptures: The political economy of realising socio-economic rights", *Law, Democracy and Development*, 6(2).

Roser, M. and Ortiz-Ospina, E. (2017) "Global extreme poverty" [online]. Our World in Data. Available at: https://ourworldindata.org/extreme-poverty (Accessed 1 March 2018).

Sachs, A. (2004) *The free diary of Albie Sachs*. Random House.

Scholz, W., Cichon, M. and Hagemejer, K. (2000) *Social budgeting*. Geneva: International Labour Office.

Sen, A. (1999) *Development as freedom*. Oxford: Oxford University Press.

Steiner, H. and Alston, P. (2000) *International human rights in context: Law, politics, morals*. 2nd ed. Oxford: Oxford University Press.

Townsend, P. and Gordon, D. (2002) *World poverty: New policies to defeat an old enemy*. Bristol: Bristol University Press.

UN General Assembly (2017) *State of South-South Cooperation*. Report of the Secretary-General (A/72/297).

United Nations Development Programme. (2018) [online] Available at: www.undp.org/content/undp/en/home/sustainable-development-goals.html (Accessed 2 March 2018).

Yigen, K. (2000) "Enforcing social justice: Economic and social rights in South Africa", *The International Journal of Human Rights*, 4(2).

INDEX

Note: Page numbers in **bold** refer to tables on the corresponding page.

Abbott Government 54
absolute advantage theory 93
absolute sovereign immunity 79
access 13, 40, 51, 53, 75, 76, 79, 93, 96, 102, 106, 128–131, 133, 136, 137, 140, 144, 155, 157, 164, 192, 193, 196, 207, 209, 217, 226, 228
accommodative 132, 135, 138, 141, 142
accountability 8, 14, 15, 53, 59, 114, 145, 183
acquisition principle 204
activation policies 161, 167
activist judicial intervention 224
adequacy 76, 112, 134, 152, 198, 223, 225
ad hoc face-to-face bargaining 7
adivasis 171–184, 206–221
administration 8, 30, 38, 84, 86, 114, 115, 117, 136, 140, 156, 159–161, 172, 174, 175, 182, 190, 206
administrative law 8, 60, 183
Administrative Reform Commissions 117
adversarial nature, judicial system 14
advocacy 8, 50
affirmative action 130–132, 141, 143
aggressive lawsuits 81
Ambedkar, Bhim Rao 111–114, 124
Anns v Merton London Borough Council 57
anti-global doctrine 26–46; constitutional status, right to strike in Israel 33; Germany, strikes 36–39; vis-à-vis a political approach, application 41–44
appropriateness 64, 65, 228

Arosemena, G. 152
article 9(3) of the German constitution 36
assumption 16, 61, 93
asylum seekers 50, 53, 58, 59
Attapady 206; government benefits, allocation 217–220; history of 206–207; original owners of land 214–215
austerity policies 76
Austin, John 2
Australia: old legal dichotomy 49–70; OSB 50, 52, 53; policy-operational dichotomy 56–60
Australian Border Force Act, 2015 50
Australian Customs and Border Protection Service 52
Australian Customs Service 52
Australian Defence Force 52
authority 3, 5, 9, 30, 38, 40, 57, 58, 61, 63, 65, 81, 82, 104, 115, 132, 185, 192, 197, 198

Bangladesh: constitutional promises 138; minorities 138; outcomes 138–140
Banking Regulation Act 99, 100
banking sector 99–100
Barclay, S. 172
Bar Ilan case 33, 34
Barthes, Roland 185
Basic Law of the Federal Republic 36
Bateman, S. 53, 54
Baxi, Upendra 10, 112
Biharis 140
Bilchitz, D. 233

240 Index

Birkland, T. 172
Birla, G.D. 113
Bollyky, T. 233
Bombay Plan 113, 114
Borgeraas, E. 160
Bose, C. J. 85
Bowles, Martin 55
Braithwaite, J. 10
Bromley, D. W. 15
Buckley, R. 61
budget 154, 157, 160, 227, 229, 232
Bush vs Gore election judgement 12

Caldeira, Teresa 191, 193
capital 75, 79, 80, 92–94, 100, 102, 103, 105, 106, 113, 114, 123, 159, 192
caste 112, 114, 116, 128–130, 133, 135, 138, 139, 178, 203, 207, 217
causal model 12
Census of India, 2011 189
Centre for International Governance and Innovation (CIGI) 78
Chakravorty, Sanjoy 195
Chamberlain, Wilt 205
Chandy, Oommen 118
child poverty, in Norway 156–157; *see also* poverty
children 6, 50, 64, 151, 154–159, 161–168, 212
Child Rights Convention (CRC) 153–156, 165, 168
child's right to adequate standard of living 153
citizenship 7, 8, 13, 62–64, 132, 140, 143
city 35, 191, 192, 197
civil aviation 100–101
civil court 16
civil society 5, 14, 29, 117, 146, 195, 224, 226, 234, 235
Clune, W. H. 223
Code of Civil Procedure (CPC) 84–87
collective action 34; of civil servants 37
collective bargaining 36, 39, 40
collective freedoms 31
collective labour freedoms 33
commissions 117, 145, 146
Commonwealth Ombudsman 61–63
community 63, 78, 134, 136, 174, 180, 185, 206, 218, 220
comparative advantage theory 93
compensation 58, 62, 194–196, 205, 217, 221
Concept of Law, The (Hart) 2
Conroy, Stephen 55
constitutional amendments 7
constitutional courts 7

constitutional democracy 3
constitutional interpretation 230–232
constitutionalism 3–5, 26–29, 32–36, 39, 40, 42–45, 129, 136, 140–142, 223–235; in Israel, public services arena 33–35; of labour rights 45; principle of 4
constitutional jurisprudence 7
Constitution of Norway, section 104 155
contemporary international legal order 74–89
'contempt of court' litigations 14
continuous mandamus 16
Cornall Report 63
Cornall, Robert 63
corruption 15, 75, 92, 211, 212
cost-benefit analysis 7
court-led judgement 13
courts 2, 5–7, 13, 16, 27, 28, 33, 35, 36, 42–45, 57, 59, 61, 77, 79, 80, 82–84, 96, 172, 227–229, 231–233, 235
CRC Committee 154, 163
criminal court 17
Crimmins v Stevedoring Industry Finance Committee 61
culture 29, 45, 63, 112, 115, 116, 128, 130, 226, 230, 231
Curators v. University of Kwa-Zulu Natal 5

Dalit 139
Dastyari, Sam 55
Davies, M. 61
"Death of the Author, The" (Barthes) 185
debt crisis 75, 76
decentralization 130, 135, 223
decision-making 7, 42, 58, 61, 106, 129, 137, 144, 234
Defence Force General 51
deformative planning 112–114
de-globalization process 32
degree of centralization 122
Delhi High Court 14
democracy 3, 8, 12–13, 18, 29, 37, 111–123, 128, 129, 136, 138, 139, 142, 143, 224, 231–234; non-statutory institutions destiny 111–125; transformative justice in 128
democratic equality 204
democratic legitimacy 43
demography 32, 33, 189
Department of Industrial Policy and Promotion (DIPP) 94
development 5, 10, 15, 26–28, 31, 32, 44, 56, 63, 78, 87, 92, 93, 99, 101–103, 105, 106, 111, 112, 115–118, 121, 122, 128, 136, 137, 140–142, 144, 146, 153, 154–156,

158, 160, 162–167, 171–174, 176, 178, 179, 181, 189, 190, 192, 193, 196–198, 207, 218, 224–226, 228–230, 232, 234, 235
Development as Freedom (Sen) 225
Dewey, John 15
DIAC 64
difference principle 204, 221
direct investment enterprise 94
direct investor 94
directive principles 130, 231
discretionary powers 58
discrimination 130, 132, 133, 135, 138–140, 143, 144, 146, 155, 164, 168, 211, 212
discriminatory colonization 129
dissent 123n2
distributive justice 7, 202–221; alienated land restoration, adivasis 217; Dworkin and 205–206; economic and social differences, reasons 211–214; frame of study and fieldwork 207–210; geographical study area 206; government benefits, allocation 217–220; land ownership and allocation 214–215; Nozick and 204–205; Rawls and 203–204; settlers, land ownership 215–217; theories of 203
domestic capital 92
Donegal International Ltd v Republic of Zambia & Anor. 80
Drahos, P. 10
Drug Price Control Order 104
Dworkin, Ronald 3, 7, 202–221
Dye, T. R. 28

economic differences 208, 220
economic liberalization 123
economic planning 115
economic rationality 6, 18
economic recovery 11
education 1, 13, 35, 93, 116, 121, 130, 140, 154, 156, 158, 159, 161, 163, 167, 207, 211, 217, 219, 225, 228, 229
effectiveness 1, 134
efficiency 2, 6, 8, 79, 92, 94, 100
elderly 34
elected representative 8, 12, 13
election 12, 29, 51, 53, 56, 130, 131, 133–135
Elster, J. 6
emergency services 37
employment 6, 28, 31, 32, 34, 36, 40, 42, 44, 84–86, 96, 102, 121, 129, 130, 132–134, 137–144, 146
enforcement 8, 30, 31, 33, 42, 52, 82, 224, 226, 233

entitlement theory 202, 204–205
equality 3, 5, 6, 42, 44, 80, 96, 112, 114, 130, 131, 133, 135–138, 143, 164, 168, 202, 204, 205, 218, 227, 228, 235
equality of resources 202, 205–206
equity 94, 101
ethno-linguistic minorities 135
European Convention on Human Rights (ECHR) 38
European Social Charter, Article 13 160
evaluation 114, 161, 165
exclusion 128, 131, 139–142, 144, 145, 154, 157, 165, 235
executive function 96

fair equality of opportunity 204
feasibility 13, 179, 230
felt-needs 14
finance 31, 61, 78, 106, 120–122, 124, 139
First Past the Post System (FPPS) 130, 131, 133, 136, 137, 139, 143
fiscal 105, 121, 228
five-year plans (FYPs) 117, 225
foreign capital 92
Foreign Direct Investment (FDI) 77, 83, 87, 92–109; banking sector 99–100; case study, four sectors 99; civil aviation 100–101; defence sector 101–103; global outlook impact, Indian soil 104–106; landmark judgements on **97–98**; legality, India 93–96; pharmaceutical sector 103–104; role of judiciary 96–98; sectoral caps **95–96**
Foreign Institutional Investors (FIIs) 99
Foreign Sovereign Immunities Act (FSIA) 80
freedom of expression 34
Freedom of Information Act, 1982 52
freedom of occupation 34
Frønes, I. 163, 164
Fudge, Judy 27, 32

Gadgil-Mukherjee formula 121, 122
Gandhi, M. K. 113
geographical study area 206
German constitutional doctrine 5
German federal constitutional court 37, 38
German jurisprudence 32
Gleeson, J. 60
global constitutionalism 27, 39–41
global integrative doctrine 26, 32, 39–42
globalization 9–11, 26–28, 30–35, 42–44, 117
Global North 4, 13, 14

242 Index

Global South 1–22, 115, 191, 223–235; transformative constitutionalism and 223–236
Gopal Singh Committee Report 132
governance 13, 26–28, 31, 32, 39, 41, 43, 44, 78, 100, 106, 107, 117, 130, 135, 140, 142, 192, 198
Government (Liability in Tort) Bill, 1965 84
GPA sale 192, 193
Great Depression 74
Green New Deal 11
grievance redressal 4
Griggs, Ray 55
Grødem, A. S. 162
group rights 141, 143, 145, 146
guarantees 4, 5, 87, 129–131, 135, 137–146, 203
Gujarat Town Planning and Urban Development Act 196, 197–198
Gupta, Akhil 181

Habermas, J. 7
Hart, H.L.A. 2, 3, 12, 39, 40, 113, 115, 133, 160
health 5, 11, 13, 30, 37, 52, 104, 106, 121, 139, 155, 156, 158, 159, 167, 211, 225, 228, 230
Heimer, M. 165, 166
Highly Indebted Poor Countries (HIPC) 74
Hodge, P. 51
Howard, John 53
human rights 6, 8–10, 26, 27, 31–33, 37–39, 41, 43, 44, 50, 53, 76, 143, 146, 151–153, 155, 161, 164, 167, 168, 207, 224, 227, 230, 231, 233, 235
human rights obligation 151–153

ideas 12, 84, 104, 111, 185, 190, 206, 211
identity 53, 128, 138, 182
Immigration Ombudsman 61
implementation 15, 16, 31, 32, 34, 35, 44, 49–51, 55–60, 106, 117, 134–136, 145, 151–155, 159, 165, 172, 174, 175, 179, 182–186, 194–198, 207, 234
inclusion 106, 132, 135, 139, 143, 154, 159, 160, 163, 227, 228
India: constitutional promises 129–130; ethnic groups 129; legislature and public employment 129; outcomes 130–132; street-level bureaucracy in 171–186
Indian Foreign State Immunity Act 87
Indian Planning Commission 111–125; chief ministers views on dismantling 118–120; less-legitimate states, planning

114–116; planning to policy 116–118; socio-economic basis, NITI Aayog 121–122; transformative constitution and deformative planning 112–114
individual rights 31, 140–143, 145, 146
inequality 11, 13, 30, 31, 44, 112, 121, 128, 129, 160, 164, 228, 234
Ingram, D. 7
injustice 11, 130, 202, 205, 207, 216
Institute for New Economic Thinking (INET) 78
institutional crisis 18
institutions 7, 8, 12, 13, 16, 18, 26–28, 30, 32, 76, 77, 103, 104, 111–123, 133, 142, 145, 146, 154, 210, 223–226, 232, 233
International Debt Commission 78
international human rights standards 27
international investment agreements (IIA) 104, 106
International Labor Organization (ILO) 27–32, 35–42, 44–45; committees 30; Convention 87 37; labour standards 32; principles 30, 35, 37, 39; standards 38, 41, 42, 45
international labour standards 26, 29
International Monetary Fund (IMF) 75, 76, 78, 82, 105, 106, 225
Israeli Collective Agreements Law, 1957 34
Israeli judiciary 32
Israeli Labour Disputes Law, 1957 34

Jain, R.B. 172
judgement 5, 7, 12, 13, 15, 16, 38, 193
judiciary 4, 5, 7, 12, 16, 32, 33, 36, 37, 39, 43, 45, 84, 85, 96, 103, 107, 129, 134, 143, 145, 146, 172, 223, 228, 229, 232, 234, 235
jurisprudence 7, 9, 27, 32, 33, 39, 44, 74–87
justice 3, 6–8, 11, 12, 15, 16, 43, 85, 101, 107, 128, 130, 131, 133, 139, 140, 202–221, 224, 230, 233, 234
Justice as Fairness (Rawls) 202, 203–204

Klaaren, J. 230
KPMG Report 64

labor market 33
labour freedoms 31
labour law 6
labour law interface 28–29
labour-related social rights 30
laissez faire globalization 32
Land Acquisition, Rehabilitation and Resettlement (LARR) Act 194, 195, 198

Index **243**

land alienation 202–222
Landes, W. M. 6
Laswell, Harold 12, 13
Latin American Crisis 81
law and policy: administrative law 8;
 constitutional mandate, public policy 4–6;
 Elmer's case 3; forward and backward
 linkages 2–7; 'gangster' notion of law
 2; globalization 9–12; implementability,
 decisions 15–16; institutional mapping,
 intersectionality 16–18; integration,
 stakeholder support 233–234; interface,
 practice 7–18; law and decisions, public
 good 6–7; legitimacy of law 2–3;
 planning laws 9; potential conflict and
 labour implications 27–28; primary
 and secondary rules, law 2; reasoning,
 practice models 12–13; regulatory agency
 functions 8–9; rights 8; role of legislature
 8; theoretical approaches, law 2–4;
 understandings of law 2–4
lawmaking 8
Law's Empire (Dworkin) 3
Lefebvre, Henri 189
legal obligation 155–156
legal realism 4
legislation 6–8, 13, 14, 27, 33, 39, 41, 42,
 52, 77, 83, 84, 87, 115, 134, 137, 153,
 171–173, 177, 178, 184, 190, 193–199,
 229, 230
Legislative Impact Assessments (LIA) 13
liberal 1, 4, 7, 39, 51, 53, 100, 101, 204, 231
liberty 4, 6, 33, 87, 104, 204, 205
litigation 14, 77
local 16, 26–29, 32, 33, 36, 37, 39, 43–45,
 85, 103, 114, 115, 129, 134, 145, 159,
 171–173, 175–177, 179, 180, 182, 184,
 185, 192
local constitutionalism 39
Locke, J. 215
low income 151–168, 224, 225; families
 151–168
Luhmann, N. 15

majoritarianism 137, 140, 143, 145
market 4, 6, 8–10, 13, 14, 28–33, 42–44,
 74–77, 81, 92, 93, 96, 100–106, 114, 117,
 123, 158–163, 167, 191–196, 205, 206, 225
Martinez, J.V. 75
Mason, J. 57
Maxwell, J. 54
mediation of powers, European model 12
medium and small size enterprises
 (MSMEs) 102, 103
Mekorot case 34

Memorandum on State Immunity 84
Metrodan case 35
migration 52, 57, 58, 160, 163, 224
Migration Act, 1958 57
minorities 128–147
*Mirza Ali Akbar Kashani v. United Arab
 Republic and Anr.* 85
monitoring 134, 143, 145
Morrison, Scott 54–56
Motor Vehicles Act, 1988 86
multiculturalism 143
Myrdal, G. 115

National Civil Aviation Policy 101
National Commission for Minorities Act 130
national sovereignty 53
Nehru, Jawaharlal 111, 112
neoliberal 86, 104, 112, 117
New Economic Policy 10
new public management (NPM) reforms
 31, 44
NGOs 104, 180
NITI Aayog 111, 120, 121–122
non-economic factors 76
non-judicial institutions 224, 233
non-state actors 5, 226
normative approach 10, 144
Norwegian Labour and Welfare
 Administration 160, 161
Norwegian welfare system 164
Novitz, T. 29
Nozick, Robert 202–221
Nussbaum, M. C. 4

Ocasio-Cortez, Alexandria 11
old legal dichotomy, Australia 49–70
Ombudsman Annual Reports 62
"Open Skies Policy" 100
operational matters concept 49; grounds
 for OSB secrecy 51–54; limits of
 OSB secrecy 54–56; origin in OSB
 51; problematique 50–51; and public
 disclosure 60–64
Operation Sovereign Borders (OSB) 49,
 50, 63
O'Regan, J. 234
ownership 94, 99–101, 106, 116, 157, 189,
 205–207, 209, 214–216, 220

Pakistan: constitutional promises 132–133;
 minority groups 132; outcomes 133–135
Palme, J. 165, 166
Paneerselvam, O. 120
Paris Club initiative 78

parliament 13, 56, 118, 130, 134–137, 139, 140, 232

participation 13, 29, 38, 77, 82, 83, 120, 128–146, 157, 159, 164–166, 168, 198, 234

participatory democracy 234

Patnaik, P. 123

persecution 140

Pezzullo, Michael 52

pharmaceutical sector 103–104

Pierce, Charles 15

planning 9, 60, 103, 111–123, 190, 193, 196–198

planning laws 9

Polanyi, K. 9, 10

policy argument 69n34

policy change 10

policy formulation 185

policy making 12

policymaking power 59

policy models 117

policy objective 5, 15

policy-operational dichotomy 56–60

policy process 1–18, 118, 172, 173, 184, 185

policy text 173, 176–179, 184, 185

polis model 6

political boundaries 230–232

political doctrine 26, 31, 44

political economy 13, 117, 122

political participation 133, 137, 143, 144, 234

political party 113, 114

population 7, 30, 34, 36, 121, 128, 131–133, 135, 137, 138, 143, 156, 157, 161, 176, 182, 189, 196, 209, 234

Posner, R. A. 6

possibility of law 16

possibility of politics 16

poverty 224; activation policies 161; alleviation, transformative constitutional approach 226–230; human rights-based approach 164–167; low income as measurement 156; minimum budget and 157; by poor living conditions 157; rate 34, 224; reasons and implications of 157–159; right to non-discrimination 164–166; social benefits, cash transfers 159–161; social policies and 159–164; South-South co-operation and 224–226; subjective experience of 157; substantive equality 164–166; universal social services 162–164

practice 1, 7, 8, 12, 14, 18, 31, 44, 49, 87, 100, 112, 124, 128–146, 152, 164, 172–175, 177–179, 186, 190, 192, 193, 197–199, 202, 232–234

pragmatism 15

primary goods 203, 209–211, 213; identification 210–211

prismatic societies 115

privatization 8, 9, 101

problem solving 4, 18, 116

production of space 189–200; individual-led forms of 191–193; state-led modes of 193–198

property 4, 6, 7, 9, 33, 34, 62, 80, 81, 84, 85, 174, 189–193, 196, 204–206, 215, 220

property tax records 191

proportional 35–37, 130, 131, 133, 136, 137, 141–144, 202, 229

proportionality test 37

public choice 8

public interest 5–7, 13, 14, 18, 27, 28, 52, 99, 101, 104, 106, 172, 230, 231, 233

Public Interest Litigation (PIL) 5, 104, 172, 230, 231

Public Service Commission Report 64

PUCL vs Union of India and others 172

race 92, 93, 106, 133, 135, 138, 203

rationality 4, 6, 7, 18, 214; legal and economic 7

Rawls, John 202–221

Raz, J. 16

recognition 2, 11, 27, 32, 34, 39, 42, 43, 79, 133–135, 141, 142, 164, 168, 172, 202, 210, 235

rectification principle 205

redistribution 205, 209, 220, 221, 225, 232

reforms 7, 31, 44, 63, 105, 106, 116, 117, 133, 145, 174

regional cooperation 235

regulation 8–10, 14, 30, 31, 36, 41, 43, 44, 77, 81, 83, 92, 94, 99, 100, 103, 105, 106, 114, 115, 140, 174, 198

regulatory agency functions 8–9

religion 4, 13, 15, 113, 128–130, 133, 135, 136, 138

Reno, W. 114

representation 14, 29, 37, 112, 114, 128–146, 191

responsiveness 221n2

rights: to life clause 5; to occupation 34; to property 174; to strike 26–45

rights-attentive bureaucracy 8

rights-based approach 164, 168

Rights of the Child 151

rights-responsive model 8

Royal Nepal Airline Corporation v. Monorama 85

rule-making process 18

246 Index

trade unions 29–31, 36, 38, 116
traditional liberal constitutions 4
transfer principle 204
transformative 5, 14, 112, 128–130,
140–143, 145, 164, 168, 223–235
transformative constitution 112–114
transformative constitutionalism 5,
223–236; typologies of 140–142
treatment 10, 79, 102, 143, 159, 180, 228, 230
Tribal Extension Officer (TEO) 176
Tribal Resettlement and Development
Mission (TRDM) 171–173, 184;
bureaucratic system for 174–177;
bureaucrats' responsibilities, ambiguity
181–183; government orders, non-
specification of penalty 183–184;
guidelines for implementation, ambiguity
179–181; Kerala land policies, history
173–174; methods 176–177; policy
goals, ambiguity 178–179; policy text
and interpretations 177–178; street-level
bureaucracy and 174–177; street-level
bureaucrats, discretion exercise 177–178
tribe 129, 130, 138, 144, 174, 176, 178, 207,
217, 220
tribunals 8, 117, 145, 146
Tucker, Eric 32

"UDAN" scheme 100
ultra vires 7
UN Convention on the Rights of
the Child (CRC) 151; Article 27
153–154
UN Covenant on Economic, Social and
Cultural Rights: Article 8 29; Article 11
154–155
UNCTAD Investment Report 105
unemployment 30, 76, 160, 228
United Nations Conference on Trade and
Development (UNCTAD) 78

United Nations General Assembly (UNGA)
78, 79
United Nations International
Covenant 29
universal 10, 15, 42, 53, 158, 162,
167, 224
Universal Declaration of Human
Rights 10
urban 146, 189–199
urban India: land records in 190–191;
production of space 189–200
US Foreign Sovereign Immunities Act,
1976 (FSIA) 77

values 5–7, 10–14, 29, 53, 78, 115, 116,
128, 129, 156, 191, 193, 196, 204, 227,
232, 234
victimization 140
violation 5, 75, 96, 107, 131, 132, 137, 154,
156, 165, 166, 181, 183, 217, 221, 233
voter 131, 143

Washington consensus 10–12
wealth distribution 202–205
Weber, M. 15
Weimar Republic 38
Weiner, Myron 116
welfare 6, 8, 30, 33, 34, 43, 44, 83, 84,
92, 104, 121, 151, 152, 156, 158–162,
164–167, 174, 176–182, 203, 223,
229, 231; duties 152; policy 151–153
Western liberal democratic traditions 4
Wilberforce, Lord 57
workfare 159, 161, 167
Work Health and Safety Act, 2011 52
World Bank 82, 104, 225
World Jurist Association conference 234
World Trade Organization (WTO)
105, 106
writ 22n41

rule of law 8, 26, 43, 76, 86, 87, 143, 145, 146, 227, 231
rural 181, 189, 190, 194, 195

Sachar Committee Report 132
Sandleris, G. 75
Sanyal, A. 113
Saskatchewan case 40
Scheduled Tribes Development Department (STDD) 174–176, 183
security 5, 6, 11, 30, 31, 38, 52, 53, 55, 56, 59, 63–65, 93, 94, 99, 101, 102, 106, 128, 132, 134, 140, 141, 144, 146, 155, 159, 191, 228
Seeing Like a State (Scott) 115
self-adjusting market 9, 10
Sen, A. 13, 86, 118, 225, 229, 230, 234
separation of powers, American model 12
service supply demand 35
Shah, Esha 116
Singh, Manmohan 10
social assistance 160, 161, 167, 228, 229
social benefits 159, 160, 162, 167, 229
social change 223, 227, 234
social citizenship 7
social co-operation 204
social differences 162, 210, 211, 220
social exclusion 165, 235
social investment approach 165
social justice 133, 224, 230, 233, 234
social policy 151, 156, 157, 159–165, 167, 202
social problem 28
social protection 225
social reasons, legislature 7
social rights 30, 155, 160, 226, 232
social security 228
social services 76, 162, 167, 225
socio-economic basis 121–122
socio-economic processes 44
socio-economic rights 76, 134, 224, 227–233, 235
socio-economic status 155, 162, 163, 167, 192
South African Constitutional Court 6, 152
South Asia: hurdles to minority participation, pathways 142–145; minorities in 128–147; political participation 143–144; practice of individual rights, re-working 143; public employment 144–145; setting minority commissions and space, CSOs 145; theory and practice, group guarantees 143–145; transformative constitutionalism typologies 140–142; transformative provisions and outcomes 129–140

South-South co-operation 224–226
sovereign border policy 49–70
sovereign debt crisis 74–76
sovereign debt restructuring 74–89; Code of Civil Procedure (CPC), Section 86 84–87; commercial activity exception 81–82; foreign state immunity, India 83–84; international initiatives 77–79; sovereign immunity doctrine 79–81; sovereign immunity, restrictive approach 82–83
sovereign debt restructuring mechanism (SDRM) 78
sovereign immunity 77
Sovereign Immunity Act 85
sovereign immunity doctrine 79–81; immunity from execution 80–81; immunity from jurisdiction 80
sovereignty 43, 45, 51, 53, 79, 101, 102
Special Forces (SF) 53
Sri Lanka: constitutional promises 135–136; ethnicity and 135; outcomes 136–137
Stalin, Joseph 117
standard of living 34, 151–168
state formation 13
State Immunity Act 77, 87
state obligation 5, 154, 155, 160, 164, 168
Stiglitz, J. 105
Stone, Deborah 6
street-level bureaucracy 171–186
strikes 26–46; collective action and international law 29–30; constitutionalization of 27, 28; fundamental right to 29; global integrative approach 28; globalization process effects 30–31; group theory and 29; in public services and public policy 28–29; in utility services 35
substantial ownership and effective control (SOEC) 101
substantive democracy 13
Sunstein, C. 15
supranational labour institutions 27
Supreme Court 5, 32, 34, 86, 104, 137; of Canada 39–41; of India 104
Sustainable Development Goals (SDGs) 224
Sutherland Shire Council v Heyman 57

tax 76, 191, 215, 220, 221
Teachers strike case 35
technology 93, 100, 102, 103, 116, 190
Thakur, T. S. 101
Theory of Justice, A (Rawls) 203–204
Town and Country Planning Act 9
Town Planning Scheme 196–198
trade 10, 29–31, 36, 38, 52, 54, 75, 77, 78, 81, 82, 87, 93, 104, 105, 116, 152